Longing for the Sky

Essays on Music, Unmusic and Antimusic

Marc Estrin

Fomite
Burlington VT

ISBN-13: 978-1-959984-57-3
Library of Congress Control Number: 2024938069

Fomite
58 Peru Street
Burlington, VT 05401
www.fomitepress.com

09-04-2024

Contents

Essays Critical

Essays Personal

Essays Political: F35

Longing for the Sky

Prefatory note

I often write essays, short and not so short, into my fiction. And for a few years — requested by my publisher — I "maintained a web presence" on Blogger, writing short pieces — weekly, or concerning some calendar event. Prompted by the first subject in this book, Ives' Essay Before a Sonata [his enormous "Concord Sonata"], I thought I'd put together a collection of these essayistic snippets and selections. Only this first essay has endnotes.

Note: my novel Insect Dreams *was initially published as a novel. The complete version, in its original form as a longer biography, is now titled* Kafka's Roach.

At the height of his powers, and while suffering no obvious personal catastrophes, Charles Ives stopped composing, for almost 40 years until his death. Why?

Concerning the Evaporation of Charles Ives

Essay After a Sonata

Ives's thought-music is traced through his Concord Sonata: the pattern discovered suggests a spiritual path of no return. Having lived out his Emerson phase, Ives discovered a kind of quietism in Thoreau which may have silenced him musically long before his death.

Right hand boldface voices — those of the Transcendentalists
Right hand italics — from Ives's Essays Before a Sonata

I — EMERSON

So much struggle in EMERSON — who would believe it? One would expect serene singing of strings, legato, high over deep harmonies. Instead, all this bashing and crashing, hitting and missing and messing around. It's a movement of elbows and fists, muscles straining to pull on the tendons of melody, deforming, transforming, throwing every conceivable twist of harmony and melody out against winds of its own making.

What is this all about? Is this "The Sage of Concord"? It sounds more like Lear or Ahab howling at the storm. What does Ives have in mind? What does he see? What is he telling us about the inner life and outer meaning of this oddball hero of his?

Emerson, Thoreau — all the Transcendentalists — were seers, scientists of the invisible, reporters from the beyond of things. Most "adult persons", says Emerson. View the world superficially, perceiving and engaging only outer vestments. While many still delight in the "simple perception of natural forms", few perceive that Nature offers to the discerning eye a world behind the world.

Things are emblematic.
Every natural fact is a symbol of some spiritual fact.
Spirit pervades Nature, speaks through Nature, but most of us can no longer hear.

Man is the dwarf of himself.
Once he was permeated and dissolved by Spirit.
He filled nature with his overflowing currents...

But the human soul in our time has shrunk, beaten down and sucked dry by "economic use". The individual soul, once coterminous and soaked with spirit, now limps along, wizened, deaf and blind, raising crutch in hand in comic, defiant gestures of so-called power. The outer body may be muscled in steel, nerved in wire, but the mind-soul is

imbruted

as the "selfish savage" attempts to claw his way back into the kingdom.

Having power over Nature is not seeing Nature, or hearing what she has to tell. Exploitation is loss, not gain, seeding and spewing death and ugliness, and cultivating the insensitivity necessary to survive.

The Transcendentalists called for a change, The parched and shrunken soul was to be revived and nurtured, and coaxed again to its old vast size. Such are Emerson's "Prospects":

> **The problem of restoring to the world original and eternal beauty is solved by the redemption of the soul. The ruin or the blank that we see when we look at nature is in our own eye. The axis of vision is not coincident with the axis of things, and so they appear not transparent but opaque. The reason why the world lacks unity, and lies broken and in heaps, is because man is disunited with himself.**

This is the sight the seers saw, the diagnosis and the prescription: to bring soul/mind/man back into Nature, to hear the secrets, to heal the split. Deep would once again call unto deep as the soul sallies into the "unfound infinite".

But then what of all this howling and raging in Charlie's report? This, he says, is where we must start, an appropriate place for a "god in ruins"

> **like Nebuchadnezzar,**
> **dethroned, bereft of reason, and eating grass like an ox.**

The opening of EMERSON presents the awe and struggle before

> **the dread universal essence, which is not wisdom, or love, or beauty, or power, but all in one, and each entirely — that for which all things exist, and that by which they are...**

This is the opening of EMERSON and that first, fierce, expanding figure is Nature, not sweet, to us, her "conquerors", but the "dread universal essence", falling and rising simultaneously, enlarging the space

5

into everywhere, and then gathering into its highest self and spinning vertiginously downwards, leaping up and falling again more ponderously to the lowest depths, pounding fortissimo on — what? — the all-too-familiar opening of Beethoven's Fifth!

What is this sound fragment doing here? In his *Essays Before A Sonata*, Ives tells us explicitly:

> *There is an "oracle" at the beginning of the Fifth Symphony; in those four notes lies one of Beethoven's greatest messages. We would place its translation above the relentlessness of fate knocking at the door, above the greater human message of destiny, and strive to bring it towards the spiritual message of Emerson's revelations — the soul of humanity knocking at the door of the divine mysteries, radiant in the faith that it WILL be opened — and the human become the divine!*

And so in EMERSON, this first movement of the Concord Sonata, Ives has stated right away the two protagonists of a great event, the meeting and struggle of the human soul (the Beethoven theme) with its would-be lover and partner, the vast and dreaded universal essence, Nature.

The Beethoven theme will always be recognizable, marked for the ear by its characteristic rhythm, varying only slightly in its intervals, as most human souls resemble one another. But Nature's theme is quite different. It is most often characterized by five descending notes, an exhalation that can be felt as a roar — as at the beginning — or as a sigh. But the intervals between these five notes can vary widely, and even the fiveness is not constant, but can be extended to sixness, nineness, twelveness, as the outbreath changes.

> *Nature loves analogy and hates repetition.*
> *She dislikes to explain as much as to repeat.*

The stage is set. We open *in media res* — no easy exposition, but directly in the deep and raging water of development, life-vests mandatory. In this eddy, weighing a few ounces, but with aspirations — the human soul. And here — no, here — wait — here, here we have Nature, weight undetermined.

But first, a word from the folks that wonder about Beethoven's Fifth. One would think it a handicap to choose so well-known and iron-clad a theme to quote and use so centrally. Won't it bring its baggage with it every time? How can Ives hope to overcome past associations?

One of the miraculous things about EMERSON is that it succeeds in doing just that — the extension of GGGEb beyond itself, its history. Ives effects a liberation from Beethoven's cage — the coiled snake lashing out and recoiling becomes a bird, a caress, a cloud. It expands in space and time to include almost any music, any formulation, three repeated tones or not. One will sense it hiding around all corners, lurking in fields and parking lots, announcing itself with any intervals, any harmonies, in any context. Anxiety: Where will it show up next? Will it be harsh? Will it scare me? Will it be forceful, soft?

Clearly, it is not a four note theme, but an eight note one — GGGEb, FFFD.... This is most important, because while the first interval is a major third, the second is a minor third, and both will be used throughout the sonata. How do these intervals make us feel?

In the Beethoven, GGGEb has an ambiguous and contradictory function. Unlike FFFD, it feels at rest. There is no need to go on. Its key is unclear; the Eb could be home — a short symphony. But by the time we hear FFFD, we know we are on the verge of something. The D is not at rest — the whole first movement springs from its tension. GGGEb — a relatively restful "here" version, and FFFD, a forward-looking, urging "there" one. Ives will use them both.

There is something basic and archetypal about the descending minor third. Children's songs all over the world pivot around that particular interval. Teasing — FD FD FDGFD — "Nyah nyah, nyah nyah, nyahnyahnyah nyah nyah." Carl Orff tunes his primary instruments to minor thirds, and begins his music lessons with FD FFD, FD FFD — "Cuckoo, where are you? Cuckoo, where are you?"

On the other hand you rarely hear descending major thirds in the mouths of babes. There is something constructed about them: they have to be composed by composers — a "civilized", complicated, late formulation. And so perhaps FFFD — that natural soul; and GGGEb — the soul passed through art, maturity, civilization.

How different descending thirds are from ascending thirds. It is ascending thirds that give us our sense of major and minor, of happiness and sadness in music. This automatic association is absent in the descent. The simple, felt distinction between happiness and sadness ceases to be black and white and opens out into judgment-withholding detail.

Rudolf Steiner says that rising intervals lift the organism toward thinking, while descending ones precipitate it towards willing. How Beethovenesque: "I WILL (major) — I WILL (minor)!" But Ives will add thinking to Beethoven's willing, with occasional ascending intervals in the Soul theme. Thinking and willing were well mixed and strongly etched in his character, and his music urges this mixture upon us.

> *Character may be the part of the soul we, the blind, can see....*
> *The soul is each man's share of God,*
> *and character the muscle which tries to reveal its mysteries.*

Back to the music then, to EMERSON, the first movement of the Concord Sonata. Let us listen for and try to describe some of the events in this push-and-pull interpenetration. [1]

B. BE! B for Bereshyt, the beginning of Genesis, B for Beethoven and Bach and Brahms. B for the Big Bang, an explosion of matter and time. Descending and ascending simultaneously, space created in contrary motion. Emerson/Ives,

Invader of the unknown,
Standing on a summit at the door of the infinite,
Lighting a fuse that is laid toward men,

The Falling begins, and in the Fall there tumbles out the first Beethoven theme, high, almost indistinguishable in the chaos, and then lower, clearer, and then again, horribly low and clear, and then finally, in between. Time pulses fast, then slower, then faster again as the human range, emerging from the avalanche, hammers out the falling thirds of willing. (Are human fall and human will connected?) And immediately thereafter, a surprising thing happens.

The Beethoven theme, that energy of granite and steel, is (amazing!) changed. Between the three pounding C's and the expected G#, we hear CDbC, an extension, a lifting of the head! as if to say "I WI(is that OK?)LL!" — a first softening in the hardness of the struggle.

But this gesture is swallowed up by the overwhelming forces of the dread universal essence, full of rhythm, but without meter, measureless. What an awe-ful thing to describe: here is Emerson/Ives,

reaching out through and beyond
mankind, trying to see what he can of the infinite and its
immensities, throwing back to us whatever he can, but ever
conscious that he but occasionally catches a glimpse....He must
struggle if he would hurl back anything — even a broken fragment
for men, to examine and perchance in it find some germ of some
part of truth ...

Perhaps the gesture was caught after all: the line rises and rises to its highest point, agitated, faster and faster, and at the peak, softens and slows, and becomes almost caressing. Feeling good, buddy? Like to sing a little minor third melody there? Not so fast! This roller coaster has a ways to go. And so it does, and we are transferred from exploding rock to tumultuous waters

despite the confused protests of the Beethoven theme, unaccustomed to its role of flotsam and jetsam.

And in this wrangling, there comes the first melding, a tentative melody, gradually born of the Soul's rising thirds, and Nature's five falling notes.

Though the intervals are not the same, there is something about this tune that has always struck my ear as a version of Steven Foster's "All the world is sad and weary/ everywhere I roam"[2], and as Ives continues to use its second half as a version of the five Nature notes, I hear continuously (and will subsequently refer to it as) "Everywhere I Roam", a pregnant emblem of the soul's "I", Nature's "Everywhere", and the sinuous and active connection between them, exploring and embracing.

"Slowly and quietly", says Ives, as Nature and "I" consider each other, almost curiously. "Could it be you?" each thinks in its own key. And in contrary motion, reminiscent of the cosmic beginning, but on a smaller scale, they begin to pull apart. Having tasted of possible intimacy, insecure, things get pretty bad — messy and assertive, and talking two languages at once. Not the way to go.

"Just one second," Nature says, "Cut! Let me show you what life could be like if you'd stop banging your fists on the floor and kicking your feet. Just sit there for a minute." And here begins the middle section of the movement, which may, says Ives, "reflect some of Emerson's poetry rather than the prose."

Whatever one may think of Emerson's poetry, there is no question of the quality of these moments in Ives. What remarkable transformations! What have the eyes of Arjuna-soul seen? Nature-Krishna as Brahma-Creator, as Shiva-destroyer, and now, behold, the face of Vishnu, the preserver. In a gentle tour de force, Nature-Vishnu sings, so gently,

"Everywhere I Roam" — first, in the old, descending five tones, then in a new arching shape, then in a six note reverse arch, as a cat might stretch its back, then in an eight note turn, so permissive, and finally a new key in six simple descending notes, changed, but the same.

A breath of silence as Arjuna-soul's jaw drops. You think you've heard something? Here comes the second act.

The span from A to C is bridged by unpredictable, almost unthinkable notes. Again, five notes, five notes, six notes, eight notes, six notes — but what notes! Vast leaps, changes of octave, surprising accidentals. But with all this, it is seen and heard as STILL THE SAME — everywhere I roam — - through these and all possible transformations.

> **Behind nature, throughout nature,**
> **spirit is present;**

one and not compound, it does not act upon us from without, that is, in space and time, but spiritually

Enter the whole orchestra, sweeping these patterns along. Arpeggiated chords support the melody until finally time gives in to the majesty of All-Time:

7/4 measures of wave-like bass are linked and coeval with 19 beats of whole and dotted half notes. It can't be, but it is. As a working notation, it simply means to allow the whole note chords to ring through for four beats like the Concord sabbath bells echoing in the hills. But seen on the page (and Ives was enthusiastic for the unplayable) it says "WHOLE, WHOLE, WHOLE, WHOLE, ALMOST WHOLE! This is it — the ganze Geschichte — pay attention — it can be done!"

The little soul sputters out some Beethoven and half-Beethoven, and Vishnu continues the display, winding down, allowing space for a few more unconvinced and unconvincing soul-peeps. "Forget it, come with me!": the soul is swept silently along in the building enthusiasm of Nature, arriving at falling patterns, digging diatonically and chromatically downward.

> *Emerson always beating down through the*
> *crust toward the first fire of life, of death and of eternity.,*
> *The strength of distance in his eyes; the strength of muscle in his soul.*

And with this knowledge the soul finds its upward moving voice,. The minor third beginning is once again connected to EVERYWHERE I ROAM, and together they climb, the five note theme often in inversion, ascending.

Abruptly, out of a piano section,

Emerson/Nature/Ives strikes a fortissimo chord "fast", "decisively

and freely". "This," says Ives, "is but one of Emerson's calls for a Transcendental Journey". The section builds onward, taking three staves to notate, and losing its meter in endless measures. Slowly and gently, the rising Soul theme couples with nature's "everywhere I roam ...every where..."

Then, "gradually faster with more and more action", the penultimate push begins, "climbing up with rush and action" to an awesome triple forte climax

which Ives tells us is "almost as though the Mountains of the Universe were shouting as all of Humanity rises to behold the 'Massive Eternities' and the 'Spiritual Immensities'".

But now there happens something most strange.

Out of this climax there emerges — the Beethoven soul theme, double forte, asserting its will and separateness, then triple forte, rising, thinking, unabashed. Nature makes a vain attempt to incorporate it in its downward line but now abashedly, almost shame-facedly, the soul persists in its separateness, now with falling thirds of willing, now with rising thirds of thinking, sometimes in its "backing-off version" with the extra lifting of the head, but most often as the bare Beethoven, barely mitigated agency, rueful, but obstinately muttering above the inexorable bass.

The movement ends "slowly (almost as a recitative)", with a deep sense of melancholy. Something might have happened, but didn't. True, there were changes — the soul's naked will was abandoned for a while, thinking was added to willing. But to all the exertions and exhortations of Nature, the answer was — finally — no. In the last six measures, Nature falls into a rocking ostinato, both funeral march and tick of immense clock. "I can wait," she says. "My time will come."

The soul slips into the bass clef, frightened, exhausted, ashamed. The ostinato continues, the last note a false one, half a step too low. Between it and the scarcely audible chord above, an awkward augmented fifth. The chord above, sadly, a minor third.

*) To be heard as a kind of an overtone

Inconclusive.

I HAVE CAUSED THEE TO SEE IT WITH THINE EYES, BUT THOU SHALT NOT' GO OVER THITHER.

Only Thoreau will make it.

II — HAWTHORNE & THE ALCOTTS

HAWTHORNE is the longest of the Concord movements; ALCOTT is the shortest. Ives gives them both short shrift in the Essays, allowing each movement only three pages of text — (EMERSON garnered 38, Thoreau, 19) — apparently they were not philosophically important to him. Hawthorne's obsession with sin and conscience was not shared by the author of The Majority, an enthusiastic endorsement of the goodness and wisdom of collective humanity.

> *This fundamental part of Hawthorne is not attempted in our music (the 2d movement of the series) which is but an "extended fragment" trying to suggest some of his wilder, fantastical adventures into the half-childlike, half-fairylike phantasmal realms.*

In THE ALCOTTS, too, Ives shies away from serious, extended engagement with the odd, intrepid father of the "Little Women".

> *We dare not attempt to follow the philosophic raptures of Bronson Alcott .... We won't try to reconcile the music sketch ... with much besides the memory of that home under the elms ... though there may be an attempt to catch something of that common sentiment — a strength of hope that never gives way to despair — a conviction, in the power of the common soul which, when all is said and done, may be as typical as any theme of Concord and its Transcendentalists.*

Nevertheless, these two movements are musically important in the narrative of the struggle to unite the soul with Nature. While EMERSON thrashes about in the personal, existential arena, HAWTHORNE (a U.S. Consul after all!) and ALCOTT add important new social dimensions to the tale. That this is no accident of arrangement is shown by the fact that the Concord Sonata follows exactly the same storyline as the nearly contemporary Fourth Symphony — as we shall see.[3]

HAWTHORNE opens in a swirl of weird arpeggios, chords and melody fragments

> *... something about the ghost of a man who never lived, or about something that never will happen, or something else that is not.*

which soften into pianissimo tone clusters played on the black keys [4] with a block of wood. Then madness again, into which Beethoven sticks a maniacal nose, banging away at triple and quadruple forte, and then — stop.

Sudden pianississimo.

A new character enters, quietly stating the Beethoven Soul theme "as a Hymn is sometimes heard over a distant hill just after a heavy storm," says Ives to the performer. Just the smallest touch, and then back to fff very fast again. But the domesticated religion of church and parlor has entered our world, and may ask for more attention. Again it comes, this time at length, "held up for a moment by a Friendly Ghost in the churchyard," only to be ousted again by a fast fff "as a trombone would sometimes call the old cornet band to march." A little bit of military music, some cute rag ("it's the rage!"), fast, loud, descending tone clusters banged out with clenched fist, and then, for the first time in this movement, "quite slowly", the old five note patterns of Nature, comin' on sweet and sugary.

And now, brought on perhaps by the military, another big new character marches on stage: Patriotism, "Columbia, the Gem of the Ocean, the Home of the Brave and the Free, the Shrine of each Patriot's devotion, the world pays homage to Thee!" Beethoven thunders in the bass, shaking his fist, and puts out an astounding, admonishing progression from some late, unwritten work (p.47, measures 5-10ish). More chaos, last short statements of "Columbia" and the Hymn, and the movement ends with a literal bang: BANG!

Compare McClendon's descriptions of the second movement of the Fourth Symphony:

> The second movement... is one of the most

striking anywhere in the literature of modern music
.... Its dominant sounds are the sounds of twentieth
century America — the roar of cities and factories, the
clash of musics — and the inner sounds of yearning,
anticipation, frustration, anxiety, perhaps madness....
Whenever hymns appear, they are promptly
    drowned out by the crashing sounds of America
on the go.... And then there are musical sounds clearly
political, indeed clearly jingoistic. America is marching, boys, and don't stand in her way! "Columbia the
Gem of the Ocean"...here takes on the tones of monster power monstrously used. [5]

HAWTHORNE takes us out of the private world of EMERSON's
soul struggle, and throws us into the deep and frothing waters of society. Ives' characterizations of this world as "fantastical", "half-childlike,
half-fairylike", "something that will never happen, or something else
that is not" are acerbic — at the least!

But then there is always the privacy of home and family in which
to hide. R&R, they call it. And so we have THE ALCOTTS, and the
"old elms overspreading the Alcott house.

> Here is the home of the "Marches — all pervaded
> with the trials and happiness of the family, and telling,
> in a simple way, the story of "the richness of not having."

As the movement opens, we hear Beth "playing at the Fifth
Symphony" — the hymn-tune version — on the "old spinet piano
Sophia Thoreau gave to the Alcott children." After all the wildness of
HAWTHORNE, we are lulled and comforted.

> There is a commonplace beauty about "Orchard House — a kind
> of spiritual' sturdiness underlying its quaint picturesqueness — a kind of
> common triad of the New England homestead, whose overtones tellus that
> there must have been something aesthetic fibered in the Puritan severity ...

19

But then, "in a gradually excited way", the Beethoven soul breaks out of its hymnlike shell, and asserts itself with the same kind of nervous intensity as in the Fifth Symphony. "I am not a domestic beast to be petted and cajoled! This house cannot contain me!" (So Thoreau will say.) All right then, we'll have some singalong, some easy tunes.

> *All around you, under the Concord sky, still floats the influence of that human-faith-melody, transcendent and sentimental enough for the enthusiast or the cynic, respectively — reflecting an innate hope. a common interest in common things and common men — a tune the Concord bards are ever playing while they pound away at the immensities with a Beethoven-like sublimity ....*

And so the Beethoven comes again, in fat C major, asserting itself pathetically in a chamber cramped with family love. Nice place to visit, but ... Outside, quietly, Nature's descending notes are heard.

III — THOREAU

This movement is about Death — death of thought, death of will, death of striving. This movement is about Comfort — relaxing into easy stride. This movement is about Life — and the goal of all life, says Freud, is death.

Henry Thoreau was Death's familiar. He died young, his once strong body shriveled and wasted. Ives remarked that

> *... a naturalist — inherently — was exactly what Thoreau was NOT. He seems rather to let Nature put him under her microscope than to hold her under his. He was too fond of Nature*

She, however, had no such scruples with him.

Yet Henry met death as an old friend with whom he was long acquainted. He slipped in gently, with no struggle, as he might have slipped in to Walden Pond for his morning bath. Sister Sophia at his bedside: "I feel as if something very beautiful had happened — not death."

Practice is the best of all instructors, and Henry was a practiced man. After the loss of two loves, after his beloved brother's shocking death, he began a long suicide, distancing himself from friends and society at large, giving up

the affection that heart longed for but knew it a duty not to grasp...

Ives defends him:

One hears him called...a crabbed, cold-hearted, sour-faced Yankee — a kind of visionary sore-head — a cross-grained, egotistic recluse — even non-hearted.... If there are those who think him cold-hearted and with but little human sympathy, let them read his letters to Emerson's little daughter, or hear Mr. Emerson tell about the Thoreau home life and the stories of his boyhood — the ministrations to a runaway slave; or let them ask old Sam Staples, the Concord sheriff, about him.

But methinks he doth protest too much: Hawthorne — who knew him — was plainer: "...an intolerable bore, who was the exception to every rule, the judge of all the rest of the universe." Even Emerson, who truly loved him, could only be politic at his funeral:

He was bred to no profession; he never married; he lived alone; he never went to church; he never voted; he refused to pay a tax to the State; he ate no flesh, he drank no wine, he never knew the use of tobacco.... There was something military in his nature not to be subdued, always manly and able, but rarely tender, as if he did not feel himself except in opposition.

Ives, still excusing him, has a theory about this:

The personal trait that one who has affection for Thoreau may find worst is a combative streak, in which he too often takes refuge. An obstinate elusiveness, almost a "contrary cussedness" — as if he would say (which he didn't): "if a truth about something is not as I think it

21

ought to be, I'll make it what I think, and it will be the truth — but if
you agree with me, then I begin to think it may not be the truth." The
causes of these unpleasant colors... are too easily attributed to a lack
of human sympathy ... instead of to a supersensitiveness, magnified at
times by ill health, and at times by a subconsciousness of the futility of
actually living out his ideals in this life.

Pulling away, pulling away.

**Why should I feel lonely? What sort of space is that which
separates a man from his fellows and makes him solitary? I have
found that no exertion of the legs can bring two minds much
nearer to one another. What do we want most to dwell near to?
Not to many men surely, the depot, the post office, the bar-room,
the meeting-house, the school-house, the grocery, Beacon Hill, or
the Five Points where men most congregate, but to the perennial
source of our life, whence in all our experience we have found that
to issue, as the willow stands near the water and sends out its roots
in that direction. That will vary with different natures, but this is
the place where a wise man will dig his cellar.**

How odd that "the perennial source of our life" is so near a neighbor to death: the image is very like a grave.

So Thoreau said goodbye to his fellows, opened the door into
aloneness, and stepped in. It was almost easy:

**I have never felt lonesome, or in the least oppressed by a sense
of solitude, but once, and that was a few weeks after I came to the
woods, when, for an hour, I doubted if the near neighborhood of
man was not essential to a serene and healthy life. To be alone was
something unpleasant. But I was at the same time conscious of a
slight insanity in my mood, and seemed to foresee my recovery.
In the midst of a gentle rain while these thoughts prevailed, I was
suddenly sensible of such sweet and beneficent society in Nature,
in the very pattering of the drops, and in every sound and sight**

**around my house, an infinite and unaccountable friendliness all
at once like an atmosphere sustaining me, as made the fancied
advantages of human neighborhood insignificant, and I have never
thought of them since.**

By and large, places, if not people, treated him well. Like a pilgrim
headed for the "sainte Terre", he would "saunter" through the world
(Thoreau's etymology), sitting, standing, lying on the edge of dissolution. In Fall, walking

**in so pure and bright a light, gilding the withered grass and
leaves, so softly and serenely bright, I thought I had never bathed
in such a golden flood, without a ripple or a murmur to it.... So we
saunter toward the Holy Land till one day the sun shall shine more
brightly than ever he has done, shall perchance shine into our minds
and hearts, and light up our whole lives with a great awakening
light, as warm and serene and golden as on a bankside in autumn.**

And in early spring,

**Fain would I stretch me by the highway side,
To thaw and trickle with the melting snow,
That mingled soul and body with the tide,
I too may through the pores of nature flow.**

Some may call it communion with Nature; I call it rehearsing
for Death, the piercing of the veil, the final wedding of soul and
world. Once, in the Maine woods, Kali showed him her face. Thoreau
describes his encounter with Mt. Katahdin in terrifying language,
unique in his writing.

**I caught sight of a dark, damp crag to the right or left; the mist
driving ceaselessly between it and me.... This was that Earth of
which we have heard, made out of Chaos and Old Night. Here was**

no man's garden, but the unhanseled globe.... It was vast, Titanic, and such as man never inhabits. Some part of the beholder, even some vital part, seems to escape through the loose grating of his ribs as he ascends. He is more lone than you can imagine. There is less of substantial thought and fair understanding in him, than in the plains where men inhabit. His reason is dispersed and shadowy, more thin and subtle like the air. Vast, titanic, inhuman Nature has got him at disadvantage, caught him alone, and pilfers him of some of his divine faculty. She does not smile at him as in the plains. She seems to say sternly, why came ye here before your time? ... Nature was here something savage and awful, though beautiful .... Man was not to be associated with it. It was Matter, vast terrific, — not his Mother Earth that we have heard of ... There was there felt the presence of a force not bound to be kind to man. It was a place for heathenism and superstitious rites — to be inhabited by men nearer of kin to the rocks and to wild animals than we.... What is this Titan that has possession of me? Talk of mysteries! — Think of our life in nature, daily to be shown matter, to come in contact with it, rocks, trees, wind on our cheeks! the solid earth! the *actual* world! the *common sense! Contact! Contact! Who are we? Where are we?*

But most of his time he spent "in the plains where men inhabit", a stranger to those men, but happy. "My happiness is a good deal like that of the woodchucks."

This constant and universal content of the animal comes of resting quietly in God's palm. I feel as if I could at any time resign my life and the responsibility of living into God's hands, and become as innocent, free from care, as a plant or stone.

And that is how Ives' last movement begins, with a long, quiet arpeggio, and a little four note figure which curls around and settles in, like a cat making a place for herself on a pillow.

*Very slowly and quietly

Restful seeming, but with darker overtones. The four note figure is very reminiscent of the shape of B-A-C-H, and of that awful place in the score of the Art of the Fugue where the music just stops — the master dead. Then, too, it is repeated three times, as if the first three Beethoven notes were magnified to show their inner shape.[6] The fourth note is missing.

The movement is mysterious throughout — little touches of light gleaming here and there on a dark forest floor. The five note nature theme falls and rises in the context of long but fragmentary melodies. And finally, the secret emerges, the context that has been only hinted at before: of course! it is funeral march with a rising rhythmic figure in the bass, and a melody so rueful and intense as to be almost unbearable in its beauty.

Now we know where those descending five notes are leading

— to the acceptance and reunification of Life with Death. This is the meaning of the struggle in EMERSON, of the brash avoidances in HAWTHORNE, and of the porous security of THE ALCOTTS. Only Thoreau in his courage and extremity could lay it bare.

The four note figure lies gently rocking. "Have you made your peace with God?", a loving Aunt Louisa asks.

I did not know we had ever quarreled.

Ives paints us a remarkable picture — visual as well as tonal — of Thoreau's process. EMERSON opened with a great contrary motion, the bass descending, the treble ascending to wedge open space, time and existence, making room for his grand vision. THOREAU, once his protégé, begins where EMERSON leaves off — wide — and in an equally great contrary contrary motion,

collapses the universe back down through the keyholes of himself — to expand even farther out again. And there he finds the funeral march awaiting him, and the Shiva dances of the Nature theme. Everywhere I roam.

Comes then the climax of the movement: the poet himself enters, playing his flute across the smoky waters of the pond.[7] All the themes of the work are combined in this long, long melody, liberated from struggle and gesture and pretense. Thoreau, marinated in healing Spirit, presides over the unification of soul and Nature. There is a decrescendo down to pppp and then a break. The flute — Thoreau — is no more. No one, said Channing, had left a better unfinished life.

The funeral march of the cosmos continues, coming to rest in an almost C major, and gently breaking into the arpeggio and four note figure of the beginning of the movement.

Thoreau lying in the palm of God.

For the last time, the Beethoven figure returns — the theme of the human soul — but this time neither rising nor falling, neither thinking nor willing, just — A-A-A-A — being — the alpha and the omega.

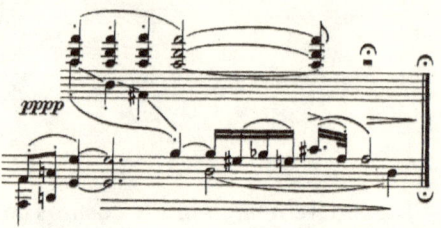

Thus Ives on Transcendentalism. All the early smashing and thrashing by a youthful Emerson is submerged in the greater understanding of a dying Thoreau. Submission is the key. The union of soul and Nature is finally achieved by giving up the assertions of the will and the inventions of thought. At the end, the Beethoven theme neither rises nor falls, but timelessly hovers as the slow ostinato of the universe pauses to listen.

Emerson was almost there, but lingering ego turned him away. The quest had to go on, lurching through the social wildness of HAWTHORNE, and surviving the restricting piety of THE ALCOTTS. Thoreau rejected them, all — ego, society, home — and became a wind harp to Nature's blowing, a flute for her to play on. The grateful words of a dying man:

> **Now chiefly is my natal hour**
> **And only now my prime of life;**
> **I will not doubt the love untold,**
> **Which not my worth nor want have bought,**
> **Which wooed me young, and woos me old,**
> **And to this evening me hath brought.**

Through his wise and painful submission, he earned at last "the Freedom of the Night."[8]

Omega and alpha. The end is not the end. The final chord, tonic and dominant combined, lets us know

There is more day to dawn. The sun is but a morning star.

IV CHARLES WALDO BRONSON HENRY IVES

At the height of his vision and strength, Ives stopped composing. Strange. The Concord was finished in 1915, the Fourth Symphony in 1916 — and from that time on there were no more major works. Cowell [9] attributes the silence largely to his health, but as Peter Burkholder points out[10], "It was not his heart attack in October 1918 that stopped his composing, for he had already all but ceased to compose." A variety of theories have been offered to explain the sad spectacle of this crippled giant, once so powerful, now reduced to cleaning up after himself, decrescendo, morendo, — for 39 years! His double-life as insurance executive/composer was supposed to have worn him out, World War One was supposed to have disillusioned him, the mockery of performers and critics was supposed to have crushed him, and crippled his will to compose. One writer suggests that his writing was "mourning for his father" and played itself out, while another actually proposes that he quit composing to make money in the stock market. [!] Burkholder, the latest writer, with the greatest advantage of hindsight and scholarship, feels any of the above may be partially correct, but that the problem is ultimately insoluble.

> *It may be that the exalted ideals and purposes for music that Ives outlined in the Essays became impossible for him to live up to, once he had made them explicit in writing .... Perhaps the very act of summarizing his musical credo choked off any possibility of further development; perhaps the explicit idealism of his writings diverted his energies from the implicit idealism of his instrumental music.[11]*

All these theories ring hollow to my ear. It is hard to imagine a man of Ives's strength and originality being cowed by opinion when he hadn't been cowed before. Why would such musical feistiness shrivel, even in a sickbed? Beethoven was sick, Schubert was sicker,

Mozart and Mahler were sicker still: they were able to continue. Ives had enough spirit left in him to do energetic insurance work until 1930 — fully 13 years after he stopped composing. Was it to make money? Ludicrous suggestion. He restricted himself and his family to a modest lifestyle, gave away his music gratis, and was most generous in supporting others. He could have been a millionaire, but took no more money from his company than what his calculations showed him to be a reasonable share of the GNP.

Burkholder's idea is a little more intriguing. The writing of the Essays did follow his last works, and seemed, in sequence at least, to end them. But did he stop because of the Essays, or did he write the Essays because he had stopped.

> [My] ... things were done mostly in the twenty years or so between 1896 and1916. In1917, the war came on and I did practically nothing in music. I did not seem to feel like it. We were very busy at the office at this time with the extra Red Cross and Liberty Loan drives, and all the problems that the war brought on. As I look back, I find that I did almost no composing after the beginning of 1917. In October, 1918, 1 had a serious illness that kept me away from the office for six months, and I have not been in my former good health since ... nor have I seemed to "get going good" in music since then. I'd start things, but they didn't seem to work out. So I stopped. I do not know how to account for it except that during the lost 10 years (since1918) what strength I had was used up in what I had to do at the office — and then the War — and it seemed impossible to do any work in the evenings as I used to do. During the last 10 years or so I have completed nothing; a set of chamber music was started and is fairly and mostly set down in a sketch some five or six years ago; and I have started a Third Pianoforte Sonata which does not seem to get along very well. In 1919-20 and especially 1921, I did write a few songs, and also at that time made arrangements of songs from old sketches, scores, overtures, etc.

What does this section from Ives' autobiographical notes [12] show? First, that he didn't really know himself what the problem was.

The war did affect him, as did the heart attack and the difficulty of after-hours composition. But no mention of the Essays or of problems which followed from their writing.

Something was going on that disturbed him in the particular sphere of composition, but which did not affect his creative energy in other ways. My suggestion is that Ives' life became unconsciously caught up in the plot and vision of the Concord Sonata.

That artists can be taken in by their subject matter is nothing new, and Pygmalion's is not the only form of involvement. Throughout the Essays, one is struck by the melding of Ives and his heroes. He often gives musical examples for their struggles — as if he were writing about composers — and sometimes literally puts his own ideas and language into their mouths:

> It is the cause, seldom the effect, that interests Emerson .... He might
> have said to those who talk knowingly about the cause of war...who
> would trace it down through long vistas of cosmic, political, moral evo-
> lution and what not — he might say that the cause of it was as simple
> as that of any dog-fight — the "hog-mind" of the minority against the
> universal mind, the majority. [13]

And again, for Thoreau:

> It is conceivable that Thoreau, to the consternation of the richest
> members of the Bolsheviki and Bourgeoise, would propose a policy of
> liberation, a policy of a limited personal property right on the ground
> that congestion of personal property tends to limit the progress of the
> soul (as well as the progress of the stomach)...[14]

Thoreau, of course, did no such thing — it was Ives who wrote about and applied this policy to himself and his family.

Whether this represents Ives' unique writing style, or a suspicious confusion of self and other (or a little of both), it is clear that Ives iden-tified himself with the Transcendentalists, and infused his thought and being with theirs, and theirs with his.

There comes from Concord an offer to every mind
— the choice between repose and truth ... [15]

There was no question which side the young Ives was on — he would speak and sing and YELL his truth and the devil take the hindmost! No repose, if he could help it, for the sissy Rollos [16] either.

It was after his encounter with the juggernaut flow from Emerson to Thoreau that things changed [17]: he decided — perhaps not consciously, but clearly enough — to stop struggling. He had hatched many original and alienating ideas. Now it was time to quietly nourish them, and let them drift slowly out into the world.

In his personal life, he withdrew into the bosom of his family, and in his last 20 years, putting even his beloved business behind him, had little actual contact with the outside world. Shortly before Ives' death, Cowell reported that "There are long periods when he is not able to stand the agitation that the crabwise progress of the human race toward peace and perfection creates in him." [18] Consequently, he refused to own a radio, and allowed visits only from old friends. He stopped walking the streets of New York after strangers began to recognize him. Summers were spent alone with his wife on their Connecticut farm.

> The house is dark, cool and spacious, and full of books, with a great window looking north over rolling meadows to a little pond frequented by small, friendly, wild animals. A noisy wren has nested undisturbed for many years just over the front door. Beyond the immediate hills are the Berkshires — a view Mr. Ives seems never to tire of contemplating. When he is able, he likes to walk out into the woods behind the house and sit alone quietly on a stump listening to the woodland sounds of summer. [19]

His own Walden Pond. Winters were spent back in New York,

hiding out, with his wife reading to him — poetry, philosophy, and natural history. For a long time he showed no interest in hearing any of the recordings of his music which had been slowly building up since 1934. It was only when his daughter gave him a record player for Christmas that Mr. Stubborn finally consented to listen.

Ives had made the transition from the public Emerson to the private Thoreau — and ever more strongly as his life went on. He set behind him the patriotic and the political — as he did in the HAWTHORNE movement and the second movement of the Fourth Symphony. While he never rejected the domesticity of THE ALCOTTS, he used that domesticity, it would seem, to work on his inner life. In the Essays he quotes Emerson on Thoreau: "His great heart him a hermit made"

> *a breadth of heart not easily measured, found only in the highest type of sentimentalists: the type which does not perpetually discriminate in favor of mankind. [20]*

Even then, he predicted he would pull back from the spirit of idealistic politics and youthful rebellion and go on to something deeper and more subtle:

> *A characteristic of rebellion is that its results are often deepest when the rebel breaks not from the worst to the greatest, but from the great to the greater ... The innate rebellious spirit in young men is active and buoyant. They could rebel against and improve the millennium. This excess of enthusiasm at the inception of a movement causes loss of perspective, and a natural tendency to undervalue the great in that which is being taken as a base of departure. [21]*

Why did Ives stop composing 39 years before his death? I propose that he was transformed by his immersion in the Concord Sonata — empowered, perhaps, towards another, more inner realm, but disabled, nevertheless, from further assaults on the unheard-of' and the unheard. A radical at heart, he stopped being a radical at hand as he acquiesced to the quietism he found, finally, in the Transcendental.

I feel this was a decision unconsciously conscious — there are many hints in his post-Concord writings of his future path. Like Thoreau's, his was a long retreat unto death, a life lived out in service of a late idea, a leaving behind of the clenched fist, and a resting, full of content, in God's palm. Poised at the juncture between the old dream and the new, Ives inserts a strange and remarkable passage in the middle of a meditation on Emerson:

> *In the early morning of a Memorial Day, a boy is awakened by martial music — a village band is marching down the street — and as the strains of Reeves' majestic Seventh Regiment March come nearer and nearer — he seems of a sudden translated — a moment of vivid power comes, a consciousness of material nobility — an exultant something gleaming with the possibilities of this life — an assurance that nothing is impossible, and that the whole world lies at his feet. But, as the band turns the corner, at the soldiers' monument, and the march steps of the Grand Army become fainter and fainter, the boy's vision slowly vanishes — his "world" becomes less and less probable — but the experience ever lies within him in its reality.*

> *Later in life, the same boy hears the Sabbath morning bell ringing out from the white steeple at the "Center", and as it draws him to it, through the autumn fields of sumac and asters, a Gospel hymn of simple devotion comes out to him — "There's a wideness in God's mercy" — an instant suggestion of that Memorial Day morning comes — but the moment is of deeper import — there is no personal exultation — no intimate world vision — no magnified personal hope — and in their place a profound sense of a spiritual truth — a sin within reach of forgiveness. And as the hymn voices die away, there lies at his feet — not the world, but the figure of the Savior — he sees an unfathomable courage — an immortality for the lowest — the vastness in humility, the kindness of the human heart, man's noblest strength — and he knows that God is nothing — nothing — but love. [22]*

Here is a visionary glimpse of what had happened, what was

happening, what was to happen. Here is the root of Ives's silence, of the change from brashness to humility. For all the beauty of the vision, there is something here that calls for mourning, a sadness in the spectacle, an emptiness replacing the might-have-been. It was a siren song of Transcendentalism he heard. The Concord current sucked him in and pulled him under.

He was soon not heard from again.

NOTES

1.   Writing about music is notoriously difficult, perhaps impossible. Words are fragmentary, and worded concepts the merest indications of larger referents. A threateningly telling indictment of this whole process is sounded by Ernst Bloch in his *Spirit Of Utopia* (reprinted in Ernst Bloch, *Essays On The Philosophy Of Music*, trans. Peter Palmer, Cambridge University Press, 1985. pp.81-82.):"...there can be no point, even in a hermeneutic respect, in the impulse to translate this recondite content back into everyday language. It is principally in doing this that people say the silliest things about the personification of sound .... Here we find twaddle in full spate about expressively pleading demisemiquavers, the brightly smiling trill of the violin, the thrice-heard unison G# after the scherzo in the C# Minor Quartet which is said to ask, as it were: what am I doing in this world? This is the province of the smug philistine who, with his explanatory chatter, thinks that he has not only said something but has also settled the matter for good by describing the Symphony in A major as "the Song of Songs of Dionysian heroism". Devices by which a piano teacher tries to improve his pupils' lame imaginations have been elevated ... to the exegetical science of musical poetics: and Beethoven is then supposed to have written it. More than that, it is supposed to be Beethoven made plain, rendered clear to the imagination, the most repugnant stuff with a neat little word for every bar, compared to which the most banal newspaper serial seems like the Annelid .... One must protest most firmly against essays of the programme-music type. They put a false complexion on matters because they put forward a kind of interpolation which is accidental, territorially inferior to music, as a legitimate way of speaking about music or as its translation into adequate categories, whereas this art will never be any more familiar than is a strange land."

    Nevertheless, given Ives's own frequent use of words in and about music, and given the verbiage of his subjects, I proceed, Bloch notwithstanding.

2.   Foster was one of the three "great" composers George Ives taught his son to love. The other two were Bach and Beethoven.

3.   For an excellent treatment of the story of the Fourth see the chapter "Charles Edward Ives: Theologian in Music" in James McClendon, Biography As Theology, Abingdon, 1974, pp 140-169.

4.   Too far out for inclusion into the text. but worth a note: is Ives thinking of slave ghosts haunting America? He does mention that this movement's

phantasmal fragments may "have something to do with ... the 'Slaves' Shuffle'" — among other things. I think of this because of the oddest true story I know, told to me by a friend who is currently a professor of piano at Eastman School of Music. At the time she was on the faculty of the North Carolina School of the Arts, sitting on the admissions committee. A prospective student arrived to audition who didn't have the usual requirements at his command, but who offered to play for the committee any Beethoven Sonata they wanted — he had them all memorized. That was impressive enough, so my friend asked him which sonata he'd like to play. "You choose," he countered. A sonata was picked, and he began to play. After 20 seconds, my friend asked, "Excuse me, could you start again?" Same business, this time stopped after 10 seconds. "Um," she said, "do you know that you're not ... playing any of the black keys?" "Sure I know it. I never touch them mothers!" Rarely daunted, she continued, "What if we, uh, painted them white?" "Uh-uh," he objected, "I'd know they was black." He wasn't admitted — which may have been a loss to radical right music, but ... I mention the story because Ives would have loved it as an example of music and American (pathological) culture.

5.   op. cit., pp.164-5.

6.   Although this may seem like a runaway fantasy of mine, the effect is quite clear to the ear. Three repeated, isolated sounds are the hallmark of the Beethoven theme, and Ives's treatment functions as a revolutionary technique of augmentation — the notes of a theme presented more slowly, AND blown up under a visual/auditory microscope, so that fine structure may be seen and heard.

7.   Leave it to Ives to ask for a flutist to come in and play four measures toward the end of a long piano sonata. Hey, what are friends for?

8.   I am aware that Ives has provided a "program" for this movement. "And if there shall be a program for our music, let it follow his thought on an autumn day of Indian summer at Walden..." Although my imagery is more metaphysical than his, it in no way conflicts with his scenario, but rather underlies it. In skeleton, Ives' story is that Thoreau, one misty morning half-conceives a "shadow of a thought" too fleeting to grasp. The beauty of the day moves him to a certain restlessness, and he tries to walk that restlessness off. But he known that instead of external activity, he must let "Nature flow through him and slowly — he releases his personal desires to her broader rhythm...." He returns to sit in meditation in the doorway of his cottage, and time passes over him, unnoticed. He hears the Concord bell as if it were a

"vibration of the universal lyre", and plays his flute — "the swan song of that day." "Is it a transcendental tune of Concord? ... Before ending his day he looks out over the clear, crystalline water of the pond and catches a glimpse of the 'shadow-thought' he saw in the morning's mist and haze — he knows that by his final submission, he possesses the 'Freedom of the Night.' He goes up the 'pleasant hillside of pines, hickories,' and moonlight to his cabin, 'with a strange liberty in Nature, a part of herself.'" (Ives, Essays, p.69.)

9.   Henry and Sidney Cowell, *Charles Ives And His Music*, Oxford, 1955.

10.   J. Peter Burkholder, *Charles Ives: The Ideas Behind The Music*, Yale, 1995. p.112.

My review of the various theories of Ives' silence is based on this book, pp.111-114.

11.   Burkholder, op. cit. p114.

12.   quoted in Cowell, op.cit., p.75.

13.   Essays, p.28.

14.   Essays, p.62.

15.   Essays, p.92.

16.   Ives' name for the collection of characters who want everything to sound "nice", and who know what's "good" in music. Quite the straw man for tongue (in cheek) lashing.

17.   The Fourth Symphony was still to come, but as I have indicated above, the story of that work strongly overlaps that of the Concord.

18.   Cowell, op.cit., p.124.

19.   Cowell, op.cit_ P.126.

20.   Essays, p.66.

21.   Essays, p.18.

22.   Essays, pp.30-31.

Other Essays on Music

General

A Hitchhiker's Guide to the Galaxy...

...of classical music. Hey, Rock-folk...Jazz-folk...Folk-folk. What do the Classical folks know that you don't? What's kept them buying tickets since 1672, and recordings since 1914, when Beethoven's Fifth became the first recorded symphony? Is there something going on that's not so boring? Interesting, even, perhaps ecstatic? Very likely.

Herewith a quickie tour of the galaxy, starting with the most obvious thing — the milky way, that great stream of western classical music from the 10th to the 21st century in periods known as "early, baroque, classical, romantic, modern and contemporary" — shoddy, approximative categories, but useful nonetheless. The brightest stars stand out, usually at period's edge.

Up half-way towards the left we see blazing perhaps the brightest star of all — Bach — the culmination and end-all of the Baroque, the great explorer of spiritual geometry, the fabricator of space and time, in the opinion of many the greatest composer ever. His world (we're talking 1685-1750) was permeated by a God coming under new attack. And so his every piece was signed "Ad Gloriam Dei". Bach's was a sixth and seventh chakra effulgence — mind, and thousand petaled lotus. Around him, and behind, the brilliant Handel, the lesser lights Corelli, Vivaldi, Telemann. A rich time, the Baroque, though — all except Bach — susceptible to the beastly charms of Muzak.

— And over to the right, there's Beethoven — born twenty years after Bach's death, dying in 1827, Beethoven, "the man who freed music." Freed it from what? From "classical music"! Look at that triangle up there in mid-sky: Haydn to Mozart and Beethoven, perhaps the greatest triple play ever. Inside classical music, there's something called the classical period — the time of these three geniuses, handing off to one another the insights of sonata form and content from which most all future western music was to spring. Middle Beethoven, a heart man, fifth chakra pounding.

For Beethoven, and the Revolution, outgrew those forms, that "classical" content, and so initiated "the Romantic period" where gaze turned inward to the passions and fantasies of the individual, with forms as varied as people and local turbulence. What a stream of first and second magnitude stars is there — Schubert, Berlioz, Mendelssohn, Chopin, Schumann, Lizst. There's the brightest of them, the "third B" — Brahms — and then, Tschaikovsky, Dvorak, and the mad and maddening Wagner. These are fourth chakra men, heart men too, though none so deep and complex as Beethoven. Some reach down to third and even second chakras — solar plexus and sex. Brahms may have created the sexiest music ever. You like sex?

(What's that streak coming off Beethoven, shooting out laterally into cosmic space? Ah, that's the "late, deaf Beethoven flare" — a stellar object unto itself, radiating out into spacetime never before, never again explored, making sound never heard by the hearing. "The only competitor to Bach," say many. "Too deep a story," say the rest. But Deaf shall have its dominion.)

Out to the right, on the edge of the Romantic, the red giant Richard Wagner — romanticism unto death. The twisted death of the romantic period, and the beginning of "modern music", an era of tonal complexity so chromatic it had to explode — so that a new world might be born. And there the new world is, further towards the right, another great triangle of first magnitude — Schoenberg, Berg, Webern forming a V for Vienna. Talk about freeing music. Beethoven freed music from the fifty years before him. These three freed music from the previous thousand years, from Pythagorean vibrations themselves. Feel adventurous? Want to impress a date? Take him/her to hear some twelve-tone music. Experience the unadvertised emotional and spiritual interstices of modern times. You may not like what you hear, but it's as real as it gets.

At the horizons left and right, things are dimmer. What Greek music was like, that music of the stature of their theater, is beyond our resolution. But over there on the left, the first bright star — Hildegard,

12th century enchantress, and higher in declination the incandescent, Josquin des Pres, the undisputed king of "early music". Swing and sway with Josquin des Pres. Behind him, his teachers, Obrecht and Ockeghem, shining over Flanders. These Renaissance composers could weave webs more fine than any spider. They used no bar lines to mark the beat — ONE two three four, ONE two three four — their time is just suspended, as intricately interwoven strands extrude from their quills. The "early-ness" of the music did not compromise its mastery. My father-in-law thought "Music died in 1521," when they laid ol' Josquin in his grave.

And over there on the right, our undigested times — the big-gies of non-Viennese "modern music", Stravinsky, Bartok, Prokoviev, Shostakovich. Further toward the horizon, the density thins out, with few stars of first magnitude. Stockhausen, maybe, Penderecki, Schnittke. Look at that weird, red white and blue star off by itself. That's Charles Ives. We'll have to see what brightens as the sky turns.

Rock-folk...Jazz-folk...Folk-folk....If you're interested in hitching this highway, in hearing unaccustomed sounds from all along the way, you can make the whole trip in this very area over the next nine months — time long enough to birth new worlds within you. Seven Days' unique sidebar calendar lists concerts where you can hear exam-ples of masterpieces from all across the sky, and follow up the periods which grab you.

OR

Consider this a hitchhiker's guide to the interstate…of western clas-sical music. What do classical music fans know that, say, rock, folk, jazz or hip-hop fans don't? What's kept them buying tickets since 1672, and recordings since 1914, when Beethoven's Fifth became the first recorded symphony? Is there something going on in classical that's maybe not so boring? That may be interesting, even ecstatic? I'd say yes.

Herewith, a time-triptik for the novice musical traveler, a sight-hearing guide along the great music highway from the 10th to the 21st century. We'll break this down into periods: Early Music, Baroque, Classical, Romantic, Modern and Contemporary Music. Approximate categories, but useful nonetheless.

We know little of the earliest western music — until church folk started writing it down at the first millennium. Two hundred years in, we find the first bright Western star — Hildegard von Bingen, a 12th-century abbess, composer of heavenly chants. By the time of the Renaissance, music had grown sacred and secular, lovely and complex, especially in the Netherlands, whose Josquin des Pres was the undisputed king of "EARLY" music. It doesn't feel so early. In fact, my father-in-law thought "music died in 1521" — with the death of Josquin. The great trio of (late) early music — Josquin, and his teachers Obrecht and Ockeghem — were geniuses who could weave webs finer than a spider's. They used no bar lines to mark the beat (as in, one two three four, one two three four). Their time simply suspends, as intricately interwoven strands of vocal line flow on in unmeasured measure.

All that marvelous counterpoint eventually produced Bach, the culmination and end-all of the BAROQUE, the great explorer of spiritual geometry, the fabricator of space and time, and in the opinion of many the greatest composer ever. In his era — we're talking 1685 to 1750 — God was coming under new attack by the new sciences. But the faithful Bach signed every piece "Ad Gloriam Dei" — "Glory to God." He made enormous choral settings of biblical passions and mass texts, intricate instrumental fugues and concertos, and pieces for solo instruments, all soaked in counterpoint and chorale, all "Ad Gloriam Dei". Around and behind him, the brilliant Handel and the lesser lights Corelli, Vivaldi and Telemann. It was a rich time, the Baroque, though ultimately all but Bach have fallen prey to Muzak.

The next mountain range is ahead, the highest peak, Beethoven. Born 20 years after Bach's death and living until 1827, he is "the man who freed music." Freed it from what?" you might ask. From "classical music!" Look at that trio out there ahead: Haydn, Mozart and Beethoven, Himalaya and volcano at once, Haydn the teacher of the others, and almost equal in innovation.

What Beethoven exploded was the CLASSICAL period within classical music, the time of these three geniuses, handing off to one another the insights of sonata form and content, its contrasts, struggles and reconciliations, from which most all subsequent Western music would spring. The symphony was born here, the sonata as we know it, the string quartet, and other chamber music forms. Imaginative music which always comes out all right. You say "ah" at the end.

But Beethoven outgrew those forms, that "classical" content, and initiated "the ROMANTIC period." Here the gaze turned inward to the passions and fantasies of the individual, with varied musical forms. What a stream of first- and second-magnitude stars is there — Schubert, Berlioz, Mendelssohn, Chopin, Schumann, Lizst. The brightest of them — the "third B" — was Brahms, who may have created the sexiest music ever, lush, lovely and insinuating. Then, Tchaikovsky, Dvorak and the mad and maddening Wagner, out on the edge, boiling. Wagner marks the twisted death of the Romantic before its evolution into "MODERN" music. The harmonic complexity of his world pushed the listener beyond any sense of key and her emotions beyond what classical or romantic music could contain.

After Wagner, music exploded. Key? What's that anymore? Gone. Tunes? Likewise. The modern tide swept away the entire consonance vs. dissonance narrative of music history.

A new sound came out of the next mountain range: Schoenberg, Berg and Webern, all from Vienna. As Beethoven had freed music from the 50 years before him, these three freed music from the previous thousand years, from Pythagorean vibrations themselves. Feel adventurous? Want to impress a date? Take him or her to hear some 12-tone music, and experience the dark emotional and spiritual interstices of modernity. You may not like what you hear, but it's as real as it gets — the pain, tension, and previously inexpressible emotions of our ravaged time.

To this day it is unclear if this "Second Viennese Circle" invented the music of the future, or wound up with images so unbearable, (even if true) as to be a dead-end spur. For there were many other modernists who spurned their extreme methods and sound, giants like Stravinsky, Bartok, Prokoviev, Shostakovich, still writing melodies, in recognizable, if more complex, keys, but with new forms and new rhythms. Perhaps it is they who best represent "modern" music.

CONTEMPORARY music remains problematical. Where are the giants, where are the mountain ranges? Some say there will never be another age with a Haydn/Mozart/Beethoven/Schubert (The "First Viennese Circle") event. They even theorize a cause: the suppressive influences of consumerist capitalism and media. Still, there are amazing composers out there, like Penderecki, Schnittke, Ligeti, Stockhausen. Under current conditions, it's difficult to establish nutritive ground. But people are still trying to find their way — as the contemporary music offerings in our area suggest.

Which brings us to the Calendar. Seven Days hereby presents a unique classical musical calendar, period by period. If you find a particular style intriguing, you can follow examples of it throughout the year. Or you can experience the whole history of western classical music in only nine months — without straying far from home. Expand your horizons.

Classical Music and Politics

Classically Absent

I opened my "Power of Music" issue [of The *Nation*] with faint anticipatory trepidation. Would lefty scan be blind, as usual, to the revolutionary message of "classical" music? Would the highly educated, morally aware, philosophically sophisticated, politically savvy editors and writers supply their readers with any reflection on a millennium of radical expression? Would the self-censorship and cultural/political omissions we expect from mainstream media be duplicated here, *mutatis mutandis,* and the double-issue be filled with obvious suspects and current celebrities? My suspicions were, alas, well-founded.

I don't get it. In "classical" music — from the tenth through the twentieth century — we have inherited a cornucopia of profundities, prompting and announcing social change at every step along the way, educating human consciousness towards ever-greater complexity of perception and thought, coaxing out our emotional and spiritual depths. The great composers have always demanded from us, and developed in us, precisely those sensibilities we need to confront the hugest issues we face — structure, otherness, variation, modulation, time, change, form, dissipation...love.

I think of the room in which the Eroica was first performed — it's aristocratic, gold-leafed curlicues, it's elaborately carved chairs. I think of Beethoven's assessment of the "princely rabble" that would seat their asses on those chairs, and the shattering indictment with which he would assault them in the name of freedom. *Seid umschlungen, Millionen,* he intoned in the Ninth Symphony, masses embracing in the kiss of the entire world. Tell it to George Bush and the IMF. Bach's intensity and structural investigations, Brahms's sexuality unlimited,

Mahler's catalogue of hetero-interactions, Wagner's engorging instability, Bartok's *mesto* dance, Stravinsky's primordial landscapes, Berg's evocation of interstitial states — one could go on and on, and in and in. Are all these irrelevant to the left, and to our goals of head and heart?

Let's talk about the means of production. Though there are surely classical stars and consumers, by far the greatest number of sounds are made by amateurs at choral or orchestral or chamber music rehearsals and performances, or playing at home — a democratic, participatory picture of growth, education, and community, growing since the eighteenth century.

Yes, the art and artists in the music issue speak strongly to us and our times. But they are not the only music relevant to the left. We need to recover the largesse of our musical heritage, and political/cultural journals like the *Nation* could play a key role here, if they so chose.

The Role of Classical Music in Contemporary Life

So you're sitting here, waiting for the concert to begin. You look around and see a lot of white hair. Yes, there are some younger people, but most are sporting notebooks — a give-away that they're likely here on assignment. And besides, for them, what's a concert anyway, if you can't get up and dance?

"Classical music" — the very word is like a knell. Audience hair is graying, symphony orchestras are closing, "contemporary music", along with attention span, is shutting down. This — where you are — is simply not hip, not relevant to today, finally bo-ring. As a brother-in-law of mine used to say, "Chamber music — chamber pots."

All right then, mourners, what IS the role of the arts today, in this incredible world, in these most perilous times? And what, especially, is the role of classical music in a world where power runs amuck, and forms shatter and disperse?

The role of classical music in these times is what it has always been — to scream, call or whisper "Wake up! You cannot escape..." The role of classical music in these times is to knock, pound or howl at the doors of the hardened heart to enable grace and penetration.

The role of classical music in these times is recognize and fight the anti-arts — those imperatives to sleep, perchance to buy, to buy it all, all the ease and violence, the self-love and disdain for others, the mindless "I" that carries our culture and our bombers around the world.

What is the role of classical anything in these times? Think: Fred Astaire, Samuel Beckett, Caravaggio, Carl Theodor Dreyer, Edward Elgar, Ferron, and while we're in Canada, Glenn Gould. Think Zora Neale Hurston, Ionesco, Joyce, Kafka, Dorothea Lange, Zero Mostel, Vladimir Nabokov, Georgia O'Keeffe, Sylvia Plath, Jakob van

Ruisdale, Sartre, Sojourner Truth, Uccello, Virginia Woolf, Marguerite Yourcenar, Frank Zappa — not to mention Bach, Bartok, Beethoven, Brahms, and add your own...

Artaud once said "No more masterpieces!" All right, then, *don't* think those above, but imagine your own. As long as it says "Wake up!" He also quoted a Balinese dancer as saying, "We have no art. We just do everything as well as we can." That might be a way to go, too.

But here you are at a concert of what some people would call "classical music". Half the hair is white — while the spiked folks are outed not by their greeny locks, but by their class notebooks. Is the audience here for entertainment (even if "required"), or is it <u>ready</u> for the revolutionary message of classical music — that glorious millennium of radical expression? Has this highly educated, morally aware, philosophically sophisticated, politically savvy crowd largely censored out the drastic challenge this concert of complexity is about to make?

In classical music — from the tenth through the twentieth century — we have inherited a cornucopia of profundities, prompting and announcing social change at every step along the way, educating human consciousness towards ever-greater complexity of perception and thought, coaxing out our emotional and spiritual depths. The great composers have always demanded from us, and developed in us, precisely those sensibilities we need to confront the hugest issues we face — structure, otherness, variation, modulation, time, change, form, dissipation...love.

I think of the room in which the Eroica was first performed — it's aristocratic, gold-leafed curlicues, it's elaborately carved chairs. I think of Beethoven's assessment of the "princely rabble" that would seat their asses on those chairs, and the shattering indictment with which he would assault them in the name of freedom. *Seid umschlungen, Millionen,* he intoned in the Ninth Symphony, masses embracing in the kiss of the entire world. Tell it to George Bush, Wolfowitz's World Bank and the IMF. Bach's intensity and structural investigations, Brahms's sexuality unlimited, Mahler's catalogue of hetero-interactions, Wagner's engorging instability, Bartok's *mesto* dance, Stravinsky's primordial landscapes, Berg's evocation of interstitial states — one could go on and on, and in and in. Are all these irrelevant to our times, to our goals of head and heart?

Yes, classical music still speaks acutely to our times. It had better — or we are goners.

"*Wachet auf!*" it says. So listen up hard. And bring the kids.

Music Hath Charms to Soothe the Stinking Breath

A recent revelation: rehearsing the Mendelssohn *Violin Concerto*, I was in the cello section mentally drooling over the carpet of harmonies we were laying down under the solo violin during the gorgeous slow movement. Not much to concentrate on other then how very beautiful this moment was.

As I breathed in the slow movement of the Mendelssohn, I realized that this music, this moment, and others like it, were SPECIFIC antidotes to the poison spewing from the mouths of politicians. I realized too, that without my frequent hits from the music inhaler I would probably be dead, or at least reduced to zombiedom. My life's balance was suspended between the poison of politics and the healing of music, which interaction created a space for my writing.

I had long been aware of "the healing power of music" inasmuch as it was the arena of "music therapy" and the tool of music therapists. But I had never been so acutely aware of its specific purgative and remedial effect.

Coming up soon are Beethoven's two birthdays, December 16 and December 17. As one of the characters in my novel, *Insect Dreams*, says: "Extraordinary people do extraordinary things." (Not to be coy, there are two different documents with two different birth dates. I celebrate both.) And this week, too, Donna and I begin rehearsals for a New Year's Day performance of Beethoven's Ninth Symphony, which will hopefully become a tradition here in Burlington. In any case, Beethoven is often on my mind.

It's somewhat predictable, then, that the combination of Beethoven, music, and healing would find its way into my writing. I want to share with you this week a particularly ridiculous scene based on a particularly amazing piece of music—a movement of the A minor

String Quartet which Aldous Huxley called "proof of the existence of God". The movement was labeled by Beethoven *"Heiliger Dankgesang eines Gesenenen an die Gottheit, in der lydischen Tonart"*—a "Holy Song of Thanks from a Convalescent to the Godhead, in the Lydian Mode".

Beethoven was known to have serious stomach problems which bothered him increasingly as he aged. I put this all together and came up with the following note in my recent novel, *The Annotated Nose*.

In this section from The Annotated Nose, *Alexei Pigov, "plague doctor" and accordion player extraordinare, hoping to pick up girls among the many nurses, has taken a job at the huge NY-Presbyterian Hospital. William Hundwasser is the (fictive) author of a (fictive) novel in which Alexei is the main character. Alexei occasionally went upstairs to the animal room to play for Herman, the spider.*

The hero, Alexei Pigov, has become the Glenn Gould of the accordion. He is befriended by a fellow lab tech, William Hundwasser, who exploits and markets his strangeness, creating from him the public figure of a medieval plague doctor come to heal The Contemporary Plague. Here he is in Hundwasser's lab, experimenting with Beethoven on Hundwasser, and Herman, the tarantula:

Studying tarantellas and subtly applying them was my first experience of being a healer. Hundwasser kept several in a terrarium in his lab as a conversation starter for the "pretty young things in their white lab coats" he enjoyed cultivating. I began with one named Herman.

Herman was a dancin' fool. He (?) would jump out of hiding — or hibernating, or estivating, or whatever tarantulas do for sleep — at the first peep of the accordion, and would then stand thoughtfully, taking the music into his ganglia. Then he would begin to sway, and after a minute to dance, and to dance appropriately to whatever I was playing, almost in rhythm, but definitely fast for allegros and slowly for adagios. When I stopped, he stopped — and waited. He could outwait me. When I left, I would just leave him there, waiting.

I figured if an insect person could react this way, with so few nerve cells, human persons must be able process such signals with far more complex consequences than simply dancing.

As you probably know, Beethoven suffered from chronic abdominal problems and severe intestinal inflammation. Fortunately Hundwasser suffered similar symptoms. An experiment was staring me right in the face. The famous *Heilige Dankgesang* in the A minor quartet, the "Holy Song Of Thanks From A Convalescent To The Godhead", was written after recovering from a serious bout with abdominal pain. Surely the tones, the great ideas of that movement, beyond being "proof of the existence of God" (Huxley), the successive integrations of disparate elements, must have something to do with disease, and with (Beethoven's) stomach disease in particular. It was worth a try.

I made an accordion arrangement of the three adagio sections, and played them daily to Hundwasser during lunch break. We used the animal room for privacy. He just sat and listened. I suppose the rats listened too, but I had no parameters to measure the effects on them.

Hundwasser, however, had lots of parameters. Or, like the hedgehog, one big parameter: the number of Rolaids he popped each day. It took a week or so before R began to drop. From an average of 20 to an average of 12. On weekends, no music, R rose again. Come weekdays, it began to fall by Tuesday. In a sustained three week experiment, no days off, R fell to 3, then climbed to 12 again with a week off. We were on to something.

Neither of us had the time for a full and lasting cure, but after we stopped the experiment, he bought a record of the Budapest playing it, and has used that routinely to calm his symptoms. Saves him money on Rolaids, and he can listen while washing the dishes during the rare moments that he washes the dishes.

Flush with success, I looked more closely into the tarantella situation, the Antidotum Tarantulae. I would need to study the phenomenon first hand.

But there aren't a lot of tarantula bites in Manhattan. There aren't many tarantas [women bitten by tarantulas] to whom I could offer treatment — especially if it were just an experiment by a newbie. What to do?

Herman to the rescue! I could get him to bite me, and then, in the heroic tradition of the great doctors and medical researchers, I could try to cure myself. I admit such research is small potatoes compared to the guy who shoved a catheter into an arm vein and guided it up into his heart, or the guys from Walter Reed's team who invited malaria mosquitoes to bite them, so they could test drugs, or even the guy who gave himself ulcers so he could prove it was bacteria that caused them. Small potatoes unless I died. But I know that though tarantula bites were toxic, they were not often fatal.

And of course, we have to remember Dr. Curt Conners, aka, the Lizard in Spiderman Comics, who lost his arm in a war, and experimented with reptilian DNA to try and grow it back, a great example of be careful what you wish for: the therapy caused him to mutate into a creature half-human and half-reptile. He became a villain, too, and even uglier than I am. I wondered if I might turn into a tarantula person — from the saliva — but it wasn't very likely.

I knew this self-experimentation would be looked down upon at the Berg Institute for Experimental Physiology, Surgery and Pathology, even though experimental physiology, surgery and pathology was exactly what I was doing. So it was 1 A.M. when I let myself into Hundwasser's lab, took Honey [his accordion] out of her case, and aroused Herman with the traditional slow, lamenting introduction to Borodin's *Polovtsian Dance #2*, "The Wild Dance of the Men". Out he came on cue, staring at me through the Adagio, and when the fast part started, gave a shiver, and went into nothing short of a frenzy, leaping high off the terrarium floor, doing 90°, 180°, 270°, and 360° spins in the air, landing on his feet, rolling over on his back, and dragging himself miraculously by hyper—extended forelegs reaching up, over and behind his head, engaging the sand. It was so amazing, I almost forgot what I had come for. He must have been a Polovetsian spider, or at least have Polovetsian blood, perhaps from the Russian steppes.

When the both of us stopped to get our breaths, I thrust my left arm into the terrarium, and, though normally a pacifist, he leaped at it, and sunk his fangs in midway between wrist and elbow. Good Herman! I had to pull him off. Within a minute and a half, I was, as they say, possessed by the spider.

Though being somewhat atypical myself, I was that night afflicted with all the typical tarantula bite symptoms: feelings of prostration, anguish, psychomotor agitation, clouding of my sensory apparatus, difficulty standing, stomach cramps, nausea, paresthesia, muscular pains, extraordinary itching, and best and worst of all, vastly heightened sexual desire. I took a cab home; the cabbie thought I was way-drunk.

Lying in my bed, I felt wounded and weary, and aware of the deep tediousness of all things. Still, after a short sleep, I was able to drag Honey out of her case, and begin a medley of tarantellas I had learned.

Somewhere toward the end of the 1490s, the great Neapolitan scholar Alessandro d'Alessandro described the treatment of stricken tarantas by the local folk musicians: "they play different dances according to the nature of the poison, in such a way that with the victims entranced by the harmony and fascinated by what they hear, the poison either dissolves inside the body and dissipates, or else is slowly eliminated through the veins." And with (wouldn't you know it?) one of the Neapolitan tarantellas, I could feel just that effect, a veritable exorcism, a return to life, possibly to love. By the next day I was weak, but feeling basically normal via my iatromusical practice.

Plague doctoring is not so much different, though I suffer less, and my patients suffer more

Guillotine Playlist

Being a musician, I think in musical terms and often structure my work guided by musical forms. As a teenager, I was completely bowled over by Thomas Mann's chapter on Beethoven's last piano sonata, op. 111, early in his Doctor Faustus. "I'd love to be able to write something like that," I thought. Fifty years later, I gave it a try with my chapter on a fictive Charles Ives sonata in my debut novel, *Insect Dreams*.

Since then, my every novel has some composer or some piece of music as part of its story or structure. In various books, I have engaged Ives' Fourth Symphony, Handel's *Messiah*, Stravinsky's *Rite of Spring*, Zelenka's *Lamentations of Jeremiah*, Mahler's *Second Symphony*, Gilbert & Sullivan's *Yeoman of the Guard*, Scarlatti's piano sonatas, Messian's *L'Ascencion*, Prokofiev's *First Violin Concerto*, and Beethoven's *Grosse Fugue*. I have planned books to be in sonata form, in rondo form, and as themes and variations.

The Good Doctor Guillotin was structured and driven by the songs of the French Revolution: The main sections are *Ça Ira* — a revolutionary song meaning it will happen, it will work out fine; *Allons enfants de la patrie* — the beginning of the *Marseillaise* — let's go!; and *Le jour de gloire est arrivé* — the glorious day has come. Unfortunately, the glory turned out to be the Terror.

Realizing that a young composer who lived and died during the Revolution's genesis and birth — Mozart — had to be part of the picture, one of the first scenes I conceived of was that of the good doctor Guillotin, progressive, humanist member of the National Assembly, playing a Mozart sonata with Tobias Schmidt, the German piano maker who built the early beheading machines. "Why are you crying?" Schmidt was to ask. "Why are *you* crying?" was to be the answer. While both characters were real, it was I who made them both musicians. The discussion that followed would concern not only the music, but the revolution occurring around them.

Not being a violinist, and not well-acquainted with the violin literature, I emailed my many musicians friends — folks I play chamber music and in orchestras with. "If you were going to cry over a moment in a Mozart violin sonata, what would it be?" I received a variety of answers, but the one that came up most commonly was the E major trio in the minuet of the E minor sonata. I listened to all suggestions, and decided that not only was that most popular suggestion eminently cryable-to, but that it would give me the most thematic connection with the social complexities of the revolution. It is now the context of the chapter "Tempo di Menuetto".

So, anyway — to my "playlist".

First, the French revolutionary songs:

The *Marseillaise* (http://www.marseillaise.org/english/audio.html) needs little explanation. The one intriguing fact is that it was written by C-J Rouget de Lisle on April 25, 1792, the very day our hero Nicholas Pelletier, the patient, the package, was executed. Claude-Joseph wrote it at his table in Strasbourg — childhood home of the builder of the execution machine.

Ça ira is an enthusiastic, if bloodthirsty, tongue twister (http://www.fordham.edu/halsall/mod/caira.html) in which we find the aristocrats swinging from lamp posts and Marie Antoinette in hell. It was the most popular "people's song" during the Revolution.

La Carmagnole was a popular revolutionary song and dance again concerning Marie Antoinette who, by the way, was unpopular not only because of her "Let them eat cake" attitude toward the poor, but because her Austrian family was likely to attack France to preserve its own and Europe's monarchies. Listen at http://en.wikipedia.org/wiki/Carmagnole. There is a wonderful Kathe Kollwitz drawing and set of sketches ("*Carmagnole*") of a revolutionary crowd dancing around a guillotine in Paris.

Next, Mozart:

Of primary use was the E minor sonata mentioned above. But

equally important thematically is a piano piece played by beginners, a little set of variations on the French folk song, *Ah, vous dirai-je Maman*. We know the tune as "Twinkle, Twinkle, Little Star". In French, there are bawdy lyrics (probably more to Mozart's liking) about what a young daughter would like to, but can't tell her mother about her new lover, but the original may have been a simple children's song, which I find thematically more interesting:

Ah! Vous dirai-je Maman
Ce qui cause mon tourment?
Papa veut que je raisonne
Comme une grande personne
Moi je dis que les bonbons
Valent mieux que la raison.

Mama, should I tell you what is tormenting me? Papa wants me to reason like an adult, but I think bonbons are worth more than reason.

There, in a nutshell, the fate of the Enlightenment Project, and our own predicament.

Musically, what is of musical/thematic interest here is that in the midst of the upbeat, tongue-in-cheek compositional facility of the twelve variations, plunked down in the middle, is one of the darkest moments in Mozart. Perhaps this crucified minute is no "worse" than some of the tortured moments in the late symphonies, but here, in the midst of a nursery rhyme tune, it is particularly devastating. The darkness concealed in the light. Both Guillotin and Schmidt would have noticed that. And they do.

Two other Mozart pieces make their appearance, both in the context of the contemporary fad for Mesmer, his healing clinic, and his animal magnetism. (Though he was run out of Paris by the good doctors of the Sorbonne, he was one of the earliest practitioners of the "energy medicine" now widely practiced in its eastern and western forms.) There was a lot of "new age, woo-woo" music played in his clinic during the healing sessions, and Ben Franklin's design for the "glass harmonica" was the Wurlitzer in the theater. Mozart wrote an *Adagio and Rondo for Glass*

Harmonica, (http://www.pbs.org/benfranklin/l3_inquiring_glass.html) which was very likely part of the mix. Woo-woo.

The inveterate Wolfgang clown wrote a send-up of Mesmer himself in *Così fan Tutte*, where, at the end of Act One, fake Albanians are killed by fake poison, and are revived by a fake doctor, using a giant, all-healing magnet.

Bach

Hard to escape him. As Bach developed his keyboard works, it became obvious to many — including the old man — that the clavichord and harpsichord could no longer contain or express the range of emotion and intensity of passion he and his works had grown capable of. Music history was screaming for a pianoforte, and organ builders and harpsichord makers put their minds and tools to it. For purposes of the story, I made Schmidt one of them, a child so inspired by his own understanding of the Kantor's needs as to make a life project of piano building. Too bad that during the Revolution, aristocrats weren't buying pianos anymore, and of course the poor never could. Find a hole and fill it. Beheading machines. That's the ticket! Makes for a sardonic consciousness.

Schmidt was not the only character involved with Bach. Sanson, the executioner of Paris, was the historical figure with the most written about him. It turned out that he (like me) was a bad cellist, but bad enough — that, mixed with his profession — no one (I thought) would play with him. What do cellists do when they have to play alone? They play the Bach cello suites. Today, any cellist anywhere can go to the nearest music store and buy any of many editions. But then? Would Sanson have been able to get his hands on them? Yes, they were written by then. And there were musical manuscripts flowing, largely through Strasbourg, between Germany and France. And any suite would be easy enough to copy in the pre-xerox age. So — it's possible that Sanson, a self-styled noble, and member of the court, might have been able to get hold of some of them. That's the best I could come up with from my musicological friends — "It's possible". Time for my author's rights: I gave him a copy to nurse his cellistic wounds with. I imagine him loving the Saraband from the D minor suite.

My soulmind is so often filled with Bach that the moment I sat down to write the Acknowledgments, I translated "I acknowledge" into *Confiteor* — which, in spite of the many settings of the Latin Credo, first and foremost means the enormous fugue/plainsong "Confiteor" movement of the B minor mass. So I wound up dividing my acknowledgments into Bach's components — the marching continuo, the fugue and the chant — and the form served me well to acknowledge the many aspects of the novel that needed acknowledging.

Minor characters

Bert Brecht and Kurt Weill's opera masterpiece, *Mahagonny*, was bound to show up in any work of mine about the Enlightenment. After all, it concerns a planned city — planned by criminals, of course — which, like the French Revolution — was to be devoted to human happiness — happiness in this case consisting of eating, drinking, whoring and boxing. It ends with the electric chair. Sound familiar? Early on, Jimmy Mahoney, like my Schmidt, senses the limitation of the project. He and his friends get together and sing a barbershop quartet (barbering, anyone?) about how wonderful, noble and beautiful their new world is. "But," Jimmy continues to observe, "Something is missing." The moment sang itself right into my text.

As did Richard Peaslee's "Fifteen Glorious Years" from Peter Brooks's astonishing Royal Shakespeare Company production of Peter Weiss's Marat/Sade. Many of the elements of this remarkable play prompted moments and larger musings in my text. Peaslee's music has that kind of memorable rightness which will forever prevent me from thinking of any other settings — much like Tenniel's drawings for Alice, or Cruikshank's for Dickens.

As did two epigraph references from *The Mikado* — inevitable in a book about beheading as punishment. "Now though you'd have said that head was dead" speaks directly to the fierce eighteenth century debate about whether the guillotine was kinder than the gallows. We are currently in the midst of an equally barbarous debate concerning our procedures for lethal injection. And we, unlike other advanced democracies, are also still debating whether the punishment fitting the crime must necessarily involve state murder to convince the public that murder is a bad thing to do.

There is a piece of music which did not, and could not, get into *The Good Doctor Guillotin*, but which I would also recommend to the interested reader/listener: the final scene from Poulenc's *Dialogues of the Carmelites*, in which a convent of Carmelite nuns, condemned for resisting the Revolution's disenfranchisement of the Church, are led serially to their deaths, singing a prayer to the Virgin while the mob screams and denounces, and the guillotine cuts and cuts, cuts through their serenity.

My wife and I couchsurfed with an orchestral conductor in Paris one of whose proudest plumbing creations was his invention of how to do the guillotine sound.

Buying a Piano Is Not a Simple Task

(Liberace)

Las Vegas provides the best demonstration of the permanent imper-manence of man in the desert — largely because nowhere in town is one unaware of its invincible presence. Wherever humans have not built, wherever concrete is not poured, the desert abides — even in the pedestrian islands in the middle of the Strip. Humanity seems a mere experiment in alien territory.

Buying a piano in the desert is not a simple task. Especially when one — before all else — must see the Liberace Museum for fear that it might close early.

Liberace's taste ran to bejeweled, red, white and blue Rolls Royces, a 24-carat gold-plated 1931 Cadillac, a collection of 42 pianos, including — in addition to Chopin's Pleyel and George Gershwin's Chickering — a mirrored concert grand which takes nine men and a fork lift to move, a white llama fur coat with a 16 foot train, a diamond ring with stone the size of a lemon, and stage outfits of mink and feathers worth three quarters of a million each. Liberace was once the highest paid enter-tainer in the world.

Its visitors are silent and reverential — almost as though they're present at the Sistine Chapel or the Vietnam memorial. They read and take notes on the information in jewelry display cases and posted near pianos and cars. Mr. Showmanship also had talent in pedagogy and museumology.

But his taste in museum siting did leave something to be desired. The famous Liberace Museum shares a small shopping center 2 miles off the Vegas Strip with Tatiana's Hair Salon, a storefront Asamblea Apostolica, an Aladdin Market, and a refrigerator magnet store. A

Seven-Eleven and The Pinball Hall of Fame lie across the street.

Being one story, the museum is not quite a towering structure. Nevertheless, it tries hard, encompassing two contiguous storefronts, one for cars and pianos, the other for clothing and jewels. Atop its entrance flies a giant pink neon piano floating on an undulating keyboard and topped by Liberace's florid pink signature. To its right, a large wall — three overlapping pages of childish music in 2/4 — nudged by a giant portrait of the child-man himself. You can't miss it — and you easily can.

But the Captain's GPS nailed it right quick, and its digital voice assistant called the turns correctly, all the way down 95 and through the heart of town, evading traffic on the problematical Strip. Not that Bruce didn't want to try his particular smarts at the blackjack table, but the string-players reminded him they had piano-buying to do.

Bruce's target, the Chopin-played late eighteenth century Pleyel, was set off behind a velour catenary supported by two ornate brass stanchions. To a civilian it clearly meant "Do Not Touch". To Captain Boynton, it meant "I can probably reach it if I lean way over." Although a catenary curve superficially resembles a parabola, Bruce was versed enough in these matters to know that it actually traced a hyperbolic cosine function. And given that catenary curves are used in suspension bridges, plus the fact that he was sort of hyperbolic himself, the Captain, having ascertained the coast was clear, decided to support himself with his left hand in the middle of the curve, and reach out with his right to the keyboard. The center, as Yeats predicted, did not hold, and the stanchions collapsed inward, sending Bruce sprawling forward enough to shove the piano bench into the pedal assembly, toppling the candelabra standing left of the music stand, said candelabra smashing on the keys ringing out a chord neither Chopin nor Pleyel had ever imagined, and the guards came running.

Bruce, ever creative, quickly gathered his rumpled self up off the floor and announced his intention to sue the museum for slippery floors. The tables preemptively turned, the guards, then the museum director made nice-nice, made sure he wasn't hurt, and refunded the price of his ticket ($15). The trio left early, Bruce's desire having been thwarted. He was not interested in llama skin coats.

Over the course of the afternoon, the trio visited four piano dealers. The Captain sat in each showroom, and tried the recommended pianos which their collective pockets would tolerate. At each instrument, Bruce played two or three minutes of the same four selections, his choice explained in the car on the way down: the Scarlatti G major sonata would be for delicacy and fluency, the Bach C# minor fugue for sustained gravitas, the Hammerklavier fugue for wackiness and unplayability, and the Brahms A major Intermezzo, just to be nice to the other customers.

At 4:30, after fifteen or sixteen little concerts, Bruce called it a day without making a decision.

"You know," he remarked, driving home, "trying out potential pianos is a lot like dating from the personals. You study and consider the specs, but then you have to go out to dinner for a first date. Not that I would know, never having been on a first date or any date."

Peter and Angela wondered silently if this were hyperbole or literally true. After all, who would go out with him? And what woman (or man?) would he be moved to woo? The Captain continued his lecture on the trajectory of dating.

"So we try some easy things like Scarlatti this afternoon, and then we see what happens when we get a little more deeply involved. That first Steinway was bright, fun to play around with, but gave up when the Beethoven chips were down. The second was mellow, but couldn't do bright, like to cut through an orchestra, not that you two are an orchestra. But we might gather an orchestra. The Bösendorfer was nice, but brown and too ornate for me, mien Gott. And the Baldwin was just too lightweight. With Beethoven I felt as if I was abusing some young woman. And I didn't like its previous owner. I could feel him in the cracks. Oily skin, pencil mustache. So — I haven't found her yet."

They all went back to the personal ads under "musical instruments", and a second trip down 95 took them to the University of Nevada Las Vegas, where the music department was downsizing in response to the drop in state funding since the crash. They were getting rid of two newish 6'1" Yamaha Conservatory 3s. One of them was IT. It was her! It was she! The Captain was in love, and after a little haggling, the price was right. And it didn't take the military to bring her home. A UNLV grounds crew moved her up and into chez Warden for only 200 bucks more.

Not that a grounds crew knew how to set up a grand piano. But Bruce pulled out his iPhone, and called up an instructional video. Then three burley guys, a mesomorph, an ectomorph, and a beautiful woman all sat around and partied.

Other Essays on Music

On Particular Composers and Works

Happy Bach's Birthday

It was more than March: it was the vernal equinox, Bach's birthday, a day which Richard celebrated annually by listening to all of the Matthew Passion. This year, however, most passion was turned toward a certain Teresa Lee Skulkington of the Connecticut Skulkingtons, his sweetie and his addiction, his team-mate and his opponent, the woman who came to dinner. Nevertheless, Bach was Bach, and not to be neglected.

After a spring fertility meal (condoms plus cream tonight) at Single Pebble, the great Old Town Chinese restaurant — spring rolls, steamed asparagus salad with ginger-lemon dressing, Royal Bird's Nest for her, Ants Crawling Up A Tree for him, kumquats for both for dessert — they walked home for the promised evening of their Savior's pain, death and resurrection. They settled in, took off their shoes, and Richard fetched his beloved Scherchen recording (Hughes Cuenod, Evangelist extraordinaire!), and placed the first disc in the machine. Teresa fiddled meanwhile in one of her drawers.

"Here!" she exclaimed. "Let's do this, instead."

"What?"

Richard looked up from the play button.

"This. My personal Grateful Dead medley. I burned it for you before I left."

"You mean instead of Bach? Or as some kind of prelude?"

"Instead."

"But it's his birthday..."

"Yes, and I brought you — now that I think of it — a Bach's birthday present."

"Well, thank you, but..."

"And it requires the Dead."

"Well, ok, but then we'll do the Passion? It's almost three hours long..."

"Sure, sure. Afterwards."

She went to the machine, installed her own CD instead of his, and turned back to her perplexed friend.

"Now close your eyes and stick out your hand."

"Come on!"

"No, really."

He did as he was told by the woman who must be obeyed. She reached into her pocket.

"There. You can look."

In his hand lay a small glassine envelope marked "U.S.P.S." Inside lay what looked like a small copy of some Andy Warhol Uncle Sam, multiple tiny images offset shoulder to head, shoulder to head, each Sam divided into hat, face and body by micro-perforations.

"I didn't know Warhol did Uncle..."

"It's not Andy Warhol."

"Who, then?"

"It's not art, it's truth — if you'll permit the distinction."

Richard drew the two inch square out of its envelope, and regarded it carefully. It seemed to be printed on some kind of blotter paper from the pen and ink days.

"Wait a minute!" he said, "Is this...?"

"What do you think? And still undetectable by pigland airport security."

"For me? For Bach's birthday?"

"For us. Four hits for you, five for me."

"But I'm twice as heavy as you."

"Wrong. I'm twice as heavy as you. And I bet I've done more acid. And I bet I can handle it better."

"Well, it's true I've..."

"It's all right."

"But I once tried some..."

"You're a good boy. We deadheads prefer lysergic acid diethylamide."

"You're a deadhead?"

70

She stuck her thumbs into proud-position in her imaginary vest .

"Teresa Lee neé Skulkington, daughter of Lawrence Charles Skulkington, of the Connecticut Skulkingtons?"

She nodded.

"At parties inside your gated Westport community?"

"When Mommy and Daddy were in Europe — which was often."

"Oh."

He looked at his unpredictable partner.

How can I keep your soul from touching mine?

"Don't worry. I can guide you through. Trust me. Now stick out your tongue. Maybe we should start with three."

She carefully tore along the perforations.

"One...complete...Uncle...Sam. There! He'll prefer that to being dismembered. Ooops! What did I say?"

"E aaan oo ithembe..."

It's hard talk with your tongue out.

"Yes, I know. The Free Dismemberee State of Kansas."

He nodded.

"Suck em hard, chew em up, swallow em down. Like a termite."

"What about you?"

She downed her scheduled five, leaving a solo Samface which she push-pinned to the bulletin board in the kitchen, and returned with two glasses of Chardonnay. He accepted his wine with love and admiration in his eyes.

"OK. You look transformed already," she said. "Have you partaken yet?"

He shook his head, and displayed his strip of Uncle Sam.

"Well, just stick it under your tongue for a minute or so, then you can wash it down with your vino."

She reached for the play button.

"Wait," he interrupted. "Can we just hear the first chorus of the Bach — just in case we don't get to it? Tomorrow isn't his birthday anymore. It's only ten minutes. Eleven."

"Go for it."

He took the abandoned CD from the top of the box where she had placed it, traded it with hers in the machine, hit play, and settled in for a micro-hit of spiritual coitus-to-be-interruptus.

The dark and pulsing E minor, velvety yet terrifying, so truthful to the painful story of the world. Come, daughters of men, help me to lament! Evocative, intertwined wailing of the still-living human damned. Look! The Bridegroom comes. How does He come? Like a lamb to slaughter.

And then the incredible, cruel contrast — the voices of children declaiming the innocence of the Lord, the first phrase of "Oh, Lamb of God, Most Holy", an island of light floating in the Styx of human darkness.

Richard reached over and hit STOP.

"What's the matter? You're right. It's terrific."

"Yeah, I..."

"What?"

"It's too much now. Maybe it's doing this with you when I've been doing it alone for so many years. I don't know. Maybe it's Uncle Sam kicking in...We can do it for Bach's half-birthday in September. I always thought autumnal darkening was more appropriate anyway."

"Have it your way."

He placed the Bach disc in its box, and substituted Teresa's in the machine.

"Now?"

"Sure. Put it on repeat, or whatever, so it will cycle around."

They settled in, snuggling, to wait for the train to arrive. She sang along, while he listened.

What do you want me to do to see you throooooo?

"Just be here with me."

And she was.

Bach Wrote

JSB on Freedom

"I want to demonstrate to the world the architecture of a new and beautiful social commonwealth. Each instrument in counterpoint, and as many contrapuntal parts as there are instruments. It is the enlightened self-discipline of the various parts, each voluntarily imposing on itself the limits of its individual freedom for the well-being of the community. That is my message: not the autocracy of a single, stubborn melody on the one hand, nor the anarchy of unchecked noise on the other. No, a delicate balance between the two, an enlightened freedom. The science of my art, the art of my science, the harmony of the stars in the heavens, the yearning for brotherhood in the heart of man: this is the secret of my music."

Bartok — Miraculous Mandarin

It must be admitted that brown-suited Gregor was out of place at the white-tie event. It was the first time the National Ballet and the National Symphony had collaborated in a production requiring large orchestral forces, and Democratic culture-vultures were still cocky-drunk with victory. But in the lobby, Szilard pulled a black beret out of his pocket, set it jauntily tipped over Gregor's right epicranium, Wigner wrapped a gay, red scarf around his cephalothoracic juncture, and the three Hungarians stepped back and looked at their creation.

"Artiste," Teller declared.

"Nothing to be ashamed of," Wigner added.

"Jah, jah, Szilard commented, "let's not make it goes to his head."

In they went, eighth row center, orchestra.

"What do we see?" Gregor asked.

"I don't know what we are seeing, but we are hearing Bartok. *The Miraculous Mandarin*." For Teller, it was always the music, first and foremost. Dancing was a superfluous footnote.

"I don't know this," said the roach.

All had to admit that they had never seen or heard the piece: it had been banned in Europe since its composition just after the Great War. The audience would soon see why.

"Why a Mandarin? Why oriental?" Gregor asked.

They looked in the program.

"Mysterious character," Wigner quoted. "Alien world."

"Like you, Samsa," Szilard noted.

Little did he know how right he was. What a setup. A lonely, sex-starved alien watching a show about a lonely, sex-starved alien.

The lights dimmed, and the audience quieted down, expectant. But instead of the mysterioso beginning suggested by the title, the orchestra plunged right in to a fortissimo, honking evocation of a modern city, alienated from nature and everything natural, sounds of raucous inhumanity. Audience members were already squirming in their seats. Gregor held his knees.

The curtain rose on a shabby room in a derelict apartment, an expressionist fantasy of squalor. The wallpaper is peeling, the furniture is comically crippled, and in the corners, piles of shabby, odd things. G was particularly struck by the filthy stuffed eagle perched next to the horn of an old phonograph. His master's voice? Ives would have loved it.

It was quickly apparent that this was the hideout of three criminals, used as a storeroom for their stolen goods. One is lying on the bare mattress, staring at the ceiling; a second is rummaging through every drawer, hoping to find — what? Money? Jewels? The third is arguing violently with a beautiful young girl, whom they have apparently kidnapped, and are holding for their occasional pleasure. He turns his pockets inside out, then pulls her violently around to rub her face with the extruded cloth. "What can I do," she cries out, "It's not my fault..." (Gregor had never seen a ballet with words). The first thief jumps off the bed, and runs at the girl. "What can you do? You can catch us some men!" And he forces her to the window and tears off her blouse, displaying her, half naked, to the street below.

Gregor was bowled over. At first attracted by the despair in her huge eyes, he was now drawn by a rush of longing for her thin — almost emaciated — dancer's body. He could see every rib, every costochondral juncture of her exo-endoskeleton. Her nipples stood out like chitinous protrusions from her bony frame. Her arms — the bones — strung together by ligaments and sinews — just like his own. She was his longed-for human counterpart, a non-fatty sister he could finally claim in soul — and body! Wait! This is a ballet, a show. She is a dancer, part of a company, not a maiden to be rescued by a brown knight in a White House. Still, he found himself breathing quickly, his tegmen rising uncomfortably against the back of the chair, and even his wound beginning to perceptibly moisten, though from the sweetest kind of pain. Off in a far corner of his mind, he wondered how he might inveigle a meeting...

The girl stands at the window, pressing her nipples against the glass; the men hide and await their prey. The music become intensely serpentine, the first of three increasingly luminous seduction themes. She waves her hands at the passersby in the street. The first thief sticks his head out of the closet. "Got anyone?" "Yes," she nods. "Good." They hide again. Footsteps come up the stairs, and she positions herself in the middle of the room.

Now he could take her, now, before she demeans herself. He could just run up on stage, grab her in his arms, and disappear with her into the District of Columbia night. Teller, with one slight cough and phlegm-trapping snort, brought him back to irreality.

The door opens and frames an old roué with wrinkled face and waxed moustache, his top hat shabby as his shiny coat, his collar dirty sporting a cheap, gaudy tie, the flower in his buttonhole speaking of ancient sexuality, long past its prime. Gregor was as repelled as was the girl.

The old man looks her up and down, repugnantly self-assured. The music fairly cakewalks. He is delighted, and amused by her putting her blouse back on. He takes off his hat; his hair is slicked and pasted over his skull. As he begins to peel off his dirty gloves, the girl, by rubbing index finger and thumb together, tries to set the terms of engagement. "Money," he says, "What's money? It's love that counts." The three thieves spring from their hiding places. Gregor was overjoyed to see them. They toss the old man among them and finally out the door, down the stairs, as the music comes to comic climax, perhaps imaging an off-stage contact, stair to pudendal nerve. The second thief imitates the old man's wooing and warns the girl to do better next time. He rips off her blouse again and lifts her over to the window. Gregor found himself pressing his private parts against the back of the chair.

The second seduction theme winds its way into the air, and the scene is repeated, this time with a handsome student. Again, Gregor was despairing, though now more from jealousy than disgust. The young man blushes deeply and casts his eyes down, just as G would have done, had he not been hidden by dark anonymity. Oh no! She likes him. She loves him! She looks at him with delight. The third thief signals from behind the student's back, thumb and index finger, thumb and index finger. "Do you have any money?" she asks. He shakes his head sadly, and turns to go. "No, no," she cries and holds him from behind, as the two begin to sway in a melancholy, ever more sexual waltz. The thieves have had enough of this, and once again come to the rescue of a heavily-breathing Gregor. Down the stairs with him! Outside, in the courtyard, we hear him sobbing faintly.

"You want love?" the second thief screams at her. "I'll give you love..." and he begins to take down his pants. The third thief draws his knife. "Don't waste her time, or I'll cut it off." A quick up-buttoning. Back to the window for the third time, that famously third repetition celebrated by fables east and west. Gregor wondered whether the three roomers in Prague had ever accosted his sister: he had never thought of it before.

He focused on her scapulae as they caressed her chest wall. Would that he could nuzzle up against deep throbbing. The exotic transformation of the seduction music turned her vertebral column into a slowly waving sine, spine, sign, and then, hup, she was frozen in horror, dactyls clawed on windowpane. What was it? What could be next? The third repetition. Gregor remembered the title: The Miraculous Mandarin, it must be the Miraculous Mandarin. The girl retreats from the window, tries to hide. The second thief pulls her out from under the bed — and the door opens.

Was Gregor hallucinating? With his right eye he saw what presumably all others saw: a black-pigtailed Chinaman of broad, yellow face, with exaggeratedly slanting eyes, unblinking, stare fixed, like that of a fish. But with his left eye, he saw a huge insect, antennae braided, hanging from under a skull cap, orangey-yellow, icteric and sick. With his beret, he covered his eyes alternatively: Mandarin, monster, Mandarin, monster, then binocularly, he allowed the images to fuse. Both Mandarin and monster were identically dressed in a richly embroidered silk garment studded with lucent jewels. Of money there was no doubt.

The girl is frightened, repulsed, yet bound by his implacable, serious stare. Would she be appalled by me? She backs away, but the thieves push her forward. The Mandarin still stands, staring, in the doorway. The third thief tickles her back with his knife. She motions the Mandarin to sit. And so he does, slowly, his set face never registering the slightest emotion, always staring at her, staring.

The girl begins her show, the seduction dance of all times, slow, but relentlessly building. She locks the door and dances on, less and less inhibited, finally spinning herself face up against the Mandarin. Seeing his unblinking stare, she bursts into laughter and plops onto his lap. My lap, thought G, I'll be kinder to you than he. It's me you want. And he covered his right eye.

From now on, Gregor watched himself on stage. Others in the audience may have thought he was a painter imaging a two-dimensional transformation.

With the laughing, half-naked young woman wriggling in his lap, the Mandarin insect begins a measured metamorphosis, eyelids flickering, breaking his fixed stare, his chest beginning to heave, his hands to twitch, his fingers reaching toward her face. He begins to shake, and frightens the girl, who jumps from his lap and backs away. Her laughter has stopped.

Mandarin insect rises and follows her around the room, his face distorted and imploring. The girl backs behind table, behind chairs, but he presses on, and finally dives to grab her ankle. She tears herself free, and he leaps at her again, alarmingly nimble and grotesque, tearing off her skirt, leaving her entirely nude. Now it is he who begins to dance provocatively, with fantastic gestures and acrobatic twists. Strange sounds come from his throat as he jingles his money at her and clutches his heart, his thighs. Tears stream from his eyes, Gregor's eyes. He is completely out of control, spinning, jumping, whirling, crashing, breaking windowpanes and glasses, spilling beer. It is impossible to escape: he grabs the girl and sinks with her to the floor. Gregor was wet at head and abdomen. Only his thorax was dry.

Did he yell out "Thieves!" before or after they jumped? A few people in the audience seemed to be looking at him. He pulled his beret off his right eye, and watched in stereoptic horror as the thieves pommeled the Mandarin, and released the girl. They hold him upside down and shake him. Gold coins roll around the stage. They pull the jeweled chain from his neck and pluck the rings from his fingers. "Let's kill him," the first thief offers, and the three erupt in horrendous laughter, throwing him on the bed and heaping blankets and pillows and rags on his face. Gregor knows he will not suffocate. His spiracles will save him. "Finished", the second thief announces when the Mandarin has stopped thrashing. Gregor wants to take a blanket to the shivering girl, but.... The thieves each eye their naked accomplice.

But so does the Mandarin. His head emerges from under the pillows, his glassy eyes again fixed on his love. "Oh no," thought Gregor, now seeing only Chinaman, "Get him, get him!" And the thieves seemed to respond, pulling the Mandarin from the bed. As soon as his feet touch the floor, the inscrutable oriental bounces up, almost six feet in the air, and again hurls himself at the girl — only to be tackled by the third, knife-happy thief. "No you don't," orders the first, as if to both subduer and subdued, smacks the knife from his colleague's hand, and pins the Mandarin's arms who, gurgling in his throat, continues to stare at the girl with fiery, goggling eyes. The third thief gathers up his knife, and to the surprise of all runs it into the Oriental's abdomen. (Gregor twitched violently.) The body slackens, the knife is extracted — and the Mandarin, jumps up again, right for the girl. From the corner, the first thief grabs a rifle — BANG! — the audience jumps — and a huge hole appears in the middle of the Mandarin's forehead. He staggers and totters — and is once again at the girl, chasing her with grotesque jumps. "Give him peace," Gregor prayed. He rarely prayed.

"Kill him," the girl cried, "you've got to kill him!" But how? The thieves grab the yellow man, wind his pigtail around his neck, and standing on chairs, string him up to the chandelier. G could imagine this scene in the more affluent East Room. Lindbergh, perhaps.

The chair is kicked from under the Mandarin's feet. The light goes out under his weight. Darkness. Silence. Holding of breath. A dim an greenly-eerie light begins to emanate from the executed, especially from his eyes, still scanning the room for their beloved. Cautiously, slowly, the thieves cut him down; he drops to the floor — and again he rises and rushes at the naked girl — who catches him in her arms, wraps her warm body around him, and gives him a deep, long kiss.

It is *Liebestod* again, the love in death in love, which allows him to rest. The wound in his belly begins to bleed. The hole in his head begins to ooze grey slime. His hug slackens, his arms drop, his legs give way beneath him. His stare is fixed — in bliss. Slowly the girl lowers the body to the floor. The music swells, the curtain falls. The Mandarin is — miraculously — dead.

Gregor was dripping. Teller was involved in string harmonics and harp glissandos, ponticellos and quarter-tone slides. Szilard remained concentrated on the cello subject of the Mandarin's suffering. His only comment was "Too skinny. That girl was too skinny." What mathematician Wigner made of the whole thing nobody knew: he was silent for the rest of the evening.

Happy Beethoven's Birthdays (Ninth Symphony)

December 16 is the first of them, the 17th the next. As Amadeus in Insect Dreams *says, "Extraordinary people do extraordinary things." That's the good news.*

The bad news is that the master decided to replace the heart-breakingly gorgeous last movement of his ninth symphony with some bombastic choral agit-prop. Granted — this being late Beethoven — there are extraordinary events in there, but like Chaplin's speech at the end of The Great Dictator, or the psychiatrist's lecture at the end of Psycho, one must ask, "Was this the right decision?"

"Beethoven's Ninth? Oh yeah — Da da da da Da da da da..." And you start to sing the Ode to Joy, with whatever words you learned around campfires or in church. Back in 1893, George Bernard Shaw ridiculed a listener who knew only the Ninth's last movement, and came to hear it only for that. He writes about him sitting there "bothered and exhausted, wondering how soon the choir will begin to sing those verses which are the only part of the program of which he can make head or tail, and hardly able to believe that the conductor can be serious in keeping the band noodling on for forty-five mortal minutes before the singers get to business."

This is a problem. For the Ninth is a work which aspires to tell the largest of all stories, one with a beginning and a middle, and hopefully an end — an end which is the most questionable section, especially out of context. It was questionable to Beethoven, who, even after it was conceived, was writing default sketches for an instrumental movement of entirely different character, and who, some years after it was finished, remarked to friends that the choral finale was a mistake. And it has been questionable down through the years, to musicians of Beethoven's generation and beyond,

The fourth movement is, in my opinion, so monstrous and tasteless and, in its grasp of Schiller's Ode, so trivial that I cannot understand how a genius like Beethoven could have written it. (Ludwig Spohr)

and to the singers of today who struggle with its bizarre and outrageous demands.

The work is a musical icon, always a special occasion to hear and to perform. Still, the question exists: Should the last movement of the Ninth BE the last movement of the Ninth — or was Beethoven caught up in some extra-musical utopian thought which, combined with his total deafness, personal isolation and urgent need for community, has left us with a flawed and freakish masterpiece? You will be able to decide for yourself this week. To help you with this, in fact, momentous decision, let me sketch out the big story of all the movements, and the personal and historical background out of which they grew.

By 1824, Beethoven had been deaf for two decades, and stone deaf for the last five or six years. There is a moving story of his "conducting" the premiere of the symphony (the chorus and orchestra having been instructed to ignore him and follow the concertmaster), beating time and turning the pages of his score even after the work was over. A soloist had to turn him around to face his cheering audience. Beethoven was a passionate man, whose years of isolating deafness had kept him from personal intimacy. His reaching out had become idiosyncratic, sometimes destructive, leaving him with "theoretical" relationships, with only the visionary goals of brotherhood and civilization.

The Ninth has become a model of such Enlightenment culture in which all conflicts are dissolved in brotherhood, love, and reconciliation, goals so archetypal that Adrian Leverkühn, Thomas Mann's dying, devil-afflicted composer, announced that these goals, precisely, were not to be. "The good and noble, what we call human...What human beings have fought for and stormed citadels, what the ecstatics exultantly announced — that is not to be. It will be taken back. I will take it back." Take back what? he is asked. "The Ninth Symphony."

Lacking a happy story of his own, Beethoven was forced into the wider world of cosmos and myth, beginning with Chaos, the formless void of primordial matter, and obeying heavenly laws, evolving into the octave of humanity. To express that coming-round, his lifelong love of Schiller's "Ode to Joy" came into play, and his creation grew into a projection of the end of history, of universal life become elysian civilization. "Where are we going, then?" asked the poet Novalis: "Always homeward." The Ninth was Beethoven's map leading to the home he always wanted but never achieved. His was not a simple, cheerful optimism, some flabby notion that things would come out all right in the end, but rather a tragic optimism, like Gramsci's "pessimism of the intellect, optimism of the will", an optimism of "volition inspired by imagination." (Schweitzer). Maybe that's why it's so hard to sing.

Deaf, isolated, some would say mad, "late period" Beethoven explores a world completely removed from ordinary thought and experience. His technique over the years had evolved beyond the bounds of anything known, before or since, both utilizing and disrupting all elements of classical design. He threw everything he had into the Ninth, "harmonic and rhythmic motion slowed to the edge of motionlessness, clouded harmonic progressions, passages in indeterminate keys, nebulous and nocturnal effects, multivalent tonal trajectories, enormously extended time spans, highly idiosyncratic fugue styles, and a supremely ornamented variation style that implies the infinite possibilities latent in even the simplest musical materials." (Solomon, *Beethoven Essays*).

All this, you will hear, beginning at the beginning.

FIRST MOVEMENT

...the very beginning, before there is a world. We hear the tremolo of the universal frame, the vastness of cosmic Chaos, gestating. E, A, open strings, open fifths, outlining, but not defining, a riddle of what's to come. Beethoven here begins the utmost three movement exploration of the fundamental components of music: interval/harmony, rhythm, and melody. In the beginning was the open fifth, uncommitted to major or minor emotion, beyond them, primeval, inhuman.

At the thirteenth measure, the dark theme emerges from darkness, a falling, dotted D minor, uncomfortable enough with itself to squirm out of key, then falling back, abandoned, committed. This is a theme which brings up memories of Beethoven's earlier struggles with "Fate", but here evoking a fate beyond personification, beyond defiance, a truly universal destiny affecting the human world, but not part of it. We are present at the creation, and we find it nothing benevolent, but rather crushing and dissipating, an inhuman beginning to the story that will end (at least tonight) with the brotherhood of Man. The scale, the range, the proportions are gigantic, the potential cataclysmic. In case we, in our current familiarity with the piece, are tempted to try to cuddle up against it, we are brutally dismissed by the grinding despair of the funeral march which marks the very end. "Beware," it says, "this could go anywhere."

SECOND MOVEMENT

Rhythm here, a demonic dance of obsessive, rhythm-dominated thrust. In case you doubt the plot, note that this movement is the only second movement scherzo in all the symphonies, thriving still on the trans-personal energy of the first, with its impersonal power. The strings do fortissimo D octaves. Silence. Then A octaves. Silence. Then the tympani, in surprising solo, whacks out a F — thus defining, yes, again, D minor. The orchestra takes off in a molto vivace uprising of blind energy, four hundred measures of hang on to your hat.

And then something very strange happens. Formally, a scherzo requires a contrasting trio before returning to its original intent. That happens, yes. But not very strange. What IS strange is that the trio is a human one, the sound, perhaps, of a peasants at a dance, an invasion of universe, of scale, a hint of benevolence, a time-leap into Mahlerian sensibility and pastiche. And if you listen carefully, you will hear in the trio theme the outline of what will become the Ode to Joy, a wonderful, gratuitous kindness after all the flinging. But it is not time yet for humanity. Rhythm (for all its beating of drums) cannot be its essential mode: the scherzo returns, chaotic and hostile as ever. The trio gives one last little try in the winds, but is beaten down by the full orchestra crashing emphatically on an open D chord, neither major nor minor. Case closed — but open.

THIRD MOVEMENT

Melody, the human mode. I am not the only kvetcher who thinks the symphony culminates, and should have ended with the Adagio/ Andante, that it is the work's true finale.. Such would not have been alien to Beethoven's late sensibility: of the last three late piano sonatas, two (op. 109 and 111) end with astounding slow movements. Thomas Mann has his stuttering pianist, Wendell Kretschmar give a lecture/performance (in Dr. Faustus) concerning why Beethoven had not written a normal, fast, last movement to Op.111, but had ended with a slow one.

A new approach? A return after this parting — impossible! It had happened that the sonata had come, in the second, enormous movement, to an end, an end without any return. And when he said "the sonata," he meant not only this one in C minor, but the sonata in general, as a species, as traditional art form; it itself was here at an end, brought to its end, it had fulfilled its destiny, reached its goal, beyond which there was no going....

Schiller himself had written, "To arrive at a solution even in the political problem, the road of aesthetics must be pursued, because it is through beauty that we arrive at freedom." Beauty. The beauty of the third movement. No one has ever contended the last choral movement was beautiful.

Fortunately, or unfortunately, Beethoven didn't agree. "This is too tender," he remarked of the third movement. His contemporary, the poet Auguste Platen, had written

He whose eyes have gazed upon beauty,
Is already delivered over to death.

and it seemed that Beethoven agreed. He needed to escape the imagined trap of passivity, of a beauty too sublime for action. The world, his world, needed changing, and neither Sirens nor lotus blossoms would suffice. And so we leave this gorgeous, inward, mystical contemplation, this rich, flowering serenity, these slow, deeply human, personal, miracles, timeless, beyond decay...

FOURTH MOVEMENT

— to be blasted away by the most gargantuan Fart in music, the chord which begins what Wagner called a Schreckenfanfare (terrifying!), blowing off not only the sublimity of the previous movement, but all that came before it. The basses and celli start literally talking — but they have no words — we don't understand what they say. Then — are we hearing right? — the symphony starts over again from the beginning: tremolo, E-A, A-E, E-A, only to be cut off, dismissed by the basses. Next, the scherzo gives it a try, again to be dissed, and finally, the slow movement, to be more gently tossed. What is it the basses want? After a pause, they tell us.

The Ode to Joy tune, for all the various sketches which preceded it, has about the attractiveness of a beer hall song. But if one wonders, with Spohr, that a genius such as Beethoven could come up with something like it, one's cynicism is dissolved as the master begins spinning out an increasingly complex set of songful variations, growing his sound through strings and winds, and finally punctuating it with brass when, lo, the Schreckenfanfare returns, and a solo bass — the first voice ever heard in a symphony — translates for us what the basses were trying earlier to say: "O friends, not these sounds. Let us rather strike up something more pleasant and joyful."

What is he talking about — "these sounds"? A little ambiguous. For it is not merely the first three movements that are being dismissed, but the very Ode to Joy theme, which has just received such gorgeous orchestral treatment. It must be non-vocal symphonic music itself Beethoven means, thus calling for the end of yet another genre, as insufficient to attain his demands on the future.

The first response of the human voice is "Freude!" — joy — , and the chorus basses begin to sing the words to the first Schiller verse. All begins at a natural, human scale, but with each successive development, the music separates itself further and further from normal song, and begins engaging other, less definable levels of experience. The text takes a surreal leap from the pleasures of the worm to the seraphic joy of angels, and we are translated into a new world, in a new, surprising key. We are directed to be as heros, joyfully racing through the heavens to victory, and the orchestra breaks into an enormous fugue with the rhythmic drive of the discarded scherzo, ending in a four part choral version of the Joy theme, its definitive statement from the billion-voiced throat of humanity. All together, now. The prisoners are free, the slaves are slaves no more.

But now things get really strange. We are exhorted to the world's largest group hug. Why? Because a loving father must be there up above the starry canopy. Not IS there, mind you, but by deduction or intuition, MUST be. On your knees! Don't you sense the Creator? Look up there. He must be there — above the stars. The music goes anti-gravitational.

So we look and listen. And what do we hear? The most bizarre double fugue in the history of music with lines quite unsingable, making little individual sense, but — as if proving something about community — evoking an undeniable, powerful, visionary gestalt. The energy gathers itself, and the work literally sprints to the finish line, prestissimo, and is over.

Is that it? Is that the legitimate successor to the unearthly, yet human heights of the slow movement? Thrilling, yes, but do you want to live there? Where is the vision of God? Not a suspicion that he must be out there, but some even secondary or tertiary vibration, as in Mahler? We've survived the cold vastness, the kinetic shoving, the opiate beauty of the first three movements. And now?

Beethoven wanted to express some exalted idea of human brotherhood in a new life sprung from the cosmic view of the three preceding movements. But I, for one, have always felt disappointed, even tricked. For all the phenomenal musical events in the last movement, theologically, it feels more like some non-denominational Sunday sermon by a hot preacher. OK, OK, this is music, not theology. But is the music of the last movement the fulfillment of the path set up by the first three? Or did Beethoven opt to use his unmatched skill and energy, in the service of an urgent, but non-musical exhortation?

He had more to say after the Ninth. Was he so convinced of the need for human voice, or its success in the symphony that, like Schoenberg, he introduced vocal song into the late quartets? No. Five staggering, metaphysical quartets were content with strings alone, one of them (0p. 132) ending with the very theme sketched for the instrumental finale to the Ninth.

There is no QED here. Tovey insists that, like it or not, we MUST listen to the Ninth as if the chorale finale were correct. Still, one wonders.

B9 Slow Movement

I wrote this note to my conductor after being frustrated by how quickly and loudly he was rehearsing the slow movement of the Ninth. It's true that winds and brass have trouble playing quietly, but...

Dan,

Yesterday's tempo for the slow movement was coming down nicely from let's-get-this-thing-over-and-get-on-to-the-real-music, or let's-have-pity-on-the-winds, towards appropriately-contemplative, with downbeats placed at the back end of the beat. Congratulations on your iron will. Finally, you do control this.

But what finally you can't control in performance is the dynamics unless the wind players better understand the country they're in. And it's not so much a question of amplitude as of attitude. If you agree with me, maybe you can get something like this across to the winds:

With clearly marked *forte* exceptions, the movement is in the world of piano to pianissimo. That is where the delicate, profound magic takes place. Bump it up to mp, and the magic becomes clouded with sound, and by mf, it's almost altogether encased in everydayness. So first and foremost, it must not get loud, or even normal. About half-way through, the winds begin to suffocate the magic. Can you get them to play as softly as the low strings start the Ode to Joy theme?

But, as I say, it's not amplitude but attitude. This is not physics, but metaphysics. I am reminded of that wonderful Flammarion woodcut of the guy sticking his head outside of the earthly sphere to contemplate in awe the heavenly,

or of the Stefan George line in the Schoenberg Second Quartet: *Ich fühle Luft von anderen Planeten.*

The winds/brass have to understand that they have entered an extraordinary universe, and are inhaling and blowing air from other planets — or at least ozone or nitrous oxide. It has to sound weird like that. Those modulations into theoretical but actually impossible realms of the cycle of fifths can't happen on expelled CO_2. They have to think alchemy.

I know this can sound ridiculous — as in the story of the young, enthusiastic conductor who, after a five minute sermonette on the mysteries of late Beethoven is asked by a grizzled trombone player, "OK. But do you want it louder or softer?" But if you agree with what I'm after, I beg you to communicate your version of this to the winds, along with getting them on board with tempo, beat placement, and basic "dynamics". Like loud or soft. Answer: soft.

Actually even the tempo issues are at play here. B sets up the fiercest of contrasts with the space-time of the first movement, and the clock-time of the second. Time. Time! — And then comes the third where spacetime dissolves. The clock ticks no more, time simply flows. Almost everything is off-beat, unsettling to the clock-timeists. Like to the guy sticking his head out of the sphere. Like on acid. Our paradox, of course, is that we need to play "on acid" and completely on-top-of-it at the same time, too bad for us. But we need to deliver that apparent-looseness.

The notes in front of us are like tiny lenses into a world B was frightened enough of to interrupt with the Schreckenfanfare. "No more of these sounds!" "Let's make more pleasant music.: "Angenehmerer"?? Even political, agit-prop B must have seen the irony of this text. Weird guy, old B.

Anyway, I hope this time we can get beyond the notes to the vision. "Über'm sternen Zelt" to the lieber Gott's neighborhood.

What Is It With Beethoven's Fifth?

They know it in the poolroom.

They know it in the bar.

They know it on the checkout line and at the beauty shop, at the garage and in pizza joint. Was there ever a phrase of music so embedded in our culture as the opening of Beethoven's Fifth? How come? How come it was the first symphony ever recorded, and how come Billy Joel said of da da da daaaa "it's one of the biggest hits in history — there's no video to it, he didn't need one."?

Well, there is Schindler, Beethoven's friend, telling how the master pointed to the opening of the score and said, "This is fate knocking at the door." A good story, a plausible hook to hang one's interest on, especially with poor Ludwig going deaf, the symphony proceeding through the lyrical sadness of the second movement, past the weirdness of the Scherzo (Big Joke — on him), and emerging in C major at the end, blazing and triumphant. We'd like that to be our story — now more than ever. Unfortunately, there is lots of evidence that Schindler made the whole thing up. Besides, they don't know this story in the poolroom.

But what is apparent, even to those who know only the first five measures, is the uncanny power of those four tones, seeding every level of the work — themes, sections, movements, and the four movements as a whole — with their compressed energy. How might one characterize that energy?

Three short, fierce notes followed by a long note, held out of time. Then once again, a step lower, the long note held even longer. In time, out of time, short, long — this tiny seed theme asserts the contrast of Contraries. And to my mind, that is what this symphony is "about" — the urgent confrontation and interaction of Contraries.

Yin and yang; despair and faith; awareness and blindness; deep and shallow; strong and weak; secular and sacred; earthly and ethereal; solid and hollow; visible and invisible; finite and infinite; noumena and phenomena; moving and still; changing and changeless; thrownness and purpose; life and death; light and dark; free and structured; serious and frivolous; work and play; celebration and despondence; peace and struggle; sorrow and joy; passion and intellect; inspiration and thought; simple and complex; lyric and dramatic; pure and impure; personal and not; direct and oblique; free and imprisoned; improbable and expected; passive and aggressive; mind and body; nutritious and poisonous; exaggerated and understated; pompous and unassuming; closed and open; Apollo and Dionysus; organic and inorganic; love and hate; sensuous and ascetic; male and female; time and space; heaven and hell — Blake said "Without Contraries there is no progression." All pairs above are implicit in the n-dimensional spiritual-emotional-philosophical space of Beethoven's Fifth, seeding its progression. As you listen, listen for Contraries, yin and yang, outbreath and inbreath at every level, and throughout. Though the first movement is the most compressed and extraordinary, contraries haunt every movement.

There is a wonderful scene early in E.M. Forster's novel, Howard's End, at a performance of the Fifth. It is the transition between the Scherzo and the Finale — and the phenomenal reappearance of the Scherzo in the Finale which gives rise to some fascinating speculation on Contraries.

"Look out for the part where you think you have done with the goblins and they come back," one character whispers, as the Scherzo starts with goblins "walking quietly over the universe, from end to end...They were not aggressive creatures; it was that that made them so terrible....They merely observed in passing that there was no such thing as splendor of heroism in the world."

And then, at the end of the Scherzo, "Beethoven took hold of the goblins and made them do what he wanted...He gave them a little push, and they began to walk in a major key instead of in a minor, and then — he blew with his mouth and they were scattered! Gusts of splendor..., magnificent victory." Were the goblins not really there then? Were they just "phantoms of cowardice and unbelief? Men like Theodore Roosevelt, Foster asserts, would say yes. But in the midst of the triumphant last movement, in one of the most surprising moments in music, escaped entirely from any traditional form, Beethoven brings them back.

"It was as if the splendor of life might boil over and waste to steam and froth. In its dissolution one heard the terrible, ominous note, and a goblin, with increased malignity, walked quietly over the universe from end to end. Panic and emptiness! Panic and emptiness! Even the flaming ramparts of the world might fail!

"Beethoven chose to make all right in the end... He blew with his mouth for a second time, and again the goblins were scattered. He brought back the gusts of splendor, the heroism, the youth, the magnificence of life and death, and, amid vast roarings of a superhuman joy, he led his Fifth Symphony to its conclusion. But the goblins were there. They could return. He had said so bravely, and that is why one can trust Beethoven when he says other things."

"One can trust Beethoven." Maybe that is the essence of all masterwork. One of my particular neuroses is that I will absolutely not watch a movie if I miss the opening shot. It is at that moment that I decide who I will be for the next two hours. Can I relax and take it all in, knowing I am in the hands of a master? Or will I have to remain critical, putting on my how-would-I-do-it-differently hat, and wondering whether I've just wasted eight bucks again? The opening of every movement of the Fifth says "Trust me." The mysterious da da da daaa of the Allegro, the strange and sad lyricism of the lower strings in the Andante, the What???! goblins of the Scherzo and the Back to Basics opening of the Finale — all are entirely convincing. All say "Trust me enough to give your entire self over." I think this explains the poolhall panache of da da da daaaa. For even this snippet, with its shrapnel Contrary, lodges itself deep in the psyche which knows that Contraries mean progression.

Ten ball in the side pocket.

Brahms — Nänie

"*Nänie*. How many people have heard it? Raise hands. None. How many people have heard of it? None. Which is why I programmed it. An inexplicably unknown masterpiece. Schiller's poem is in the form of a Roman threnody, and Brahms sets it in just 181 bars of profound emotion. You'll like it.

"Sopranos, let's start at letter B. Just sopranos. Mary, give them a D. I'll tell you what I hate already."

The chorus giggled.

"You're going to come in too loudly." George raised his arms. "Six beats, quietly."

He traced out a preparatory measure. As he reached five, he said "Too loud." They had not started singing. When they did, it was from the dark, tomb-like quiet of the bottom of their register.

Auch das Schöne muß sterben... A long, Brahmsian line, rising and falling in three undulating waves.

"Good. What does that mean?"

"It says here Even Beauty must die."

"I'd quibble with the 'even'. Auch means 'also, too, as well'. As well as what? What usually dies?"

"Old folks."

"Sick people."

"And when a young, beautiful person dies?"

"It feels...wrong."

"But *das Schöne muß sterben*, Schiller says, and Brahms agrees. And together they'll give us three scenes of untimely death — the death of a spouse, the death of a lover, the death of a son, each with some touching detail.

"Modern ignoramuses that you are, I'll tell you what you think you're singing about when we get to it: you can't tell the players without a score card."

Why did they love his insults?

"Let's continue with the first section. See how the entrances are spaced four bars apart until the basses push in after only a half measure? Death is like that. Let's have everyone this time."

George gave the preparation and the downbeat. The sopranos entered on a distressing variety of pitches. George cut them off.

"Oi. Beauty must die, but you don't personally have to kill it. Mary, another D."

Better. The chorus grew its polyphony in slow crescendo, then fell precipitously into hard-hearted realm of Hades, the Stygian Zeus. A strange lament, this, in a major key, but sublime, elegiac, in the spirit, if not the tonality, of mourning.

"Gentleness ahead." George warned, as the piano filled in the transition. "Easy does it."

The basses began, too growly, reaching up out of low-register darkness:

One time love did move the ruler of shadows —
But at the threshold, he took back his gift.

George cut them off.

"What's that about, any guesses?" he asked.

"Sounds like Orpheus losing Eurydice at the exit."

"Erudition prize #1 to Tim Eckelberg, MD. Why did he lose her?"

"He looked back," said an alto.

"So what's wrong with looking back?"

No offers.

"Think about it. And try to imagine the story as you sing this section. The beauty of Orpheus's song, his love for his young wife, her snakebite death, his courage in going where no man had gone before to attempt a rescue. His culpable impatience."

Amazing what context can do for the complex act of singing. As the chorus read through Eurydice again, it was with the softened heart that tempted even the the Ruler of Shadows, abductor of Persephone.

"If I had a hat on, which I wouldn't in a church anyway, even a UU church, I'd take it off to you. You sound great. So next section then, change of key — a gentle F major for the goring of the genitals. What a card, old Brahms. Any guess where we're going?"

"Let's see," said Manon of the long neck. "It looks like the sad story of Aphrodite and the stripling."

"And who is the stripling?" George asked.

"Adonis, my fave," yells BB Eckelberg, Tim's boisterous ex-wife. In the good days, the old days, they used to read Bullfinch aloud. Now they sat as far apart as a small chorus could keep them.

"You have a passion for young, beautiful men?"

"No, I love to see arrogant males punished, especially by wild boar tusks." The chorus smiled embarrassed, unwilling spectators to the good-humored hatred flavoring the congregation with toxicity.

Aphrodite could not staunch the cruel wound ripped by the boar in the dear boy's body

...grausam der Eber geritzt.

Brahms, typically modest and shy, chose understatement here, short, sweet and bloody.

"Next month," said George, "in honor of this piece, I have scheduled the first annual Mt. Diablo Adonis celebration. BB will help coordinate it, won't you? In honor of your fave?"

"What's the deal?"

"July is the Roman month to honor Adonis and all things beautiful. Aphrodite herself fell in love with that Mr. Teen-Universe, and stupidly handed him over to Persephone for child care. Guess what. Persephone also fell in love with him, and wouldn't give him back. Zeus decided they should time share. Aphrodite loved him. Persephone loved him. The thing he loved best was hunting. 'Don't go hunting today, sweet boy' — that's Aphrodite. 'Tosh, controlling woman, unhand me.' We know what happened — bor-ing. Hearing his groans, Aphrodite rushed to him, right through the briars, but she was too late. We are not told what she did with the scrotum. The blood from his wound colors the red anemone, and from her lacerations, the red rose."

"Awwww," sighed the basses in concert.

"That, my base friends, was not the reaction of your classical ancestors. They saw the story as foretelling the coming of another spring, even after July had turned toward darkness and death. They also sensed the presence of death in the fullness of life. Savor abundance, anticipate death — that was the message of the festival of Adonia. For the ancients, if not for you.mSo — three weeks from tomorrow, we'll all pack potsherds with a little soil, and plant fast-growing seeds — fennel, lettuce, wheat, barley... We'll water our gardens of Adonis for eight days, and then abandon them. Then we'll get together the following Sunday, mourn the shriveled seedlings, wail and cry, and maybe sing Nänie as best we can. We'll make little 'Coffins of Adonis' out of cardboard, and lay effigies inside them. Next — with hair unloosed, and bosoms bare, especially the sopranos and altos — we will Trauermarsch to the stream and float the seedlings and effigies away while we sing Theocritus's Hymn to Adonis, the Dying God...

The chorus was used to putting up with him. They worked their way through Thetis — rising in majestic F# major from the sea, mourning the fall of her son Achilles and leading her Nereid sisters in a key-rending wail, more Wagner than Brahms, fifty goddesses chromatically bewailing the unspeakable transience of beauty. Beauty fades. The Perfect must die. Then, four mysterious, improbable measures back to our most distant D major home — for the summation.

Poet and composer part ways here. Schiller tells us bitterly that though singing a lament is a noble thing, most go down to Hades quite unsung. Nasty.

Brahms turns the table on this un-Ode to Joy by repeating the penultimate line, and making that the end.

Auch ein Klaglied zu sein im Mund der Geliebten is herrlich

To be a song of lament in the mouth of the Beloved is herrlich.

Herrlich: marvelous, glorious, lovely. wonderful, beautiful, magnificent, gorgeous. And that is the end of the piece — all those things, quiet, reposeful, heartbreakingly radiant, and *herrlich* — most Brahmsish.

"You love this? George asked.

An enthusiastic, universal 'yes'.

"Then go home and study it. I want notes by next week."

Debussy — Prélude à l'apres-midi d'un faune

The 17th and 18th century paved the way: the motto (in the celebrated words of Kant) "dare to know." And enlightenment thinkers did just that, opening new vistas of science and a rational understanding of the universe. The 19th century intensified the motto: "dare to master" — and the financial might of capitalist industrial revolution empowered the quest for domination of the natural and political world. With his revolutionary message, Beethoven epitomized this vision of human creative power. Take a theme and develop it, twist it and explore it, find its inner possibilities and squeeze them out, prod its reflexive interaction with the tool of the will — the creator transformed by its history. With Beethoven the "development section" of classical sonata form grew to engulf the work, and from Beethoven sprang Wagner's manipulation of leitmotifs, and Schoenberg's permutations of the twelve-tone row. The message: man the master.

My favorite Debussy image is of the young man at a concert, whispering to a friend, "Let's go — he's beginning to develop!" What? Leave at the most exciting, revealing, genius-testing moment? What does this guy want? A little insight from his school days when he submitted a composition to his professor which flouted all rules. When asked what rules he observed, he said, "None — only my own pleasure!" "That's all very well," was the retort, "provided you're a genius."

I don't know what grade he received in this battle, but we all know who won the war. The premiere of "The Prelude to the Afternoon of a Faun" helped initiate the birth of a certain kind of modernity — some would even say post-modernity — in which there were no grand rules applying, no agreed-upon values, no fixed forms. As the music flows from moment to moment, mood to mood, at its own "pleasure," eschewing "development," embracing only the barest symmetrical form, so do we flow as a culture: enveloped in our private dreams, resisting "government," despairing of "solutions," heedless of what may come, going with the flow. Twenty three centuries earlier, Chuang-Tsu wrote "Am I a man dreaming I'm a butterfly, or a butterfly dreaming I'm a man?" More than a century ago, Debussy dreamed his prophetic dream. And here we are today.

Is it an accident of fate that Debussy died in agony, of cancer, in the middle of a war?

Handel — Messiah

George Says Goodbye to His Chorus

Since by man came death...
"Again."
Since by man came death...
"My friends, not falling apart is not being successful. Again."
Since by man came death...
"You sound like a bunch of vowelless drunks. Basses, what was that? Remind me I have to get my sump pumped."
Since by man came death...
"Altos! I think we're going to change this to the Mt. Diablo Toothpaste Society. Fix it here and it moves over there."
Since by man came death...
"O, my God! That's great! What are you doing? Do you know what you're doing? Is that luck or talent? Whatever you did, keep doing it. Again..."
Since by man came death...
Since by man came de-eh-eh-eth...
"Go on..."
The piano struck C major.
"Stop! Betty, that chord sounds like BOOM. Can you make it more like THWACK, the guillotine stoke of life?"
Betty nodded. Thwack not boom. I can do that.
Since by man came de-eh-eh-eth...
THWACK!
By man came also the resurrection of the dead,
By man came also the resurrection of the dead.
"Good enough. Not bad. A little more cosmic bandwagon next

time. Go on."

For as in Adam all die...

THWACK!

"Stop. Betty, D minor is not C major. Can you make it more, um, medico-theological?

Betty nodded. Medico-theological.

For as in Adam all die-ay-ay-aye...

"You got it. Keep going..."

even so in Christ shall all be made alive,

even so in Christ shall all be made alive,

even so in Christ shall aw-aw-aw-aw-all be made alive.

"Hey, you sound like you believe it? Do you believe it? Wait...you're Unitarians, you don't have to answer that question. OK, skip over to 'Worthy is the Lamb'...Betty?..."

D major, medico-comico-theologico-tragico..BROWOOOM!

Worthy is that Lamb that was slain

and hath redeemed us to God, to God by his blood,

"Great. Keep going..."

to receive power, and riches, and wisdom, and strength,

and honor, and glory, and blessing...

"Stop. What is this, a shopping list? Sale items at Crazy Eddie's? These are all different. They're in size place starting small at 'power'. 'Blessing' is over the top — throws us down an octave. Again, from the shopping list.

to receive power, and riches, and wisdom, and strength,

and honor, and glory, and blessing....

"Good. Go, men..."

Blessing and honor, glory and power be unto him, be unto him

that sitteth upon the throne, and unto the Lamb,

"Stop. Sounds weenie. Secular weeniness. Altos, can you help the poor men? It takes a village..."

Blessing and honor, glory and power be unto him, be unto him

that sitteth upon the throne, and unto the Lamb, forever and ever

forever and e-ver...

"Good. Here we go."

The chorus began the Amen pianissimo, as instructed, plotting its enormous crescendo. George conducted it at the slowest tempo anyone had ever heard, but somehow it held. The counterpoint became more complex, the single word wrapping itself around itself, inserting itself within itself, combining and contrasting in single song and stretto, majestic, growing ever more profound.

And then it came — the moment George claimed was the richest in music, the great fermata-ed silence before the final cadence, the grandest of grand pauses, the empty measure of empty measures, the black hole of infinite density, the loudest silence in creation. George's slow, slow tempo had expanded the time frame out beyond that of any previous performance in two and a half centuries — out to the nth nanosecond of stretch-before-collapse, the ur-dominant moment of conception, penultimate to forever.

After which,

Amen..., sang the chorus,

A — men.

Silence.

For ten seconds, forty-two human beings were bug-eyed at what they had just done. George nodded.

"Who needs drugs when you're a musician?" he said. "Do that at the concert, and I'll pay the legal fees. Take five minutes and then I have an important announcement."

The chorus made for the juicy-juice and the pissoirs. Thirsts slaked and bladders emptied, they took their seats, all ears.

"Amen," George said. "The end. So be it. Tomorrow's concert will be my last with you for a while."

General gasp and murmur.

"I found out last week that I got my Guggenheim, and yesterday, I got word from "Looie", the Libera Università Internazionale, that they want me in Rome — starting next semester — an offer I can't refuse. So I'm outta here. If you know anyone who wants a nice Maybeck sublet, let me know. I'll stay in touch. While I'm gone, I've arranged for a good friend, the distinguished Hungarian musicologist, Leoj Ztlem, to conduct. He's in the Bay Area the next few years working on Pythagorean music theory, and those of you on the Social Action Committee interested in the harmony of the universe will have a ball. I'll be leaving right after the holidays. I think Tim Eckleburg will be having a little farewell potluck, so you can talk with him if you're interested. If I don't see you then, I'll see you all when I get back, and one way or another, we can make music again.

George's Messiah

George loved Messiah. It was nothing a Jewish boy in Levittown had been expected to love, but it happened. Until he was fifteen, he had steered clear of this goyish mania. But one day, a lovely young girl with long, dark hair handed him a leaflet for an afternoon performance a bus ride away in Queens. Maybe she sang in the chorus. It must be all right for a Jew to go into a church, he thought, if it's for a concert, and not to eat the body and blood. He wouldn't tell his parents. They'd never know.

The young man was ravished by the experience. He used the word in every possible meaning: he was seized and violently done to; he was overcome by horror, joy and delight; he was pre-sexually bewitched, for the long-haired one was in fact singing soprano in the front row, and never had such an angelic voice issued from such sensuous purity. This concert was of the Easter portion of the work, and from "Behold the Lamb of God" to the last "Amen"; he was transfixed with wonder. From the three bar mitzvahs he'd attended he knew Jews didn't make this kind of sound. Synagogues were filled with the discordant rumble of davenning, each worshipper finding his individual prayer voice and rhythm, chanting, whispering, singing, crying, repeating phrases over and over, lost in the brumming of the crowd. Sometimes a cantor sang. But this — this! It is music, music that hath ravished me! He got home at an unsuspicious five o'clock, and never mentioned his encounter.

He had tried to hear Messiah every year since then, but with all the changes that had occurred along the way, he had managed to bat only about .300. So what a boon — right here, in his own community, that he could conduct an annual Messiah! The sad part was that he could never share this joy with his family, old anti-clerical mom and pop ever more rigid in their disdain for religion. The idea of their very own son promoting Christ the Jew-killer might, he thought, send them each into heart failure. So this was his one activity he never called home about.

Choosing to do the Easter portion of Messiah for Christmas was George's little revenge on America. Though written as an Easter piece, and traditionally performed in Europe during Easter time, in coming to America Messiah had shifted seasons, and along with them, content. Though the Puritans had banned the celebration of Christmas, post-Puritan America has embraced it with a vengeance, currently exhorting all to worship at the mall of one's choice. Perhaps in the land of the Easter Bunny and the lethal injection, crucifixion is seen as barbaric. Christmas, not Easter, is where most American celebration is concentrated, and with it, most concertizing. Messiah has become a Christmas piece, and most American performances restrict themselves to its first section concerning Advent and the birth of Christ. The meat of the oratorio is left out, and the introductory portion is capped with the Hallelujah chorus — a masterwork written to praise Christ's ascent to his heavenly throne, unreported in these Hallmark card performances. "A premature ejaculation at best," George thought when feeling generous. But if Americans were determined to hear part of Messiah at Christmas, he was going to be damn sure it was the Easter portion that attacked them.

At 6:30 on the evening of the concert, Betty cell-phoned in to say that she had had a flat on I-680, that the AAA said they'd be there within fifteen minutes, and that being the case, she'd be at the church by ten after, and could they hold the performance? As if there were a choice.

So George came out at 7:05, and announced that the concert would begin at 7:20 because, as the contemporary world amply demonstrates, the Messiah always comes late. Then he did a remarkable thing, unexpected, certainly, because of his refusal of the first part of Messiah, but unexpected, ever, in any form, under the eye of God. He sat down at the Steinway, and played the slow opening of the opening "Symphony" of the work. Twenty-four stately, double-dotted measures marked grave — this the limit of his keyboard technique. When the moment came for the Allegro moderato to begin, George stood up, walked to the curve of the piano as if for a vocal recital, placed his right hand on the rim of the case , and performed that three-part fugue all by himself. He whistled the soprano voice out of the right side of his mouth, the alto out of the left, and vocalized the bass part with accurate, wordless humming. You don't believe this. It is true. Upwards of a hundred people heard it with their own ears. He must have been practicing this in the shower for the last twenty years in preparation for that night.

Look, Messiah is one of the grandest works of western culture. It is simply not appropriate for a serious conductor to whistle the overture in public performance. But the effect, rather than being ridiculous, was to create a churchfull of gaping at the wonder that is man. No problem was too great for one who set his mind to it, no achievement too difficult. The room was riddled with people who had dedicated themselves to Bay Area excellence: none could gainsay George Helmstetter's accomplishment.

Betty arrived, pumped and wired. The chorus filed on to the risers. In spite of George Bernard Shaw's opinion alleging "the impossibility of obtaining justice for that work in a Christian country," mid-Messiah instantly summoned the audience to pain and passion including even them, the guilt-free of the world. "Behold the Lamb of God", the sacrifice upon whom all sins would be heaped and slaughtered into renewal, the Lamb whose blood would be smeared on door jambs to frighten Death away, the Lamb that would conquer the wolves, the conquering Lamb.

What about this Lamb? Handel took great pains to describe its scorn-filled whipping. *"He gave his back to the smiters, and his cheeks to them that pluckèd off the hair."* Blood and hair clotting together on the prison floor. Here is perhaps the only major artwork which celebrates saliva as such: *"He hid not his face from shame and spitting,"* spit in the face, a cadence, ach-ptoo! The listeners were assured, in no uncertain terms, that the Lamb was burdened with their very own doings: Surely he hath born our griefs, and carried our sorrows. The fierce F-minor cries, the painful, discordant suspensions: He was wounded for our transgressions; he was bruised for our iniquities, a catharsis of pity and terror.

Even the Jewish mothers of many in the audience would not have been able to evoke such a sense of guilt. The thoughtful were carried emotionally along, while at the same time wondering about the phenomenon of the Messiah. Is this suffering lamb the Saviour of the world? How odd. The Messiah's function is to be victorious. Christians thought of Christ. Jews thought through their own lens of the "true" reference, the continued oppression and persecution of Israel throughout the Christian and pre-Christian centuries — the Nazi destruction, the pogroms of the nineteenth century which had brought their parents to the New World, the persecutions of the eighteenth century, the seventeenth, and on back to the Exile, where the image of the Lamb converges with that of scattered Israel.

"And with His stripes we are healed." What is that about? Why should one's agony be inversely proportional to another's? Conservation of Wound? Conservation of Tears? Conservation of Pain? Beckett has told us: "The tears of the world are a constant quantity. For each one who begins to weep somewhere else another stops. The same is true of the laugh."

Handel lingers over the word "healed" as if to lay soothing balm upon Christ's — and our — wounds. Yet even this very moment, was beyond a definitive scan. The perverse listener — and who is not perverse? — could easily hear the melismatic syllables of "healed" as "hee-hee-hee-hee-heeled", in effect a subtle but demonic, underlying cackling, as if to say that no matter what the unction, the wound is too great to be cured — you'll see. Hee-hee-hee. George was haunted by this dopplegängbanging effect, but was unable to phrase his way around it. The Lamb of God, and the sheep who have gone astray.

"All they that see him, laugh him to scorn. They shoot out their lips and shake their heads, saying": Enter the scornful, the brutal choral metamorphosis from a confessing people of God to an unruly crowd in obscene play at a public execution. So does Jekyll turn unexpectedly to Hyde.

"He trusted in God that He would deliver him: let Him deliver him, if he delight in him." Such assertive contemptuousness! The trivializing, de-legitimizing of God, putting his capitalized pronoun on a

syncopated weak beat, now ironically, self-flatteringly strong. What pristine nastiness, abundantly clear. *Thy rebuke hath broken His heart. He is full of heaviness. He lookèd for some to have pity on him. But there was no man, neither found he any, to comfort him.*

Not only was this George's favorite moment of Messiah, with the single most touching note in music slipping into place in the piano's middle voice, a pensive entwinement of suffering and beauty. In the pause after pity on him, a luminous E rises half step to a questioning, consoling F, as if at least one human heart might go out to Jesus from the frigid emptiness answering his gaze. But it was also the theological key to the work: Here was the heart of it. As every culture has known and proclaimed, something is wrong with the human race. Things are not as they should be. There have been many intellectual explanations — mythological, religious, philosophical. But here is the psalmist's prophetic assessment: the primal fault is that we disdain God. We have turnèd everyone in his own way. The biblical word for this is "sin."

*Since by man came death...*The listeners had to interpolate the moment of death. But George found this not egregious. The whole textual strategy of the Messiah is one of brilliant, evocative avoidance. Charles Jennens, an otherwise unremarkable British gentleman, had provided his friend George Fredrick with a libretto of theological genius, portraying every shade of devotion from piety, resignation and repentance to hope, faith and exultation. And all this without resorting to narrative, as in the Passions of Bach: Christ did this, and then he did that, the misery composed directly into the music. The Messiah commands attention because of what it does not show, for the most part indicating, rather than depicting events. And therefore the death of Jesus, that epoch-making moment, really could exist as a lacuna between his unrewarded search for comfort and the triumphant Lift up your heads which followed. Praise be to Handel for demonstrating this.

Lift up your heads; The Lord gave the word; Their sound is gone out. And so, for the Jews, the Ark takes its place in the Temple, for the Christians, the Son takes his place in Heaven, and the preachers tell the world — but some do not hear. Why do the nations so furiously rage together? Tim Eckleburg stepped out to sing, less than accurately but with conviction, to sing of the kings of the earth, of the rulers that counsel together against the Lord. Again, the demonic chorus: Let us break any bonds with the Anointed, and cast away their yokes from us. And what will happen? This time Willy Higinbotham, a "real" tenor from the Cal music department, stepped forward to describe the smashing and breaking that will ensue, an image which always reminded George of the piled up debris confronting Walter Benjamin's Angel of History.

And then, the great moment, the moment incoherently misplaced in American versions, the phenomenal Hallelujah Chorus. The piling up of debris? Hallelujah! For the Lord God Omnipotent reigneth — which at first blush is not a very encouraging vision of the future. But what if it were to become the case — that the kingdom of this world is become the kingdom of our Lord, and that over such a peaceable kingdom He shall reign forever and ever? It did give one pause, in the midst of the war on drugs and the war on terror.

Almost three hundred years earlier, King George had stood in his excitement, dragging the court to its surprised feet around him, and now the audience at the Mt. Diablo Unitarian-Universalist Church took this traditional ninth inning stretch incapable, however, of diverting the impregnable momentum of the music.

For all the radiance of the performance, there was one moment that stood out above all others. Dr. T.J. Eckleburg, with his strong baritone, came in too soon after George's breathtaking pause before the final cadence, shattering the loudest silence in creation. After the concert, BB commented to another alto: "I've sung Messiah many times in my life," she said, "and I've always waited for someone to come in too soon. It was very satisfying to me."

Messiah at Los Alamos

And with His Stripes We Are Healed

This is the first excerpt from Insect Dreams, now in its original form, called Kafka's Roach. Gregor Samsa is Kafka's man-turned-roach, from his novella, The Metamorphosis. I rescued the dying Gregor from under the couch, dusted him off, and got him over to America, where he undergoes 700 pages of adventures in NYC, Washington, DC, and finally New Mexico, where he works as a health consultant to the Manhattan Project. The scientists worked 16 hour days, seven days/wk. But they took off Saturday nights for special events. All the characters except Gregor were real but I did make much of this stuff up. Nevertheless, the book is an accurate reflection of the goings-on. Unfortunately.

Gregor was excited. He loved *Messiah*. It was nothing a Jewish boy in Prague had been expected to love, but it was nothing any boy in Prague could miss. As a child, it had seemed to him that each April, every church in *Staré Mesto* had entered some frenzied *Messiah* competition. Until he was fifteen, he had steered clear of this goyish mania. But one day, a lovely young girl with long, dark hair handed him a leaflet for a performance at four PM, in five minutes, right there, right at St. Mikulás, right around the corner from his house. She looked very Jewish, this one. Maybe she sang in the chorus. It must be all right for a Jew to go into a church, if it's for a concert. His parents would not be home until six. They'd never know.

Gregor was ravished by the experience. He used the word in every possible meaning: he was seized and violently done to; he was overcome by horror, joy and delight; he was pre-sexually bewitched, for the long-haired one was in fact singing soprano in the front row, and never had such an angelic voice issued from such sensuous purity. This concert, too, was of the Easter portion of the work, and from "Behold the Lamb of God" to the last "Hallelujah", he was transfixed with wonder. Jews didn't make this kind of sound in their churches. Synagogues were filled with the discordant rumble of davenning, each worshipper finding his individual prayer voice and rhythm, chanting, whispering, singing, crying, repeating phrases over and over, lost in the brumming of the crowd. Sometimes a cantor sang. But this — this! Could it be his Jewish faith was shaken? Unspeakable. It is music, music that hath ravished me! He got home before the rest of his family, and never mentioned his experience, even to his sister Grete, a budding violinist.

He had tried to hear *Messiah* every year since then, but with all the changes that had occurred along the way, he had managed to bat only about .300. So what a boon — right here, in his own community, an annual *Messiah*! The sad part was that he could no longer sing it, as he had in his late teens and early twenties, in the face of his father's rage. Not that his father was an observant Jew — it was strictly High Holidays with him, and whatever social practice was necessary to maximize profits. But for some reason, the idea of his very own son singing — singing! — about Christ, advertising a false messiah — the faintest whiff of this image sent him into catastrophic fury. In fact, one of these seizures, the most terrifying one in Gregor's memory, had been on the very night before Gregor's change. He hadn't made the connection. But still, not to be able to sing this, to be kept from pouring his heart into the clean and glorious lines...Metamorphosis had many boons, but being unable to sing *Messiah* was not one of them. His voice was too scratchy.

Gregor came early, picked up a program, and sat down in the front row. The tables had been pushed back, and the room was filled with dinner and folding chairs, even on the balcony. As he read through the program, people slowly filtered into the room, some in suits and dresses, many more in uniform. The growing rumble reminded him of davenning.

"Behold the Lamb of God", ok. Hey, where is "He was despised" and "He gave his back?"...must not have an alto soloist. (For the first time in ages, Gregor grew aware of his own back, and the smiting by his father.) Surely..."And with his stripes"..."All we like sheep", good, good. What? Genia Peierls is the tenor soloist? She sings "All they that see him?" Easy, G, take it easy. "He trusted in God", ok, and at least we get "Thy rebuke", even if it is with Genia... "Lift up your heads?" What? Where's the death? Where's "He was cut off out of the land of the living?" How can they skip that? If she can sing the other tenor solos, why not that?

Gregor thought he had better give up reading the program, so he could listen with a receptive heart. They would do what they would do.

Choosing to do the Easter portion of *Messiah* for Christmas had been a trans-Atlantic compromise. Though written as an Easter piece, and traditionally performed in Europe during Easter time, in coming to America, *Messiah* had shifted seasons, and along with them, content. Though the Puritans had banned the celebration of Christmas, post-Puritan America has embraced it with a vengeance, currently exhorting all to worship at the mall of one's choice. Perhaps in the land of the Easter Bunny and the electric chair, crucifixion is seen as barbaric, but Christmas, not Easter, is where most American celebration is concentrated, and with it, most concertizing. *Messiah* has become a Christmas piece, and most American performances restrict themselves to its first section concerning Advent and the birth of Christ. For some reason completely incomprehensible to Europeans, the meat of the oratorio is left out, and the introductory portion is capped with the Hallelujah chorus — a masterwork written to praise Christ's ascent to his heavenly throne. "A premature ejaculation at best," commented Hans Staub, concerning this practice.

But if this was their country, and if Americans were determined to put on part of *Messiah* at Christmas, the new influx of Europeans were going to be damn sure it was the Easter portion that was performed.

The piano in Fuller Lodge was, appropriately, a living example of both the Heisenberg Uncertainty Principle, and Neils Bohr's — excuse me, Nicholas Baker's — Principle of Complementarity. You were never quite certain what the pitches were because you could not have accurate tuning of two or three of the multiple strings at the same time. If one was in, the others were surely out. Then too, the instrument existed in some duple state averaged between Hammerklavier and Harpsdischord, as Joyce was pleased to call it, a soft touch bringing out the clinging, plucking quality of frayed felt, while a strong attack manifested the sound of bare wood core on metal. You could never elicit the two at the same time, and a complete description of the instrument would have to include aspects of both. Otto Frisch, an excellent Mozart pianist, was quite the sport to agree to play on it. But no one was about to move Teller's Steinway grand over through snow and frozen mud for a forty minute performance at the Lodge. Besides, such accompaning sounds took the burden off the chorus to sing in tune. No one would think of blaming Frisch, and no one could really indict the singers.

At 7:20 the chorus entered a restless hall to great applause, and the full-bearded Moll Flanders, computation leader in the Theoretical division and thus Dick Feynman's boss, dressed in unwonted, too large tailcoat and white tie made his way to the front. Even the GIs whistled and stomped. Moll had permanently endeared himself to the whole community with a show he had put on in the early fall: "The Moll Flanders Ballet Workshop [the poster said] presents the premier of an original ballet — 'Sacre du Mesa' — to the futuristic music of George Gershwin." Everyone in his company had had ballet training except him. But he pointed out with impeccable logic, that in order to dance General Groves, [Groves was in Washington], he didn't need ballet training, since the General himself had had none. QED. Tonight he would surpass that feat.

The "house lights" went down, and in the first of only two wrong decisions that evening, he broke the suspense with two mere announcements: The concert was beginning at 7:20 because, as the contemporary world has amply demonstrated, the Messiah always comes late. The audience simply took this in, confounded. Also the chorus All we like sheep had to be scrapped at the last minute because too many had gone astray and the shepherd was still out looking for them. Chuckles from the cognoscenti. He signaled to Otto, and the Overture began, grave,

115

perhaps more striking than usual for being in an indeterminate key. Then, a truly extraordinary event occurred. When the moment came for the Allegro moderato to begin, Moll walked over to stand at the side of the upright piano, placed his elbow on top, and performed that three-part fugue all by himself. He whistled the soprano voice out of the right side of his mouth, the alto out of the left, and vocalized the bass part with accurate, wordless humming. You don't believe me. I was there. I am not a gullible man. I heard it with my own ears. He must have been practicing this in the shower for the last twenty years in preparation for that night.

Look, *Messiah* is one of the grandest works of western culture. It is simply not appropriate for a serious conductor to whistle the overture in public performance. But the effect, rather than being ridiculous, was to create a lodgefull of gaping at the wonder that is man. No problem was too great for one who set his mind to it, no achievement too difficult. The Fuller Lodge was riddled with people who had dedicated themselves to excellence: none could gainsay Moll Flanders' accomplishment.

The music jumped from E minor to G minor, an artifactual glitch of abridgement, noticeable to few in the audience since "Behold the lamb of God" had caught them up, every last one of them it seemed, in its net of falling lines. Were there some there who had never heard Messiah before? What were they expecting? Something churchy? That is not what they got. Rather they were bathed in an ominous summoning to pain and passion, set in a post-whistling context which included even them, the sinful of the world. Those who knew recognized the voice of John, the same voice that cried in the wilderness, "Comfort ye, my people." The Lamb was about to be chosen, the Passover Lamb, the sacrifice upon whom all sins would be heaped and slaughtered into renewal, the Lamb whose blood would be smeared on door jambs to frighten Death away, the Lamb that would conquer the wolves, the conquering Lamb.

What about this Lamb? Handel took great pains to describe its scorn-filled whipping. "He gave his back to the smiters, and his cheeks to them that pluckèd off the hair." Blood and hair clotting together on the prison floor. Here is perhaps the only major artwork which celebrates saliva as such: "He hid not his face from shame and spitting," spit in the face, a cadence, ach-ptoo! But without an alto soloist, the audience was cheated of secretions. Instead they were assured, in no uncertain terms, that the Lamb was burdened with their very own doings: Surely he hath born our griefs, and carried our sorrows. The fierce F-minor cries, the painful, discordant suspensions: He was wounded for our transgressions; he was bruised for our iniquities, a catharsis of pity and terror.

Even the Jewish and Italian mothers of many in the audience would not have been able to evoke such a sense of guilt. The thoughtful were carried emotionally along, while at the same time wondering about the phenomenon of the Messiah. Is this suffering quadruped the Saviour of the world? How odd. The Messiah's function is to be victorious. Christians thought of Christ. Jews thought through their own lens of the "true" reference, the continued oppression and persecution of Israel throughout the Christian and pre-Christian centuries. The currrent Nazi attacks, the pogroms of the nineteenth century which had brought their parents to the New World, the persecutions of the eighteenth century, the seventeenth, and on back to the Exile, where the image of the Lamb converges with that of scattered Israel.

"And with His stripes we are healed." What is that about? Why should one's agony be inversely proportional to another's? Conservation of Wound? Conservation of Tears? Conservation of Pain? Beckett has told us: "The tears of the world are a constant quantity. For each one who begins to weep somewhere else another stops. The same is true of the laugh."

Handel lingers over the word "healed" as if to lay soothing balm upon Christ's — and our — wounds. Yet at this very moment, G's wound began to weep. As he searched his soul for cause, he heard someone in the soprano section, he couldn't tell who, articulating the melismatic syllables of "healed" as "hee-hee-hee-hee-heeled", in effect a subtle but demonic, underlying cackling, as if to say that no matter what the unction, the wound is too great to be cured — you'll see. Hee-hee-hee.

And now, skipping over the strayed "All we like sheep", Genia Peierls stepped out in front of her row to sing "All they that see him, laugh him to scorn. They shoot out their lips and shake their heads, saying": Enter the scornful.

Genia, the Russian wife of the emigré German theoretician, Rudolf Peierls, and mother of the brilliant, beautiful, precocious Gabrielle, age 12 going on 40, had recently arrived with the British mission, and was already the most talked-about character on the mesa. No matter what the issue or activity, Genia was there, in the front row, taking things energetically in hand, running everything with ringing voice and Russian disregard of the definite article. The less generous, or more easily intimidated, spoke of her as a terror — always telling other people what to do. In this instance, she had insisted in singing the tenor recitative preceding "He trusted in God", because, as she forcefully observed, "How will audience know who speaks?!" And although she was right — it was important to identify the excerpted voice of the chorus — the transition did little to soften the brutal choral metamorphosis from a confessing people of God to an unruly crowd in obscene play at a public execution. So does Jekyll turn unexpectedly to Hyde.

He trusted in God that He would deliver him: let Him deliver him, if he delight in him. Such assertive contemptuousness! The trivializing, de-legitimizing of God, putting his capitalized pronoun on a syncopated weak beat, now ironically, self-flatteringly strong. What pristine nastiness, abundantly clear. Genia stepped forward again to sing Handel's comment, justified only by her own: "Is very important!" *Thy rebuke hath broken His heart. He is full of heaviness. He lookèd for some to have pity on him. But there was no man, neither found he any, to comfort him.*

And surely she was right to do so. Not only was this Gregor's favorite moment of Messiah, with the single most touching note in music slipping into place in the piano's middle voice, a pensive entwinement of suffering and beauty. In the pause after pity on him, a luminous E rises half step to a questioning, consoling F, as if at least one human heart might go out to Jesus from the frigid emptiness answering his gaze. But it was also the theological key to the work: Here was the heart

118

of it. As every culture has known and proclaimed, something is wrong with the human race. Things are not as they should be. There have been many intellectual explanations — mythological, religious, philosophical. But here is the psalmist's prophetic assessment: the primal fault is that we disdain God. We have turnèd everyone in his own way. The biblical word for this is "sin."

Gregor felt connected to Genia Peierls for the first time. Perhaps he sensed for a moment why she was the way she was. At the same time, he, in that moment of E to F, felt terribly, agonizingly lonely. And his wound, not so much stripe as crater, bled its brown tears.

The listeners had to interpolate the moment of death. But G found this not as egregious as he had expected. The whole textual strategy of *Messiah* is one of brilliant, evocative avoidance. Charles Jennens, an otherwise unremarkable British gentleman, had provided his friend George Fredrick with a libretto of theological genius, portraying every shade of devotion from piety, resignation and repentance to hope, faith and exultation. And all this without resorting to narrative, as in the Passions of Bach: Christ did this, and then he did that, the misery composed directly into the music. Messiah commands attention because of what it does not show, for the most part indicating, rather than depicting events. And therefore the death of Jesus, that epoch-making moment, really could exist as a lacuna between his unrewarded search for comfort and the triumphant "Lift up your heads" which followed. Praise be to Moll and Genia for demonstrating this.

"*Lift Up Your Heads*"; "*The Lord Gave The Word*"; "*Their Sound Is Gone Out*". And so, for the Jews, the Ark takes its place in the Temple, for the Christians, the Son takes his place in Heaven, and the preachers tell the world — but some do not hear. Why do the nations so furiously rage together? Jim Tuck, the gawky six foot comedian of the newly-arrived Brits, he of explosive lens research, stepped out to sing, less than accurately but with conviction, to sing of the kings of the earth, of the rulers that counsel together against the Lord. Again, the demonic chorus: Let us break any bonds with the Anointed, and cast away their yokes from us. And what will happen? This time Willy Higinbotham, a "real" tenor, stepped forward to describe the smashing and breaking that will ensue, an image which reminded Gregor of the piled up debris confronting Benjamin's Angel of History.

And then, the great moment, the moment incoherently misplaced in American versions, the great Hallelujah Chorus. The piling up of debris? Hallelujah! For the Lord God Omnipotent reigneth — which at first blush is not a very encouraging vision of the future. But what if it were to become the case — that the kingdom of this world is become the kingdom of our Lord, and that over such a peaceable kingdom He shall reign forever and ever? It did give one pause, in the midst of the battle of Stalingrad, the submarine warfare, and the maiden flight of the V2.

Two hundred two and a half years earlier, King George had stood in his excitement, dragging the court to its surprised feet around him, and now the European aficionados led the audience in Fuller Lodge in this traditional ninth inning stretch, though many of the GIs, worshippers in someone else's church, didn't quite know what was going on, and rose with quizzical expressions under their crew cuts. Fiercely cued by Moll, Rudi Schildknapp's five trumpet notes came in right at measure 57, and though several of his cohorts applauded defiantly right then and there, they were shortly cut off by the impregnable momentum of the music.

For all the radiance of that performance, at that time, in that place, there was one moment that stood out above all others. Willie Higinbotham, with his strong tenor voice, came in too soon after the breathtaking pause just before the final cadence, shattering the dramatic silence in the Lodge. After the concert, Otto Frisch consoled him with congratulations. "I've heard *Messiah* perhaps thirty times in my life," he said, "and I've always waited for someone to come in too soon. It was very satisfying to me." The story even followed him to Washington where he went to lobby for civilian control of atomic energy late in '45. I heard it there several times in scientific and diplomatic circles.

In spite of George Bernard Shaw's opinion alleging "the impossibility of obtaining justice for that work in a Christian country," the night's

Messiah excerpt had been an exhausting forty-three minutes for Gregor. He leaned back against brown wetness — to decompress. But before the audience could conclude the event was over, Chaplain Capt. Jonathan Maple walked onstage, making his way through the departing chorus members, who were taking places at the back of the hall. Chaplain Maple was a gaunt thirty-five, with a high forehead under short black hair accentuating his skull-like visage, his somber eyes magnified by thick, round glasses. He had recently arrived on the mesa, a permanent replacement for the guest ministers, rabbis and priests whose coming-and-going Groves felt might compromise security. He had an office in the Big House, and was available by appointment for consultation. This, however, was his first general public appearance, and even those who might otherwise have fled stayed around to assess this new member of the community. I had mentioned Moll Flanders' two mistakes of the evening. This was the second.

Chaplain Maple began innocuously enough:

"I want to thank Dr. Flanders, Dr. Frisch, and the thirty-four members of the Mesa Chorus for their gift to us tonight."

Audience applause for those at the back.

"But I also want to acknowledge the appearance of someone invisible — more than someone — three, four, perhaps a dozen invisibles whose voices have been haunting the evening. Can you think who they are?"

No answer from the room of thinkers and doers.

"I am referring, of course, to the psalmists and prophets who supplied Mr. Handel with his texts, and us with our spiritual itinerary."

Some mumbling among the crowd. The one comment I clearly caught was, "Now we have to sit through a sermon?" Others seemed intrigued.

"Have ye not known? have ye not heard?

Hath it not been told you from the beginning?

Have ye not understood from the foundations of the earth?

It is he that sitteth upon the circle of the earth

And the inhabitants thereof are as grasshoppers..."

The quotation came out of the blue, entirely unprepared by the previous remarks. Furthermore, the Chaplain's voice had taken on a new quality — or was it the Chaplain's voice at all? The closest approximation was the disembodied voice heard at all hours of the day and night over the Project PA system, but here shorn of its electronic quality. Perhaps it was a practiced ventriloquy used in his denomination. In any case, it seemed to come from the three sides of the balcony rather than from the speaker in front. Gregor, at first joining the audience in the search for the source, was drawn to attention by the characterization of "grasshoppers". After a pause for the exotic voice to dissipate, Chaplain Maple continued.

"Those were the words of First Isaiah, the author of much of Handel's text 'Hear, O heavens, and give ear, O earth: I have nourished and brought up children and they have rebelled against me.' Thus begins the first and greatest of the books of prophets: a testimony with visionary authority, proud genealogy, cosmic scope — and an indictment of the rebellious children of the Lord."

A few soldiers stood up to leave, but were signaled back down by imperative sergeants.

"I say 'First Isaiah'. Do all of you know that the 'Isaiah' of the Old Testament is not one, but at least three different people, writing scores of years apart? [Silence.] I hope I am not shocking anyone. These are the words of the First Isaiah, who began to preach in the reign of King Uzziah, in the eighth century BC. First Isaiah was a visionary moralist, calling upon a country in the summit of its power. Uzziah had built the economic resources of Judah as well as its military strength. In Jerusalem there were engines, invented by skillful men, on each of the towers, capable of shooting arrows long distances, and heaving great stones.

"But Uzziah's strength had become his weakness. He grew proud, and angry at meddling priests, and as his anger mounted, leprosy broke out on his forehead. And King Uzziah was a leper to the day of his death, and being a leper, he dwelt in a separate house, for he was excluded from the house of the Lord.

"In the year that King Uzziah died, First Isaiah had a vision: he saw the Lord sitting upon a throne, high and lifted up. Above the throne

122

stood the seraphim, and each one had six wings; and with twain they covered God's face, with twain they covered His feet, and with twain they did fly. Insect-like angels, shielding men from the radiation of God."

Scientists and military brass took wary note. Radiation? The radiation of God? Did the Chaplain know something he shouldn't? Gregor, tachycardic, again noted the insects.

"Those were years of power struggles and shifting strategic alliance. The huge kingdoms of Egypt and Mesopotamia, Babylon and Assyria, alternately triumphed, while tiny Judah played its cards as cleverly as it could, seeking protection without humiliation. First Isaiah lived through the reign of four Judaic kings, and he counseled each to rely not on military protection, but on God. History, he proclaimed, was a stage for God's will and God's work; the rising and falling of willful nations was mere detail."

The West Pointers in the audience struggled to recall their Military History courses.

"The louder First Isaiah spoke, the farther he was pushed from centers of power. So he let it be known that politics itself, with its arrogance and disregard of justice, was the problem — not the solution. And why, Ladies and Gentlemen, and Children of all ages, why is that?"

A grand pause. When no answer came the chaplain continued.

"Because politics is based on the power of the sword. You know First Isaiah's words: some of you have laughed at them. He announced the day when nations 'shall beat their swords into plowshares and their spears into pruning hooks.' Are you still listening? First Isaiah proclaimed the day when 'nation shall not lift up sword against nation, neither shall they learn war any more.'"

It had become clear that this was to be no short, simple thank-you speech from the religion Division. Some in the audience became restless, some transfixed. The GIs knew they could not leave, and the civilians felt they could not abandon them.

"What were First Isaiah's flight instructions from the Lord?" continued Maple. "Now hear this, friends:

'Go and say to this people (this people is you):
Go and say to this people

Hear and hear, but do not understand;
see and see, but do not perceive.
Make the heart of this people fat,
and their ears heavy,
and shut their eyes;
lest they see with their eyes
and hear with their ears,
and turn and be healed.'

"What?? What could these instructions mean? Isaiah checked them twice. Prophets are normally charged with making people see and understand; they aim to mobilize their hearts, not put them to sleep. 'How long?' Isaiah asked, appalled. 'How long this tactic?' God's plan was uncomfortably clear:

'Until the cities be wasted without inhabitant and the houses without man, and the land be utterly desolate.'"

Maple paused to let the thought sink in.

"It is hard to be a prophet," he added. And again that voice from nowhere and from everywhere:

'Why is my pain unceasing,
My wound incurable,
Refusing to be healed?'"

Gregor could not believe his ears.

""I cry by day, but you do not answer:
and by night, but find no rest.
I am a worm, and not human;
scorned by others and despised by the people.'

Why, Isaiah, why? Could it be, my poor Isaiah, that only an outsider, only an exile, can claim the humanity society denies?"

Gregor was breathing quickly.

"God's plan was decimation; First Isaiah was assigned to cover the news. Reduce Israel to a remnant, and let things begin again. And the Jews were scattered, and their Temple destroyed."

Pause. Silence. Many Europeans' thoughts shifted course toward Europe.

"But in the Exile, a prophet arose who lifted the meaning of the events from mere political history to a cosmic drama of world redemption. This was Second Isaiah, the poet responsible for chapters 40 through 55, for much of the Messiah text, a lyrical visionary of the heart. For Christians, Second Isaiah spoke the words that most clearly presage the coming of Christ. The historical, human order is to be overcome by the suffering servant, in Christian thought, the crucified Saviour.

"It is not just a few thousand Jewish exiles to whom this prophet speaks, as they sit weeping by the waters of Babylon. Second Isaiah addresses every exile all over the world, every human at a loss to find God, every blind man trying passionately to penetrate the darkness of the future. That, Ladies and Gentlemen, is you.

"The root of the problem, indeed the root of all evil, is your false sense of sovereignty, and stemming from it, your pride, your arrogance, your presumption.

"'They worship the work of their own hands,' the Prophet says, 'that which their own fingers have made. They have chosen their own ways, and their soul delighteth in their abominations.'

"But the Lord is weary of such offerings. Where is contrition? Where is regret?

'Bring no more vain oblations;
Your incense is an abomination unto Me.
When you spread forth your hands,
I will hide My eyes from you;
Even though you make many prayers,
I will not listen.
Your hands are full of blood.'"

Things were becoming truly uncomfortable. This might have gone over in some small southern Baptist church, but this was the Fuller Lodge at Site Y. Chaplain Maple seemed to sense this, and pulled back.

"Let me say a few words about history. This is what the prophets discovered: History is a nightmare. We generally assume that politics, economics and warfare are the substance of history. To the prophets, it is God's judgement of man which is the main issue. They look at history from the point of view of Justice, judging its course not in terms of wealth and success, victory and defeat, but in terms of corruption and righteousness, violence and compassion.

"We should not expect the darkness of our history to be dispersed soon by any clever technical or political strategy. We will not receive answers concerning the future because we ask questions of those who cannot know, the vain gods of the nations.

"The only solution of the historical problem today lies in the prophetic concept. Second Isaiah speaks to the exiled remnant of our time, to those in prisons and concentration camps, to those separated from husbands or wives, from children or parents, to those toiling in despair in foreign lands, to those in the hell of modern war. He speaks to every one of us in this room.

"How should we respond to his words? Ironically? Dismissively? Angry at their seeming pretentiousness, at the immense gap between the proffered solution and the catastrophic reality in which we live?

"Two and a half centuries ago, we opted for means to control nature and society. It was a right decision, and we have brought about something new and great in history. But we excluded ends. And now the means claim to be the ends; our tools have become our masters, and the most powerful of them have become a threat to our very existence.

"A century and a half ago, we opted for freedom. It was a right decision; it created something new and great in history. But in that decision we excluded the security without which man cannot live and grow. And now the quest for security splits the whole world with demonic power.

"What is the world you are making? Wars, victories, more wars. So many tears. So little regret. And who can sit in judgement when victims' horror turns to hate? What saved Second Isaiah from despair was his messianic vision of man's capacity for repentance.

A Lieutenant Colonel unknown to me walked out. Perhaps he had to relieve himself, but of what was unclear.

Only one thing stands in the way. Do you know what that is?

What stands in the way of repentance is the worship of power. Why are human beings so obsequious, so ready to kill and ready to die at the call of kings and chieftains, presidents and generals? It is because we worship might, we venerate those who command might, we are convinced that it is by might that man prevails. "

This was heresy to the more uniformed in the crowd.

"The most striking feature of all prophetic polemic is the distrust and denunciation of power in all its forms. You who work here know what I am talking about. The hunger for power knows no end; the appetite grows on what it feeds."

Maple's between-the-lines was growing ominous.

"Now as then, the sword is the pride of man; arsenals, forts, chariots and bombs lend supremacy to nations. War is the climax of human ingenuity, the object of supreme efforts; men slaughtering each other, cities blown to ruins. What is left behind? Agony and desolation. And you think very highly of yourselves, don't you? You are wise in your own hearts and clever in your own sight. But into your world, drunk with power, bloated with arrogance, comes Isaiah's word that the swords will be undone, that nations will search, not for gold, power or harlotries, but for God's word.

"It seems inconceivable, doesn't it? But to Isaiah it was a certainty: War will be abolished. You shall not learn war any more because you shall seek other knowledge. Your hearts of stone will melt, and hearts of flesh will grow instead. Are you ready for the metamorphosis?"

Richard Feynman got up to leave.

"But wait!" the Chaplain called after him to no avail. "We have forgotten an Isaiah, the Third and last Isaiah, the strangest and most mysterious of the three. In transit from the second, he begins with gentle, female imagery:

'Rejoice ye with Jerusalem, and be glad with her, all ye that love her: rejoice for joy with her, all ye that mourn for her.

That ye may suck, and be satisfied with the breasts of her consolations;"

[A titter from the young girls in the audience. Feynman paused at the door.]

"As one whom his mother comforteth, so will I comfort you, and ye shall be comforted in Jerusalem.'

"Happy ending. Nice and tidy. The American Way. But the Bible is not born of shallowness. [Feynman completed his exit.] I skip to the end of the book and read you the comments of Third Isaiah. After all Flesh has come to worship the Lord, God schedules a little field trip:

"'They shall go forth, and look upon the carcasses of the men that have transgressed against Me: for their worm shall not die, neither shall their fire be quenched; and they shall be an abhorring unto all flesh.'

"The unending destruction of flesh. The eerie excursion of the chosen to look upon the World's Fair, the abhorrent, endless process of corruption.

"'Through the wrath of the Lord is the land darkened, and the people shall be as the fuel of the fire: no man shall spare his brother.

And they shall snatch on the right hand, and be hungry, and they shall eat on the left hand, and they shall not be satisfied: they shall eat every man the flesh of his own arm.

"Therefore hath the curse devoured the earth, and they that dwell therein are desolate: therefore the inhabitants of the earth are burned, and few men left.' So that the Lord 'may do his work, his strange work, and bring to pass his act, his strange act.'"

Little Paul Teller started to cry. Mici carried him out.

"Well may you cry, my young friend. It's a grisly scandal of a text. The reality of Third Isaiah's judgement is indeed grim, but it is dishonest to pretend that reality is otherwise. Where do you in this room fit in this reality?" With a wave of his arm, he indicated the entire room. "What's wrong with this picture?"

The tension exceeded the punctured silence before the final Hallelujah. But there was no Hallelujah — only the disembodied voice again:

"'Woe to those who call evil good and good evil,

Who put darkness for light and light for darkness!'

'The stone will cry out from the wall,

Woe to him who builds a town with blood,

And founds a city on iniquity.'"

Chaplin Maple strode quickly from the silenced room. He was not seen again on site. The dance that followed had a forced and frantic quality. Gregor left early to go home to bed. I remained to assay the effects.

Humperdinck — Hansel and Gretel

The Wich

From SKULK. Richard, my Noam Chomsky character, and T.L., my Ann Coulter character, attend a student performance at Wichita State University, while they both stalk a department store Santa, who they think may be stalking them.

She poked him in the ribs with her pointy elbow. The audience quieted for that magic moment in darkness, before it all began.

And begin it did, the famous overture, with a chorale of four-part horn sweetness, the "Now I Lay Me Down To Sleep" tune, known or unknown, of all our childhoods. On the scrim, DAWN OVER WICHITA, 12-hours misplaced, or perhaps the advertised "attitude", a sarcastic comment on the sleepwalking days of Kansans. In any case, what a gorgeous opening: the famous *Abendsegen*, or evening prayer, sweet, sweet — but not sugary-so. Rather sweetly rich and creamy, like premium chocolate, or a cantaloupe at maximum bouquet, an aural caress. The projected sunrise was lovely too, the gleaming river, the Hyatt Regency with its sparkling waterfall. THE BIRDS GREET THE SUN, says the scrim, and the great Kansan sky becomes slowly filled with birds, a gentle nature film, like PBS. As the overture builds with Wagnerian harmonies, the birds become more intense — wait! — there's a flying birds shot from Duck Soup, couldn't be, I must have imagined it. The Meistersingerish counterpoint thickens, as does the sky, and my God! it's the title bird-melee from Hitchcock, wait! was it really? I thought I...and the flocks fly north — could that be Margaret Hamilton on her broom in among them?? — as the camera pans lyrically eastward over the city towards the wrong side of Wichita's tracks, the music lusciously Wagner-without-Nazism. Sunrise over slums is also beautiful — as long as you're in long-shot. But the overture winds down, gently, strangely chromatic, again calling forth the *Abendsegen* — a prayer, however twisted — as the camera climbs a filthy stairway to an attic apartment. The scrim rises on the opening scene.

"That was something," Teresa said.

Richard could only nod his head.

Ives Fourth Symphony

I first discovered Ives when performing his Piano Trio at Goddard College, back in the seventies. You could tell he was a real character from the music alone. Then I read his Essay Before a Sonata, got more seriously interested in him, and especially his Concord Sonata. I wrote the first piece in this collection in the early eighties, and read it with piano performances of the excerpts, to a UU church audience. Thus prepped, a full performance followed. Who knew all this could happen in Moscow, Idaho? Then, when I got around to writing Golem Song/Kafka's Roach *in the aughts, he popped up as a main character. Ives had co-founded the largest insurance company in NYC,* Ives & Myrick. *He composed while commuting by train from his home near Danbury, Connecticut. Gregor has his first meetup with Charles Ives:*

"Hey, Mister..."

"No, thank you, I..."

"I'll give you a good deal."

Should he, or shouldn't he? His last encounter, well over two years ago, had been disastrous; he had felt desexed ever since. The thought of a woman's soft flesh had become repulsive once more. He didn't know this person. He could get a disease. She was vaguely attractive, but... Wasn't this illegal? What if he were caught? Without papers, he could be deported...Still...

"They're great seats. Fourth row, center."

"What?"

"Fourth row, center. We have an extra ticket."

"Ticket for what?"

"Oh, forgive me. I thought you were heading for the box office. You were reading the poster."

And, in fact, Gregor had stopped to puzzle out the poster in the Town Hall display. "Pro Musica International Referendum Concert." What sort of referendum? Wasn't that when you voted on some proposal? Music to vote on proposals? What sort of proposals? He couldn't vote, he thought, but still he was interested. He had just stepped away from his myopic inspection when the woman...

"Debussy, Ives, and Milhaud. You never get a chance to hear this music." He had never even heard of Milhaud...but Ives?

"Ives?"

"Charles Ives. The insurance genius-composer. You've heard of him?"

"Is he about two meters tall, and he is writing an amendment for your Constitution?"

"I haven't met him, but it sounds like it could be."

"I think I have met him. Does he like baseball?"

"That I do know. My husband and he played on the same team at Yale."

"Yale. That was the team at the game I saw."

"Then it was probably Charlie Ives. Don't you want to hear some of his music?"

"Yes. I would like to. But I have no money at the moment."

"Oh. Too bad. We do need to get something for the seat."

"I'm sorry."

"That's all right. I'll tell you what. If I can't sell it, I'll leave it under your name at the box office. Can you check back in an hour or so?"

"Thank you. That's very nice of you. Gregor."

"Just Gregor?"

"Samsa. Gregor Samsa."

"S-a-m-s-a." She, writing it on the back of a chewing gum wrapper from her purse.

But Gregor did not check back. He didn't want to sit next to this woman. For one thing, her afternoon perfume was already making his antennae itch in a mid-winter breeze. What would it be indoors, with a fresh dose? For another, he couldn't really sit front and center at some international Town Hall performance with the shabby clothes he had taken to wearing in his new metamorphosis into freedom. He could go up to Ulla's and retrieve his good suit for the evening. But, no, he couldn't just breeze in and breeze out, and there wasn't really time to talk before eight — he hadn't seen her for several months. He should probably go see her. But all this did not quench his curiosity about the insurance genius-composer who was writing a Constitution amendment. Nor did it stop him from going to the concert.

In the last months, G had become expert at slipping in and out of buildings unnoticed, of caressing the shadows, and being caressed by them. He knew the midtown alleys like the claw of his pretarsus. He knew the back doors of Town Hall. He knew the ushers stood in them pre-concert, in the coldest weather, to smoke. He had a black overcoat and a flute case for such occasions. Walk in quickly, authoritatively, nod the head, flash the flute case nonchalently. They had never challenged him before, and wouldn't now. What usher wants to be dressed down for hassling some distinguished international musician? Then, up to the second floor via the stairs at the back of the hall. Slip into the auditorium as the usher seats another customer, and wait behind the curtain on the back wall. What a wonderful thing to be flat. Even six feet tall, Gregor could get behind an arass without making a bulge. In the dark, with two stick-like legs protruding at the bottom, he was totally undiscoverable. He had only to edge over and stick his knee outside the tapestry for excellent acoustics — even if he couldn't see.

He would go to the concert. Then afterwards, he would visit Ulla, take some time, share the last months — and say, he might retrieve that card Mr. Ives had given him at the ballgame. Hadn't he given him a card? It must be in the pocket of his brown suit. He was wearing his brown suit, wasn't he? Ulla would remember. She was his clothing consultant for his date with Alice. Yes, he'd get the card, and if he liked the music, he would call up Mr. Ives and tell him.

And so it happened. Gregor arrived at the back door of Town Hall at 7:25, walked right by two ushers finishing up their Chesterfields, and found his curtained place at the back of the orchestra. Not fourth row, center, but it would do. There was his reluctant patroness in Row D. That little man is her husband? Well, she didn't say "husband", did she?

He wondered if she had sold the ticket. He'd look at intermission to see if a seat either side of them was empty. For now, the soft darkness.

This concert of January 29, 1927 was a courageous love-labor of E. Robert Schmitz, a French pianist who had shown up at Ives & Myrick looking for insurance. When the conversation turned to music they were startled — both. Ives had discovered a brilliant pianist and promoter, and Schmitz a fascinating and undiscovered talent most generous with money. The night's concert was to be played by 50 musicians from the N.Y. Philharmonic under the baton of Eugene Goosens, an up-and-coming conductor-composer. It had been originally proposed to premier the whole Symphony, but the Comedy movement took up so much energy, there was no time left for rehearsing the even more demanding last movement: only the first two would be played. Besides, Goosens couldn't make head nor tail of the music, and thought his men would be lucky if they could just get through it. He didn't tell Ives — whom he had found personally impressive and charming.

Charles and Harmony had come to all the rehearsals, but, in their typically bashful way, hid themselves in the green room where they could hear scarcely anything. Goosens had to come backstage to consult, so scared, they were, to come out and face "the men."

Ives was last on the program, which began with Debussy's late, elusive cello sonata, a strange, other-worldly work in which the cello, chameleon-like, metamorphoses into violin, into flute, into even mandolin. The house was half-full, but the applause for Pierre Fournier, the intrepid young French soloist, was thunderous. Gregor loved this 1915 work, and wondered he had not heard it in Europe — for it appeared in the same year as himself.

He was less impressed with the second work, Darius Milhaud's incidental music for Aeschylus' *Eumenides*. Whips and hammers were used in the orchestration, and a small chorus was required to groan, whistle, and shriek in several keys at once. Too much striving for too little effect. The audience seemed to share his view, the applause being barely more than polite.

Gregor stuck his head out during intermission, but decided to remain hidden, and not mingle with the crowd. He saw a dark portly personage down front slowly make his way to the rear among a small circle of reporters. That must be Mr. Milhaud. He knew what Debussy looked like. Besides, wasn't he dead? After the hall was almost empty, he spotted Mr. Ives and his wife sitting anonymously in the right rear, near the exit, positioned, he thought, to flee. He was curious what he might hear.

The hall lights blinked, and the audience took its seats for the largest work of the evening, the opening movements of Ives' last symphony, finished thirteen years earlier, some time while sideshow Gregor was performing Rilke for his own questionable audience. From the opening challenge of cellos and basses, he didn't know what hit him. This fierce question gave way to a distant choir of strings, flute and harp, whispering fragments of the hymn, "Bethany", *"Nearer, my God, to Thee"*. Gregor didn't know the words, of course, but the feeling of intimate divinity was patent, all the more telling for the preceding, striding immensity. *"E'en though it be a cross that raiseth me..."* It would have been good for him to know the text. *"Still all my song shall be nearer, my God to Thee."* Maybe it was too soon for him to know this, the cross. It gives me the shivers, though, to think of G behind the curtain with such thought-forms broadcast by so many transmitters seated in the hall:

Though like the wanderer, the sun gone down,
Darkness be over me, my rest a stone;
Yet in my dreams I'd be
Nearer, my God, to thee...

Or, thinking of his to-this-day-impenetrable immigration:

Or if, on joyful wing cleaving the sky,
Sun, moon, and stars forgot, upward I fly,
Still all my song shall be,
Nearer, my God, to Thee.

A small group of players continued Bethany's shimmering veil throughout the first movement, independent of their colleagues,

136

a hidden spiritual presence revealed only when the larger orchestra quieted. Had G been able to see, he would have been assured of their existence, but his insect-fine sensibilities could still detect them, lyric, meditative, behind the acoustically looming foreground. Ives must be on a quest, too, he thought, a quest for wholeness, a way to bring such diversity together. This is a work of high mystery.

A solo cello sang a drawn-out melody based on "Sweet By and By" — where Father waits "over the way" in a dwelling place on the beautiful shore. Gregor would learn more of this that pre-election morning. Not three minutes in, behold! a choir, out of nowhere, asking the question Gregor had been feeling:

Watchman, tell us of the night,
What the signs of promise are...

Gregor could hear the words, understand them. What about the night? And the answer:

Traveller, o'er you mountain's height,
See that Glory-beaming star!

Yes, but it is so distant, a mere pinpoint in a universe of darkness... The chorus, too, was skeptical:

Watchman, aught of joy or hope?

But the answer, unequivocal:

Traveler, yes, it brings the day,
Promised day of Israel.
Dost thou see its glorious ray?

All this within a rich fabric of orchestral sound woven from fragments of other hymns, gently polyrhythmic, polytonal — as is the world. And in less than five minutes, the movement was over, evaporating in the question, *"Dost thou see its glorious ray?"* Dost thou, Gregor Samsa? Dost thou? Yes. Yes, I do.

But what now? Do we see the glorious ray? See it in our ears?

What followed was one of the most extraordinary events in western music, probably in all music — ever. Maestro Goosens, when questioned afterwards about it, was quoted as saying, "My dear boy, I didn't know what happened after the downbeat."

What happened was all that ears could possibly hold, the damndest racket ever to come out of an orchestra before or since. It's not clear how much Gregor "got", standing behind the tapestry at the back wall of Town Hall. But the main thrust was clear: there was a tiny voice which kept appearing, a hymn-singing, delicate voice. It would lift itself up in frailty, and harmonized in shifting quarter-tones, would make sincere attempts at hymnody. But each time — it would be smashed, crashed, bashed, trashed by ever-greater pandemonium, massive musical agglomerations of dizzying, polyrhythmic marches, ragtime piano riffs, secularizations of other hymn tunes, jingoistic clear-the-way for America, America on the march — even a foreigner, a less-than-legal immigrant could hear that.

And when America marched, it was in a confusion of keys and meters, with tens of different rhythms going on at once, and half a dozen tonal centers at the same time — appropriate in a country where everyone seemed out for himself. Awash in a maelstrom of competing keys, the total effect was far beyond tonality, an utterly complex shaping and clashing of sound masses. It was the sound of our twentieth century, as even Gregor could understand, the roar of our cities and factories, the clash of our people, races, cultures, a satanic bellowing-out which added up to sheer madness. In such a context, old tunes seemed transformed: "Columbia, the Gem of the Ocean", once a song of joy, now roared monstrous power, monstrously applied; the old Stephen Foster tune — *"Down in the Cornfield, hear dat mournful sound"* seemed here not about massa's death, but about the travesty of White supremacy in the racist south — and north. In short, the movement seemed a nightmare crushing of the inner sounds of yearning, hope, and vision, an intimation not of immortality, but of eternal punishment.

Poor little tune in the solo violin (it was *Beulah Land,* which G did not know) — out there all alone, waiting for the inevitable, singing with your head in the guillotine. Why are you there? What are you doing in company such as this? You — fragile, sentimental, but undaunted, with your somber accompaniment and strange quarter tone noodlings. Did you come only to be trampled under our heavy industrial feet, crushed by the venalities of our small-town Babbitry with its blaring booster bands? Or is your presence ironic, a sweet reminder that religion shares complicity in our tragedy? Or are you just there, as truly you are, nine-hundred-lived, watching, waiting for the racket to die out on its own? At the end of the movement, Gregor did not know.

He did know he was shaken. He knew he had been present at a miracle of pedagogy — Mr. Ives was trying to tell him something about his new country, about himself, about his quest. He knew he would go see him, as he had been invited to, six and a half years ago.

He watched the Iveses sneak out amidst the booing. He heard the following exchange in the lobby: "Is Debussy dead?" "Yes." "Is Ives dead?" "No, but he ought to be." He knew Charles Ives would be his teacher.

Ives — Like a Sick Eagle

Gregor applies for, and accepts a job in Ives' insurance office, quickly becoming a favorite. Climbing the stairs to work,

He thought of Mr. Ives' song. Mr. Ives was so nice to give him a signed copy of his book of songs. "To Mr. Gregor Samsa, my prize student. March, 1929. Ch. E. Ives" That was his favorite, "Like A Sick Eagle" — he could sing it just the way Mr. Ives would like it. Even better. Mr. Ives wanted quarter tones, but Gregor could easily do eighth tones, sixteenth tones if he were careful.

I love this song too. It was how G and I discovered our friendship. We must have been the only two people on the mesa who had even heard of Ives, much less knew this song, this tiny masterpiece, a one-page study in descending tones, short phrases with weary, chromatic pauses between them. The score is marked, "Very slowly, in a weak and dragging way", shining exhausted light on Keats' disheartened poem:

> *The spirit is too weak;*
> *mortality weighs heavily on me*
> *like unwilling sleep,*
> *and each imagined pinnacle and steep*
> *of Godlike hardship*
> *tells me I must die...*

"Like a sick eagle," Gregor sang, *"like a sick eagle, looking towards the sky."*

Ives wrote it, I believe, while his new wife, Harmony, was in the hospital, undergoing the hysterectomy that would render them childless, with an unhappy, adopted daughter. "What a way to start a marriage!" thought G.

Insect Sonata (Ivestrin)

In appreciation of Gregor's helping him through a period of depression, Ives writes a (fictive) Third Piano Sonata, "The Insect Sonata", and dedicates it to Gregor. Together they attend the premiere performance of the work at Town Hall. Using the Concord Sonata as a model, it was easy enough to come up with a detailed description of this one. Several musician friends of mine were surprised and disappointed to find I had just made it up. The following excerpt is narrated by Gregor's friend, John Aschenfeld, official historian of the Manhattan Project.

The Insect Sonata

The lights were going down. A young usher flashlit the route to their seats in the back row. There was a moment of rustling silence, and Nicolas Slonimsky — the extravagant Russian emigré pianist, composer and conductor with a passion for ultra-modern music — walked on from stage right. Perhaps staggered might be a better word, for he had done nothing but eat, sleep and drink this difficult work for the last three months, trying to get it into his brain and under his fingers. He had conducted several Ives premieres, and had the composer's trust. He was not a sissy. He drank strong samovar chai. Still, a man needs sleep.

But one can stagger and still be on fire, and Slonimsky, even punchy, was a force to be reckoned with. He bowed to the audience. Without a word of introduction, he walked upstage of the Steinway Concert Grand and returned with a large brick and two pieces of two-by-four, one 47 3/4", the other 45 1/2", the longer painted in white, the shorter in black enamel. He put the wood on the piano bench, and carefully leaned the cement block on the sustaining pedal. Climbing out from under the keyboard, he retrieved the wood, and placed the longer piece, narrow edge down, along the white keys, and the shorter one, wider side down, along the black. He was ready to begin the first movement: Creation.

Standing over the keyboard, the piano bench behind him, he took a huge breath, and crashed his whole body weight, elbows first, down onto the wood. Some in the audience gasped, most jumped. The piano let out a sound such as had never been heard on the planet. At no time, ever, had all eighty-eight notes of a Steinway Concert Grand been simultaneously sounded and sustained publicly.

The Boeing 747 is such a well-designed plane that, should all its engines simultaneously fail at 35,000 feet, the huge beast has enough wing-lift to coast for 600 miles before having to land. Similarly, the Steinway Concert Grand. Quadruple fortissimo to start, the opening ultra-chord took a full two and a half minutes to decay into nothingness, though the absolute endpoint depended on each listener's distance and auditory acuity. Slonimsky stood above the keyboard, his eyes closed, and allowed his spirit to spread to the farthest physical and spiritual reaches of the expanding vibrations.

When he could hear no more, (he was the last in the hall), when what he would call his etheric body had reached its maximum distance and had begun to contract significantly, he removed the two-by-fours, replaced them upstage, reached under the piano, pushed the brick to the side of the pedal, and took his seat at the keyboard.

Before I continue, let me confess that I was not present at this historic performance. I am piecing this narrative together from Gregor's reports, from a study of the score which was finally published in 1967 by Universal, and from some recent listening to the only available recording, just released by Gilbert Kalisch on Nonesuch. (Even John Kirkpatrick, the only man to truly master the Concord Sonata, could not handle it.) And while I am digressing from the concert, let me say, too, that while it is nowhere indicated in the copious commentary in the score, it is clear that Ives's famous opening was also the first direct musical reference to the "Big Bang" theory of Creation.

This notion, now the leading cosmological hypothesis, had come in 1926 to the Belgian mathematician/priest Georges Lemâitre in a religious vision. It accounted for Hubble's red-shift findings, and explained the recession of galaxies in the framework of Einsteinian General Relativity. He published his theory in 1927 in an obscure Belgian journal ("Un univers homogène de masse constante et de rayon croissant rendant compte de la vitesse radiale des nébuleuses extra-galactique", Ann. Soc. Sci. Bruxelles, 47A, 1927, pp. 49-56), which, in 1930, was "discovered" by a graduate student of Arthur Eddington's — who then announced it, just a few months before the concert, to the world. The public loved its straightforward image of the "primeval atom", the "cosmic egg", containing all matter in the universe, whose disintegration marked the beginning of time and space — which may explain the general acceptance of this cacophonous moment. Without being told, people understood that the opening of a movement called "Creation" might consist of some kind of big bang. The actual experience, apparently, was something else.

The big bang gives way to a world of vast, austere empty space. Out of silence, there appear atomic fragments of pre-melodies, one note, three notes, two, a gentle report of almost-vacancy. Beethoven had attempted same in the opening moments of the Ninth, but Ives takes this micro-macro view far further, developing not a larger, more convincing, musical phrase, but the idea of "phrase" itself, and the very conception of tonality — bi-, tri-, quadri-tonality — as the pre-melodies stake out their tonal grounds. The section is marked "In the Egg-Case, Molto Adagio", and in it we recognize the eggs of the Egg, streaming outward, developing the charged direction of their own contents. Punctuating the slow metamorphoses of individual capsules were quiet outbursts of tremolos at the seventh and ninth, creating halo-like shimmers of light. Since there are six such crescendo-decrescendos in the movement, I assume they clock the six days of creation, after which there is rest. On the fifth of such presumptive days, the day when God said, "Let the waters bring forth abundantly every moving creature that hath life," the music thickens markedly. It now has enough mass for rhythm to emerge, at first simple syncopations, and finally a poly-rhythmic cosmic dance, a combination of simultaneous musics, as Ives was wont to do, but here slower, softer, more anatomized, not the repulsing chaos of the Fourth Symphony "Comedy", but a far more inviting, massaging, soundspace enveloping the listener in a finally friendly creation. On the sixth presumptive day, with the addition of "creeping things" to the bestiary, a clear, easily recognizable rhythmic figure, a quarter note, a rest, and quick pickup to the next quarter: the telltale rhythmic signature of of an insect heartbeat, gathering.

The middle section of this ABA movement is marked "The firmament walks up a mountainside to view the firmament", an odd, but evocative, piece of topology. We hear the slow, gentle, aggregation of kaleidoscope-massed chords and tone clusters, the total effect of which is to rough out, in strange harmonies, an accompaniment to a still absent melody. The bass tries out "Oh Maker of the Sea and Sky", only to have it fade away, incomplete. The tune returns again, "Creator Spirit, By Whose Aid...", and advances a few bars further, before dissolving in its own accompaniment. In this middle section, the overall serenity is occasionally pierced by inexplicable explosions, surprising, sometimes barbaric, leaps of tone sequences from one end of the keyboard to the the other, recalling George Ives's experiments with the humanophone — accenting in yet another way the pervasive feeling of spaciousness. Wisps of quotations — Handel's frogs and locusts, Mahler's lindens, Haydn's whales and worms, Beethoven's cuckoo, Ives' friend Carl Ruggle's lilacs, Saint-Saëns's, Tschaikovsky's and Sibelius's swans — make fragmentary appearances, a half a dozen notes, like the sprinkling of stars which form a constellation.

Then, as if from a different level of space-time, the first mood returns, now enclosed in a trinity of superimposed sets of perfect fifths, a pedal point pervaded by heartbeat, giving birth, as if from a resistant hardwood table, to a hesitant, but slowly complete, chorale setting of "Watchman, tell us of the night", the melody floating in and out of tonality, sober, maestoso, cognisant of the triple mysticism of its cloak of open fifths. "Watchman, tell us of the night" — here not an anxious question, but a humble entreaty, its feet washed in mystery.

144

With this, Slonimsky closed the movement, quietly, firmly, then placed his hands in his lap and waited the full three minutes requested in the score. For the first of these, the audience was completely silent, hypnotized by the evocation, "spaced-out", to use a contemporary expression in its most correct and literal sense. In the second minute, people grew uncomfortable. Some worried that something was amiss, while others gathered their suspicions of a put-on. A small flurry of whispering was shushed out by the faithful, and the silence cycled round again on a deeper level.

The pianist opened his eyes and once again placed the the brick on the sustain pedal. He stood by the side of the piano while two stage hands pulled pins from their hinges, and placed the huge piano lid against the wall, stage right. The performer now had in front of him, an enormous horizontal harp, ready to speak of "Revelation".

But not just a harp. A harp inside an enormously powerful, sophisticated structure, evolved over centuries, a structure capable of containing and supporting more than eighteen tons of amassed string tension. A structure of multiple strings in two overlapping fans. A structure of spruce and steel very like a coffin.

I am a poor pianist, and I leave all maintenance of the Yamaha to Emil, our most excellent tuner. But I have often been attracted, amazed, even thrilled by the technical genius of the modern piano-forte. And yet, each time I put my head under the lid, I feel strongly: coffin, an ominous, but somehow freeing impression nurtured and sweetened by the involuntary rush of the last Schumann song in the *Dichterliebe*, the one about "the old evil songs, the wicked, depraved dreams." Heine and Schumann want to bury them all in a large coffin, a coffin larger than the Heidelberg Cask, longer than the bridge at Mainz, a coffin so huge it must be carried by twelve giants and buried in the sea. A coffin for all those songs and dreams — and Heine's love, and Schumann's suffering. What better coffin, then, than a massive piano case? When I play the caressing postlude to that song, the end of the whole song cycle, my spirit is wafted under that black lid to be massaged and prepared for its final free-dom. I wonder if Ives had any sense of this in writing the second movement, if all its boisterousness is ironically placed inside a tomb, and must be so understood.

In any event, the entire second movement, "Revelation", marked "Scherzo TSIMAJ", takes place inside the case, and requires of the performer an utterly unprecedented technique, and of the composer an extended notational system. It also demands a new vocabulary from the would-be reporter. Just as we have few words to describe taste or pain, or most of the 473 sounds cats can make, so the verbal lexicon is completely inadequate to describe the rich sound palette of an undamped piano harp in a sophisticated sound chamber, urged by fingers which can pluck and stoke, flick and scratch, flesh, bone, and nail, by fists that can bang, and palms that can slap, by forearms grazing and elbows jabbing, and even by hair brushing lightly, across or along the strings. Add to those the percussive sonorities of various striking objects: the metallic echo of wedding ring on harp bolt, the ticking or tocking of chopstick and toothpick, the liquid rebound of strings released by soft dough. And all this in a universe sympathetic with vibration, where each sound creates families of related sub-sounds, ripples upon ripples, slow beats after fast, high upon low upon high. No description can communicate such aural complexity.

Because a performer would quickly be lost in a forest of undifferentiated stringing, the strings were colored black and white to mirror the familiar keyboard; though paint had been lost over the hammers, and in areas of maximum vibrational displacement, the visual effect was still striking, and Gregor asserts that certain combinations of vibrating strings, though each only black or white, can create short flashes of color. I don't understand the physics of this; perhaps it occurs only for the blattid nervous system, or solely in mosaic eyes.

Even if I can't describe the sound in great detail, I can provide a roadmap to this extraordinary piece thanks to Ives's clear musical and extra-musical ideas and his detailed marginalia.

After the long silence of, I suppose, the Sabbath, the movement opens triple pianissimo, with a quietly pulsing, timeless, Eb, the same sustained note Wagner chose to represent the beginning of the world from abysmal depths. ("Mark my new poem well," he wrote Liszt

(11 Feb. 1853): "it holds the world's beginning, and its destruction.")
Most curiously, the tone is notated as Fbb for reasons which will later
become clear.

All of a sudden, there is a loud, old-fashioned, short fanfare, the
kind of musical cliché which would invariably be followed by "And
now, Ladies and Gentlemen...", over which is written "Welcome to the
Grand Old Opryetta", and the sound drops back to the Fbb, now pulsing in the first movement's rhythmic cell of the beating roach heart.
Suddenly, the note pushes unexpectedly off into the rising Eb arpeggio of the hero theme from Ein Heldenleben, only to fall flat on its
face as the sixteenth notes tumble down, splat, back to a more agitated
pulsing. The manuscript then notes "In The Cage", and the Fbb pulse
takes on the perturbed syncopations of the pacing beast in that short,
1904 piece — and then stops short, as the pianist begins the most banal
version of "How Dry I Am", a tune well-known in those late years of
prohibition. In the margin, "This song is in Fbb — and that's very flat!"
The tonic pulsation is tailed in closest stretto by an Ebb echo while a
ghostly soprano plucking plays out the maudlin Mother's song of two
decades earlier, "Where's My Wandering Boy Tonight?", and the stretto
adds a Dbb to produce a series of micro melodic fragments of three
falling tones. Then, in a sonically amazing series of jostling overtones,
the stretto organizes itself into a gradually emerging modulation in
which Fbb is ghostily changed to Fb, and Fb metamorphoses into F
natural, dragging its stretto neighbors with it into the emanating tune
F, E, E, D; F, E, E, D.

The music stops abruptly, and the new section is marked "Feeding
Frenzy, Allegro Scrumptuoso", as an increasingly agitated rhythmic
figure is mixed into the more and more dissonant sonic halo and the
performer begins what must be the most fiendishly difficult task in
the repertoire. "Antennae accelerando," Ives orders, and the music
breaks out into quick-march version of "I Hunger And I Thirst", and
"Come Thou, Font Of Every Blessing". Then, a clarion call from chop-
stick-struck strings: "Hark A Thrilling Voice Is Sounding", and the
whole grand harp breaks into a Yale Football March, with a tapped out
supra-melody of "Rush Down Boys". In the score is written, "All hands

on deck!!!", and all hands are surely there, and knuckles and elbows too for a chaotic concatenation of barn dances, popular parlor tunes (with highly unpopular treatments), polka-dot polkas, cross-rhythmic children's songs and devilish ragtime, "allegro (conslugarocko) — wag those knees", all swirled together in stubbornly original juxtapositions, "wrong note" harmonies, and polychords. Ives writes "play adagio or allegro — very nice", so the performer has completely free choice about what comes out of the black box.

Slonimsky's manic disposition, fueled by months of caffeine, made this performance a never-to-be-equalled thrashing about in the cupboards of Americana and the annals of technical prowess. Honky-tonk whip-chords, sharp, unexpected jabs at irregular intervals, "Presto con Blasta", "Con Furyo-fffff". Again, an abrupt halt; in the manuscript: "Back to the hero — all good Opryettas got to have a hero." So, scratched out with fingernail on the thickly wound lower strings, we hear the belching song of an overstuffed roach, the F, E, E, D theme now revealing itself as the second phrase of "Three Blind Mice" — "see how they run", mice in this case metamorphosed into roaches running in mighty molasses motion.

Then, crash! the fastest and most difficult passage of all, a long section of rapid, sprawling chromatic chords, out of which the left hand pulls quintuplet dances of jaunty wild demons, while the right hand slap-accentuates every fifth sixteenth note, and the entire raucousness comes to a vociferous climax in a repeated polytonal canon on "The Streets of Cairo", a belly-dance tune, which emerges to dominate the scramble. In the manuscript: "EVEN HERBERT HOOVER WILL GET THIS," — though I must admit I don't. Under everything, the now-identifiable eructations of our fat, sated hero belching out the Czech national anthem and a well-sauced version of The Moldau, accompanied by an ironic rendition of "Old Folks Gatherin'" from Ives's Third Symphony. "Ain't it a grand and glorious noise?" he writes, and only the most determined musical curmudgeon could disagree. He finishes up with a section entitled "Southpaw Pitching" a left-hand solo recitative of highly improvisational character which brings our modified hero face to face with his revelation.

But what is the revelation? A revelation most ambiguous. I must return the reader to the indication "Scherzo TSIMAJ" at the opening of the movement. We know from the Piano Trio (1911) that TSIAJ means "This scherzo is a joke". But what of the added "M"? "This scherzo is mostly a joke"? What is the non-joke meaning? That outside the egg there is thirst and boisterous life, hunger and frenzy and fight? The intent, I think, becomes clear in the inspired last movement, "Redemption". The stage hands fit the lid back on, and raise it to its full height.

"Bring Art into life and Life into art (no elite redemptive space!)" floats mysteriously above the movement title, in small letters at the right hand top of the page. Then, "III. REDEMPTION", that short phrase announcing a gift to humanity as full of import as the "6. Der Abschied" in Mahler's masterpiece, Gregor's beloved "Song of the Earth".

It is unclear if Ives ever heard any Mahler. He may have during 1909-11 when Mahler conducted the New York Philharmonic. Ives said he avoided listening to new composers because it threw him off stride, as the old war-horses did not, but he probably heard more new works than he cared to admit. It is known that Mahler had discovered Ives. In 1911, just before leaving New York, he noticed a symphony score by some unknown, apparently untutored, American composer on the table at the Tams Music Office, and took it back to Europe with him for an intended performance. Had he lived to perform Ives's Third, the course of twentieth century music — and Ives's life — would have been quite different. But Mahler died that spring of the heart ailment he knew was hovering, the sickness that provoked Der Abschied, and the transcendent meditations of his Ninth. But how quick he was to recognize — in music that sounds so different — the commonality between them: that love of humble, commonplace melody, the project of incorporating "the whole world" in a musical work, transforming as needed, honoring the "bad old songs" and using their energy to invigorate and transform more complex "classical" genres. They were both great foes of Hog-Mind.

"Allegro fortissimo with marked energy". Back at the keyboard, the movement begins, with a complex clarity fresh to the ears after the misty vibrations of an unrestrained piano harp. Reversing the usual procedures, as he often does, Ives begins with the most complex statement possible, in which many subsequent motives appear — immediately, simultaneously, with four part polyphony growing to five parts by the third beat and nine by the fourth beat — of the first measure. There is enough germ material for an entire symphony here, all in one measure. While other composers might begin with a simple motive and develop its implications in the course of a work, Ives starts out with multiple complexities that seem like late developments which, as the movement proceeds, become more and more open, more clear, more straightforward. Another version of the Big Bang.

The second measure is still enormously complex, but even now a movement toward simplification begins. Like galaxies condensing out of the initial explosion, patterns start to appear. The nine parts of the end of the first measure form themselves into harmonic blocks, with the three lowest voices shaping a bass chord, the four higher parts moving together into a soprano-alto chord, and two tenor voices snaking interstitially in between. The three blocks move with so much variability and independence that together they form a kind of hyper-counterpoint, with each block the equivalent of a single contrapuntal voice. Thus does nine become three, dissonant in a basically consonant way.

There follows an animando section, crescendo, with the upper choirs rising and the lower ones descending until they each drop off into empty space, extruding the tenor duet out in front to begin the second section, an overlay of funeral marches incompletely metamorphosing one into the other, as does the cockroach, to an irregular, discordant accompaniment below that growls quietly in its own universe. The funeral march from the Eroica changes its famous descending trochees (to be sounded so movingly at Gregor's death) into the steady, falling eighth note spondees of the middle phrase of the Chopin funeral march, and from there transforms to the more familiar, haunting iambics of the last movement of the Scriabin First Sonata. Accompanying this noble procession, like Sancho Panza alongside the Don, is a second line of more burlesque commentary, the mock-funeral from the Mahler First, chirping along from above, while "The Worms Crawl In, The Worms Crawl Out" rocks deep below, like an ominous carved cradle. The F, E, E, D theme returns, the "See How They Run Funeral March", in pendular motion, transposed back to Fb, Eb, Eb, Db, then easing down to Fbb, Ebb, Ebb, Dbb, that Fbb=Eb, the base note of the Earth, extended out, its trailing afternotes appended behind it, twitching grace-notes-after-the-fact, descending into the underground.

Silence.

Then shocking surprise: the fierce opening of the movement occurs again, "fortissimo possible", causing, I am told, several members of the audience to wet their underwear or worse. As before, the sound grows richer as the choruses form, as the contrary motion fills the space. But this time, the outer choirs do not fly off into upper and lower regions, but produce — a second, even greater, surprise — a voice.

This was Slonimsky's singing debut, for when are concert pianists ever asked to sing? "For God," he bellowed out, "is glorified in man," a line from Browning's long dramatic poem, Paracelsus. As Beethoven had needed the human voice to bring the Ninth to culmination, so Ives had transcended the limits of the piano sonata. Some wonderful singer might have been engaged to enter here, as a flute player does at the end of the Concord Sonata, but no. Ives specifically notates "No helpers allowed!" as if to demand that any performer demonstrate — in his or her own person — the ability to metamorphose and transcend.

I'm told it was an impressive performance. The vocal line and harmonies are such that standard technique would not have sufficed in any case — the premium was on musicianship and a sense of the dramatic — both of which Slonimsky possessed in excelsis.

He sang of Paracelsus, that German-Swiss physician and alchemist, a real-life Faust of the sixteenth century, who established the role of chemistry in medicine, a restless seeker after knowledge who would not stop until he discovered "the secret of the world." A proud man, brilliant but arrogant, "singled-out by God", he thought, "to be a star to men", Paracelsus was always at the center of controversy. He took no prisoners. He was deeply hated.

At the end of his life, he offered up a testament to the world, imagined and articulated by Browning in the long, inspired, final speech of his poem.

For God is glorified in man, he asserts,
And to man's glory vowed I soul and limb.
To man's glory — and to his own.

But then, Paracelsus' final self-assessment:

Yet, constituted thus, and thus endowed, I failed:
I gazed on power, I gazed on power till I grew blind
What wonder if I saw no way to shun despair?
The power I sought seemed God's;

So that was the meaning of the huge outburst at the beginning of the movement, the human counterpart and echo of the Big Bang: it was man trying to play God, a performance whose accompaniment must become a funeral march.

I learned my own deep error, Slonimsky sang, in a new section, *andante molto,*

And what proportion love should hold with power in man's right constitution;

Always preceding power,

What an admission for this power-seeking man! Paracelsus. Slonimsky. Perhaps Gregor? Was this old man Ives's warning to Gregor?

And what proportion love should hold with power in man's right constitution;

Always preceding power,

And with much power, always, always much more love.

Those last, deeply reflective words, "al-ways, al-ways....much.... more....love. The two "always" drawn out in slow funereal iambs, the length and hesitation of "much" and "more", the final fall of a major sixth onto the long-held D of "love" — fallen, yet still a half-tone above Eb — how similar the mysterious, immense space created is to that of *Der Abschied*, with its closing, hypnotic chant of ewig.....ewig.., a final testament of the greatest depth and wisdom.

From the Big Bang of Creation, through the complex Revelations of the manifested world, from the arrogance of the Seeker to the final simplicity — Love. I have heard the Dalai Lama explain, "My religion is very simple: my religion is kindness." This was Ives's gift to Gregor, the bug that crawled out of his table, his thank-you for being reminded of that glory-beaming star, the promised day of Israel.

The audience was rapt, enchanted, blessed. It took the hearers a full minute of silence to begin to tentatively applaud. In that minute, wherever their souls were, they were unaware of one detail, known at that moment only to Slonimsky and Ives: After the final note with its long fermata, after the double bar, was written, in small letters, *vers la flamme.*

Then, applaud they did, wildly, with Bravos!, stamping and whistling. One enthusiast actually yelled "Encore!", but the indignant stares he got soon convinced him otherwise. "But the ticket says..." The ticket was wrong. No encore was possible.

Gregor was transported; the Iveses were ecstatic. Slonimsky returned for a bow, and indicated the composer at the back of the house. Used to slinking out of concerts amidst the booing, the old man was not quite sure how to acknowledge such acknowledgement. Harmony nudged him: "Stand up. Take off your hat."

The applause lasted for two more Slonimsky exits and entrances. Musical history had been made. How surprised our trio was then to find that only a few people came up to greet them. The center of interest seemed to be elsewhere — around someone in a wheelchair sitting in the aisle, keyboard side, towards the front. Gregor couldn't see through the crowd who it was. The Iveses were about to go backstage to congratulate Slonimsky when the wheelchaired figure pushed his way through his admirers, up the carpeted slope and around the back of the hall to where Charles, Harmony and Gregor were putting on their coats. It was the Governor, the Governor himself, Franklin Roosevelt.

Mr. Ives! Mrs. Ives, I take it? And you must be the subject! He reached out and shook hands with each, moved, and moving, with genuine gratefulness for his extraordinary experience. Even G's outfit did not phase him: he grasped his claw.

Hold that shot, that handshake, that famous handshake, the handshake that would determine the rest of Gregor's life — and death.

Josquin Des Pres — Missa Une Mousse De Biscaye

This selection from The Annotated Nose. *It pretty much represents my own initiation into Renaissance Music, and the four years of constant choral singing that went with it.*

"Gotta get to a rehearsal."

"What sort of rehearsal?" she wanted to know.

"Hamilton Vocal Ensemble. Pretty terrific. A grad student in the music department pulled together a group of singers to do early music. Nice bunch. Pure voices. No vibrato. We're working on a Josquin mass."

"What's that?" Delia asked, her musical knowledge going back to Bach and no further.

"A Josquin mass? Josquin des Pres? You don't know him?"

Delia blushed, an odd response, but appropriate to the moment.

"Greatest composer of the Renaissance. 'Swing and sway with Josquin des Pres' — that's our motto. Do you sing?"

"Well, yes. I do."

Soprano, alto? Probably alto, right?"

"Yes.

"Can you sight sing? Just sing off a page?"

"Yes. Pretty well."

"Well hey, maybe you should come by. Monday, Wednesday, Friday, twelve to one at the Chapel. Know where that is?"

"Yes. My father teaches at the college. French."

"Who's that?"

"Dr. Robinson."

"Really? He's terrific — at least I hear."

"He's a great dad."

"I'll bet. Wow, Charlie Robinson's daughter…. So do you want to come? To Vocal Ensemble? See what it's like?"

"I'll think about it. I've got a lot on my plate."

"OK, then. See you when I see you. Great to meet you."

The fact is that Delia's plate had just been licked clean by a large Golden Retriever Shepherd and its master. And she spent the next several days — and nights — thinking about nothing but the latter. But did she have the courage to step in that direction? A week had passed. She had glimpsed him once when he and his Woody were leaving the green as she approached. She would not yell out, or run after. But when her father delivered a reminder-invite left for her in his departmental mailbox — that was too much to bear. On an early November afternoon, she pulled open the great white door to the Hamilton Chapel, and then the door into the sanctuary.

This was the miracle. She had walked into the middle of a miracle — *Et homo factus est.*

The central moment of the Nicene creed is the mystery of incarnation: *Et incarnatus est de spiritu sancto, ex Maria virgine.* And the center of the mystery, the miracle at the heart of all miracles, is evoked in the next line: *et homo factus est*, he was made man. Josquin had transcribed his heart-stopping awe at this event, calling a halt to his unmatched weavings in musical spacetime, and proceeding quietly, on contrapuntal tiptoe, as it were, to describe the mystery. It was much the way Delia entered the chapel — hesitant to presume or to intrude. The effect of Josquin's awe on her own, of his tentative, breath-holding witness on hers, was staggering. She had never heard anything so beautiful in her entire life as the sounds that caressed her from those echoing walls. She groped her way into a pew, and dropped down onto the kneeler. From her hidden position, framed by wood and velvet, leaning her head against the hymnal, she absorbed the crucifixion, the death — and with a shock, the spirited resurrection. And with that ascension, she herself was pulled back from the deep and shot outward, an arrow of longing, toward the source of the sound. At the *Amen*, she scrambled herself up onto the pew until the rehearsal was over.

"Delia!" Jens cried out, when he noticed her at the back.

"Hey, you came! Have you been here long? What did you think?"

What was she to say?

"I came in when Mary gave birth to Jesus."

"Is that in there?"

"*Ex Maria virgine...*"

"I don't know Latin. But I guess, yeah, Mary, virgin...ok."

"You mean you sing this without knowing what it means?"

"I only know how beautiful it is. Incredible. That's enough for me."

She could have left him then and there, before it even started. But she didn't. Instead, she joined the chorus, and spent the next months of dog-walking sharing with him what she had gathered in twelve years at Catholic school, in her last two years of reflection, art history classes at the college, and her own studio work exploring religious and spiritual themes. He, in turn, shared with her his deep appreciation of early music, from chant to the most complex Flemish polyphony, and allowed her to glimpse yet another face of God in the world.

Mahler — Kindertotenlieder

Friedrich Rückert, the poet who lost two tiny victims to diphtheria, and Gustav Mahler, whose wife warned him in vain against tempting fate (their own child died shortly thereafter) report a far more complex journey than Elizabeth Kubler-Ross's fraudulent New Age itinerary of Denial, Anger, Bargaining, Depression and Acceptance.

In the five songs of the *Kindertotenlieder*, a grief-stricken parent meditates in the early morning on the loss of his children during the night. His first profound impression is one of irony: in the midst of his pain, the sun will soon come up and shine brightly on all, all the to-be-happy-today people. "Only I have experienced this horror this night." Does he deny? No. He strengthens himself against taking night into the center of his being; he tries to see his pain in the truthful context of oncoming, but ironic, light. Thus, the first stage for an enlightened soul is not denial, but expulsion of the threatening pathologic.

In the second song, Rückert and Mahler understand the premonitory two-facedness of the light sparkling in their children's eyes. They are flames of concentration, arrows of longing for the larger world from which they had recently come. Thus, the deeper second stage is not anger and tantrum, but an intuition of the complexity of spiritual space-time.

In the third, most painful, song, triggered by a small event, understanding and intention give way to outpouring anguish. Father is sitting in a room. His wife comes in, stands in the doorway, and father looks not at her face, but at the empty space at her side where the child's face should have been. The horror of that emptiness leads Mahler to what is perhaps the most painful phrase ever composed, extended and again extended to the limit of singer and hearer alike — what depth of human pain is there, pain of transience, pain of finitude, pain of mortality, the universal senselessness of the human condition. And thus, the third stage: not bargaining, but shattering. One must truly die to be born again.

Kübler-Ross is right in this: humans often try to trick themselves, an activity similar to, yet more complex than simple denial. But as Sartre points out, and as Mahler and Rückert already know, lying to oneself, walling-off of consciousness is a tricky, improbable maneuver.

The fourth song illustrates the double perspective of true suffering: "I often think that they've only gone out for a walk. They've just gone on ahead, up into the bright sunshine above the clouds." But the griever sees himself thinking it, knows it to be a story, but a story with consoling power. No depression here, no self-deception, but a soothing opiate, like the woman pouring oil on Jesus' head, the conscious use of imagination to lighten suffering.

Just before the end, in the fifth song, a reactive brush with anger, an externalization of the psychic storm within, a true, passionate and crucial assertion: "it's not my fault!" "I wouldn't have sent them out in such weather — they were carried out, against my will." *Man hat sie hinaus getragen.* Who did the carrying? Man — they. Who is they? Everyone, everything that is not me. A cry from ego in an ego-despising universe.

And with this fierce and futile protest, the true light dawns. An eerie, chromatic d minor is transformed into the gorgeous sunrise of D major — the sun that was rising, but superficially, at the beginning of the work. From ironic light of sky and predictive light of eyes, through emptiness of absence, past tender light-imaginings and stormy darkness to the genuine light of spiritual understanding — that is the path our tour guides take us.

Are we too cynical for this journey? "No storm can frighten them now? They're resting in God's hand? Baloney! — they're just food for worms, and pity me!" If we are unable to see by the dark light of the *Kindertotenlieder*, then we are truly the shallow, deprived souls observed by Kübler-Ross who angrily deny, plead and whine, get depressed (and on Prozac), and finally, often by dint of inexcusable forgetting, "accept". The deeper we breathe in this music, the more we will understand when our own time of sorrow comes.

This is dangerous music the dwarf had sung — dangerous because so transforming and beneficent.

Mahler — Second Lenox Resurrection

In The Education of Anold Hitler, *Arnold, at Harvard, meets and dates Lenny Bernstein's 'Cliffie daughter, who gets him into the Tanglewood chorus for rehearsals and performance of Mahler 2. This young man from Texas had never heard Mahler before.*

Parking crew '72 was as expected: long days in the sweltering sun; nights hot, cold, and rainy — all needing interventions of great skill. But workplace success could not compete with rehearsal hall radiance: come end of June, Arnold found himself involved in another lot more nourishing, almost, than he could bear. "Celestial Soup" he called it, a dollop of vision beyond all pain, beyond all terror, a post-apocalyptic weave — of resurrection.

Where had Mahler been all his life? Never in Texas, that's for sure. And even New York had heard little enough until twenty years before, when a young Lenny Bernstein exhumed him from the cisterns of disdain. Too long. Too turgid. Too vulgar. Too. Too. Too. Who among the tueurs had even heard him?

The long playing record had given the fiery new director of the NY Phil a tool to pierce the nation's armor, and Lenny had — almost single-handedly — awakened this giant to prophesy to the sixties, to its turning, yearning youth. Early on came the call to resurrection, the Second Symphony. Lenny had made it his own.

It is a long and painful work — before resurrection come many kinds of death. But Arnold had come to the work tail first: the pain he did not know, only the glory — for his chorus came in only at the end, after the massive funeral march, after the dies irae and its spasms of horror. He did not know the "long dead hour of happiness" of the second movement, or the sinister *moto perpetuale* of the third, or the "scream of anguish." Nor had he faced the terrifying questions initiating his own fifth movement, the ferocious march in which "the dead arise and stream on in endless procession," the terror of their call for mercy and forgiveness, the last trumpet, sounding into a universe empty even of birdsong.

None of this had Arnold heard. His choral part began after all that, in the magic moment between worlds, when out of deathly silence there sounds the softest entrance in all music: *Auferstehen*. "Rise again, yes, thou shalt rise again. " That is where he came in, that is where his consciousness began, at a place unbalanced, but marvelously so.

Piano rehearsals were at seven in the West Barn, conducted by John Oliver, head of the new Tanglewood Chorus. There were only ten minutes of choral music to perform, so rehearsals proceeded quickly from mastering the notes to perfecting the expression. How does one sing "*misterioso*"? "*Misterioso*" is not just soft.

Arise, yes, you will arise from the dead, my dust, after a short rest.

Is the speaker alive or dead? .

The lord of the harvest gathers in the sheaves of we who have died.

How to sing from the other side of the grave? This was the challenge for the second and third rehearsals. Particularly moving for Arnold was the final assertion

Was du geschlagen

Zu Gott wird es dich tragen!

a strangely ambiguous phrase interlacing heartbeats and blows as the vehicle to God. What God? For him, just now, it could be Mahler.

The concert was scheduled for Sunday, the Fourth of July. Was this Lenny's huge, seditious pun — Independence Day as the final liberation, Resurrection? He had arrived early in the week in his beige Mercedes, top down, grand entrance, waving royally to the clicking of student Instamatics. MAESTRO 1 , his license plate read. On Tuesday and Wednesday, he rehearsed the orchestra; on Thursday afternoon, the chorus. It was Arnold's first experience of the charismatic great.

Since Lenny was late — as usual — John Oliver used the time to warm up the group and take them over a few of the rough spots. The maestro appeared in a baby blue sweater, jeans, cowboy boots, with a red handkerchief tucked into his rear pocket, and a big grin on his tanned and handsome face. He spent the first ten minutes hugging and chatting with old friends while the chorus waited patiently in its seats. Somehow this was all right. During that ten minutes, he smoked two cigarettes — right under the ABSOLUTELY NO SMOKING! signs of the old wooden barn. That, too, was ok. For Lenny, the standard rules never applied. From the moment he walked into the barn, the universe widened, and anything was possible. This was a professional chorus, already well-rehearsed. The night's work would concern something beyond performance.

His socializing over, Lenny climbed up on his stool, picked up the score from the conductor's stand, and began davening with it, rocking back and forth, touching it to his forehead: *Baruch ato adonoy, elo-heynu melech ho-olom...* He peeked up over the closed volume.

"Did you know I was a closet rabbi?"

The chorus laughed.

"No, seriously. I've got these rabbinical instincts to pray and bless and teach."

He went back to davening. The growled tune went slowly from chassidic-liturgical to the opening bars of *Auferstehen.* The chorus applauded his gambit.

"This voice is what you get when you cross a khazen with a chazer." More laughter, this time from the Jewish cognoscenti.

"Cantor and pig," said a neighbor, eyes rolling, who'd heard this joke before.

"Well, good evening, everyone, and welcome to this mighty raft of sincerity on which we will negotiate the upcoming patriotic storm." He held up the score. "Let's put out of our minds all the death-dealing we're being offered, embrace the antidote to death, and try to dilute all the red, white and blue poison in the air."

He put the closed score on the stand.

"Peace. From death, peace. Not the peace of the dead, but the peace of the beyond — beyond the beltway, beyond the Pentagon, beyond

Fortress America — triumphant peace. Let's take it from rehearsal 31."

Lenny raised his arms. The downbeat was the merest opening of his already opened hands.

Auferstehen....

ja, auferstehen....

"That's great. That's terrific. Now let's make it four times as great. Four times as soft."

Auferstehen....

ja, auferstehen....

He cut them off.

"Glorious! Better than glorious. Sensational! But you know what? It sounds like humans. Let's try not-humans, just molecules vibrating. Just sonorous forms, barely in motion."

Auferstehen....

ja, auferstehen....

He cut them off again.

"Let me ask you something. What comes just before this?"

Arnold hadn't heard what came before.

"A rest?" an alto offered tentatively.

"Is it a rest?"

"No, there's no rest there," said a bass. "Just a double bar."

"And what is the double bar fencing off?" asked Lenny.

"The previous section."

"The orchestra."

"The world of death."

"Ah!" shouted Lenny, "Another world. The death-world. The world before *Auferstehen*. Listen, this is a chance to change things, to right them. You, with those parts in your hands, you are the new Gods. Think about what you want to create. You don't have six days. You have only the next 22 bars. What do you want?"

"To stop the war."

"A clean planet."

"Yes, yes, yes — that's what we all want." Lenny — not deprecating, but in the spirit of 'Give me more...' "We're not going to get it just wishing. We need a new tool, some fantastic new tool, equal and opposite

— no, greater than — napalm or nuclear weapons. On Sunday you can let it loose. What is it?"

He closed his eyes and waited.

"Here's what," he said. "You are going to make a new kind of music that will seep out into the world and change everything , some kind of never-before-heard articulate utterance that will go much further than anything now understood, that will free music to heal the ragged wounds of our existence. Dig? You are about to create a historic hour of eloquence with a revelatory music that will call forth visionary hearing from the world. When you do this, when you create this audacious hearing, all music — from *Tristan* to *Eleanor Rigby* — all music we already know will sound out its secret content. What we now understand as music will seem childish by comparison."

He looked, one by one, into the eyes of every singer.

"There is an ultimate language, super-human, a language made of passwords into the tonal nature of everything that flows — and that, my friends, means everything , every person, every thought in the universe — before, during, and after its manifestation. You — right now — you are about to bring this new sound language to birth. It's been calling us for a long while, designating, teaching, but we hear it only occasionally in a few, exalted moments of the greatest masterpieces. Nobody can understand it yet, even you, its creators. *Auferstehen.* Let's hear it."

Lenny raised his hands, closed his eyes, and held his breath. A hundred and twenty breaths waited on his. Then, with no visible signal except a slight rise and falling of his spine, a hundred and twenty voices conspired in a sound wave of infinitesimal amplitude, an etheric vibration so subtly pervasive that it met with no resistance from the self-protecting world. *Auferstehen. Ja, auferstehen.* Arnold's hair stood up on arms and neck; he felt the marrow pricking in his bones. He had sung these notes before, but never in such a context. A quiet cutoff.

"That, sweethearts," said the Maestro, "is wholly exalted expression."

And he lit a cigarette.

At seven, the full forces gathered in the moistness of the Shed. Two hundred and twenty four people awaited the apotheosis of the week. Some awaited delivery from the world's anguish.

John Oliver warmed up the chorus, and Lenny arrived, again twenty minutes late. Though he had been on site for a week, there was still much hugging and embracing and touching. Arnold thought perhaps he couldn't function without that kind of fuel. But if he took energy from people, he gave it back with interest.

The chorus had been invited to take their places on stage at the beginning of the rehearsal, even though it might be several hours until they were needed. The opportunity to watch Lenny rehearsing the BSO — in the Mahler Second, no less — was one of the perks that had brought them to Tanglewood that summer, and not to festivals elsewhere. Not one chorus member was absent, not one had chosen to show up "after break".

While Lenny was schmoozing, Seiji Ozawa, in rumpled whites, was trying to move the conducting students onto the already crowded stage, the better to observe. He himself began to carry folding chairs. Sensing a conducting class coup, the student instrumentalists carried their own chairs up, to colonize what little space remained. The BSO pros looked annoyed, but students were the name of this particular game — and the money was good.

Lenny leapt up on the stage, with all his engines roaring. No blue jeans this time, but a tan gabardine suit and blue shirt with open collar. He hung his coat over the back of the conductor' s chair, shook hands with the first chair strings, climbed up on the podium, and opened the score. Though he would perform without it, he needed it now for rehearsal numbers and the small details of orchestration.

"Too bad it's still light out," he began, "because this music is no daytime art. But neither is night music all nocturnal. Let me hear the first three measures as if you were playing them at high noon."

The violins and violas attacked the tremolo fortissimo, quickly evanescing to pianissimo as the celli and basses attacked the second measure figure triple forte, leaving in their wake only the delicate tremor of the upper strings.

"Stupendous!" the conductor yelled. "The sun protests the cloud passing over. Now...let it become six at night." He waited, eyes closed. "Let the shadows lengthen, the sun go down, let the sky slowly darken. Ten o'clock. Eleven. *Um Mitternacht*. Ready, midnight cowboys?" He raised his arms. "Now!"

The orchestra attacked the opening again. Astounding! The same notes, the same vibrations, the same loudness, the same tremolo, the same low ascending figure — were all different, completely different, midnight different. This was nothing short of magic. But was it black magic or white?

"Yes!" cried Lenny. "You've got it. This music comes out of the dark. It must be understood and felt in the dark. The somber heave of the nocturnal ocean...can you feel this darkness surging in Mahler's soul? Only his infrared eye could penetrate these depths...."

With that introduction, Lenny drove the orchestra along like a night-embracing demon, exploring the mysteries of small moments, repeating the same phrases over and over, each time uncovering a new layer of burning beauty, or chilly cosmic meaning. He rehearsed by asking questions: "Why is this written this way?" "What do these notes mean?" "Why does he do it differently this time?", questions and answers, sometimes from singers, students or players, often from himself, Lenny quoting bits of poetry and literature extempore, improvising silly lyrics, filling them in on the history of this melody, that orchestration. He invented alternative harmonies to show how right Mahler had been to choose the ones he had. For all the demonic power unleashed, there were belly laughs throughout the rehearsal, great sighs, excited spirits together on the trail of discovery. This is why ensembles loved him.

Yet there are limits, even to pedagogic bliss. By midnight, faithful chorus members were checking watches — they had not yet sung a note. Administrations feared Lenny for his overtimes. Players were ambivalent — the pay was great but these were long rehearsals! The celestial *Urlicht*, celestially sung, had just faded away into nothingness. "I am of God," Frau Ludwig had sung, "and to God I shall return. Dear God will grant me a tiny light which will light my way to eternal, blissful life."

It was past time for a break, or even a breaking off until morning. But Lenny was faithful to his doppelgänger's intentions: the Master had written "the 5th movement follows without any break."

So no stopping: a "Cry of Anguish" *wild herausfahrend,* leapt savagely out at the unsuspecting: the cellos and basses ripped triple forte up to a naked C, and the entire orchestra crashed in — four flutes, four oboes, five clarinets, four bassoons, ten horns, six trumpets, seven percussionists, organ, harp and "as many strings as possible" — in a grinding and terrible explosion. Within twenty seconds, the smoke began to clear, and threads of light emerged, painting a sweeter, if still murky, landscape.

The orchestra quieted further. Six horns, ppp, had sounded the first ghostly appearance of Resurrection when Lenny coughed. A routine cigarette cough. But as the orchestra became softer and softer, the cough became louder and louder. He sat back on his stool and gripped the back rest with his left hand to steady himself, while conducting with his right. He coughed more harshly, more effusively, now gripping the conductor's stand in addition to the chair, conducting only with his thrashing head and flying, gray hair. The six offstage horns let out their fanfare, the "Voice of the Caller", Mahler had labeled it, " The end of every living thing has come, the last judgement is at hand, and the horror of the day of days has come upon us." Lenny could no longer conduct. He was completely consumed in paroxysmal coughing. He staggered off the podium into the arms of Seiji Ozawa, who had leaped up on the stage, and now led him off, down the steps, into the auditorium, coughing.

The concertmaster announced a ten minute break, but the orchestra and chorus sat pinned to their chairs, watching in terror as their beloved maestro seemed about to come apart. Bernstein gestured frantically at his jacket hanging over the stool on stage. Thinking it might contain some lozenge or medicine, a student ran to get it for him, then careened back, as did all others who could see, as the conductor, barely able to manage, tore a pack of L&Ms out of the jacket pocket, managed to get a cigarette in his mouth, and, unable to work the matches, gestured imploringly, then violently for someone to light it for him. The scene was so grotesque that stunned onlookers were paralyzed. The Maestro took this as disobedience, and out from under his uncontrolled movements there rose a more willful rage, a tantrum, which seemed, paradoxically, to calm him. "Goddam it, I need a cigarette to cough better!" he cried between coughs. "Somebody light this fuckin' thing for me!"

"What a piece of work is man! How infinite in faculty, in form and moving... And yet, to me, what is this quintessence of dust?" It was many a chorus member to whom such thoughts occurred. To go from the tiny light leading to God to "Somebody light this fuckin' thing for me!" — this was startling.

It was one in the morning, and all was beyond repair. Lenny abandoned the rehearsal, set the call for eight the next morning, and then went off to party. Arnold wandered, shattered, home to bed.

Messiaen — L'ascension

A month before his bar mitzvah in January of 1961, Simon and Yvette Barenboim, refugees from Vichy, and 30th Street friends of Mrs. Lobkowitz, invited her star pupil along to a concert of French organ music at the Church of the Ascension, in Manhattan. "Sure," said his parents, "why not?" This is why not:

Organ is not a healthy thing for a good Jewish boy. It knows no limit or restraint. Julius had a guest's distant sense of such immensity during the smaller pieces by Guilan, Daquin, LeBègue, and Duruflé. But the major work of the evening took him through the gates, and sprawled him prostrate in the most interior grand hall of Christendom. Jewish music does not presume to utter or describe the holy name. Jewish music is humble. Messiaen's *L'Ascension — Quatre Meditations Symphoniques* is not.

For almost half an hour, Julius was bathed in a sound-world of ecstasis, culminating in the "Prayer of Christ Ascending toward his Father." Closely massed seraphic sounds, slow, chromatic ascensions to heights of unresolved, sweet dissonance. Now I am no more in the world, he thought, a bird of spirit flown from time into eternity.

Soft cascades of blue-orange chords enveloped him — saturated, radiant colors almost blinding to the ear; the desire for light, for stars, sweet, opulent, voluptuous sound in a world of tonal ubiquity, vastly open to other modes of experience, a universe of infinite time, infinite extent, and infinite power. An exit from the amusement park, at least, a ticket out, thought Julius, a step through the looking glass: the trick is to be unborn.

All this in the context of earlier movements: *"Serene Alleluias Of A Soul Desiring Heaven"*, *"Transports Of Joy Of A Soul Before The Glory Of Christ, Who Is His Own"*. Scarlatti's allusive conversations with God seemed utterly superficial. Messiaen was not healthy for a good Jewish boy.

Mozart And Auschwitz:

Mozart E Minor Violin Sonata

The calendar offers up some provocative coincidences — provocative and tartly instructive. January 27th, for instance, has given us both Mozart's birthday, and the liberation of Auschwitz. Mozart and Auschwitz. Could there be two poles further apart? Two poles at the blazing core of German-speaking culture, that playing field for the possibilities of the human.

Those familiar with Mozart know that his writing is not all sweetness and light. The late works, especially, peer unflinchingly into that wildness and pain that was his life, that led him, at 35, to a pauper's grave, whereabouts unknown. So to find the dark moments in Mozart is not hard.

One of the characters in my recent novel, *The Good Doctor Guillotin*, Tobias Schmidt, the German piano-maker who wound up building the first guillotines during the French Revolution, describes a concert in Paris by the 22-year old Austrian visitor in which he played a set of his variations on the bawdy folk tune *"Ah je vous dirai, Maman"*. (We know the melody as that of "Twinkle, Twinkle, Little Star".) He talks about how "in the middle of the unending C major of this trivial folk tune, Mozart had thrown himself and his listeners into a precipitous C minor variation which ripped open the pleasant, clever world, and exposed the darkest forces lurking in the background."

Yes. Fairly standard, even in Haydn, and more to come in Beethoven. Yin and yang: the black dot in the middle of the white. High German culture — and then Auschwitz.

But then, there is the other dot — the white one in the middle of the black. The paradox is that this one can prove even more painful.

In another scene in the novel, Schmidt is accompanying Dr. Guillotin's violin in a room in the captured king's prison palace:

"Why are you crying?" Schmidt asked.

Guillotin had put down his violin.

"Why are *you* crying?" he asked his pianist.

"I'm not crying. That's sweat," Schmidt said, wiping away a tear.

I'll tell you why they were crying. They were crying because in the E minor violin sonata there is a moment too beautiful to play—the trio in E major, haunting, unbearably poignant and lovely.

Guillotin had gulped at the key change, started to tear up at the first rising sixth of the theme, and by the repeat of the first phrase had to lower his instrument.

Schmidt was crying because—like the C minor moment in the Ah, vous dirais-je variations he had heard Mozart play—this moment, too, seemed to open a trapdoor revealing all those lurking dark forces, then shut it quickly again—but in reverse and inside out. Here it was a trapdoor not into darkness but into a universe of light, of the possible, of all that could be but isn't.

They were crying because they understood this: That such a world is hidden from us, unattainable, glimpsed only in Mozart's cruel caress. A dark E minor minuet: the dance par excellence of the aristocracy. Grace, beauty, decorum. Delicate but controlled and controlling. And then the intolerable knife thrust of the exquisite trio—revealing the old order for all its implications, its unsuspected possibilities of disaster.

"Is that what we're crying about?" Guillotin demanded. "An exposé of the old order? I thought we knew that. I thought we were trying a new order."

"That's what I, at least, am crying about," the piano-maker said. "It's not the ghastly court and the canting nobility I'm mourning, it's the stability and structure, the placidity and contentment, the state of grace they would pretend. I'm crying because I understand the loss. I fear it; I fear such transience, fear mortality—in this context of most beauty. I'm crying because we will now have to face the great trembling—at hand—and inescapable."

Guillotin dried his eyes, wiped the rosin off his strings, and, taking this cue, Schmidt closed the piano, an instrument he had built for the music room of the Tuileries palace.

The awfulness of beauty. The unbearable face of unattained, unattainable possibility. The white dot in the middle.

I wonder if those who are having so much difficulty giving up their dreams are paralyzed by the same awful contrast between the dot and its matrix.

Prokofiev — First Violin Concerto

Alexei Pigov, whom we have met before playing tarentellas for tarantulas, had continually failed to find the right pickup strategy for getting a girlfriend. At Music & Art HS, he had set his sights on a young beauty, the orchestra concertmistress. He had learned what piece she was working on, had mastered the piano reduction, and was hoping to impress.

The Courtship of Graulexei Pigov

It must be admitted that surprise does not bring out the best in us. When he showed up at Room 12 at 2:15 on the dot, Elizabeth had not yet arrived, and Grailexei became Graylexei right there, in the hallway, obsessing on grayish thoughts, his morning's balloon leaking fast.

He had eaten little during lunch, so as to shunt no blood from brain and fingers to digestive tract, and now she wasn't even here. Their first date, and she had stood him up.

Oh, but there she was, coming down the hall! Gray turned to grace, and grace to gracias, gracias a Dios!, and thank God, too.

"Hi, Al. What's that you've got there?"

"What do you think?"

They went in. She was unpacking her violin.

"Um, a cat-carrier?"

"No breathing holes."

"A huge typewriter?"

"Close, but not really. It's my piano."

He opened the case. Honey had never looked so black and white and shiny.

"It's...an accordion."

Let it be said, that even at Music & Art, where an accordion had never been seen, and where viola jokes were king, a small side-chapel was reserved for accordion jokes. Even the exquisite Elizabeth Schrank was aware of the following story: "A man parks his car in a rough part of town with an accordion on the back seat, forgetting to lock the door. When he returns, there are two accordions."

Thus, her "It's...an accordion" was not a simple declarative sentence describing a local object. It was a tastefully understated disclosure of horror, of taint, of musical pollution, of which Starry-eyed Al was oblivious.

"Right. A Hohner Honica. Top of the line."

"But I thought you said you played the piano."

"This is a piano accordion. There are button ones."

"I mean, this score is for violin and piano. Like this piano here."

She pointed at the small Steinway. He had an answer all prepared.

"Say, which can do all the flute passages better, this guy here, or my guy?"

Not persuasive.

"But...it's...the part is too hard for an accordion. It needs the full range of..."

"Try me."

Groucho stood there like an accordionist landed on Mars, proposing to collaborate with a greatly puzzled and tentative Martian colleague. The seconds of silence seemed like minutes. He looked imploringly at his beloved.

"Well, ok, let's see what it sounds like.

Al harnessed up, feeling a bit undelicate compared to her. Honey was, after all, a machine, a music machine, but a machine nonetheless. Compared to Elizabeth's exquisite violin...But he knew he had her now. She set her music on her stand, and offered him the piano part.

"No thanks. I know it," he said.

 What?

He could see he had impressed her already.

"But what if we need to go back to a certain measure?"

"I know the measure numbers. Don't worry."

For her, the Martian, he had transformed from an alien earthling into a something from Neptune. Pre-tty weird! But ok.

"Ready?"

"Ready."

Graulexei laid down, so gently, a prelude, a soft aureole of sound to accompany her opening melody. All those accordion breathing exercises, techniques he had labored over: Cheyne-Stokes breathing, yogic, Kussmaul and agonal. Days and days of bellows practice on these alone enabled him to provide a delicate setting for her gem of a melody. What a tune, he thought, what a face, what a body, that beautiful hair. Shimmering tremolandos of hair, shimmering tremolandos of sound. At the end of the opening statement, it was her turn to accompany him, and for the first time she looked upon her partner. What she saw was so surprising that she almost forgot where she was. He, Alex Pig something — whatever his name was — he who never took off those stupid nose glasses and kind of oozed around like a creepy teen-age amoeba, staring at whatever, and playing this, her favorite music. On some back burner of her consciousness, she was low-flame astounded. But Prokofiev was still on high, at the front of the range.

Come the middle section of the movement, the piano reduction of the orchestral score was bursting its poor seams to contain all that was going on. Fierce cross-rhythms, wild leaps of exclamation, prestissimo skittering of arpeggios and scales heading this way and that. First rate pianists always had a hard time with this section, and excused themselves with the feeling that, well, it was only an approximation anyway. But Alexei made it his own. His may have been the first hands to actually play every note in this maniacal display. They looked to Elizabeth like wild spiders high on speed and acid. And not just two. God knows how many there were — a clutter of them, a gaggle, moving so dexterously and so fast as to be a visual blur. Elizabeth's eyes widened attractively, her mouth opened seductively, and — not so attractively — a little bit of spittle drooled toward her chinrest. She quickly licked it back. But Alexei didn't see; his eyes were closed.

She played through the dreamy end of the movement staring at him in a kind of trance. Alexei's eyes remained shut, and a whole-body, beatific smile enveloped his being, the lips under his nose mustache, the tilt of his head, the alternate rise and fall of his shoulders as he opened and closed the bellows, and the sway of abdomen over pelvis on the piano bench as he surrounded her, wind-like, harp-like, in delectable filagree. The final twisty flute run dissipated in the air like a wisp of sweetest-smelling smoke.

He open his eyes and gazed at the woman to whom he had given this gift of love. She stared back at him. What was she thinking? She was thinking of this accordion joke: "What's the difference between an accordion player and a terrorist? Terrorists have sympathizers." 30

Purcell — Dido and Anaeas
at High Desert State Prison

In my Speckled Vanities, *the team looking to buy a grand piano in Las Vegas, has decided to give a concert at Peter's place of employment, Nevada's largest state prison. Bringing high culture to prisoners to prompt to reform was — and still is — a theory inadequately thought through.*

Never had the best-laid plans of mindful men gone so awry as during the performance of Dido and Aeneas on March 16, 2010 in the gym at the High Desert State Prison, Nevada's largest, at Indian Springs, Nevada.

Purcell's short opera was to be the high point of a visionary joint program to combat violence against women by inmates at the prison, and soldiers at the neighboring Creech Air Force Base, home to the 432nd Air Expeditionary Wing, the nation's first air base dedicated to unmanned aircraft. Drones in the air, drones at their controls, and drones droning away behind bars — all had their violence against women. Which needed combatting.

An opera written in 1689 for the students of Mr. Josiah Price's Boarding School for Girls in London might seem an odd vehicle with which to explore the personal and systemic urgencies of sexism, chauvinism and deathism, yet if carefully examined, and judiciously performed, it just might do, uniquely serve the purpose, all threads tied into one revealing pattern, illuminated by most evocative music of love and longing, of perfidy and bitterness, of raucous drink and demonic laughter.

Aeneas, you may recall, fought bravely at Troy until the last, until Hector ordered him to flee with a remnant of Trojans to establish another Troy overseas, out in western land.

After much blowing around, and many adventures, his gang will

177

end up founding Rome — but on the way, alas, the ship makes landfall on the African coast at Carthage, where Dido, queen of Carthage, falls in love with Aeneas, and he with her.

The lovebirds stay and play for a year while witches conspire to destroy the queen, Carthage, and "all in prosp'rous state", [an objective much approved by the prisoners]. An imp sent by the Witches with orders from Jupiter for Aeneas to get Troy back on the agenda, and pack up for Italy. Ordered by the chief of gods, what is Aeneas is to do but bid his love adieu and move on? And herein the Air Force Base and Prison's project's point: violence against women, and in this case against an exemplary woman whose psychology is laid bare.

In an agonizing "How can you do this to me?" scene, Aeneas breaks, will stay for love, will give up his destiny and disobey the orders of his god no matter what. But Dido will have none of it, will no longer entertain a man who had even once *thought* of leaving her, for whatever reason, for whatever cause. [The chorus sings "Great Minds against Themselves Conspire". Discussion to follow the performance.] She forces him out. Aeneas leaves. Dido dies. In one of the most heart-rending arias ever composed, she sings "When I am laid in Earth, may my Wrongs create no Trouble in thy Breast. Remember me, remember me, but ah! forget my Fate."

The prisoners, the soldiers, the guards, the administrative staff, the musicians, the small attending public never did get to hear the final lamenting chorus "Soft and Gentle was her Heart. Keep here your Watch, and never, never, never part."

Why? Because as Angela Warden rent her garments, her beauty blazing, and as Jane Lapieux bent over her from behind, revealing a maiden bosom under her stola, one prisoner yelled "Take it off babe, take it off!" and another, empowered by the outburst of the first, stood up in the front row, unzipped his pants and wrestled out an enormous schlong, for some reason, musical or other, already engorged, jumped up on the platform and invited one or the other women — or both — to "Suck it, bitch, suck it!"

This was too much for several other prisoners similarly afflicted with priapism, who then rushed the stage, cocks at various angles, to get beyond each other at the women. Needless to say, this then was too much for the brave men in uniform pledged to protect American women among others, and to promote family values via unmanned equipment like drones. A team of khakis jumped the psychos, and dragged them off the stage. The prison guards, also in khakis, joined the melee against the blues. It was color war! Other blues jumped up to defend their own — not against the guards, who might effect a long-term revenge, but against the faggot soldiers who were too shit scared to actually go to war, and could murder people all day on the other side of the world, and then go home to sleep with their wives and take their kids to soccer practice. And then there were the whites on the browns and the browns on the blacks and the blacks on the whites.

Some in the audience tried to make for the doors, but their way was blocked by fallen folding chairs, and then fallen fleers, and they would have found the doors locked anyway, if only to ensure an audience for questions & answers, and discussion.

Ending his introductory talk before the show, Peter Warden had asked the prisoners to please shut off their cell phones (laughter), and asked the guards politely not to shoot Bruce Boynton, the piano player. (No laughter.)

Nevertheless, about two minutes in, a shot rang out from someone licensed to carry a gun, or who had otherwise obtained one, and something cracked the dry black wood of the upright and howled itself across the strings. Another shot splintered the instrument and sent the harp screaming, snapping, and tearing. Bruce fell to the floor, his glasses clattering on ahead of him, the piano player, shot.

Angela, Peter, Jane, Bruce, a quartet no longer, and never again to be. Great Minds against Themselves Conspired. Who were they, and how and where?

Scarlatti — Piano Sonatas

From The Lamentations of Julius Marantz, *concerning young Julius'*
piano lessons

Schubert could never afford a piano. Philip Marantz would fix that —
at least for his little blue-eyed boychik. That Ludwig Boltzmann took
piano lessons from Anton Bruckner and then committed suicide, that
he couldn't fix, but he bought an old Chickering upright anyway from
Morris Kaplan, Used Furniture, on Surf Ave. As Mrs. Lobkowitz down
the block shepherded his son through Anna Magdalena, he recalled
Karl Barth's famous surmise: that while the angels may play only Bach
in praising God, among themselves they play Mozart.

Julius, however, after three or four years, preferred Maestro
Domenico, the great Scarlatti. He loved to fly his fingers over the keys
like drunken spiders, full speed ahead in breathless virtuosity, scam-
pering from one sequence to the next, and then, drunk and tipsy to fall
into some quirky, slow, contrasting extreme. He loved the octave leaps
into tinkling sky, and the daring plunges into ocean of rumbling bass.

The Sonatas were called "exercises or diversions", and that they were
for Julius — 555 of them, a lifetime's worth of fun. Julius adored the master's dedication printed on the inside cover of his Selected Works:

> *Reader: Whether you be Dilettante or Professor*
> *in these Compositions do not expect any profound*
> *Learning, but rather an ingenious Jesting with Art, to*
> *accommodate you to the Mastery of the Harpsichord.*
> *Neither Considerations of Interest, nor Visions of*
> *Ambition, but only Obedience moved me to publish*
> *them! Perhaps they will be agreeable to you; then all*

the more gladly will I obey other Commands to favor
you with more simple and varied Style. Therefore show
yourself more human than critical, and then your
Pleasure will increase. Live Happily. D. Scarlatti, 1738.

Was this a mensch? The whole family thought so.

Yet not all the works were scintillating and lighthearted, and even the gay ones were often tinged with undertones of tragedy. In fact the majority of selections in Julius's book were slower, rather than fast — poetic, nostalgic, dreamy even, much like their 12-year old performer. His favorite was the F minor Sonata, a work he had been given early on, before his fingers could master the extravagant velocities called for by some others. Although it was relatively simple, Julius continued to find it overwhelming in its meditative melancholy. The sextuplet theme went up — G, Ab, Bb — and came down — Ab, G, F, up and down, up and down, so simple, he though, but so profound. On the one hand up and down, on the other from instability to repose, a little striving, and a letting go... Even a 12-year old can understand mortality. Levi-Strauss thought the invention of melody the supreme mystery of man.

Horowitz: "Many composers of his period speak to God. Scarlatti speaks to the people, the children of God. There are instances when he does speak to God, but more often he chooses not to." Julius thought him wrong.

Schubert — Der Leiermann

One of the greatest of Schubert's songs, the shatteringly simple leaving-off of the Winterreise *song cycle.*

Der Leiermann
Wilhelm Müller (1827)

> *Drüben hinter'm Dorfe*
> *Steht ein Leiermann,*

There, outside the village, there stands a hurdy-gurdy man.

> *Und mit starren Fingern*
> *Dreht er was er kann.*

And with numb fingers, he cranks away as well as he can.

> *Barfuss auf dem Eise*
> *Schwankt er hin und her;*

Barefoot on the ice, he sways back and forth.

> *Und sein kleiner Teller*
> *Bleibt ihm immer leer.*

And his little dish remains forever empty.

> *Keiner mag ihn hören,*
> *Keiner sieht ihn an;*

Nobody wants to listen to him, no one looks at him,

> *Und die Hunde knurren*
> *Um den alten Mann.*

And the dogs growl at the old man,

> *Und er lässt es gehen*
> *Alles, wie es will,*

And he lets things be, just as they will

> *Dreht, und seine Leier*

Steht ihm nimmer still.
He cranks away, and his hurdy-gurdy is never silent.
Wunderlicher Alter,
Soll ich mit dir geh'n?
Strange old man, should I go along with you?
Willst zu meinen Liedern
Deine Leier dreh'n?
Will you crank your hurdy-gurdy to my songs?

[*My literal "translation". As a word, "hurdy-gurdy" doesn't make it for "Leier". Just listen to the song:* https://tinyurl.com/2p82679u]

Night Dreams of Another Life

Every now and then, I am awakened at 3 am by the sound of a shopping cart rattling past my house. No voices. Just a lonely, ghostly, shopping cart. It has that eerie sadness Woody Guthrie used to sing about — like "that long lonesome train a-whistlin' down." Except it rattles.

The sky is dark, the street lights bright outside my window. All other noise has ceased. Squad cars prowl silently, if at all. Donna is sleeping, and the cats breath quietly at our heads and feet. Wordsworth said it: "The holy time is quiet as a nun/breathless with adoration." Except there is a shopping cart. Rattling.

Who is out there, pushing? Who is searching the recycle bins and garbage for nickel bottles and cast-off clothing? Who must be up this early in the morning to ensure his meager catch?

In daylight hours I would probably revert to my social/political thought chain: the ghastly state of current American capitalist politics, the ripping away of the safety net from under the free-fall of the poor. But in the middle of the night, my thoughts often go to the amazing end of Schubert's song cycle, Die Winterreise, the Winter Journey.

In the standard frame of nineteenth century romantic poetry, a lover, spurned by his beloved, must "get away" from his memories of her, must avoid the possibility of seeing her with her new husband. He wanders out into the winter, his tears freezing in the icy landscape.

He has dreams and nightmares. He longs for mail, though he has no address. He communes with birds and beasts; he hallucinates. There are many amazing and moving images in these 24 connected songs, but none is more mysterious and compelling than that of the last song, "Der Leiermann", the Hurdy-Gurdy man. Of all the songs, it is the quietest and simplest, a bare vocal line alternating with a little organ-grinding refrain in the piano.

After all the wildness of nature and passion — this last strange encounter: with an old man outside a village, playing his music as best he can, his fingers numb, standing near his empty cup, barefoot, on the ice. Nobody listens to the organ-grinder, nobody pays any attention to him — except the dogs, who come — to bark and growl. But the old man just lets it all happen without complaint, grinding out his simple tune, never stopping. Coming upon him, our heart-weary traveller is dumb struck.

We think it is a simple little story, a narration about some striking character met along the path. The first surprise comes in the last verse. Is our sad young man repulsed by the organ grinder, frightened by his situation, thinking "there, but for the grace of God, go I"? No. "Strange old man," he says to himself, "shall I go with you? Will you grind out music if I sing?" And the second surprise is — that's it. That's the end. The hurdy-gurdy phrase runs it's course and this incomparable masterpiece just stops — quietly, with a question, a question leading out into infinity.

As I lie in bed listening to our local Leiermann, his shopping cart singing its sad, repetitive song, I — this person snuggling next to his sleeping wife, nuzzled by his trusting kitties — I want to go out there and join him. I want to experience the emptiness and beauty of the street late at night, the sense of the world stopped around me, the non-hustle and non-bustle and time of my own creation. I want to give up my deadlines and assignments, my enslavement to the little property I own. I want to simplify my life, and have the basic tasks of my cro-magnon ancestors, to live from day to day, to hunt and gather, to relate to the turning of the sky.

Not to romanticize the brutal life forced on the poor by devil-don't-care capitalism. My late-night dream does not contain having to figure out where I can poop, or where to get a shower after two weeks without. I don't have to scrounge for quarters for the laundromat, or worry about my things being stolen while I sleep on someone's porch to stay dry. I don't even have to hang on to my empty bottles and cans — but can give them, a pathetic, inadequate gesture, to those who build their lives around them.

Still, there is freedom out there, late at night. Dream-freedom. We humans have always paid a lot for freedom. At this very moment, somewhere on earth, there is blood being spilled — for freedom.

Schubert Piano Trio in Bb

From Speckled Vanities

On a glorious November Saturday evening, Peter and Angela were married at a regular PARTITA! evening. None of the other singers and players suspected what was happening.

Her clothing that night was not out of the ordinary, but like much of female fashion at the time, it was imbued with sufficient magic to transform, without changing a ribbon or a bead, into a magical garment, as the occasion demanded. As she took her violin out of its case, every fold of her skirt, every tuck on her blouse, was lurking with power, enveloping her in a glow more than nuptial. Peter and Bruce were dressed normally, if slightly spiffier than usual.

The three sat down to read the exquisite slow movement of the Schubert Bb trio.

Bruce, mischievously smiling, lay down two measures of a gently rocking lullaby, and Peter entered, pianissimo, in a high register, with a melody to melt the heart. With a little flourish, having grown to forte, he sank down again to accompany Angela's statement, their two lines caressing one another far more intimately than physical bodies could approximate. Bruce added his version in gentle octaves, smiling all the while, as the couple licked around the melody with playful, insistent tongues. The tune would flirt with minor keys, but briefly enough to simply affirm its compassionate sunshine.

The middle section is stormier, forced by the piano on the others, but with the kind of exertion which only strengthens the singing pair above it. Nevertheless, as her part relaxed to let the piano lead, Angela felt a passing strangeness she had never before experienced. This, she knew, was her wedding ceremony, yet here and now, of all places, she felt unfaithful to her groom. As she was transported by the music, she imagined he couldn't understand as well as she the greatness of what moved her, or what was truly going on. All colors, all furniture, all faces, her very bow and strings had been enhanced by the moment, and no, she was not on drugs, she was riding on Schubert, the curves of his melodies and their gorgeous modulations. In some unutterable way, everything seemed different, loftier, expanded. She felt free, and strangely free from Peter, his cello, and his designs on her, attractive as they were. He — and all else — seemed to be on the other side of some membranous veil. A little longer, and she might have slipped out of her own being, beyond reach, a space of inviolate solitude, an emptiness of boundless truth.

But the A section returned, and she was called again to be in charge, the one responsible for pivoting on a long C, crescendo-decrescendo, to bring back the opening theme a tone higher, and for inviting Peter to come join her in these more daringly harmonized regions. Back to earth she dipped and rose, but with a complex seed planted within her, as if by some holy ghost.

Schubert had taken the three through his ten minute conjugal sermon, and it was time for the "I do"s, the public pledging of allegiance not to country, but to spouse. They had chosen their moments. Angela's was in the third measure from the end, using her little sixteenth note figure to articulate "Yes, yes, I do," singing the pitches in her beautiful voice, and emphasizing her commitment with a long, accented Bb.

Peter chose the next occurrence of that figure to offer his "And I do, too," singing it in harmony with Angela above, and while it was Angela again who nailed it down with another long, accented Bb an octave higher than her first, Peter repeated the phrase in duet with his cello, and then with his cello alone. There was a short silence in the world, and then the couple played their affirmation figures together, to bring the service to a close on a long-held fermata. And they were both astounded.

Only Bruce noted that their final instrumental statements, their affirmation figures, were in contrary motion, hers climbing to a high Eb, his descending to an Eb four octaves below it. Bruce's notes spanned the inner space between, and he wondered what all that distance meant. But then, as scripted and assigned, he channeled the ministering angel, and in his best mock-Austrian-fat-man-with-little-spectacles accent, said "Hiermit erkläre ich Sie zu Mann und Frau."

And then he added, unscripted, unexpected, "And may that glory which rests on all who love, rest upon you, and bless you, and fill you with happiness and a gracious spirit...and despite all changes of time and fortune, may all that is noble and lovely and true abound in your hearts, and abide with you, and give you strength in all your days together. Amen."

I don't know where he got that text from, I don't know if mathematicians are capable of composing such a text. All I know is that he said it, and perhaps we have now detected something somewhat cryptic about him.

Everyone else in the room eventually realized what had come to pass. It did take a moment for the Ellefson apartment, somewhere on Durant St., Berkeley, California, USA, Planet Earth to re-establish, and then there were tears and applause and hugs and deep breaths and backslaps when it did. Bruce then announced, "For income tax purposes, Angela will be taking Peter's last name."

There was politically correct laughter, but in fact, such was the case.

Strauss — Metamorphosen for 23 Solo Strings

In 1943, the 80-year old Richard Strauss was shattered by the destruction of the Munich Hoftheater, the building which saw the births of *Tristan* and *Meistersinger*. "This," he wrote, "was the greatest catastrophe that has ever disturbed my life, for which there can be no consolation and, at my old age, no hope." Those ruins were the emotional catalyst for his great, late work, *Metamorphosen*, a threnody for European culture destroyed in physical and psychic bombardment.

About this work, the critic Roland Manuel wrote, "Perhaps Strauss lived for 85 years simply to create this glorious work. Perhaps his excess...his offenses against good taste have all been just stages on the road that has led to this old man's discovery of wisdom."

The strange harmonic transformations of very few themes ripen towards a fragment of the Eroica funeral march, etherially harmonized and marked "In Memoriam", a theme whose rhythmic and melodic skeleton haunts the entire shattering, half-hour work. One emerges from it dizzy, perhaps exhausted like Strauss, but spiritually stronger than before.

Listen to a septet version (for those who can read music, easier to follow score). At measure 9, you'll recognize Strauss' version of the Eroica funeral march theme. https://tinyurl.com/yx7hwy3v

Stravinsky — Rite of Spring

This excerpt from Insect Dreams/Kafka's Roach *describes the (fictive) performance that (a here fictive) Genia Peierls produced for a (fictive) Saturday night at Los Alamos. As you can tell, I love this masterpiece. Many great recordings available. The event is here narrated by Gregor's friend, John Aschenfeld, (fictive) official historian of the Manhattan Project.*

I was speaking of *The Rite of Spring*, a ballet and score universally considered a "seminal work" in twentieth century culture, though not always with awareness of the full metaphorical content of this usage. *The Rite* was born in 1913 (the same year as Gregor was conceived), and though it was part of a generalized artistic reaction against effete bourgeoise culture, it seemed to call forth, with its abrupt, harsh rhythms and remarkable instrumental sounds, it evoked more than any other work the threat of barbarity lurking just under the surface of civilization. It hit the public like a hurricane: its opening night sparked a riot at the Théâtre Champs Elysées. Audiences had never heard anything like this music which could evoke — or admit — an aggressive, chaotic, innate human savagery of uncontrolled primeval force. The work was banned in Stalin's Russia and in Hitler's Germany, where it would not do to acknowledge such barbarism already in practice.

The plot concerns a pagan ritual of pre-Christian Russia, a ceremony to put winter behind and call forth spring: a virgin is sacrificed by stern elders and a primitive, uncivilized mob, a community which propitiates its gods with orgiastic liturgies of cruelty and murder — so that the cycle of birth, growth and death may proceed.

If such distant, prehistoric activity seemed menacing in a civilized European theater, how much closer it might appear here, in the environment of Pueblo culture, where humans and beasts were dependent on the nourishing earth, here where the civilized society on the hill was preparing to embrace gods of such power as had yet to be experienced.

Genia Peirels was well aware of the correspondences. An outsider among scientist wives, she was positioned socially, and by temperament, to see the larger themes of Project activity. Her choreography hid behind the tradition of satirical events at the dance halls, but her goal was seditious — perhaps a call to rebirth, but also a withering comment from an unheeded Casssandra. She and Stravinsky pulled the wool over most people's eyes — certainly over the eyes of most of the performers. But for some few in the audience, Gregor for one, and for myself, cast as "Scribe", perched over the event on a high judge's seat borrowed from the tennis court, the message was clear enough — and devastating.

The dance was held in Theater No. 2, the larger of the two recreation halls, the one used for school phys-ed, Tuesday night colloquia, and pickup basketball. Tonight, the backboards had been covered with camouflage cloth. It is possible that this was history's first presentation in full-surround sound, for although the recordings were monophonic 78 RPMs, Genia had borrowed twelve speakers from various homes and offices, set them up four, four, two and two along the walls, and had the electronics boys wire them up to Rad Lab's biggest amplifier and Moll Flanders' best-on-campus Victrola with mechanical changer. A stickler for details, she had even installed a new needle.

At the 7:30 starting time, there were few in the audience, a cause for some tsk-tsk-tsking by those of us who had arrived promptly. But it turned out that the small audience was the population remnant from the enormous cast milling about the doors, waiting for their entrances. A small audience was a good thing, too, since most of the benches had been commandeered for alternate use by the imperious producer-designer-director.

The house lights went out, and the room was plunged into the darkness of the first evening of spring. Genia, her shadow, projected by the amplifier's tiny red light, seemed accidently but appropriately monstrous on the south wall. She flicked the lever, the first record dropped, and the eerie sound of a bassoon playing high above its natural register snaked its way into the room, sounding something like music must have sounded before the beginning of time.

The first of many flashlights came on, its operator dark behind it, and began to slowly explore the room. As more instruments joined, erupting arpeggios from the womb of darkness, more flashlights were added, playing out their spidery criss-crossing of sounds and beams and clearings, building to a short riot of calls in unstable light, tune fragments from the depths of centuries, all of which stopped short, the lights coming abruptly together at the centerline. Behind them we sensed humanity, invisible, embedded in nature, pre-dating the creation of a personal God. The solo bassoon began its song again, and the pool of light split in two and slowly edged its two halves upward to reveal the now-bare faces mounted on the backboards: to the east was Oppie; to the west was Groves.

This scenic revelation occasioned the audience's first and last laugh, which I punctuated with the scratching of my scribal pen. What I was noting down, they didn't know. I wrote on like some manic, unstoppable soloist, accompanied by the gears of the record changer.

Although I was merely a "mysterious" scenic prop, I had taken it upon myself as historian to record my own feelings, and those audience reactions I could fathom, as well as the inadvertent behavior of the cast as they went through their appointed rounds. While the military and worker contingent were previously unfamiliar with the work, most of the scientists, and all of the the Europeans, had heard it before, though none were old enough to have seen the ballet which quit the boards in the twenties after two production failures: audiences would simply not accept what they had been asked to witness. Still, the piece had claimed its own in concert version, and became a great favorite of avant-garde conductors enthusiastic to assault the standard repertoire. Gregor had heard it often enough to dislike it thoroughly — but he, like others, had never really imagined it as a stage work, with human bodies as flotsam and infusoria to the sound. What would Genia come up with as a guiding image?

At the opening of the second dance, "The Augurs of Spring", her plan began to reveal itself. Enter Enrico Fermi in chinos and black leather jacket who, with a snap of his fingers, caused a spot of light to fall directly downward in the center of the floor from the one mid-court bulb Genia had left screwed in. The orchestra began to pulse with accented string chords, mechanical in obsessive meter, but wildly unpredictable in accent, and the first of the raboti entered, carrying one of the missing benches. As the worker left, another appeared with another bench, and another with another, and so on, until it became clear that, under Fermi's direction, the were erecting a structure built from benches, a structure similar to the pile he had conceived and created at Stagg Field. A group of eight children, gloved in yellow, entered from the south door, and proceeded to blow up green balloons and insert them into the matrix of benches, just as Fermi's uranium spheres had been cradled among its graphite bricks. This activity went on through this and the following six dances, utilizing the set-aside benches of Theater No. 2, all the benches of Theater No. 1, a few from North Mess, and a large load of lumber from various construction sites — so that by the end of the first half, "Adoration of the Earth", a ziggu-rat reaching halfway to the ceiling had been created by the mechanical work of robot-like men.

While the levels are rising on we meet two major groups of protag-onists. Revealed by exposed bulbs of the south door exit light, we see a group of young men in GI uniforms, on hands and knees, being taught by a masked old hag with grey face, huge nose, gaped-toothed mouth, and hair of shredded cloth. From the chicken feet she holds in both hands, one can gather that this is the Baba Yaga of Genia's youth, the nightmare witch of every late-night Russian child. The group moves jerkily to the orchestral pulse, as the wise woman instructs them in divinations. The class intensifies, the jerking grows larger — and is brought to a halt by a sudden percussion crash. Three young girls — Gaby, Nella and Jane — appear in street clothes at the north door with lit candles flickering, and with their entrance, we hear the first extended melody, an old calendrical Slavic song, as they move lyrically towards the center, the boys' beat still pulsing quietly behind them. The

GIs take leave of their cackling teacher and slowly approach the girls, a Russian chorale tune sounding on four trumpets behind them. At the sight of the boys, the girls place their candles in the middle of the rising structure, and staying well separated from them, begin a reactive dance to the male approach.

The music self-stimulates and grows to Bacchanalian frenzy, as the boys mock-threaten the three, lunging at them, and pulling them out of their small group into their own larger one. Perhaps these were the very gestures that had frightened les jeunes filles, and led them to their quizzing of Gregor. Here, the first appearance of the male impulsive principle, a succession of string chords and syncopated drum beats. The boys' unclear intentions induces a sexual panic of vociferous brass and twittering woodwind, frenetic horn calls, short staccato ejaculations interrupted each time by heavy single punches which take over the music's texture. The young men grasp the girls — then freeze, as the Victrola arm retracted and side three dropped, a classical Brechtian alienation effect reminding the audience that no matter how involved they get, this is only a show that invites reflection.

With an extended four-flute trill calling up a primeval melody on clarinets, the "Round Dances of Spring" begin, those slow and grave incantations which connect the dancers to the huge earth beneath them. A dragging rhythmic figure is repeated over and over as the young men and girls form separate circles of contrasting motion, the males angular, the women more lyrical. The songs become threatening as the male group adds performers with lab coats and flashlights, and splits into two: scientists and soldiers. Three circles spin around themselves while revolving, planet-like, around the rising ziggurat. At a frightening moment, the orchestral pressure triples, and the three groups leap up on the first three tiers of the structure, women above, military next, and scientists on the lowest level, like electrons quantum-kicked to higher orbit. The slow dance continues, and the men return to earth as the orchestra quiets, while the three girls watch them from above.

Gregor remarked to me that the massive rootedness of this section reminded him of trying to pick up a small cube of uranium for the first time, a shockingly heavy mass that resisted any attempt to free it from the earth. Above the girls, the raboti kept slowly building as the next side dropped.

Military vs. Science while the workers work on: Genia had caught the essential dynamic of the Project. And now there ensued, to urgent rhythmic beating, "The Ritual of the Two Rival Tribes" — competitive dances, rough skirmishes and flashlight-beam duels of blue and white light. The tymps have loosed the rhythm, and eight horns cry out war. As the men stop to breathe, the girls and the yellow-gloved balloon children plead for peace, but there is no stopping the barbaric tubas and loosed testosterone until, in the "Procession of the Oldest and Wisest One", Niels Bohr is pushed in, descending a high, rolling stepladder used to service the cyclotron. As the orchestra holds a quiet, long chord, and the others tremble, he spreadeagles out at center court, and kisses the floor. The earth responds with a long, harmonic, triple piano "yes".

With this kiss comes "The Dancing Out of the Earth", an immense energy of life force, in frenzied celebration, drunk with spring, finally freed from its wintry bondage. There is a wild pulse of drumming in three vs. four, with orchestral outbursts and detached off-beat chords. The whirlpool becomes a boiling cauldron as, to syncopated shrieks on brass and woodwind, the dancers in separate, asymmetrical, electrified clumps leap and fall convulsively out the exit doors as the breathless scene ends.

Several things of note: In this last earth-orgy, there were no more soldiers, no more girls, there were no more scientists or workers. All individual being had regressed from personal sensibility to a liberated collective Unconscious. The musical strategy was exactly that of a cyclotron or cloud chamber: dissonant, brief, irregularly formed musical 'objects' were fired off at one another in a high energy field, collided and released their latent energy. The collision of simple rhythmic and melodic cells, set up fantasmagoric interference patterns — waves and particles at once — while the fierce rhythm encased a basic melody in a way that could scarcely be imagined.

The room was dark and silent, the basketball court now empty except for the ever-watching eyes of Oppie and Groves, which now in darkness, with no other distractions, glowed clearly from their luminescent sclera. The house lights came abruptly on, and Genia walked on stage dressed as a cigarette girl, hawking "Stravinsky popcorn", "Diaghilev yablaki" and "Nijinsky limonad." The audience laughed, and was left to gather in customary groups to discuss the show.

Still in character, I tried to drift stenographically among the conversations. Klaus Fuchs, a German emigré and, as it turned out, Soviet spy, was shocked at the dancers' undisguised joy at "the vulgar splendor of war", and felt the music to be a "virtuoso accompaniment to regression". Much as he admired the Russian people he felt "alienated and shocked by the absence of taste so important in the tradition of German music since Beethoven." An American technician's wife asserted she "had never felt so physical," and went around making people feel her carotid pulse. A psychiatrist-turned-physicist felt the work was "dream-aversive" while his conversation partner, a man I did not know, felt that on the contrary, it was quite frightening precisely because it set up "a regressive dream-collective as a positive accomplishment." One thirteen year old boy thought it was "a lot of laughs."

I found Gregor outside, pacing. He seemed anxious, skittish and depressed, but didn't feel he could leave. "Something is coming," he told me, "something frightening and unknown, some coming giant, of elemental force." He would not say more. Surely he was not referring simply to the bomb here, though that too was soon expected. Was he referring to Yeats' rough beast, its hour come at last, slouching toward Bethlehem to be born? Usually transparent, he could become annoyingly cryptic when disturbed.

The lights flickered and the audience took its seats again while I mounted my judge's stand for "The Great Sacrifice", the dreaded second half. After initial darkness and a repeat of Genia's unintended monster show in red. The room was illuminated in the murky light of the single bulb directly above the now twelve foot, balloon-stuffed ziggurat. The record dropped like a pellet of potassium cyanide into sulfuric acid.

In the dim light, in tensely watchful silence, the youths milled around, melancholy, desolate, to the strange color of muted trumpets and horn calls. An old Russian tune suggested a human world, but clearly we were in the realm of the subconscious, an area of feeling where the palpable and tangible disappear, and where humans, in a gloomy, shadowed world devoid of objects — except for the sinister ziggurat — move timidly, with the caution of uncertainty and fear. The gloomy coloration seemed less an expression of mourning for the upcoming ritual murder, than some mood of the unfree — a quiet bleakness of imprisoned creaturehood. And now the three girls entered, trembling, to dance their circle in the mystery and panic of nature's night as felt by adolescent maidens: it is precisely through them that the strain of nature's growth can be most clearly sensed. They move around the ziggurat, which now seems a sacrificial pyre in the garish light. They move to a languid legato melody on six solo violas, against a background of pizzicato cellos, they rise and fall from tiptoe, dropping their right hands and jerking their heads. Then — eleven huge chords, one of the most threatening moments in music, and they leap up to the first level of the pile. It is time for "The Naming and Honoring of the Chosen One".

To ecstatic shrieks on the wind Gaby, Nella and Jane leap convulsively up and down the sides of the ziggurat to chugging, fragmented rhythms. In the chaotic changing of levels, Gaby seems left above, almost randomly chosen. Gaby, daughter of Genia. What was this mother saying? Gaby would be the sacrifice. She looks down at her friends on the levels below, and the hysterical outburst on upper winds and brass express her fearful dismay. But the elders enter, and soldiers, scientists, workers and children gather round the pyre to praise and glorify her.

And now come the priests to evoke the ancestors, a group of eight masked figures, who emerge from tunnels in the ziggurat to surround the scene. Who they are is unclear. One looks, perhaps, like Einstein, one like Beethoven, one something like Hitler. With a series of declamatory fanfares, the tribe recalls their ancestors in a slow, reflective march. The music pulses quietly, irregularly goosefleshed by shivers on flute and english horn. Moll Flanders climbs the ziggurat steps to kiss Gaby, and in returning to ground, carries an exhausted Jane to safety.

Enrico Fermi likewise claims his Nella, and carries her down to safety. The priests march ceremoniously through the crowd to a striding, pounding rhythm, setting up shifting patterns within the mob. The pulsing and shivering returns, bass clarinet dipping down and back from the underworld, as all face the pyre and focus their gaze on the platform twelve feet above.

Gaby seemed to be in a trance, seated alone, eyes closed, on an 8 X 8 platform, a light directly above her head throwing grotesque facial shadows. "The Sacrificial Dance of the Chosen One" calls her with its opening staccato chords in wild, chaotic rhythm, calls her out of a universe of time to a world so rhythmically shattered as to be beyond any countable measure. Her eyes open slowly, and as she tilts her head sidewards, we see her dawning sense of mystery, then horror, then panic in the face of the unknown just ahead of her. Her first odd act is to reach out to the community below, not for help, but to focus their attention — look here and here — to assist them in the celebration of her death. The orchestra begins to bubble with blood-curdling ejaculations — threats and laughter from the erupting forces of nature over which she fatally presides. She is galvanized into twitches and leaps of increasing frenzy, her attention withdrawn from the group below, and ejected out beyond self to the cosmos. Hysterical turns on the violins and piccolos ascend in a nightmarish way, and she begins to spin, to spin more and more dizzily on the unrailed platform — where is her mother, where is her father to catch her? — as time becomes ever more complex and unbalanced, in a mounting, centrifugal confluence of exaltation, ecstasy, sexual climax, sacrifice and death. It is a mad dance, non-dancerly, naive, the dance of an insect or a factory blowing up. At last she falls, exhausted, her being dispersed like windblown seed. She tries to rise, but in vain. Her last breath, a tiny gurgle, a little upward run on the flutes. There is a short silence, and then a final convulsive chord, sharp as the blade of a guillotine. The ritual is accomplished.

No one dared applaud. In the stunned silence the Godfaces were raised off the backboards, floated to the center of the room, and tented quietly over the dead young girl, Oppie and Groves in unwonted necrophiliac caress.

198

That was it. On a budget of less than ten dollars, Genia Peierls had exposed the tragedy of modern being, exposed the barbarism of human life, of our life, the violence of the soul, exposed the cruelty of nature, the community as a hovering sword, the instinctive savagery of a tribe wedded to Eros and Death, and fate — le Destin — , powerful, primordial, random, as the ruler of a godless universe, exposed a sacrifice anti-humanistic to the core, a sacrifice entirely without tragedy, the final stage of a power-struggle between nature and humanity.

The lights came on. The huge cast assembled to embarrassed applause, with slight increase as Gaby got up and descended the platform. Moll Flanders presented the three girls with bouquets of spring flowers sent up from Santa Fe. As if rehearsed, the three of them walked over to Gregor, and presented their flowers to him. He was overcome. What did it all mean? Outside, the equinoctial moon shone brightly.

Tarentellas and Wedding Music in General
As Played by The Fungus Pygmies

Alexei gets a wedding gig, and meets a musical partner in crime.

A gig! His first real gig! One where there might be — would be — single girls, desperately seeking. He'd have to play tarantellas. He studied up. He studied the music — the normal tarantellas, Napoletana, Calabrese, Sicilian. But in addition, Liszt's frantic "Tarantella, Venezia e Napoli", Chopin's, Rachmaninoff's, and Schubert's Presto tarantella at the end of the *Death and the Maiden* quartet.

He studied tarantulas too, his spider fingers itching with joy. For the dance originated as poison control for tarantatas — women from Taranto bitten by the hairy beasts. Neighbors would surround the victim, play and dance, and watch the movements of their patient. Once the correct rhythm, speed and tune were found, survival was certain. Using Pignocchio's arachnid hands to denature tarantula venom seemed a genuine homeopathic interaction, *similia similibus curentur*. Sam Hahnemann would be proud; no one at the wedding would know.

His performance strategy was simple: one of contrast and surprise. He began his wanderings through the reception hall playing Gesualdo's "Moro Lasso". Only he knew the secret words, and their referential meaning. This is your life, Alexei, and all of you out there:

> *Moro lasso al mio duolo,*
> *E chi mi può dar vita,*
> *Ahi, che m'ancide e non vuol darmi aita.*
> *O dolorosa sorte,*

Chi dar vita mi può, ahi, mi da morte.
[https://tinyurl.com/8t9a8a5e]

The music was extravagant, emotionally shocking, early seventeenth century chromaticism not heard again until Wagner and Strauss. Some passages included all twelve notes in a single phrase, anticipating Schoenberg. Sharp dissonances of pain, violent rhythmic contrast, uncomfortable harmonic juxtapositions, as of A minor and Db Major at the beginning of the piece. Wedding music it was not.

But to set up a wedding — what could be better? Pain — then release and joy, a sequence highly recommended by the sages. At a signal from Antonio, Pignocchio let rip a medley of the hottest tarantellas from every region represented in the room. Even dotards left their wheelchairs to dance. Groups formed, chains spun clockwise and counter. The puppeteer puppet sped them up and slowed them down like some demonic personal trainer. Children danced descants around the grownups. The Pied Piper wouldn't have been more successful. In fact, several rats were seen dancing in the kitchen. And these were New York City rats, normally ironic and blasé.

During a break, and following their Milanese tradition, the best man, Harpo-like, snipped the groom's tie into pieces — to great cheering — and the pieces were sold to pay the musician. Pignocchio was bravissimoed into the spotlight, the crowd undaunted by his mask, and presented with over a thousand dollars of checks and bills. In among them were business cards scrawled with "Contact me for more work." When asked to comment, he could only say, "*Grazie, grazie.* I wear not motley in my brain," a remark that left them — for some reason — laughing and applauding.

As the blood alcohol levels ascended into heaven, Alexei wandered the tables, boosting hilarity with his sneezing song which began with a verse set to Mozart's dark minor variation on "Twinkle, Twinkle, Little Star":

Twinkle, twinkle, starnutire [note: Ital. to sneeze.]
Oi, my eyes are getting bleary

And my ears are getting stuffy,
And my nose is getting puffy...

Suspended on the dominant, here he broke into a polka chorus much fitted to his instrument:

Achoo!
Achoo!
Achoo, achoo, achoo!
Ah-ah-ah-ah-ah-ah-ah-ah-ah-ah-ah-Achoo!
Scusi.

The guests, protected by invisible alcohol shields, didn't seem to mind being sneezed on. Perhaps they thought the germs couldn't get beyond his mask. How did they think he breathed? In any case, they laughed and laughed, and slapped him on the back.

The dancehall was filled with eligible, dark-eyed beauties, many friends of the bride. And Pignocchio had memorized six killer pick-up lines. Surely one of them would work:

"If you were a new hamburger at Burger King you would be Burger Princess.

"I wear Fruit of the Loom underwear. What kind do you wear?"

"I'll be Beethoven, you be Mozart. Let's have a conversation."

"That's a cool outfit. You look like Eudora Welty. I'll bet everyone tells you that, right?"

"Is it hot in here, or is it just you?"

"I miss my teddy bear. Will you sleep with me?"

The first three provoked laughter wherever applied. The next two were met with vacant stares, while the last, uttered in desperation toward the end of the evening, elicited from one bella ragazza only

"Excuse me, I have to throw up."

Perhaps she had drunk too much chianti.

As she staggered away, Pignocchio felt a tugging at his sleeve. He turned to see a shriveled old man, beckoning to him. Leaning over sideways so as not to bash the ancient with his bellows, he put his ear to the speaker's mouth.

"Più in alto che se va," he croaked, "più il col se mostra!"

The higher you climb, the more your ass shows. It wasn't clear to whom he referred.

But Alexei felt upbraided. He recalled an incident from early childhood when his mother took out after him for giving his checkers wild rides in his little red wagon instead of playing quietly with them. A "high fanatic" she had called him, some mistranslation from the Russian, and he stood there, truculent, swearing to be one when he grew up.

Wedding Music

"When I am done, she will be a real woman, a real girl, free of her genetics, entirely marvelous, stunning, bewitching. Your nose is child's play in comparison. She is the spirit that will lead both of us on. Get used to her. And you and I can make beautiful music together."

"What do you mean? What kind of music?"

"All kinds. Surgical music. Medico-cultural-political music. Music music."

Another re-lighting of the pipe. Alexei was getting nervous. This was more than he had bargained for.

"I want to play with you," the doctor continued. "We can make a band, play gigs such as no one has ever imagined. We can help keep marriages together — like Gesualdo."

He smiled warmly, with tobacco-yellow teeth. Alexei began to fiddle nervously with his bandages.

"Marriage is a sacrament," the doctor continued, "Non è vero? But half of them dissolve. You know why?"

Groucho's ghost welled up uncontrolledly.

"The chief cause of divorce is marriage," an old Graulexei muttered.

"Unh-uh" declared the doctor, shaking his bushy head. and blowing out sweet-smelling smoke.

"You may not have played enough weddings to realize this, but marriages break up because of wrong wedding music. Stupid music.

Nazi Wagner music as the bride comes in, Jewish Mendelssohn music as she walks out. Lohengrin: sorcery. "Here Comes The Bride!" Marriage aborted ten minutes later. Midsummer Night's Dream: lovers drugged, lost, unfaithful. Whoopie!"

More puffing.

"My little theory, *ragazzo mio*. How can marriages survive such confused beginnings? We're lucky that only 50% split up. You and I will play the right music, unimpeachable music, music designed uniquely for each wedding pair. Healthy marriage birthing is the divine right of musicians, and we have never been allowed to exercise it." He broke into a hearty laugh. "And it'll be fun. *Un scherzo glorioso.*"

"What do you play?" Alexei inquired.

"Kontrabaß. Juilliard, '47."

"You think that will go with accordion and harmonica?"

"Yes. Brilliantly."

More smoke.

"How did you...?"

"Einstein Med School '53. I was impressively tall. Five years of residency at Jacobi."

"Why did you...?"

"Couldn't make any money as a musician. Smoky jazz joints unhealthy. Beethoven's Fifth aside, why would anyone want to play professional bass?"

The doctor leaned back, and studied his patient through his wrappings.

"I'm going to call in Miss Robinson, all right?"

Alexei was too confused to resist.

The Fungus Pygmies

Francis Mangiafuoco was a somewhat strange man. He had been the tallest baby in the bassinet, and stayed that way in carriage, on tricycle, and tooling around the streets of Milano. He was handed a full-size double bass in his scuola elementare orchestra because full-sized was the only bass they had, and he was the only student hefty enough. It became his friend, the only one who would play with him on a regular basis.

They called him "'Pazzo' Mangiafuoco", but he wasn't crazy — just different. In a post-war time when all things German were repugnant, he chose to study German, and made a deep teen-age exploration of German music, literature and philosophy. No sappy Bottesini or Dragonetti concertos for him. He went right for the Bach Suites for solo cello, difficult enough for an instrument tuned in fifths, and some almost impossible for one tuned in fourths. He took on the Beethoven cello sonatas, and, like Alexei, had worked up the Brahms double concerto with a lovely violinist he was interested in.

As a bass player, he was extraordinary. One could cite huge hands and giant, instrument-enveloping height as responsible. But no. What characterized his playing was delicacy and stunning clarity, with long, lyrical lines of an almost vocal quality and seamless changes of bow. His sound was clean, clear, silky, focused. From early on, he was winning all the local competitions, and then the national ones.

When all his hormone-steeped friends were going ga-ga over Puccini and Verdi, he found himself far more attracted to the great Germans: Handel, Gluck and Mozart, Fidelio and Freischütz, Strauss and Berg. And especially Wagner. He loved the masterly Hans Sachs, Parsifal the holy fool, and his even more foolish son, Lohengrin. He shared the unwelcome wanderlust of the Dutchman, and Tannhäuser's wary relationship to love. He understood the sweet poison in Tristan's chromatic passion. But above all else, he loved The Ring with its infinite meditations on lust, greed and power. He felt himself Wotan, Alberich, Fafner, Siegmund, Brunnhilde, Siegfried, Mime and Loge all in one. They made him that much more huge. Especially Wotan.

He read Kant on the categories of the mind, and Schopenhauer on the will. And beyond all, enthroned in parallel to Wagner, he discovered the madman Nietzsche with his projection of the Übermensch — the perfect companion for his six foot, six inch frame — and a subtle and not-so-subtle indoctrination.

Given his audition tape and record of achievement, he was a

shoo-in at Julliard. And another one at the Albert Einstein College of Medicine. They liked well-rounded applicants.

Hysterica Musico

Rehearsals were a gas. Nitrous oxide. Much laughing. Each reveled in the other's technical skills and unorthodox musical imagination.

And some of the laughter was chemically induced by a different gas, bananadine. The doctor had a prescription for curing shyness and much else, including stage fright, and for liberating the daimons within:

1. Take 15 lbs. of ripe bananas, eat and save the skins. Frank consumed ⅔, his partner the rest.

2. With a sharp knife (of which the surgeon had many), scrape off the insides of the skins.

3. Put all scraped materials in a large pot, add 4 gallons of water, and boil until material has attained a solid paste consistency (3-4 hours).

4. Spread the paste on cookie sheets and dry it in an oven at 300° until it turns to fine black powder.

5. Smoke it.

They used a two-hosed hookah Frank had obtained on his last trip to Cairo. Three or four puffs did it, though Cryillano thought his high might have something to do with having eaten five pounds of bananas.

The gig was the wedding of an elder colleague's daughter. There would be plenty of women there of many ages — enough for both of them. The couple had expressed no particular inclinations concerning the music, "Just something to come in on, and something to go out to. And whatever at the reception." Nice. Easy. The Fungus Pygmies felt free to call the shots.

Frank suggested the Meistersinger march as a processional, a completely positive, C-majorish work, with none of the catastrophic destiny of "Here Comes the Bride" in Lohengrin. Cyrillano thought this might be a good introduction for him to the dreaded Wagner, so he took out the score and brought to the first Pygmy rehearsal the remarkable accordion and bass "deorchestration" he had made. The good doctor found it more than satisfactory, and was sure it would increase the chances of a solid, if C major, marriage. For a recessional, they worked up a version of the imaginary Kije's wedding, reckoning that since marriages subsist primarily in the imagination, the couple would have a salubrious send-off. They tacked on the "Troika" so as to get everyone the hell out of the church asap so they could pack up and get over to the Elk's Hall for the reception.

Since "whatever" was the only guideline for the reception music, and there would be plenty of alcohol, and plenty of talking, they felt free to be more devil-may-care. So they worked up a medley of Looney Tunes, followed by some Hoagy Carmichael for relaxation, then on to a rendition of the orchestral suite from Lulu (since the bride, Frank assured his partner, was a lulu), followed by some faux Liberace for interlude, and culminating, while people were plenty drunk but still standing, with an improvised, but elaborately planned Sinfonia Discordia in five movements, Chaos, Discord, Confusion, Elaboration and The Aftermath. The idea was to create something completely unharmonizable — sounds no system could encompass. High on bananadine, they were sure Confusionism would lead to liberation. And sure the party would love it.

At the end of the third and last rehearsal, Frank said,

"You know, *figlio mio*, you are *magnifico*, terrific. There's nobody like you."

The accordion player explained that that was because he had been born parthenogenetically, without a father. That bananadine was good stuff.

Tchaikovsky — Symphony Number 5

from the endnotes to And Kings Shall Be Thy Nursing Fathers, *Tchaikovsky's imagined entrance into the realm of Death.*

In an earlier form, a conductor of mine wouldn't use this for a program note. He said it would upset the old Tchaikovsky ladies. I would think it impossible to ever become an old Tchaikovsky lady without deeply sensing this. Gimme a break. Old Tchaikovsky ladies are different from old Mozart ladies.

"There is something repulsive about it."

This was the composer's comment about his Fifth Symphony after returning from a European tour conducting it.

True, Tchaikovsky was often neurotic about his compositions, announcing his joy with them to his brother, Modest, then doubting them — and himself — after performances. Schizy. He could fly like a swan, but once on the ground, he would waddle.

Waddling is one thing, but what is "repulsive" about the Fifth? Some clues present themselves.

In a notebook page dated 13 April 1888, the year of its composition, Tchaikovsky outlines a scenario for the first movement: "Introduction: Complete resignation before Fate, or, which is the same, before the inscrutable predestination of Providence. Allegro: (1) Murmurs of doubt, complaints, reproaches against XXX. (2) Shall I throw myself in the embrace of faith??? A wonderful program, if only it can be carried out."

A hopeful beginning. In opening the work, Tchaikovsky cuts to the core. The opening theme in the low clarinets recurs in every movement, commenting on other themes, or challenging them.

Thus, the opening theme carries a narrative function beyond its musical one, and it doesn't take much imagination to hear it as embodying the Fate Tchaikovsky invokes in his primordial program. So let's call it the "Fate theme", and see how it functions throughout the piece.

Tchaikovsky always wore his heart on his compositional sleeve: the sublime slow movement is the expressive core of the whole work. The opening string chorale before the famous horn solo warns the audience to take this movement seriously, even religiously.

Halfway through this erotic movement, the orchestra begins a stringendo and crescendo culminating in fortississimo (fff) trumpets blaring out the Fate theme. It's worse than hearing the steps of your parents entering the room when you are making out with your lover, or a cuckolded spouse returning home early. There's only one possible effect of this interruption: to scare the hell out of the audience, and make it regret its emotional vulnerability. "Oh no you don't. You'll be sorry." The avenging angel bares his sword.

If that's the way the Fate theme can function, what is the meaning of its triumphant takeover of the last movement? Critics have always found this the least successful. Is it because it's overwrought and only barely convincing? Protesting too much, and as such, repulsive?

I think there is little mystery what the XXX refers to in Tchaikovsky's note to Modest. Throughout their extensive correspondence, both closeted gay men dealt in code with their "sickness". "X", it was called, or sometimes "Z", in unmistakable contexts. But in this case, there is more to it than that. What was going on for Tchaikovsky at this time?

It had been three years since Tchaikovsky had produced a major orchestral work — his *Manfred Symphony*. Manfred, a strange, programmatic inclusion in the series of numbered symphonies. Why Manfred?

Manfred is the subject of a dramatic poem by Byron, the story of a Swiss nobleman tortured by mysterious guilt. "Thou lovedst me/Too much," he declares concerning his sister, "as I loved thee: we were not made/To torture thus each other, though it were/The deadliest sin to love as we have loved."

Tchaikovsky was sympathetic to Byron's love for his half-sister, and this for him brought up the dangerous theme of incest. At the time of writing Manfred, Tchaikovsky was already deeply in love with his nephew, Bob, his sister's son, then 15, Tchaikovsky's favorite age for sex with boys. The composer dedicated his Sixth Symphony to him, and awarded him the lion's share of his will. Problematical family dynamics. "XXX" indeed, and a perfect vehicle for Tchaikovsky's brooding about his sexuality. The noble outsider, rejected by a conventional world. He later disowned the piece, calling it "abominable...I loathe it deeply." Sound familiar? Repulsive?

And what followed the Fifth? His fantasy overture, Hamlet, overlapping the scoring of the Fifth, and beginning again with a "Fate" theme. Over the first page, Tchaikovsky had written. "To be or not to be?" The Fifth — sandwiched between Manfred and Hamlet.

Within five years, Tchaikovsky was dead, probably by his own hand or tongue, possibly of arsenic, possibly of cholera, nine days after premiering his death-haunted Sixth Symphony, his requiem.

Tchaikovsky and the Asshole

The asshole, in the first instance was me. I remember, after I got "sophisticated" in my senior year of high school, having been introduced to Bach's *Wachet Auf*, then graduating backwards into the interstices of Renaissance music and earlier, and then forward into the Beethoven String Quartets, being able to sing every movement of all sixteen if challenged, then taking up the cello to be able to play them as well as know them — through all of that, through all my hanging around with kids from Music & Art, and music majors at Queens College, through getting a $50 prize at graduation for being "the non-music major who contributed most to the musical life of the community (I played in orchestra, chamber groups, and sang in chorus and small vocal ensembles) — throughout all of that, I was not only deaf to Tchaikovsky, but even had the arrogance to make fun of him, singing one or two of the heart-on-the-sleeve moments in a loud, blaring, nasal voice, the kind little kids use for "nya nyanya nya nya" teasing, and quoting the saw, "Tchaikovsky was a great genius. Too bad he had no talent." What an asshole.

But I got my comeuppance. First of all, I learned in orchestra that Tchaikovsky was goddamn hard to play, and that within and around those difficult passages were measures of astounding originality. For one of hundreds, possibly thousands of examples, in the six-note opening phrase of the Sixth Symphony, which sounds to any listener like a simple downward scale, with a little flip at the end — F# — E-D-C — BC — it turns out that the F# is played by the 2nd violins, the E by the firsts, the D by the seconds, the C by the firsts, the B by the cellos, and the last C by the firsts again. And each melody note is strangely harmonized by the other instruments not playing it. Is that weird or what? Is that not deep complexity masquerading as the simplest simplicity?

And the movement before that — a waltz in five. Who ever heard of a waltz in five? How would one dance it, or even take it in as a strange, odd-shaped inner environment?

And at the end, *pppp*. Four piano markings. I mean there is piano, pianissimo, pianississimo, but there is not even a word, a musical term for four p's, beyond human hearing. Had any composer ever written four p's before? if so, I am not aware of it.

Tchaikovsky — no talent? What an asshole I was!

But the second instance asshole was more world-shaking. In the ongoing debate about the cause of Tchaikovsky's death, most agree that Tchaikovsky died of cholera, towards the end of a cholera epidemic in Moscow, 1893. But how did he get it? The most common answer for Tchaikovsky old ladies is that he drank "a fatal glass of unboiled water" at a fancy restaurant, with classical symptoms and death to follow. But since when do fancy restaurants not boil their water during cholera epidemics? So a little doubtful there. Where else might he have picked up cholera, if, as is likely, cholera he had?

Cholera is a fecal-oral disease. Shit to mouth. Wash your hands after pooping. But if your sexual habits include 14-year old poverty boys picked up from the docks, as we know from his letters to his also-homosexual brother Tchaikovsky's did, then fecal-oral might have a very different itinerary. The Sixth Symphony is pretty deathy throughout. Tchaikovsky suspected, knew, or feared something. He died three weeks after its premiere.

On Vaughn Williams Reconciliation

My 80-something conductor, Robert deCormier, has decided to take a stand against the war(s) — from the podium. The Vermont Symphony Orchestra Chorus is now preparing a concert consisting of Haydn's *Missa in Tempore Belli* (Mass in Time of War), and the Ralph Vaughn Williams *Dona Nobis Pacem* (Give Us Peace).

The former is a work written in 1796, when Napoleon's armies were invading Austria, and threatening drums were sounding on the outskirts of Vienna. These drums are featured in the mass, especially in the Agnus Dei, calling forth an especially poignant setting of the Dona Nobis Pacem. *Agnus Dei, qui tollis peccata mundi*....The "sins of the world", indeed.

But it is the Vaughn Williams I want to speak of. The texts of this extraordinary piece are drawn from three sources, the mass's *Dona Nobis Pacem*, which frames the five movements, some swords-in-to-ploughshares biblical texts towards the end, with the bulk of the work devoted to four texts from *Leaves of Grass*. Whitman, of course, was witness to the barbarities of the Civil War, and spent time on the battlefield, nursing the wounded.

The combination of one particular visionary text with music unbearably beautiful makes it impossible for me to sing this movement. I have not yet been able to control my choking up, so I just have to mouthe the words, and deal judiciously with my tears. (That's one good thing about the cello. When these kind of moments arise in orchestral playing, you can choke up all you want and still play on.)

Here is Whitman, poem 137, "Reconciliation": the chorus sings

WORD over all, beautiful as the sky!

Beautiful that war, and all its deeds of carnage, must in time be utterly lost;

That the hands of the sisters Death and Night, incessantly softly wash again, and ever again, this soil'd world...

What confidence Whitman had that the WORD, the WORD over everything, a WORD the size of the sky, must — must! — in time overcome all deeds of carnage, that after much death, and darkest night, the world will be washed clean again — this soil'd world.

The text is set over triplet arpeggios in the strings, quietly washing against the slow four beat pulse. Two against three, three against four — the great Brahmsian secret of the emotional heart, masterfully used, sweetly, caressingly, so affecting in its contrast with the dissonant harmonies of much of the rest.

The "reconciliation" comes as a baritone soloist sings this text

... For my enemy is dead—a man divine as myself is dead;
I look where he lies, white-faced and still, in the coffin—I draw near;
I bend down, and touch lightly with my lips the white face in the coffin.

And the chorus returns with "*WORD over all...*", this time *a capella*, so vulnerable, so difficult to maintain pitch, to be there, in tune, for the orchestral return... But what a consummate Vaughn Williams gesture — the nakedness of the WORD, the nakedness of us all.

Tears, yes, but finally not healing peace of mind, but, for me, despair. For I realize it is exactly this confidence that is utterly lost. Whitman could attend the wounded and the dead in 1862 and still know that the carnage would — in time — come to an end, that the soil'd world would be washed clean of blood.

But I fear that there is now no hope for remedy, that the WORD has been so clouded by *our* "words", so shredded by our weapons, so marginalized by our plans for world domination, and the plans of others to defend against our plans, that the sisters Death and Night have become our permanent landlords, jailers, executioners, and changers of the scene: "That's all, folks."

What a loony tune we — and our children, and theirs — have been launched into when the WORD has been chased from the sky.

Wagner —Prelude to Tristan and Isolde

Gregor Samsa goes to see a Fifth Avenue plastic surgeon about amputating his middle pair of legs so he can be more attractive to women.

Do you still want to be drastically modified?"

"It may help me..."

Dr. Lindhorst stepped resolutely to the desk and pressed a button under the leg space. Miss Mozart stuck her blond head through the door.

"Yes, Doctor?"

"Miss Mozart, please prepare procedure T for Mr. Samsa here." Miss Mozart nodded both her head and eyelids in a gesture that sharply brought Alice to Gregor's mind. The residue of hesitance was washed away in the sweet ache that rose from heart to throat. Still, he was frightened at what he had committed himself to.

"All right, my friend, already a shadow of your former self, Maxwell Lindhorst at your service. Maxwell Lindhorst, who lacks the knowledge, the wisdom, and even the right to decide what is best for his patients. Many consider cosmetic surgery an act of vanity. Some see Pride there, or Envy, or Gluttony for praise, or Sloth finding the easy way around, or Anger taking a knife to self instead of other. In your case, I suppose, it is Lust in the driver's seat. But I do not judge — because only you can know. This will all be free, gratis, as I promised. I merely ask you sign this consent form. Don't worry. You don't have to sign in blood. I'm not interested in your soul."

The doctor took several sheets of paper from a desk drawer and placed them, along with a fountain pen, in front of Gregor. G drew his large reading glasses from the special pocket inside his jacket, and perused the pages. It was not clear what he actually understood: much of the document was in technical, medico/legal language.

"Can I die from this?"

"Of course. One can die from many things. Joy, for instance. Or love. However, it would be an extremely rare event."

Gregor took up the pen, but had trouble unscrewing the top.

"Here, I'll do that for you," said the obliging doctor. Miss Mozart knocked lightly, and again stuck her head into the room, this time from a door among the bookshelves which Gregor had not noticed. Her bun was gone, transformed into a stream of golden hair.

"The room is ready, Doctor."

"Thank you."

She disappeared behind the door.

"Shall we go?"

"Now? Right immediately?"

"There's no time like the present. Except the future. Except the future."

He walked to the bookshelf door, opened it, and beckoned his patient through. Gregor expected some sort of operating room, with huge lights over a surgical table, green tile walls and floors. Instead, he found a room more like a recording studio: a wooden chamber with acoustical tile and strategic baffling, in the middle of which a Bösendorfer concert grand faced the only seat in the room, a contraption quite like a dentist's chair, yet obviously far more comfortable.

Miss Mozart, now clad in embroidered Irish robe, held a hospital jonny over her arm.

"Mr. Samsa, will you step behind the screen, remove your clothes, and put this on?" She handed him the jonny.

"All my clothes?"

"Please."

Gregor, truly embarrassed, backed himself behind the four-paneled Chinese masterpiece. He could have sworn it had depicted a serene and holy mountain. But now, from behind, the image had transformed into a fierce mountain of a tiger, dismembering a small deer. He folded his clothes, dropped them neatly on the floor, and slipped into the skimpy covering.

"I can't reach to tie this behind."

"Come out," said Miss Mozart, "I'll do it for you."

Gregor didn't mind showing this beautiful woman the smoothness of his tegmen. He strode more confidently out, and presented her his open back."

"Oh!" She jumped back. He had forgotten his wound. With the day's already disturbing events, the bandage was more than saturated.

"What's the matter?" Dr. Lindhorst came quickly around to look. He held the jonny open at arm's length.

"Having a bit of a problem, there, Gregor? What's going on?"

"My wound, it..."

"What happened?"

"My father was frightened."

"And he threw an apple at you."

"Yes. How did you know?"

"I read about it. In the story. There's a book about you. Did you know that? I knew of you when you first came to be. Long before my daughter."

"I do not see this book. Do you have a copy?"

"In the story you die. The chambermaid throws you out with the garbage."

"That is *Dreckhaufen*. I am here. Oh, but perhaps it was by my parents. They think I am dead. We trick them, Anna Marie and the borders and I. It was not good they must have me around. They continue their lives."

"Many people think you're dead."

"Not the Gregor Dancers."

"The Gregor Dancers don't read German books. Anyway, that was, what, eight years ago? Why hasn't your wound healed? Mind if I take off the bandage? Miss Mozart, will you fetch some fresh dressing? Thank you."

This was the first time Gregor had ever shown his wound to anyone. It was the first time he had been asked about it. He rarely thought about it except as a hygiene problem, to be cared for like dandruff or body odor. So here was an unexpected benefit of his visit to the surgeon.

"Rose-red, in many variations of shade, dark in the hollows, lighter at the edges, spots of blood, small necrotic areas...and...we've got to clean this out."

"I clean it twice a day."

"But there are maggots in it."

"Occasionally, there are maggots. They come and they go. It does not hurt me. I think this is the way it is — it will not get better."

"It will take a tegmental graft."

Miss Mozart returned with a tray of sterile gauze and saline, and deftly cleaned and dressed the wound while the doctor spoke.

"We may be able to do something about this later, unless it's a somatization of a spiritual wound, which would be a serious category error to treat. The immediate issue is the amputation. Can you concentrate on what I'm saying while Miss Mozart works?"

Gregor drew his attention back from the light playing in her hair. Yellow light attracts insects. "Yes. I listen."

"You still want to go ahead, Mr. Pygmalion?"

Gregor nodded.

"When Miss Mozart finishes, I am going to ask you to lie in this chair, and get as comfortable as possible. Then I am going to ask you for a vow of silence — complete silence — for one hour. We will be going through a pre-procedure which brings our chances for success to almost 100%. Other surgeons have a range of results; I do not. You have chosen the right pair of hands, Gregor, and the right strategist behind them."

Miss Mozart was finishing the final bandaging. A work of art.

"Are you willing to be silent for an hour, to concentrate entirely on what you hear?"

"I will."

"All right. Come lie in the chair. Miss Mozart will adjust it for you. Comfortable? Good. We're going to strap you in for your own safety."

There was a long silence during and after the buckling. An expectant tension filled the room. Dr. Lindhorst sat down on a small padded projection coming out of the chair, took hold of one of G's bare legs, and spoke quietly towards its knee.

"All cultures except our own western, sanitized and scientized one have understood the intimate connection between processes of the body and those of the soul. When the soul consents, its physical shell will follow. Without that consent, there is unpredictability and chaos.

My surgical results are more successful than those of my colleagues because while they start by opening the skin, I begin — and end — by opening the soul.

"The eyes may be the portals of the soul, but they are exit portals only. Seeing is an important, but finally trivial sense. Eyes can be opened or closed, objects can be visible or not, the world can be dark or light. Nature would not give a central place to such a contingent sensibility. No, the chiefest and deepest connections are made through the ear — which can hear at all times, in the dark, around corners, when eye is blind, which can hear aggregations of distinct vibrations — distinct pitches in chords — when the eye would average them into one. Blue and yellow becoming green — what loss is there!

"Today we are going to engage your soul — through your ears. I'm fully aware that in your case, the word is metaphorical. Insects have no ears, I know. But they have fine hearing organs at the leg joints. That is one reason I am reluctant to amputate: we are talking about partial deafness, reduced acoustic acuity, closing one third of the doors into the soul.

"Still I am willing to go ahead, Gregor Samsa, if, in your wisdom, you would so like. But I am aware that there is much still unsaid between us, and many consequences of the unsaid. I am aware of your sleeplessness last night, your Bettschmertz, as it were. I am aware of your mysterious friend in Washington, D.C. , and of your wanting to be loved.

"Gregor, Love is brother to his sister, Death. Eros and Thanatos, my friend. Longing always leads somewhere, and that somewhere is not always longed for. You must appreciate this — deeply — before you take an irreversible leap of mutilation in the service of love. If you understand and truly accept, your tissues will heal. If you do not understand, if you do not truly accept, you will carry yet another unhealing wound." He paused to let his words sink in. "Miss Mozart, you may begin."

The slim, intense woman took off her shoes, and sat down at the Bösendorfer, barefoot. Smoothing back the sides, and reaching behind her neck, she encircled the long fall of her golden hair with her fingers, moved it from her gown, and let it fall loosely onto her half-bare back.

Though Gregor could see every detail with his immense peripheral vision, he felt himself drifting back into a hazier space deep inside his cuticle. Long echoes of Lindhorst's hypnotic voice rippled slowly in circles of ever-softer sound.

Miss Mozart placed her right hand on the keyboard. The first gentle A reached up a plaintive minor sixth, and hung there, suspended in non-time, until its own weight eased it down to the supporting net of the note below — only to immediately fall through that net — oh surprise! — to the accented half step below, the awe-full D# of the Tristan chord, the chord of chords, that miraculous find of ambiguous, melancholy longing. Miss Mozart's left hand joined her right to urge the F and B below, while her right fourth finger struck the G# that would resolve upwards, and upwards again beyond what might have been its goal. The *Tristan* chord, F-B-D#-G#, a chord so extraordinary that one can search in vain through music to find its like. Search was its name, and its mode, and its function. Search. But for what? The beauty of despair? The despair of beauty? What trembling question was being asked by this voice in the night? In the long pause which followed, Lindhorst whispered,

"Be in the silence, Gregor. Let the sweet pain soak in at your soft joints." Then he signaled to Miss Mozart to continue.

The second phrase, a step higher, infinitely slow, exaggeratedly, tormentingly slow, left Gregor hanging as did the first, the Sehnsuchtsmotiv, the Leitmotif of Longing, calling him from the vast darkness of What. His wound began to weep into its new dressing. His dorsal gland began to moisten. The meat at his leg joints began to soften, as if to bid welcome to the knife.

"Something is dissolving, Gregor. What is it? Don't answer." He couldn't have.

A third time the phrase called out, higher still, and longer, reaching upwards by two more notes, as if its fingers were stretching from an already outstretched hand.

"It hurts, my friend, does it not?"

As if to answer, the phrase returned, the same last, rising pattern, an octave higher, and then only the last two notes, a half-step reaching upward, and once again, the two reaching notes, an octave above, harmonic tension so great as to be humanly unbearable. And yet it hung there, radiating, in the silence — until beginning again, it pushed beyond itself, and with a final leap, reached beyond itself, above and below, to a land that could be footed, an almost safe place — an accented chord of F-A-C — but with a B above, a skyhook which let gently go, and allowed the hearer — and the universe — to collapse down to the floor of an ever-rising, but graspable flow of molten melody, the Motif of Love.

"Now you can swim, Gregor. Your wings are beginning to spread." And indeed, G could feel pressure at his back, once associated only with sexual excitement, but now with something more mysterious, sexual in part, but as larger as the sea is to the drop. Miss Mozart's fingers called forth the Bösendorfer's magic, and the melody rang forth in quiet, sensuous richness, as if from twelve pianissimo cellos, though there was not a cello in sight.

The clock had ticked off ten minutes, but there were no minutes here, only an expanded, warping space-time, similar to Gregor's flight, but now colored with the depth of new emotional and spiritual dimensions. The labyrinthine melody rolled on and on, reaching ever higher, falling back and reaching again, a melody of melting and surpassing tenderness, sweeping up in its wake the mists of the sublime — that world so far beyond perceptual or imaginative grasp, that our sense of its beauty is deeply mixed with dread. Alarming and reassuring both, it sweeps along, in ecstatic prolongation, immensely complicated, dissolving tonal language — and any other — as if God himself were exhuding enharmonics. Complicated, yet beyond complicated, and thus simple: exaltation, transformation, an intoxicating brew of idealism and lust, delirious forces striving to embrace, exchanging the Kingdom of Day for the Kingdom of Night.

Fingers flying, Miss Mozart piloted this extraordinary tone poem back to its unsafe harbor, the *Sensuchtsmotiv*. The Prelude to Tristan and Isolde sank down to its embers.

"After such love, why is there still longing?" Lindhorst whispered, tears in his eyes. Miss Mozart turned quietly to the very last pages of the piano score, and in hushed tones, began Isolde's song of Love's triumph over Death. "Mild und leise," Gregor knew the words, "wie er lächelt, wie das Auge hold eröffnet..." She sang beautifully, as extraordinarily well as she played, and not having to overcome an orchestra, she was able to evoke the most delicate nuances of emotion and inflection as Isolde gazes upon her lover, transforming his death into eternal, living, life. In the intimate murmurings of the first serene phrases, slowly rising through unbelievable ascending passages of modulating sequences, wave upon wave, lyrical, rhapsodic, ecstatic, to climactic heights of passion and transfiguration, Isolde makes her decision to die, to melt with Tristan into ultimate ground of being, to leave behind the torment of the finite doomed to infinite yearning. Together they will be at home in the vast realm of unbounded night, borne on high amidst the stars, and then down, down, to where there is no down

In dem wogenden Schwall,
in dem tönenden Schall,
in des Welt-Atems
wehendem All —
ertrinken,
versinken —
unbewußt —
höchste Lust!

Release! Death powerless against the Inextinguishable — love's vast, immeasurable redemption. Yet even here, after this inspired surging of metaphysical perception, even here, in the midst of yes, even here, appear the ineffable harmonies of the Sehnsuchtsmotiv, longing beyond longing, even in final exhalation — longing. Then silence. Profound silence.

Miss Mozart sat still, staring at the piano, her wrinkled hands in her embroidered lap.

"Gregor, are you still there?"

Dr. Lindhorst checked his abdomen for the rise and fall of breath.

"Gregor, listen to me carefully. This music is all very well and good, but it is a paen to annihilation. Do you understand that? There is redemption there, and transcendence, but it is transcendence of individuation itself. Do you want redemption from being and its torments? A sinister kind of redemption, that.

"Do you remember the *Little Mermaid*, Gregor? I'm not joking. Hans Andersen's Little Mermaid who wanted to be rid of her fish tail and have two props to walk on, like humans, so that the Prince would fall in love with her? She gave up her tongue for the Sea Witch's magic drink so her tail would part and she would gain what men call pretty legs. But every step she took hurt — as if she were treading on sharp knives. And in the end, the Prince marries someone else, someone who can speak and sing, and the Little Mermaid's heart broke, and his wedding morning brought her death and dissolution to foam on the sea. Gregor, do you think this has anything to do with you? Are you prepared to dissolve for love like the Mermaid? Like Isolde? Do you want to be foam on the sea?

"And speaking of treading on sharp knives, I trust you are acquainted with the phenomenon of the phantom limb? All patients have sensations seeming localized in the amputated limb, often like muscle pain with the phantom feeling cramped or uncomfortable. But some patients suffer chronic, severe pain, unresponsive to therapy. Are you prepared to reach out to assuage your pain, and find nothing there to touch? Do you think you can swindle the Devil, and escape from being meat?

"And, Gregor, speaking of the devil, just what is your connection with his sulphurous realm? Have you ever asked yourself how you got this way? What crime you had committed? What deal you are pursuing? What are you, an externalization of the beast in man? I know, I know, you're a nice person. They're all nice people. But why...you? For this," here he rapped on the hardness of G's thorax, at the level of amputation, "why you? Don't answer. I'll tell you why you. Because you ask too many questions, and have too many quests. There's a composer named Charles Ives living up in Connecticut. Wrote a piece some fifteen years ago called "The Unanswered Question", for which, unfortunately, Miss Mozart has no score."

"I couldn't play it." She got up from the piano and disappeared through a black, heavily-paneled door.

"*The Unanswered Question.* You need to know this piece, Herr Samsa, and meditate on it. Do you read score? There are no recordings, and probably never will be. Mr. Ives sent me a copy of the score. I'll show it you some time. It's clear enough. Ives, too, is on a quest. He wants to banish the conflict between consonance and dissonance, between sound and silence, between questioning and answering, between finality and eternity. Why? Why? What's wrong with these conflicts? I'd like to put all you questors in one large room, and photograph you weekly in your Unreal City."

Perhaps it was because Miss Mozart was no longer there, perhaps it was the stridency in Maxwell Lindhorst's voice, but Gregor was coming around from his mind-altering polyesthesia.

"I could not speak, and my eyes failed, I was neither living nor dead, and I knew nothing, looking into the heart of light, the silence. *Öd' und leer das Meer.*"

"What?"

"That's what you look like — the Wasteland. Are you with us again?"

"Can I talk?"

"Yes. You're such an obedient German."

"I'm Czech."

"German Czech. Gregor, a lovely woman has stooped to folly; must you folly too? There are people in a burning building who will not come out unless the weather is just right. Must you be the one to rout them? There are many false grails, Gregor. Did you know Wagner was going to write an opera about the Buddha's last journey? He never did. I can imagine Schopenhauer coming out on stage, and lecturing like Hans Sachs about salvation through renunciation. The greatest good is never to be born at all."

Dr. Lindhorst got up from his seat, grabbed the two handles protruding from the rear of the chair, and began to push Gregor toward the black door.

"But since, Herr Samsa, you are already born," and here he broke into his own text setting of the Prize Song, in high Heldentenor:

The greatest good
lies in full and absolute negation
of personal...
...ity and will
until even..
tual dissolution.
Out in the void,
like mer-may-ayd foam on wave
and wave until
the heart amending
the soul descending..."

"I'm not ready."

"What?"

"Don't take me in there. I'm not ready."

"You're not? I though you were."

"You thought wrong."

"Are you ready for a modus vivendi asceticus? Noli me tangere? Ethos of purity contra pathos of impurity? An anxious, neck-breaking game, continually on the edge of the impossible?"

"You're mocking me."

"Like hell I am."

"I want to get up. Please to unstrap me."

"With pleasure."

Zelenka — The Lamentations of Jeremiah

In my Golem Song, *the quite strange Jewish racist, Alan Krieger, intent upon committing mass-shooter murder of blacks from his bedroom window, brings his boombox ghetto blaster up to Harlem to warn the multitudes of their fate, and to check on whether God approves. Zelenka's Lamentations of Jeremiah (his favorite piece of music) provides the text for all to ponder, which, of course, is nobody, since who understands Latin, including God?*

Lenox and 125th. Still Indian Summer. Still sunny. You'd think Shvartzaville would have its own weather. In Darkness let me dwell. The ground, the ground, shall sorrow, sorrow be. Indian Summer — is that still politically correct? Look at this place! Good thing all those vendors got kicked off the street, it'd be a thousand times worse.

Well, here we go, this is it.

"God? God, are You listening? This is Your chance to show Your stuff. Here's the mission plan. I'm gonna walk west on 125th from here over to the A Train on Eighth, excuse me, Fredrick Douglass — that's two 's'es — Boulevard. I'm gonna cross the street back and forth a couple of times and get into whatever crowds are the biggest, and maybe do some window-shopping. Now — here's where You come in, pay attention: if You don't like my plan for *Kristallnacht*, — You know, salvation through abomination, suspension of the Law and all that — then I want You to strike me down. I'm serious. Dead. I mean, You don't have to do it Yourself. I'm sure there are many freakin-merkins in the next two blocks who would be willing to do it for you, free of charge even. So you get what I'm talking about? I'm either going to get from here to Eighth and down into the subway safely en route to Fordham Road, or I'm not. If I make it, I'll figure You want me to go ahead with Plan X. Clear? And although those occhi chorni are already staring at me, probably because of the color of my skin, or my Popeye forearms bulging out below my rolled-up shirtsleeves, or maybe it's even my propeller yarmulka, I will help clarify the issue for You and for posterity by acting somewhat outrageous so as not to disappear into the crowd.

"Did You know that October 19th is Jan Dismus Zelenka's 317th birthday? Of course You knew that, You know everything, but maybe You weren't keeping track. But now that I mention it, I'm sure You're as happy as I am. It's the little things in life that keep you going, don't You think? So, because it's Jan Dismus Zelenka's 317th birthday, and because it's thematically appropriate, and because when in Rome..., I've got my big CD boom-box here my brother Walter sent me out of pity and terror of my being any less than up to date — and thereby evading comparison with his material acquisitions — I've got my big black box with its sub-woofing attack dogs to boom out Zelenka's *Lamentations of Jeremiah* to the locals of color who of course don't know jack shit about classical music, well, not exactly classical, since Jan Dismus ain't exactly classic, more's the pity, but You know what I mean. They prob-ably also don't know jack shit about Jeremiah, and so I'm trying to kill three birds with one stone here — a music appreciation session, a bible lesson, and of course seeing if I can get myself killed.

"Now was Jeremiah stoned to death or what happened to him? So I'm going to stand in for the old boy here in this miserable resem-blance to Jerusalem, similar only to the extent that it has mosques, and damn well better convert to God — or Sodom and Gomorrah, here we come. 'Alan the Prophet' doesn't sound as good as Jeremiah or Eziekiel, but it's better than 'Bruce the Prophe', wouldn't You say? Or 'Chip'? Anyway, You only have to put up with it for two blocks, OK? Gimme the benefit of the doubt, I don't have much practice. I'll talk loud.

"So You ready? Does this interest You? Lemme just get this fuckin machine on to the right mode, let's see, CD, up the volume, up the bass equalization whatever the hell that is... and push Play! Mm, mm, mmm, that man sure knew how to scratch them viols.

228

"*Incipit* is right. It's only the beginning, my melaninic friends, only the beginning. *Bereshyt*. Stuff up your ears with earwax if you care not to hear, or tie yourselves to your own mast cells — because if you don't, it's —

"And standing in today for Jeremiah the Prophet, who was unavoidably detained on the way to the theater, is none other than Alan Krieger, Boy Wonder and Sometime Healer, for your edification and his own.

"*Aleph*. The first letter of the Hebrew alphabet, my friends. And where are all the Hebrew children? Must be out there weeping by the waters of Babylon and 125th St. Now Ladies and Gentlemen, such as you are, surely you know that the Hebrew letters, unlike your own paltry ABCs, such as they are, are not just transliterations of vocal sounds, but symbolic projections of biologically structured energies in different stages of organization. What? You didn't know that? Shame on you! What do they teach you in your crumbling schools?

"*Aleph*. Number one. The sound before all sounds. The archetype of the unthinkable, unrepresentable life-death. The abstract principle of all that is and all that is not.

"Whoops, I stepped on a crack there. Break your mother's back. My mother, not your mother. Hope she blames Walter, not me. Walter's my shitass brother, my mother's current keeper. But that's not your problem. You all are not my mother's keeper. Or my brother's. Step on a crack, you will find a black (selling crack, of course). Step on a black, you will get the sack. Not you, me. You don't work. I suppose I don't work anymore, either. But we digress.

"The city is lonely that was once full of people. The Harlem Renaissance down the tubes. Cain't get whitey up here any more sans gentrification. They don't believe in spooks, they just don't believe in spooks.

"*Facta est subtributo*. Oh, my goodness, you have become vassals, servants, slaves. Sound familiar, my friends? Why is that? Why have you always been, why will you always be, the underclass? Think there's any reason? Or is thinking too hard?

"Oop — here comes *Beth*. No, not that Beth, the twenty year old hot stuff with the six kids. *Beth* the second letter, the archetype of all dwellings, though you don't seem to care much about dwellings, but consider too, the archetype of all containers, nickle bags, hair pomade cans, prison cells. The physical support without which nothing is, without which *Aleph* life-death can't manifest. That's m-a-n-i-f-e-s-t, you literacy impairedniks, to show or display itself. Even as you do, half a million show-offs displaying themselves in three square miles. Intense, intense. Like overcrowded rats.

Do you like this music?

Hey, ma'am, you like this music? You do? Well, praise the Lord!"

"Praise the Lord, too, bro."

"I'm not your bro. I'm Walter's bro.

"And won't he be sorry? Sorrow and Pity and Terror. And here we are crying in the night. You, not me. I cry in the day only. You cry in the night because your deadbeat lovers have all split sans child support and there is none to comfort you, ceptin maybe the next lover.

"Oops, step on a crack, they'll call you a quack, though you, not I, are the ones into voodoo. Quack, quack, quack — you've said the magic word, Alan. Voodoo. Voodoo? We do. We charge you yield, in Queen Victoria's name. Sylvia's is around here somewhere. And if you listen very carefully, you can hear the duck quacking inside the wolf's stomach, because in his hurry, he mistook her for a plate of chitlins. Hey, even my mother's food tastes better than soul food, and she doesn't even *have* a soul.

"Better cross the street. People seem to be avoiding me on this side. Besides, those kids have to hear about how everybody has become their *inimicis*.

"Watch out, you fuckin idiot! Humans before vehicles!

"Top of the food chain! Give these apes a '62 Chevy, and they think they're Mario Andretti.

Ghimel, you on the south side of the street. *Ghimel*, the organic movement of every *Beth* goosed by *Aleph*. You ought to understand that, you jiggling jelly-rolls. Get them big, black *aleph*-ends inside you, you squirm around like *Ghimel*. Ghimel that old soft shoe, a one, a two, a doodly doodly doo — like that.

"I say there, sir, do you speak Latin?"

"Watch out, mufucka, you gonna get fucked over."

"Are you threatening me, sir?"

"No, man, you too big an asshole to take my time."

"And a pleasant day to you, too, sir.

"In exile, that is. Among the nations but *sans requiem*. Damn! Step on another crack, you'll become a hack. Me? Never! You'll be sent to Iraq. Fat chance. Blood pressure's too high, and besides, I'm too old. You'll turn into a macaque, and get AIDS. Only if I have sex with the locals. Step on a crack's an aphrodisiac. Maybe that explains this semiotic semi-erection. Hey! *Omnes persecutores ejus apprehenderunt eam inter augustisa.* Blame it on the Jewish landlords!

OK, made it to Seventh Ave. Adam Clayton Powell Boulevard. I can't believe they'd name anything after that crook, the prince of dubious practices. Keep the faith, baby.

"Hey, you, big black guy! Keep the faith!"

"You too, brother."

"I do, I do.

"You should only know. Look at that fucking state office building. Mario Cuomo shows his good faith to his loyal blacks.

"Hey man, you like this architecture?"

Well, that was a withering sneer! Hates it so much he won't even answer me. With architects like that, who needs Albert Speer? And Ah, The Teresa Towers, aka the Teresa Hotel, once the largest hotel in the world open to blacks.

"Hey, old mama, remember when Commandante Castro stayed here?"

"Sho do. He come dance at the block party."

"How come he stayed here?"

"Didn't want to stay with the rich people."

"You like that?"

"Don't you?"

"The gates are destroyed, Grandma, the virgins are dragged away."

"What you talkin?"

"Seventh Avenue ain't what it used to be."

"Well, ain't that the truth."

"Nice talkin to you."

"Peace, brother."

"Cross on the green, Alan. Fart shittr, by my green candle, this is too easy. What do I have to do to get struck down? I'll yell louder. *OPPRESSA EST. OP — PRESSA EST!* Old Z knows whereof he speaks. Skipped *Daleth*, no problem, only the symbol of all physical existence. Pop dismissed it all. But *Hay*, here, *Hay*, number five, the archetype of universal life. Make *Hay* when the sun shineth. Where would the Universal Life Church be without *Hay*? And all those guys that manufacture *Hay* pendants? *Hay* mucking around with *Daleth* can play the game of existence, together with *Aleph*, the intermittant life-death.

"What do you think of that, sir? Do you believe in intermittant life-death? I'm interviewing for the New York Times. Damn."

"What's the matter?"

"Stepped on another crack. Break your mother's back."

"What you talkin bout my mutha?"

"No. I was just saying the poem: Step on a crack, break your mother's back. You say that poem too? Not just melanin-deprived sons of Jewish mothers?"

"Man, it don't mean nothin. It's just a poem."

"Ah, I see. Poetry don't mean nothin. Something inherent in poetry, no doubt."

"No, man, it's just a kid poem, not a poem poem. Dont' you know nothin about poetry?"

"I'll go home and study, my friend. Thanks for reminding me.

"What's that? It's a fuckin rat! It's four feet long! I thought it was a giant dachshund, but it's a fuckin rat.

"Hey kids, look at that rat, just strolling along Martin Luther King Jr. Blvd. *Iniquitatem ejus.* Hey, man, look, there's a rat there. Arent' you going to do anything about it? You see that rat? Oops. Into the alley Did you see him?"

"How you know it was a him?"

"There aren't any girl rats. Rats are hims, and mice are hers. What do they teach you in biology? It was a big, sharp-toothed, guy rat."

"Well, shit, man, go call the CDC. Here's a dime."

"CDC? CDC? Whatta you know about the CDC? I'll take the dime, thanks."

"My mom lives in Atlanta. Don't spend it all in one place."

"What is this? I come down here with my boom box to preach to the heathens, I expect to be killed, and I wind up getting spare change. Without asking. And I missed the end of the first Lamentation. They missed the end of the first Lamentation. Should I rewind? Fart shittr, you can't rewind these things, and I never get the right button, and I always just go back to the beginning of the cut.

"Onward. Anyway, there'll be more bawling about conversion to the Lord later. CDC. Do Re Do. Do re do fa fa, ti do ti mi mi... Now there's a sequence Zelenka would never use.

"Hey, my little chickadee, am I in the vicinity of the famous Apollo ballroom?"

"Up a ways, right across the street."

"Thank you. As you can see, I'm from out of town. Did vou know that *Vav* expresses the fertilizing agent, that which impregnates? I wouldn't get too close to this boom box, if I were you."

"What's vav?"

"Oh, doctor, I have no idea how I could possibly have gotten pregnant."

"I'm not pregnant."

"You will be, you will be. With bazoomers like yours, before the year is out."

"Oh, Alan, any kiddie in school can love like a fool, but hating, my boy, is an art. Step on a crack, get ready to attack. Avoid the cul-de-sac. Don't go slack. If need be, sit on a tack. And he thought I didn't understand poetry!"

"Hey, man, I like your beanie. How much you want for it?"

"My dear, dark sir, this here is no beanie. This is a propellered yarmulka. Interstellar Propellar, I believe. It represents the foreskin detached from the eight-day old, the covenant in the flesh. The propeller represents *Ruah*, the breath of the Lord hovering over creation. The elephant represents the Republican Party."

"So how much?"

"Not for sale to the uncircumcized, my friend. I have not been mentally stripping you, but fifteen cents to your dime your shlong is ganz geputzed. And you're missing *Zain*, the seventh letter, the achievement of every vital impregnation, the opener of the field of every possibility, including the Seven Deadly Sins, and their secular variant, the Seven Deadly Enemies of Man. Remember Billy Batson walking down that long hallway to meet Shazam? Those statues: Pride, Envy, Greed, Hatred, Selfishness, Laziness, Injustice? (You'll note the remarkable absence of Lust.) Don't look stupid at me. Captain Marvel. Why do you think Billy Batson the crippled newsboy was turned into Captain Marvel, the big red cheese? To combat the Seven Deadly Enemies of Man. And Woman. Look around you, sir. You see any problem? Nuff said? And no, you can't buy the beanie. Go kill some kid for his sneakers.

"Gotta cross the street. See what's playing at the Apollo. Round many western islands have I been, which bards in fealty to Apollo hold. Oh, Billy, Ella, Duke, Count, Aretha, where are you now?

"What the...yikes...Ow

"Shit!

"Thus far in his great mercy has God led me. Look at my goddam arm. It's bleeding. It's scraped. I can't believe this."

"You ok, sweetie?"

"I don't know."

"You look dishevelled."

"Sorry. This is a new experience for me. Don't they put guards around open manholes? I'm gonna sue the shit out of the city."

"There was a guard, sweetie. You bumped it aside. You ok? None of your parts damaged?"

"Scraped off a piece of my psoriasis. Where are we? Whoops, Jerusalem sinned greviously and therefore she became filthy. That couldn't be me, I'm serving the Lord."

"Not filthy. Ignominius.

"A Latin speaker!"

"Cognates at the very least."

"OK, thanks. That's nice of you — merely ignominius. But the beginning of *Teth* coming up. The archetype of primeval female energy. Makes things clearer. "*Sordes*" is why *ignominius*."

"Like sordid."

"*Sordes*, thou good Samaritaness: dirt, filth, squalor. It *would* take primeval female energy to notice that."

"Well, you *are* filthy, sweetheart. Can't deny it. Filthy clothes, filthy mind. Can I pull you out, and we can be filthy together?"

"I weigh a lot."

"I weigh 220, darling."

"Women don't weigh 220. You're not even fat."

"I'm not even a woman."

"Whoa... what's going on here?"

"Grab on to my boa. I'll haul you up."

"Thanks but no thanks. I'll climb out myself."

"Now don't be silly and prejudiced, a smart Jewish man like you."

"How'd you know I was Jewish?"

"Who else knows Kabbalistic meanings of the Hebrew alphabet? Besides, you look Jewish."

"Well you don't. Actually, you do dress a little like Miami Beach. And that patch, echt Hathaway cyclops."

"Ah, *c'est moi, cherie*. And on the first guess, you smart cookie, let me eat you up! And Miami! The most exquisitely beautiful people in the world! Here, grab hold."

"That thing will never support my weight."

"Specially reinforced with steel chain for self-defense. One can never be too careful with these violent, transvestophobic masses. I've killed three people with it. Up you go."

"Into the wild blue yonder..."

"...Flying high, into the sky."

"Oi. Thanks. You sing beautifully — for a Marine."

"My name is Jack. You can call me Doreen. Jack — black, Doreen

— queen. Neato mnemonic, *n'est-ce pas?* And shut that damn thing off. I can barely hear myself think."

"Now? Just when we're starting the *Lamentations for Good Friday*?"

"It's October, silly."

"Of course it's October. October 19th. Zelenka's birthday."

"Who's Zelenka? Shut it off."

"No. Zelenka's the greatest composer in the history of the world, as you could tell if you weren't so ego-involved."

"Nobody can tell. There's too much distortion. It sounds like the underground works at Mount Pinotubo."

"I have to crank it up so they can hear. HE THAT HATH AN EAR, LET HIM HEAR. ARE YOU LISTENING OUT THERE?"

"What do you think?"

"No."

"Correct. So what are you doing?"

"I'm making a test."

"What are you testing?"

"None of your business."

"You're cute."

"You're repulsive."

"No, you're repulsive."

"How can I be cute and repulsive at the same time?"

"Cabbage Patch dolls are cute and repulsive at the same time."

"Well, you're just repulsive."

"Why?"

"Cause one-eyed men shouldn't dress like women."

"Why? Oh, what does the Scotchman have under his quilt? Shlong, shlong. You think Socrates wore a three piece suit? Or a Hell's Angel jacket?"

"But you also act like a woman."

"Hauling 200 pound putzes out of the sewer?"

"I don't want to have sex with you. I'm normal."

"You're normal? On what planet?"

"Look, Jack..."

"Doreen."

"Doreen. I've gotta finish my plan here. I've got a lot hanging on it."

"I've got a lot hanging on me."

"There are more important things in this world."

"Like what?"

"Like trying to influence the struggle between good and evil."

"Which side are you on?"

"What do you think?"

"How boring."

«*Chacun a son gout, mon ami.*»

"Chacun a son goo, too."

"Look, I can't tell you what this is all about. I just have to see if I can get over to Eighth Avenue, get onto the A train, and get to Fordham Road in one piece. A third of a block to go."

"Give me a call when things settle out. Here's my card."

"IBM???"

"Why not? Big building. Plenty of closets."

"I'm not into sex with men."

"I can see that. But I want to know more about your experiment. I'm a good listener. I ask good questions. Personnel Consultant. It's right there on the card."

"Well, maybe I will. I have to see."

"If you decide to sue the city, leave me out. Good Samaritaness. Despised and rejected by all, but worthy nonetheless."

"Gotcha. Besides, you'd only testify against me."

"There *was* a guard rail, hon. You were just too whacked out to see it."

"Thanks. Maybe I'll catch you later."

"Bye, whatever your name is."

"Alan. Krieger."

"The Warrior. A dangerous profession. You can get killed being a warrior. See you later."

"*Jerusalem, convertere ad Dominum Deum tuum. Jerusalem, convertere ad Dominum Deum tuum.* Hey you kids, *convertere ad Dominum tuum,* and I don't mean crack."

ESSAYS CRITICAL

Heidegger and Death

My laughable attempt to sum up Being and Time *in a few pages. Nevertheless, Heidegger's concept of "Being-toward-death" reigns throughout Gregor's story.*

Gregor examined the volume in his hand: *Jahrbuch für Philosopie und phänomenologische Forschung, Band VIII.*

"I tried to read it several times at the end of the twenties," Weisskopf continued, "but it was hard, and there wasn't enough time to really study it. I knew only a little about Heidegger then, but I soon found out more than enough: The man is an absolute Nazi."

"Why, what...?"

"I was living in Berlin in '32 and early '33. The bands of brown-shirted students were roaming the streets, beating up Jewish students — or anybody that looked Jewish. My office looked out on the university courtyard — a front row seat. The police didn't interfere, of course, and more than once I had to pull a Jewish student into my office so he could escape through the back door. Heidegger was put up for University Rector, but the faculty resisted. The students took them on — these same violent Nazi students, clamoring for their man, Heidegger. I'm not sure how many of them knew exactly his politics, but he was a young, radical professor, extremely popular with all those students fed up with academic conservatism. They wanted to ask the big questions, to overthrow traditional thought. Heidegger's lecture notes were being circulated in mimeograph — they seemed truly revolutionary. The more the faculty was threatened, the more the students were for him. And he was for them, demanding active participation at all times — active participation from all militant philosophy students! Discipline. Service. He replaced Husserl at Freiburg, and as Hitler rose, so did he. In May of '33 he was appointed Rektor of the University. His inauguration address was so important it was printed in the *Berliner Tageblatt* — and we knew where things stood."

"What did he say?"

"I can't quote you chapter and verse, but it became the bible of Nazi university reform. It was about self-determination of German universities, and need to develop leaders to bring Germany to its spiritual destiny — the German radical students who were already marching. So-called academic freedom had to be expelled because it was, he thought — - I remember this phrase — 'no more than taking it easy, being arbitrary in one's inclinations, and taking license in everything.' This is academic freedom? The most extremist students had to lead the faculty to discover its real destiny in service to the state. He ended by quoting Plato: 'All greatness stands firm in the storm...' The language was Nazi language — stupid and obsequious, heroic nationalism, the general, empty ravings of a party hack in power. This, from the genius author of *Sein und Zeit!* "

"What did he do as rector?"

"What did he do? He expelled all the Jews on the teaching staff, he made every faculty member fill out a questionnaire on his racial origins and take an oath about his racial purity, he made the Nazi salute obligatory before and after class, he organized a University Department of Racial Matters directed by the SS, he took all financial subsidy away from Jewish students and gave it to SA and SS militants, he set up mandatory classes on racial theory, on military science, on German culture... Let's see...What else?"

"Thank you. That's enough."

Ellen brought in a plate of crackers and cream cheese, but G was too upset to eat them, and took his leave as soon as was polite, his "gift" trembling in his claw. The mid-January sky showered him with Heisenbergian cosmic rays as he made his short way home from Weisskopf's, placed the questionable book down on the table, and lay down in the straw to think.

For all of Weisskopf's vehemence, Gregor was still curious. More than curious: he could swear he felt a definite force, pulling him toward the black object on his table. How could he reconcile the two opinions of Weisskopf and Arendt? Vicky was one of the most widely educated Europeans on site, a gentle man of culture, an excellent pianist. She was a major thinker — he had heard of her. Maybe she was his lover back in her student days, when, in the twenties? But why would she be still so enthusiastic now, after his Rectorship, in light of his Nazism? He had to at least look between the covers. He opened the book at random: "67. *Der Grundbestand der existentialen Verfassung des Daseins und die Vorzeichnung ihrer zeitlichen Interpretation.*" "67. The Basic Content of Dasein's Existential Constitution, and a Preliminary Sketch of the Temporal Interpretation of it." Better start at the beginning.

Like Vicky, he found the reading hard, even as a native speaker. It was not just that he had been away from the language for many years, and was superficially rusty. Heidegger's strategy seemed to involve destroying or digging under, around and through the everyday language which formed a concealing crust over the problem he was pursuing. Gregor decided that on first reading he would skip the parts that were too complex to easily follow. Still, and in spite of the noisy party going on at Fuller Lodge, he was able to make a first beachhead in the difficult terrain. Surprisingly, it was for him the most intense of page-turners.

He read of Heidegger's fascination with *Dasein* as an object of investigation which might reveal the nature of Being itself — not the collection of qualities that different beings manifest, not the grammatical convention, the empty copula of "The ball is blue", but "is-ness" itself — what "is" is — behind all manifestation. "Reveal" — in the way that Arendt had used it — creating a clearing in the world's "hiddenness" so that pure Being might be experienced. *Dasein* seemed for Heidegger a specifically human characteristic, humans — the being that inquires into *Dasein* — but he knew it was broader than that, for it seemed to relate even to him. *Dasein*, *da-sein*, there-being. But where is "there"? In some abstract, German philosophical space? No! There is here, in the world. *Dasein* was all the possibilities G was in all his relationships with people, objects, events in his everyday world. This seemed potentially rich, perhaps even rewarding. Thank you, Doktor Arendt.

The language was strange, twisted, violently hyphenated as only German can be. There were new, made-up words existing in neither German or English — like *nichten*, "to nothing". He learned that not only he, but everyone, had been "thrown" into the world, so that *Dasein* was a *Geworfenheit*, a "thrownness", into the infinite facets of "thing-ness" and "factness", and that because of our deep association with things, and others-as-things, we come not-to-be-ourselves. Gregor's flesh tingled under his carapace. He read Heidegger's intense portrayal of *Dasein's* self-estrangement in "publicness" in which every kind of spiritual priority is suppressed in a leveling down of sentiment and expression, in which "every secret loses its force" as "something that has long been well-known." The passivity and even barbarism of the "they", were just extensions of their everydayness, bearing no moral responsibility and no ethical guilt.

Gregor needed to take a breather from such searing intensity. He took a five minute stroll under the cool sky. The party at the Lodge seemed to be winding down. He thought of the *Daseins* inside, enveloped in their small-talk, in the prefabricated flux of conventional sentiment and mindless curiosity, indulging in what Heidegger was now characterizing as "inauthentic life", an inevitable and distinctive component of "being-in-the-world". He felt distant from them, and in this distance was aware of his *Angst* — a repudiation of his *Dasein's* "theyness". Did he need fur-ther alienation from his fellow creatures? Nevertheless, the book called to him, and he returned to its perusal, refreshed.

"Inauthenticity" — bad? No, necessary, Heidegger explained, as if preternaturally commenting on Gregor's recent thoughts about the Fuller partiers. Alienation was positive because *Dasein*, when made aware of its loss of self, was motivated to strive to return to authentic being. "Fallenness" into "facticity" was an absolutely necessary precon-dition for the struggle toward true *Dasein*, toward repossession of self. It reminded him of the *felix culpa* of the Christians, Adam's "happy fall" which set up the ongoing drama of human redemption by God. But here, there was no "God", only a call to authenticity.

And then — there it was — the term he had been looking for, the condition he had been wanting to know about since reading the letter: *Sorge*, care. Care seemed to be the relationship between the inauthenticity of being-in-the-world and the striving for *Dasein*. How tantalizing this was. It seemed it might answer questions that had flitted, ghostly, through his heartmind, never standing long enough to be posed. We feel *unheimlich*, Heidegger says, "homeless", "unhoused" in *Angst*, and *Dasein* reacts by anchoring into a *Dasein*-for, *Sorge*, "care-for", "concern-for and -with", a concern for others something like solicitude — all in moving towards a larger *Sorge*, a caring-for, an answerability-to Being itself, a Being that transfigures beings. Desire and hope are the reaching out of Care, a reaching out toward freedom. Gregor felt inundated in a newly-discovered reality of his own essence: I care, therefore I am. Care, says Heidegger, is the primordial state of *Dasein's* being as it strives towards authenticity.

Years of unadmitted pain seemed to melt away as Gregor reconceived his own story in the bright light of this black-covered volume. This was respite larger than another walk under Orion's sword, and he plowed on, ecstatic, to Part II, the section on Time, with its central image, the punch-line as it were — the section on "Being-towards-Death." His joy-ride came to a screeching halt.

Sein-zum-Tode. Being-towards-Death. According to Heidegger, *Dasein* can achieve wholeness only when it faces its "no-longer-being-there", its *nicht-mehr-da-sein*. There is nothing with more potential for authenticity than one's own death. No power of "theyness" can take away this fundamental truth — that all authentic being is a being-toward-its-own-end. Heidegger quotes a medieval homily which Gregor had often heard in Prague: "As soon as man is born, he is old enough to die." Death is perhaps the identifying phenomenon of life: *Dasein* cannot "be" without its end.

The they-world is not unaware of this phenomenon, and has created many evasions of authentic death: euphemisms, social taboos, medical optimism and death-talk. Gregor thought of his friends working in the "Gadget Division", creating a death machine without equal in the history of the world, yet never — never! — mentioning the word. No Dead Christ realism here! A true being-toward-the-end, says Heidegger, is one which continually tries to keep in focus its own finitude "in an impassioned FREEDOM TOWARD DEATH — a freedom which has been released from the illusions of the 'they'" Freedom. Freedom. Gregor had never felt so strongly the chitinous fetters which bound him. Being-towards-death was the absolute condition of freedom.

And here Victor Weisskopf's voice came to him, in an I-told-you-so aria on Teutonic death-obsession, images of Dr. Lindhorst, the operating room table, Hans Holbein, the *Leiermann*, the *Liebestod*. But even within this morbid miasma he still felt the inalienability of his personal death as a profoundly bracing, even liberating, awareness, and in the uncertain glimmer of the end of night, he read about *Dasein's* authenticity manifesting in conscience, summons and resoluteness. In resolutely projecting itself forward toward its own free death, *Dasein* attains its personal and social destiny. The 7:25 siren reoriented him to everyday space and time in all its fallenness. "Oppie has whistled," as Fermi was wont to say.

The Wonderful Wizard of Oz

Behind the Emerald Curtain

In 1892, eight years before he was catapulted to fame by *The Wonderful Wizard of Oz*, Lyman Frank Baum must surely have read this Preamble to the Populist Party Platform:

> *We meet in the midst of a nation brought to the verge of moral, political and material ruin. Corruption dominates the ballot box, the legislatures, the congress, and touches even the ermine of the bench. The people are demoralized. The newspapers are subsidized or muzzled; public opinion silenced...and the land concentrated in the hands of capitalists.*
>
> *Urban workmen are denied the right of organization for self-protection; imported pauperized labor beats down their wages; the fruit of the toil of millions are boldly stolen to build up colossal fortunes. From the same prolific womb of governmental injustice we breed two classes — paupers and millionaires.*

Sound familiar? Make you mad? It made him mad, too, and four years later, he marched in torchlight parades for William Jennings Bryan, the Populist candidate who lost to McKinley. "You shall not press down on the brow of labor this crown of thorns," Bryan said, "You shall not crucify mankind on a cross of gold." The crowds cheered, and so did Baum.

The Wonderful Wizard of Oz is a product of that man and his times, both an abiding fairy tale (the first crafted from American themes), and a clever, wry, ironic allegory of economic, social and political affairs in 1900 America. As readers or viewers a hundred years from now will have little understanding of "modified limited hangout" or "Monicagate", so audiences today have little feel for the cultural context of Oz apparent both to Baum and his initial readers. What did they understand which we don't, though the story still charms?

Turn-of-the-century America was a land awash in conflict over race, class and money. Midwestern farmers were organizing to resist the aggressive capitalism of east coast financiers, a struggle symbolized in the 1890s by the Populists' Free Silver Movement. Gold belonged to international bankers in the big cities; silver belonged to the folks out west, and expanded currency came to be seen as a symbol of economic justice for the masses of the American people.

Baum was most sympathetic to this agrarian world view, with its critique of the false and destructive values of international capital. Look at what happened to the Tin Man — a worker turned from a human being into a heartless machine by the Wicked Witch of the East — the dehumanizing effects of capital and industrialism. Dorothy's journey reveals the dangers and promises facing the heartland from sectional powers. Oz is a confusing, alienating, and beautiful, but dangerous, world, not unlike our own.

With the establishment of the Federal Reserve System in 1910, the original monetary issues had so receded from public consciousness that the makers of the 1939 film felt free to change the most basic metaphor of the book: Baum's silver shoes became the famous ruby slippers (better in technicolor!), while the Witch's golden hat was replaced with a crystal ball. Still, the skeleton remains: Oz is the abbreviation for ounces — the measure of silver and gold; the constraining, yet dangerous path that leads to the city of central power is made of yellow bricks; all the inhabitants of the capital wear glasses the color of greenbacks which colors their view; and finally, the leader is a fraud, his power a product of secrecy and spin.

Baum was of the school of thought of Louis Mayer (MGM): "If I want to send a message, I'll use a telegram." Consequently the political allegory is always secondary to the general story, and is readily abandoned whenever it might detract from "wholesome" teachings for children — his stated goal. Thus, one might ponder the apparent contradiction: though the Wizard rules by fear and deceit, he is actually "a good man." Is this just a little "nicey-nice", or does it represent a deeper understanding of the struggle between humanity and power? Our current President offers us similar questions to ponder.

Certainly the Wizard is benevolent in recognizing the Scarecrow's real intelligence, the Tin Man's real capacity for feeling, and the Cowardly Lion's real courage. In the Populist tradition, he empowers ordinary people with their own enduring values of common sense, compassion and courage. And so, each is able to achieve the master goal of the story: finding home. At the same time, Baum's humane vision is achieved by shifting the focus away from systematic questions: why is the country divided into sections and warring races, why are good people ruled by evil rulers, why, even, is Kansas, the heartland, such a miserable place? Thus he anticipates postmodern political paralysis: just heal yourself, and everything will be all right. (And thus, the power structure endures.)

But I feel we must respect Baum's instinct for this overwhelmingly successful work: *The Wonderful Wizard of Oz* should not be overweighted with such questions. There are many paths to existential, cultural or political home. Dorothy's journey has moved people for a hundred years — across class, race, sexual, educational and regional lines — because it illustrates, simply and imaginatively, T.S. Eliot's thought from "Little Gidding":

> We shall not cease from exploration
> And the end of all our exploring
> Will be to arrive where we started
> And know the place for the first time.

Letter Exchange

Two Kafka Parables

A LETTER EXCHANGE
between
GREGOR SAMSA,
HEALTH MAINTENANCE CONSULTANT,
THE MANHATTAN PROJECT,
and
HANNAH ARENDT,
concerning
HER PARTISAN REVIEW ARTICLE (v.11, FALL 1944),
"FRANZ KAFKA, A RE-EVALUATION ON THE OCCASION OF
THE TWENTIETH ANNIVERSARY OF HIS DEATH"

P.O. Box 1663
Santa Fe, New Mexico
August 30, 1944

Very Honored Doktor Arendt:

You possibly find this funny or rude, but two months ago I buy new copy of THE TRIAL and try to set on fire. I fill a buket with paper and kindling paper, make nice fire, perfect for auto-da-fe, and throw book into flames. It fast puts flame out, my room fill with smoke, the fire brigade arrive and I have bad time to explain my actions to firemen.

However, I explain to you. I just red your "re-evaluation" in the Partisan Review and feel — while you make certain points against grain of most opinion — you in the end to join a critics crowd who worship an idol that walks on the world with poisonous steps.

For you, Herr Kafka is important Jewish outsider using his only weapon - thought - against a "falsely created world". You see his characters as "facing society with an attitude of constructive defiance, open aggression", ready for takeing a stand against such a world "for the sake of human values". You make M. Kafka a man of the Enlightenment, an emancipation moralitist who writes of his utopian, romantic faith in Reason.

But this is surely not true. The heroes of this writer are not ever fighters. The book is fascist and its characters are terible creations of such terible world. What kind of models are they for a reader? Herr Kafka's characters react to the most terifying events as if they were simply normal. They perform their duties without understanding, in blind obedience. To follow the rules is more importent than what the rules are, more importent than the moralitat of the rulers. In Herr Kafka's world there is no freedom because there is no real self to be free. There is no real personality, no real love. Human beings turn to apes, dogs, moles, mice - even insects — who struggle in ungeklärte interpretations, full of nothing but not-productive hypotheses. This is a world of no-freedom, and whatever transformation Herr Kafka offers leads only to dammnation.

I agree with you that Herr Kafka "sounds the alarm" and describes the world "as it is, and as it should not be." But does it make free to portray the madness of the world? Very much not. Mister Kafka makes a destructive, bleak image of the way things simply ARE. He offers no political or social vision, no encouragement for members of any human community, just a nihilism makeing alienation and dehumanization. His characters are victims of inexplicable forces, helpless in fear and chaos. They are not able to reflect. They can only sit "outside the Law", silent and listen.

Herr Kafka's stories may be of service to intellectuals with their feelings of helplessment and self-loathing, but they just justify the ways of a banale, bureaucratic, not-understandable fascist system. Readers could become Mr. Kafka's victims, unfit for life, tied to death, tangled in his endless confusions and confusions not proposeing any solutions to the problems and will never, in Kleist's beautiful words, help humans "Ein Feld zu bebauen, einen Baum zu pflanzen, und ein Kind zu zeugen." His dis-ezed universe, un-penetrable, abnormal, offers no human dignity to a race in dire need of such. Does everything need question, the whole Gestalt of the West?

You and I certainly share the same goal: to free human spirit from dictator institutions and machine rule. But the totale pessimism of this Prague insurance agent, convinced of the impossibility of all assurance — does that serve human needs? In short, Herr Kafka is bad for the world. I hope you will agree, go against current opinion, and truly "reevaluate" this overrated writer.

Highest regards,
George Samson

****

365 W. 95th St.
New York 25, N.Y.
20 December 1944

Dear Mr. Samson,

Thank you for your provocative letter. I hope you will have patience with the extended answer I believe such a letter demands.

I must admit I found your auto-da-fe amusing, though not for its slapstick quality. Rather it demonstrates an unfortunately typical misdirection of goodwill: destroying the messenger does not invalidate bad tidings.

We agree, I think, on the message Kafka brings to a misconstructed world: the ancient admonition to "Know Thyself." The truth of our time must be disclosed or uncovered from within its all-pervasive and seductive trappings. It requires a scalpel as sharp as Kafka's to do such deep surgery. Modern man stands amidst the confusion of the time and seeks guidance, and Kafka provides not only guidance, but the intellectual momentum for constructive escape.

Let us look together at two of Kafka's little parables, in some ways contrasting, even contradictory, and in some ways additive. Here is the first:

"He is a free and secure citizen of the world, for he is fettered to a chain which is long enough to give him the freedom of all earthly space, and yet only so long that nothing can drag him past the frontiers of the world. But simultaneously he is a free and secure citizen of Heaven as well, for he is also fettered by a similarly designed heavenly chain. So that if he heads, say, for the earth, his heavenly collar throttles him, and if he heads for Heaven, his earthly one does the same. And yet all the possibilities are his, and he feels it; more, he actually refuses to account for the deadlock by an error in the original fettering."

Even so is the world, a place where freedom and security is protected by chains which, while not seriously limiting earthly activity, keep one from falling off. But Kafka tells us that earthly freedom — that granted by "the world" — is not enough. For there is a dimension of other-than-earthly activity which also belongs to any citizen of the world: he is bound also to this transcendent realm, and gives up his citizenship at his peril. That is Kafka's first great message: not one of limitation, but one of transcendent connection, a connection which also protects from too great immersion in the ordinary. True, there is conflict, tension, even paralysis in this situation, and you, Mr. Samson, may see the protagonist as defeated by his sadistic author. But the protagonist is not defeated. He is actually aware of the possibility that there is no error in the structure, that if deeply perceived and adroitly handled he may be able to bountifully operate within these strictures, as a poet does within the limitations of sonnet form. It is not stubbornness or stupidity behind his analysis. It is the smell of real freedom.

The second story is this:

"He has two antagonists: the first presses him from behind, from the origin. The second blocks the road ahead. He gives battle to both. To be sure, the first supports him in his fight with the second, for he wants to push him forward, and in the same way the second supports him in his fight with the first, since he drives him back. But it is only theoretically so. For it is not only the two antagonists who are there, but he himself as well, and who really knows his intentions? His dream, though, is that some time in an unguarded moment — and this would require a night darker than any night has ever yet been — he will jump out of the fighting line and be promoted, on account of his experience in fighting, to the position of umpire over his antagonists in their fight with each other."

The most obvious level of this tale concerns man embattled between the forces of the past and the imperatives of the given future. It pictures a crushing, suffocating thought-world miraculously evaded. However you choose to interpret the story, Mr. Samson, it again urges corrective action. True, the night will have to be at its darkest — to provoke, to inspire and to hide — but such a condition is already a regular occurrence in our dark times. And the man who can dream such a jump, such a discontinuity, such a transformation, that man is more than halfway toward its realization. Let Kafka whisper in your ear, and things may evolve which have never appeared before.

Forgive my presumption in suggesting that you concentrate not on the fetters, or the darkness of the night, but rather on the taut potential for situational metamorphosis. Kafka discloses what our blinded eyes have ceased to see, and such revelation has the power to trigger the springs of action.

As it has not yet appeared in English, and would be difficult in any case to penetrate, I imagine you have not read BEING AND TIME, the work of my friend and teacher, Martin Heidegger. It is impossible to summarize this complex work, but let me alert you to its existence, and hope you will spend some time with it when you can. To whet your appetite, let me simply mention that a key node in the work concerns the experience of "Angst", a word with no English equivalent, approximately rendered by "uneasiness" or "malaise," a feeling of non-normality occasionally experienced by reflective and serious people, perhaps you yourself. Common things may seem uncanny, odd or unfamiliar, as if from some other planet. Heidegger argues that Angst is a crucial experience in pushing beyond the "they-world", a blinding, deafening, stultifying continuum of idle talk and stereotyped expectations. One who is transformed by Angst is given the space to escape such a world — by seeing how strangulating it really is. Kafka's heros are characterized by nothing so much as Angst, and are therefore given an opportunity to transcend denied to most people. Inasmuch as the reader identifies with these characters, they too, are asked to see the world as unheimlich — uncanny, but also etymologically "not-at-home", and themselves as no longer unquestioning members of the "they". Kafka's animals are the supreme metaphors of potentially redemptive self-alienation. The animal metamorphoses you mention — into "apes, dogs, moles, mice — even insects" are not simply "regressions" — these characters are adventurers out of the "they-world" into the the possibility of other experience and deeper understanding. There may be many "unresolved interpretive furies" and "unproductive hypotheses", but Kafka's writing would not be "true" were it otherwise.

You may be interested in Heidegger's understanding of the fruits of Angst, painful as they may be. Angst draws out, e-ducates, the authentic self, which then interacts with an authenticated world via Sorge, or care, both caring-about and caring-for.

Again at the risk of being presumptuous, let me say that you seem to be a caring person, perhaps just by nature, or perhaps after having experienced some kind of transformative Angst. My counter-suggestion to you is that you be the one to re-evaluate this extraordinary prophet and teacher, and to engage him not as an enemy, but as a friend. "An enemy," as the Russian proverb says, "will give in, but a friend will argue." Kafka never does give in, does he?

I remain yours sincerely,

Hannah Arendt

Peter Watkins' *La Commune*

The Paris Commune — a citizens' revolt against a royalist government, the organizing of that revolt, and the crushing of it by government forces, all in the course of three months in 1871.

After staring at a screen for 345 minutes, my wife and I — completely revved — looked at one another, and both asked the same question: "Are we doing enough?" What an outcome from seeing a film we expected to tax our endurance.

Peter Watkins' *La Commune (Paris 1871)* is unlike any other political film I've seen. I've previously been appalled by suffering depicted, awed at Davids fighting huge Goliaths, frustrated, and angered and stressed. But never before have I felt so personally challenged to think acutely through my beliefs, to measure my own action against my ideology.

Watkins achieves this effect via an astonishing conceptual move which greatly expands the potential for the art of political film. Assembling a group of 200 non-professional actors, he asked them to research their roles in the great insurrection, and to so understand the history of their characters as to be able to speak for them in interviews, in modern language, perhaps, but accurately, and with passion.

His players thus had to grapple with six different personae, three personal and three collective:

— the historical figures, individually, and as class members at a defining moment of history;

— themselves, as actors presenting those figures, playing them out while simultaneously judging them, à la Brecht;

— themselves, as themselves, as individuals come together for an ambitious, artistic/political project, and also as groups, say of men vs. women.

In the course of making the film, these 200 people had to build their own commune, to establish decision-making groups around their work, and the agenda of the project itself.

What we see is startlingly unrealistic. We are shown around the "studio" by a pair of commentators from "Commune TV", dressed, as is everyone, in nineteenth century garb, but utilizing hand-held mikes for their reporting. Written commentary flows throughout the film, describing historical events in great detail; the viewer comes out well instructed as to actual history, sometimes with modern comparisons. In general, the rhythm proceeds from these historical introductions to the scenes described, action and interviews, with frequent cuts to contrasting reports from effete anchors on National TV. Thus, *La Commune* is also about the media: some news for communards, different news for the haute bourgeoisie. Commune TV itself is also critiqued, with one reporter wanting to self-censor to better serve the struggle, and the other arguing for objectivity.

In the course of scenes and interviews, we experience the difficulty of creating a just society in the midst of competing world views, strategies at odds, and varying levels of commitment — and the threat of external force. At the same time, we come to understand the individual struggles which must occur at such potentially world-changing moments. Beyond the designated enemy, who else is the enemy? Does a revolution require a guillotine?

Once the social/historical background is laid, the radical nature of the project emerges with increasing intensity, as Commune reporters start to intercut their interviews with different kinds of questions: Not What are you, the character, thinking?, but what are YOU, the actor, thinking about what's going on? What IS going on — not for the character you are playing, but for YOU? Would YOU do today what your character did in history? Such questioning begins gently, so that the actors can be reflective about their answers, but finally it intrudes, overwhelms, fiercely, passionately, right at the peak of the barricades. In the feverish pitch of their historical action, almost hysterical actors are badgered, mercilessly, about their personal reality.

The film emerges as a theater of cruelty, as these amateurs try to access such schizophrenia in the midst of their characters' life and death struggles. The level of emotional and intellectual intensity is unmatched, especially compared to the smoothness of normal, professional productions. And it is here — in this harassment — that the film becomes uniquely interactive. For viewers, rather than settling into the problems of the characters portrayed, are caught up in the inquisitorial demands of the interviewer, and absolutely MUST ask themselves the kinds of questions my wife and I were forced to face. Paradoxically, it is via such a non-realistic theatrical contrivance that Watkins achieves total breakdown of aesthetic distance. Astounding.

During the final third of the film the momentum becomes so great and potentially exhausting that the audience is given occasional breaks as the cast comes together to discuss the actual making of the film, the contemporary and personal politics (especially sexual) that got swept under the rug, or hidden behind the historical story. Yet, though the tempo goes from allegro agitato to andante, one's interest is further intensified by meeting the individuals involved, and comparing their experiences with one's own.

For theater and film folks, *La Commune* is an outstanding primer of Brechtian technique, with a compositional strategy reminiscent of the Living Theater's *Paradise Now*, or Peter Brook's *Marat/Sade*. The emergence of Artaudian effects from Brechtian theory is nowhere better seen.

Yet the prime importance of this work is as an organizing tool. If political action in your community is plagued by low energy or lack of commitment, a viewing of *La Commune* should solve that type of problem, for no one can leave it at the same ethical or intellectual energy level as before. The political difficulties depicted are daunting; some might find them depressing. Yet witnessing them so clearly can warn us of our own, contemporary, traps.

This is a film of first rate importance for current political struggle. Stream it, rent it, show it, if you possibly can.

Where She Stops Nobody Knows

Aug 31, 2007
Margo Lee Sherman, an old friend, an extraordinary actress, and one of the original puppeteers, came up this summer to do a one-woman show at the Bread & Puppet farm. Here is a promo piece I wrote for her coming:

Christmas season, 1966. The Vietnam war is heating up. At St. Patrick's Cathedral in New York, Cardinal Spellman calls for Victory, Victory!

On the great cathedral steps, among the shopping crowds, a young woman in black holds a bloodstained doll, while her partner in white carries a sign reading : I AM MARY. MY BABY WAS NAPALMED IN VIETNAM.

The police arrive to stop the Nativity performance, threatening arrest. The women descend, and place the bloody Christ-child on the sidewalk.

A cop: "You can't leave that there!"

"Why not?"

"It's littering."

I AM MARY MY BABY WAS NAPALMED IN VIETNAM. The young woman carrying the bloodied infant was Margo Lee Sherman, and the event was one of the earliest creations of Peter Schumann's Bread & Puppet Theater — and in my opinion, one of the greatest pieces of political street theater in history.

Margo Lee Sherman is an extraordinary actress because she is an extraordinary person. Her way is slow, her voice deep, her timing devastating. If you asked her for the time, and she said simply "8:15", you might break out crying. She has that kind of an affect, that kind of tone, that kind of diction. The smallest of her gestures is enormous.

And here she is, forty years and thirty one-woman shows later, still noting the same tears flooding the world, speaking them, sharing them, and calling them forth, still horrified.

Her choice of material is varied and subtle. For example, *What Do I Know About War?* was born from a story about Capt. Terrance Wright, who returned from Iraq and couldn't stop hiccuping. Hiccuping, that's funny. what a riot. Well, apparently not for Capt. Wright, who was later found in a Fayetteville motel room — dead — from what the Army called "an unknown illness."

OK then, hiccuping. Odd, maybe even grotesque. But what is hiccuping? Spasm of the diaphragm followed involuntarily by spasm of the glottis. Spasm. Spasms. Like Iraq? Involuntary, out of control, impossible to stop by willing. Chronic hiccuping? One's humanity is left behind. Drinks in the hand are spilled and cups are broken. People make fun, and then avoid you, a victim of forces beyond your control.

The tiny actress makes big noises: explosions, gunfire, IEDs. Where have I heard these sounds before? Ah — those little boys with their Tonka tanks and Mattel space guns, making sounds that defy orthography, usually followed with "...you're dead!" Little boys — like those 18-year olds with automatic weapons, making — in their great wisdom — life and death decisions for whole families, whole towns of "dirty ragheads" and "sand-niggers." That's where I've heard those sounds before. Little boys.

Such subtleties, conscious and unconscious, reverberate through-out the piece because, as a current Bread & Puppet sideshow sings, "Everything, everything, everything is everything." Margo knows this, intensely, and the planet knows it, and humans need desperately to learn it.

An hour-long show, and for many of us a long trip to see it. But in its many contexts — the silences it must provoke, the discussions driv-ing home, the expanded understanding, beyond casualty figures, of the human costs of war, the new wariness with which to hear claims of its "success" — the show is a long one, and huge. Like Margo Lee Sherman herself, tiny, tenacious, and deep.

Franz Kafka Does Thanksgiving

He eats the droppings from his own table; thus he manages to stuff himself fuller than the others for a time, but meanwhile he forgets how to eat from the table, and so in time even the droppings cease to fall.

What can we make of this tiny tale? For one thing, "he" is greedy enough to be crawling around, picking up droppings, and stuffing them back into his mouth. He is rich enough for excess, and sloppy enough to be spewing it around. Sounds a bit like America, profligate with her resources, her goods, her arms, her ideology, showering the rest of the planet with the consequences of such "richness".

Kafka's parable says this can't go on. We cease to understand the bounties on our table. We no longer say "Much obliged." Obliged for what? Obliged to whom? We're the one who needs to be thanked—by the Third World for "market reform"; by the poor the world over for the loans which enable them to keep paying loans; for our arms to prop up their corrupt, American-approved governments; for their opportunity to deal with our wastes, and clean up after our parties.

But the reckoning will come: if Kafka says so, then the reckoning will come. For all the lust for short-term gain, there are signs aplenty that the planet and its people will protest, and rise up against impossible systems of injustice.

For this at least, let us give thanks.

Happy Birthday, Existence!

"I'm depressed." A most common comment. Depressed about what? The answers are various: our dangerous, deaf, moronic leadership, the ongoing wars, religious strife, public and private corruption, joblessness, lack of child care, housing, perverse spending priorities, the entire fate of the earth. So I thought I might bring some cheer this month by calling for a birthday celebration, a BIG birthday celebration—the October 23rd anniversary of the birth of ... EXISTENCE.

That's right. On October 23rd, 4004 BC, at 4PM, Eastern Standard Time, or midnight in the Garden of Eden, God created the heavens and the earth. And the earth was without form and void.

Such was the conclusion of James Ussher (1581-1656), Archbishop of Armagh, Primate of All Ireland, and Vice-Chancellor of Trinity College in Dublin, after profound and exhaustive study of scriptural genealogies and Middle Eastern and Mediterranean histories. His conclusion was incorporated into an authorized version of the Bible printed in 1701, and thus came to be regarded with almost as much unquestioning reverence as the Bible itself.

Six thousand and twenty-seven years old! That's a lot of years. And after all that time, what have we come to? *The Decline of the West*.

Way back in 1919, Oswald Spengler saw it all, the grand pattern, the "inward form of History", repeating through all recorded time, and in every major culture, including ours.

"For everything organic the notions of birth, death, youth, age, lifetime are fundamentals..."

He saw all cultures come into springlike being, youthful and vigorous, flower in their summery, unique ways, and then autumnally decay. Their winters were frozen into rigid, petrified forms, and these forms he called "civilization". Our Western culture had been born around the tenth century, flowered in the gothic and the Renaissance, became "civilized" in the eighteenth century, and in the nineteenth century, with the industrial revolution, had begun the process of spiritual decline. The upcoming death of Western Culture was as certain as that of any other living organism. History was Destiny, unfolded through the cycle of human cultures, all of which shared a common rhythm and pattern. We cannot choose our destiny, we cannot alter it. We have no choice but to make the best of our historical situation.

Stark. Dramatic. No wonder it attracted so much attention. In this wintertime essay, he drove his metaphor hard. When the freezing point of a culture is reached, like water, it expands and can shatter its container. Though spiritually exhausted, it gathers the technical and material capacity for outward reach, desperately grabbing at life. And so begins what he called an Age of Caesarism. He predicted the coming of totalitarian states, not by looking at the social movements around him, but by taking the longest possible view. He predicted a coming age of imperialist wars in which nations would complete their spiritual death, and finally fall to pieces, yes, like Rome, but also like every other culture, finally succumbing to the invasion of new forces, alien, hostile to the old, full of springlike, spontaneous creativity and religious devotion. In the inevitable final battle between civilized engineers and God-inspired barbarians, the engineers would go down clutching pens and pencils. Artists would also succumb: this was not a time for soul. Art would be frustrated by society's rejection, or corrupted by its licentiousness and power—a spiritual vocation gone astray. The Zeitgeist is inevitable, a time of perverted men in a hopelessly perverted age, liars calling liars liars.

Spengler spoke of the endless repetition of the "already-accepted", of standardized art, of petrified formulas which would ignore and deny history. "Events," he said, would become "the private affairs of the oligarchs and their assassins," and would arise from administration, not society. He foresaw professional armies operating with an entirely different morality than civilian society. In 1917, he noted, "In a few years, we have learned virtually to ignore things which before the war would have petrified the world."

Oh well, happy 6027, anyway.

Discovery of Pluto

From Insect Dreams/Kafka's Roach

Perhaps even more than bagels, Gregor loved going into Paddy's Bagel Bakery on Sixth St., off Avenue B. The name was improbable enough, but the large brown bagel hanging out front, growing out its intensely green four-leaf clover broke the bounds of all rational construction. And the sign was just the beginning of the outlandish Paddy experience. He would descend a short flight of stairs to a basement level areaway piled with years of tossed-in trash, a genuine archeological dig site. There was a narrow, almost clear path toward a door which over the years had carved a radial swing space in the mass of miscellany, and as G headed for his goal he thought — as we do today concerning four wheel drive — how lucky he was to have six legs, in case he needed them. He pulled open the door and was hit, full body, with a caressing blast of steam which felt um-um-good on a freezing Sunday. He closed the door behind him.

Once inside, he could see, as usual, absolutely nothing. The steam was thick, almost impenetrable, and the two 15 watt bulbs hanging from the ceiling served only to make it opaque as well. Remember, bagels have to be boiled before baking, and here in this low-ceilinged basement storefront sans ventilation, it was the steam from two great vats that took front and center — and above and below. And behind. Gregor knew that others were in the shop, but he assumed he was the only customer since all he heard was continuous nattering back and forth in a language of gibberish. It could have been a whole hoard of Niebelungen dwarves, or more likely a large cohort of leprechauns jabbering away in Gaelic. Shadows flitted and projected through the thick, atmospheric fog, but shadows of what — no one could tell.

"A dozen plain bagels, please," he shouted into the hubbub. He didn't know if he had been heard. He repeated his order, and waited, antennae alert, mosaic eyes moist with cloud. A hand appeared out of the mist, holding a brown paper bag. Whose hand this was, he'd never know, but he took the bag from it and replaced it with twenty five cents. The hand withdrew into the mist without so much as a thank you. He had turned to grope his way back into the street when the door swung open in front of him, and G made out the form of a newsboy, silhouetted against the light, waving a paper. Or was he simply fanning away the steam?

"Whuxstree, whuxstree, read all about it, new planet called Pluto! Pluto the new planet!..."

Perhaps it was the shock of sudden light or the dizzying high of steam in the spiracles. More likely it was the stroke of that word: Pluto. Gregor sank down to the ground, and crawled, invisible, until he hit a wall, and pressed up against it. The newsboy, eliciting no customers, backed out, slammed the door shut, and G was left in the misty darkness.

"Pluto. Pluto. I come from Pluto." The voice echoed deep inside him, reverberating off the inner surfaces of his chitinous shell. "I come from Pluto." Perhaps his earliest complex thought, trailing darkest clouds of glory. He would tell his parents, over and over, "I come from Pluto." His mother would say, "Don't be silly, mein Schatz," while his father would refuse to understand. And indeed, how could his parents understand, for the planet, with its chthonian name lay still in the darkness, outside the known reaches of the solar system. But not for child Gregor with his clear memories of long periods of overwhelmingly beautiful night, the sky half filled with a huge moon, looming through swirls of greenish gas. The strange, pale glow of a vastly distant sunrise. His movement lithe, half-floating in near-weightlessness. Cold. The cold. He remembered the cold, an intimate dwelling place among barely shivering atoms.

The whole scene came crashing back on him now, again swaddled in darkness and faint mist, but this of the warmest, wettest kind. He lay on the floor under a dark shelf above, antennae quivering with a faint, paresthetic scent of sulfur. Where was it last he sensed that smell? Sulfur, oxygen's downstairs neighbor in Mendeleyev's great table, aggressively sniffing out the world with its two electrons, and being sniffed, in turn. That smell...

If a doddering old History of Science professor may be allowed yet another intrusion, even into Gregor's interplanetary swoon...

The discovery of Pluto was one of the more remarkable stories in a science replete with same. When Herbert Hoover was sworn in as our thirty-first president on the 4th of March, 1929, he would have told you, if asked, that there were eight planets in our solar system, and being an ex-mining engineer, could have listed them, in order: Mercury, Venus, Earth, Mars, Jupiter, Saturn, Uranus and Neptune. Perhaps he used one of the many mneumonics available to recall them: "My Very Educated Mother Just Served Us Noodles". Or "My Very Easy Method: Just SUN".

Yet at that very moment, there were two earthlings who could have assured him otherwise: Vesto Melvin Slipher, the world-renowned director of the Lowell Observatory in Flagstaff, Arizona, and Clyde W. Tombaugh, a 23-year old farmboy from Kansas.

The story begins even before there was a Kansas, back in 1781 — March 13th to be exact — when the British astronomer, William Herschel, became the first person in modern times to discover a planet unknown to the ancients. He called it Uranus after the personification of heaven, and like that personification of heaven, it proved to be a bit erratic, straying tens of thousands of miles off its mathematically predicted course. Some unknown force must have been distorting its path, and in 1845 (sixteen years before the state of Kansas) the French astronomer, Urbain Leverrier, worked out the likely mass and orbit of a hypothetical planet beyond Uranus. Given that roadmap, Neptune was found and named in the following year — but again seemed to pull away from a purely mathematical dance. And worse, its mass was too small to account for Uranus's meanderings. There was still something out there, invisible, sucking on those two huge spheres. But given the reach of contemporary telescopes, nothing else could be found. And as the resolutions gradually increased, so did the number of points of light. How many 17th magnitude dots can one analyze?

In the early part of our century, two Americans once again took up the search, an occasion for two of those extraordinary coincidences which seemed to decorate G's life like mysterious jewels. Percival Lowell, the literary, world-travelling scion of the distinguished Lowell family of Massachusetts, had been inspired by the discovery of "canals" on Mars to devote his life and personal fortune to studying the red planet. Because of the stillness of the air above, and the rarity of cloud cover, he had built a private observatory outside Flagstaff, Arizona and equipped it, at great expense, with the most advanced equipment available. At this site, he developed a theory, published in 1906 (Mars and Its Canals — still interesting reading), of intelligent life forms on Mars cultivating long rows of vegetation, using irrigation from annually melting ice caps. You may laugh at a theory which seems more appropriate to the The National Enquirer than to the Annals of Astronomy, but it was not until Mariner 4's 1965 fly-by that it was conclusively disproved.

Lowell moved on from Mars to an elaborate mathematical study of the orbit of Uranus. He attributed its irregularities to the gravitational pull of some unseen planet beyond Neptune, calculated its probable position, and organized a systematic search by his observatory staff, directed, after 1916, by Vesto Melvin Slipher. Fourteen years after his death, "Lowell's Planet" was discovered.

Coincidence number one: Percival Lowell was the brother of A. Lawrence Lowell, the president of Harvard, whose hidebound review put Sacco and Vanzetti to death. The Harvard brother was the leading member of a committee to advise the Massachusetts governor on the case, and had he or any member of his "Lowell Committee" failed to find the defendants guilty beyond a reasonable doubt, they would have been spared. They did not fail. Heywood Broun asked "From now on, will the institution of learning in Cambridge, which once we called Harvard, be known as Hangman's House?"

Coincidence number two: How is one supposed to compare field photographs of half a million stars? Lowell, whose plates over the years surely contained a faint image of his planet couldn't make out its slight traverse through the zodiac.

Do you remember Hans Lindauer, Zeiss designer of the planetarium projector and donor of lenses for Gregor's reading glasses? Hans Lindauer. Here he is again in our story — coincidence number three — the inventor of the Zeiss Blink Comparator. Vesto Melvin Slipher was wise enough to purchase the new device shortly after it appeared, and using it, Clyde Tombaugh "blinked" Planet X (as it was then called) into visible existence.

The Zeiss Blink Comparator was an ingeniously simple device. Photographic plates of identical sky fields from two different nights were put into the machine, which focused them into the same eyepiece. They were then "blinked", quickly alternated, into the eyepiece, and any celestial object which had changed place over several days would appear to jump back and forth, thus calling attention to itself. Hans Lindauer — a clever mind. Needless to say, there were technical difficulties to be overcome — precisely matching up star fields, allowing for slight atmospheric differences in visibility night to night, identifying defects in photographic plates, and so forth. But a determined perfectionist like young Clyde went through three quarters of the zodiac using the highest standards of patient, technical precision, and on February 18th, 1930, less than a year after he was hired to do this scutwork, the 23-year old tow-head with thick glasses and callused hands loaded the Blink Comparator with plates taken January 23rd and 29th, and out jumped Planet X from the star-dense constellation of Gemini, smack in the middle of the Milky Way, a 15th magnitude dim "star" that changed its position against a fixed background.

Clyde Tombaugh. Did he jump around like the star, and rush to announce his decision? Not Clyde. He put in two more weeks of patient work, searching for the image in intermediate and outlying positions, and only after he had proved its existence to himself, seen its slow, continuous inching through a 248 year course around the sun, did he go up to the director's office to nonchalantly announce, "Dr. Slipher, I've found your Planet X."

For the next few nights, Slipher, Clyde, and other lab staff checked and rechecked, and the director was ready to put his reputation on the line by announcing the discovery to the world. But when? With an astronomer's love of the calendar, Slipher chose March 13th, 149 years to the day from Herschel's discovery of Uranus, and, coincidentally, Percy Lowell's birthday, a date which the wily director knew would much please Lowell's widow — the observatory's continuing benefactress.

Announced on a Friday, along with a request for name suggestions, the news provoked a flood of telegrams to Flagstaff, one from the grandfather of eleven year old Venetia Burney, of Oxford, England. Venetia was studying mythology in school and over breakfast suggested that Pluto, king of the underworld, might share his name with the new planet because it was "so distant, dark and gloomy".

After much sifting through suggestions, this was the one that stood out, partly because of its aptness, but largely because the astronomical sign for Pluto is ♇, the initials of Mrs. Lowell's beloved husband, and thus provoking   more continued funding. The largest objection to be overcome was the name's possible association with "Pluto Water", a widely advertised laxative.

So "Pluto" it was, announced in the Sunday papers, the headline screamed out by the newsboy into the darkness of Paddy's Bagel Bakery.

One more word about Clyde W. Tombaugh. Through a mutual friend, I came to know him quite well in his later years. He became a quiet, sweet old man, twisted by kyphosis, one of the astronomical world's great punsters. I remember him talking about finding Pluto in his heyday: "It was like a coaxing a wheedle out of a naystack." He never learned to use a word processor, or even a typewriter. I received one of his detailed, long-hand letters early this year, just before his death. He spoke about the irony of his life spent working in cold and darkness in a desert world of blazing sun. It reminded me of Gregor.

ESSAYS PERSONAL

The Gutter to Success

On Being Very Temporarily a Bad Boy

Strange. We called it "the block" — our block, Wallace Ave., RIGHT AT PELHAM PARKWAY. But it wasn't a block, a word that might well describe the masses of apartment houses reaching six stories high. Nor did our block take in three of the four other streets which made up the rectangle upon which those buildings were deposited. Our "block" was just the third of the length of the street on and in which we lived, functioned, and played. We are already established in the realm of local abuse of language.

Our block had sidewalks, I'll grant you that, but they weren't the side of anything except in contrast to the other side of the street. Not side at all, but center of all our activity, forcedly linear. So — blocks that weren't blocks, and sides that weren't sides.

Between the two sides was "the gutter" an open space somehow not devoted to anything vulgar or base, but the landscape for stickball. The hits, instead of being singles, doubles, triples, or home runs, were measured in "sewers" — the distance between manhole covers down the midline of the street. The gutter was shared with the occasional car that, driving down the block, would easily assert its dominance, as we stickball players scattered to the small spaces between the parked cars lining the street.

The sidewalk dropped off into the gutter at the "curb" which then meant only a "curb", unrelated to the act of putting an end to something, or rounding it off.

Aside from stickball, the WALLACE AVE. sidewalk was our area of play. And that sidewalk was divided into wall-to-curb squares, which

I now realize were planned by planners to absorb thermal expansion, but which, for us, were the simply the natural boundaries of the board games to be chalked in those squares. We called them "cracks" in the sidewalks, though they weren't cracks at all. But they were more than just depressions in the concrete. They had magical powers: "Step on a crack, break your mother's back." I don't know who was the first to come up with that, or what his problem was, but it was established folklore by my time, and who, other than a budding matricide, would not be cautious over it? At least if his head were on straight.

This seems like a good time to mention my use of the pronoun "his". There were absolutely no girls out on the block. I knew girls existed because I saw them in class photos, but there was never, never, one visible on the street. My wife, an ex-girl, insists that, not yet being interested, I just didn't see them. I don't buy this. I certainly saw a lot of other things, concerning which I was equally interested or uninterested. Grownups, cars of all makes, stores, little old men shuffling into schul, a parkway with trees, rocks and grass, the elaborate façade, courtyard and hallways of my apartment complex. But never a girl. Some in my gang might have had sisters, but if so, they were hidden up in some tower somewhere. If they existed, didn't they ever play out on the street?

The first girl I was "in love with" was in my class in junior high school, and she lived in another neighborhood, a foreign land, two subway stops further north. (The "subway", typically malaprop, was an elevated line running noisily 25 or 30 feet above a main drag.) I never saw her in the street either, even when we were both in the same JHS class. Girls and streets, like oil and water, mutually exclusive. The closest I can get is 40s photos of crowds walking Fifth Ave. And those were women, not girls.

The last thing I can say about the sidewalk is that you could stand on it, walk on it, run on it, sit on it, on the curb, or back against the wall, but you could never lie down on it, prostrate or prone. Not because it was dirty (which it was), not because you "would get germs" (which you would) (you could put your face on your forearm), but because — I don't know — you would be swallowed up in its extensive horizontality? You might never get vertical again? It was just unthinkable. You *could* lie on a park bench, or on the grass, if you could find any.

It was a warm September day in 1944. I was five, and about to start first grade at P.S. 105. I had calf-length tweed knickers over knee-socks, Buster Brown shoes ("I'm Buster Brown. I live in a shoe. That's my dog Tige. Look for him there, too."), a white shirt and green tie (school colors — to be worn every Tuesday for assembly). Jews like me were being gassed in death camps, but I hadn't yet heard the news.

As is the norm for New Yorkers, especially kids, I crossed over to the school in the middle of the street, but probably out of enthusiasm, without "looking both ways." I ran out into the gutter. A car screeched to a halt, stopping just short of me. It happened to be driven by Nellie L. R. Goodwin, the school principal, a stern and majestic figure who, I now discover, was born in 1880, two years before Franklin Delano Roosevelt. If you were bad, your classroom teacher would somehow and appropriately punish you. If you were really bad, really, really bad, you got sent to "the principal's office" the demesne of someone so powerful, powerful as YHWH, she could not be named directly. The principal's office was my first stop in a long history of schooling. (For most, not the best way to start your school career.)

The rest of a long story is shortly told: Nellie L. R. Goodwin dressed me down for running across the SCHOOL street (HOLLAND AVE.) without "looking both ways", and finished by asking me if I had anything to say. My response: "I like to live dangerously."

I don't know where these words came from. I was the ultimate good boy, never doing anything wrong, even by accident. It would never have occurred to me to do anything forbidden, or even questionable. I was a wimp, a "good Jewish boy". We didn't even *have* "sin" in my neighborhood, as they must have had across the parkway where there were churches and nuns (scary!), and someone I understood to be "the virgin Mary" standing under an upended bathtub — though what a virgin was lay years ahead. Even a woman named Mary was exotic.

"I like to live dangerously" now seems to me the voice of some Satanic other, inhabiting my body, or the earliest example in my life of a floating signifier — a semantic dirigible floating along, at that moment over my head, a "meaning" without a referent.

But those words made me instantly famous. My dressing down turned into hand-clapping praise which followed me from principal to first-grade teacher, and on up through five grades more. They catapulted me from normal into the group of "special progress" kids, who skipped a grade, and went to OLINVILLE JHS (P.S.113) out of the neighborhood, and on to Bronx Science, and on and on, to the Rockefeller Institute for Medical Research, and further.

Now some might conclude from this cv that I was just a regular old smart kid on a smart kid itinerary. But I assure you, I was always and completely misplaced, everywhere way over my head. Comparing myself to my college and grad school and professional compadres, I was a relative moron, dressed in some outsized costume, propelled by... it was only the wind that came from Nellie L. R. Goodwin's clapping hands, during her dressing down of my running into the gutter, right in front of her car. That's all it took to be my version of success. But for the gutter, I might have....

Watch Your Back in the Bronx

Jews and Italians

I subscribe to a wonderful little quarterly magazine, Back in the Bronx, which calls forth articles and letters from its subscribers narrating growing-up experiences from the (nineteen) thirties to the sixties or occasionally seventies, by which time all had changed. With only one exception, the texts are laudatory, bubbling with good memories. All except mine. Not that my Bronx childhood was unhappy, quite the contrary. But where in the magazine was the yin to all that yang? I submitted the little essay below.

What was fascinating was all the criticism both I and the magazine received. Why write anything negative? Why perpetuate childish animosities? That's not what a magazine "celebrating" growing up in the Bronx should contain. I stand chastened. Maybe. Maybe I should have submitted to some lefty Jewish journal of sociology. But such a journal would never publish anything so anecdotal and sans footnotes.

Anyway, here's a very slightly, trivially darker side of what was once a glittering, glittery Bronx. And the land of Edgar Allen Poe.

While the general theme of *Back in the Bronx*, as announced on the masthead and reflected in its content, is "Celebrating the Experience of Growing Up and Living in the Bronx", all was not always to be celebrated. A major part of my growing up in the forties and early fifties was worrying about being beaten up by "the Italians" if I accidently crossed into the wrong neighborhood.

In my time, my Pelham Parkway neighborhood was approximately 100% Jewish. Second, now third generation Jews, probably moved up from the lower East Side, not quite the ones who moved out to Long Island or even up to Westchester. No people of color, except the families running the two Chinese restaurants. All over, Jews. Jews within Jews. If there was any crime, á la Dutch Schultz or Meyer Lansky, we kids didn't know about it. To this day, I assume there was none because where would they have hung out? Where, for that matter, would they have parked?

But east of Barnes Avenue, things began to change, and across the parkway, on the north side, there was even a church, with a statue of Mary in a bathtub shrine. Mary. The Virgin Mary!

A few blocks further east, on the north side of the parkway was the "private house" of Jake LaMotta, middleweight champ, future subject of Scorcese's *Raging Bull*.

Jews didn't have Raging Bulls. Israel was just getting started.

And also Jews didn't fight, didn't carry switchblades or zip guns, a la West Side Story. What did we do, most of us? Be good, smart boys and girls, some occasionally naughty. And we didn't invade Italian neighborhoods to bash them with, or read books aloud to them. Our Jewish settlement was settled and non-invasive.

We were not non-invadeable, though. The PS 105 schoolyard was Jewish home territory. The steps going down into it supported Jewish tushies, the ball games were Jewish ball games, run by Jewish rules. That is, until — occasionally — Italian kids showed up, the Jews were signaled off the basketball courts, or the ball fields, and a kind of mini-occupation began, all rules suspended, and new exclusionary territories enforced by fiat.

We never fought back, never disputed lost territory. We retreated to the steps or simply went home until the occupation was over. There was no violence because there was never any resistance. The conquerors came, saw, conquered, and left, cigarettes dangling from their lips, cigarette packs rolled into tight t-shirt arms, the shirts molded to muscular, non-Jewish bodies.

I was the only kid on the block who did not go to Hebrew School after school, and who was consequently not, as we illiterately said, bar-mitzvahed. If some few may have enjoyed the extra learning (I doubt it), it was certainly universal form to complain about more prison, to make fun of the teachers, and of the black-garbed old men shuffling to the tiny synagogue near the corner of Wallace and Lydig Avenues. Of course I now wish I had gone to Hebrew school, so I would know what all those Israeli protest signs were saying, not to mention being able to more deeply penetrate our almost impenetrable Bible, but back then I felt blessed by not being blessed.

My parents, raised as flappers and Commies, thought the whole bar mitzvah thing was "superstitious nonsense", and certainly didn't pressure me about Hebrew school. My father, a historian, would insist to my Yiddish-speaking grandfather, that there was no archeological evidence whatsoever that the Jews had ever been in Egypt, and would then delight in playing the bad child at family seders, where he would pepper the prescribed haggadah texts and foods and sequences with jibes, gambols and songs that were wont to set the table on a roar. A regular, scholarly, Jewish Yorik, appreciated by some, tsk-tsked by others. So no Hebrew school, and no guilt. I don't remember how I filled the time when all the other kids were unhappily occupied.

But not to lose the thread — there was no one else around, no one who was not at Hebrew school, the ghettoization was complete. And perplexingly, there were no girls. They were quiet but visible in classes, but they vanished completely outside of school. Where did they go?
Back to some Jewish junior convent? No one in my gang of I guess eleven of us, since we had a football team — with uniforms (!) — no one seemed to have a sister, visible or invisible. I swear I talked to my

first girl when I left the neighborhood to go to Bronx Science. Very perplexing to this day.

Back to the Italians. Being judged an "SP" (special progress) kid, I had my 7th and 8th grades combined, and went to a junior high school, on Gun Hill Rd., one stop further north on the Lexington Ave. 241st St line. We were the little Jewish "fags" sent into the belly of an Italian neighborhood. Gun Hill Road. What a setup! The natives actually had (zip) guns, and made it known to us foreigners, what and where the power was. We pretended to be neighborhood regulars, eating hero sandwiches at a corner store across the street from the school - a "fifteen-baloney", or "twenty-five-baloney" — that's 15¢ or 25¢ — if you can imagine that, right along with the Italian kids. And then one of us — Melvin — tall, handsome, great athlete — got stabbed, actually stabbed in the back with a shiv. Like ambulance stabbed.

It was a definitional moment for us Jewish kids, our first real, not just potential, violence, and for all we knew, life-threatening. And of all people — Melvin! Today, an act like that would prompt two weeks of air attacks. We didn't have an air force. Whereas before, inter-cultural violence was corralled into safe and unsafe neighborhoods, now, and for the next two years, it could occur anytime, anywhere, in school, on the street, or in the middle of a baloney sandwich. The world had turned actively adversarial. Our protected little Jewish world was imploded, exploded. This — not first sex or parental divorce (Jews didn't divorce) — was childhood's end.

Onward to Bronx Science (1955). But again, from the names in the yearbook, predominantly Jewish, if non- or even un-orthodox. In my graduating class of approximately 500, there was one black kid. Vincent. Everyone was smart (you had to test in) and nice, and the cocoon was spun and folded in again. We all went to college, and most of us, probably to graduate or professional schools. In my senior year, I had a first girlfriend, though she was "saving herself for her husband."

I'm sure others have similar stories. The Bronx is still made up of neighborhoods, and always was. Neighborhoods define themselves via rules and norms which often conflict from one side of the street to another.

What I don't understand is why — in many years of reading *Back In The Bronx*, I've never come across a story describing what seems to me a core dimension of kid life in the Bronx. Why do all the stories seem completely celebratory? "It was so wonderful growing up there, and here are all the details of its wonderfulness." The names of the candy stores and movie houses — ah! As poverty has grown, as social systems have broken down, why aren't there stories reflecting that? The movies — and in many cases, our lives — tell us things in the big world are otherwise. Not to mention the chauvinistic orientation of our military and foreign policies.

One of the consequences of the ghettoization described above is that I have no idea of what those Italian kids were thinking and feeling. Was it really the arrogance and scorn I have always imagined? Or did they just have a different way of dressing which involved keychains, pegged pants and cigarettes? Did their neighborhoods, or the little Catholic schools they may have gone to not have a giant schoolyard we were blessed with, and so they needed ours to play basketball? And most of all, did their religion create in them a consciousness of sin and shame which needed confessing and expiation, while we were rather burdened by the opposite — the assigned role of being God's "chosen people", requiring not confession but continued expression?

I live in Vermont, but compared to my wife, a native Vermonter, I still feel like a Bronx kid. I miss the "gutter" in which we played stickball, where the hits were valued by "sewers" — one sewer a single, two a double, etc. Up here, we live in a neighborhood clearly defined socio-economically (poorest in Burlington), but fiercely progressive in its politics, and in who it elects. Yet I have absolutely no sense of any boundary lines to Burlington's neighborhoods, as I did in the Bronx.

Is that because no matter where I go, I know nobody will stick a knife in my back? What a strange method of map-making and subjective geography.

The Only Three Things I Learned in School

Pocket Epistemology

The best teacher I ever had was a philosopher-historian named Hans Meyerhoff. Mondays, Wednesdays and Fridays at noon, he held forth on "Existentialism in Literature" in the largest hall on the UCLA campus. People would pack the room, sit on the stairs, eat lunch standing at the back, to hear this man. Each week he would begin a new book. He would stride across the stage to the lectern, slowly reach down and pull the book from his briefcase, open the book decisively in front of him, and say, in a thick German accent,"Vhat does ziss book show?" With this question, he taught me how to read. "Vhat does ziss book show?" is one of only three things in 25 years of schooling (other than typing class in junior high school) that I have found valuable as an adult.

Of the other two, one is also in a German accent, though from a different émigré. An old-world biology professor once remarked, upon observing a student report, "Per zent meansss von hundert samples. Do you haf von hundert samples?" It made me look at statistics differently for the rest of my life. "Among the 12 students in the seminar, 60% brought laptops to class." Right. 74% of statistics are made up.

The last gem was imparted by an otherwise non-distinguished physics professor, as a random observation on scientific method: "Two colleagues," he said, "a scientist and a non-scientist are riding along in a car when they spy a flock of sheep along the side of the road. 'Oh, look,' says the non-scientist, 'the sheep have just been shorn.' 'Yes,' says the scientist. 'At least on this side.' A clarifying insight.

These three stickies all share a concern with epistemology — the questions "How do we know what we 'know?" and "What constitutes valid "knowledge"? In this day of claims and counter-claims, of politics accurately described as "Liars calling liars liars", of fake news with more news than real news, we had better be alert to the epistemological frame of our life-worlds. Throw that switch, and the bullshit-detectors start madly beeping.

How To Fail in the Religion Business Without Really Trying

My Short First and Only Ministries

After the failure of my first ministry ("too political"), I was sent to a high-powered career placement institute. Several hundred dollars and many inkblots later, a team of psychologists came up with their recommendation: I should think seriously about becoming airline flight attendant. High-flying, but insufficiently theological; close but no cigar.

After the failure of my second ministry ("too political"), I figured it was two strikes and you're out. "This guy will either be great, or a disaster," someone on my fellowshipping committee had quipped. The either had succumbed to the or. Two years and ten thousand bucks out the window. And yet, and yet...

And yet Starr King more than equipped me for every subsequent activity of my life.

It was my first experience of a fulfilled institution, a beloved community of idealists and seekers empowered by its radical yes. I left Starr King starry-eyed and polypotentiated — if parish ministry wasn't right, I could slip into medicine, ambulance work and teaching. The school gave me a taste for playing over my head (the secret of ascension), and my musical activity expanded accordingly. Writing sermons accustomed me to flying by the seat of my pants, and easily morphed into writing Writing — essays and plays and now novels — all exploring big, Starr-Kingy material. Inexhaustible.

Brecht has a wonderful scene title in Mahagonny: *"Alle wahrhaft Suchenden werden enttäuscht"* — all those who truly seek will be disappointed. And even <u>that</u> was embedded in SK's gift. For disappointment will never quash seeking — not if one has been launched from the celestial city on Berkeley's Holy Hill. A Starr King diploma may be a prescription for failure, but I wouldn't have any other kind.

Gripes from the Grammar Police

Like How to Talk and Such

It's hell being an editor, especially of often political texts. It bleeds over into real life.

1. If you are going to open your mouth on the issue, please learn to pronounce "nuclear" as NU CLE AR, not as NU CU LAR. Nucleus/ nuclear.

You wouldn't say an atom has a NUCULUS. It sounds illiterate, and undermines your authority to speak about the issue.

I know this mistake is common, and even saying "nucleus nuclear nucleus nuclear..." is a tongue-twister.

But I have to admit that there may have been a worse boner: Perhaps apocrypal: but there was supposed to have been a hardcover edition of a science textbook (expensive!) titled on cover and spine as UNCLEAR PHYSICS.

2. BEGGING THE QUESTION
To beg the question" does NOT mean "begs that some question be asked". It names a logical fallacy where the answer is presumed in the question. As, for example:

"The reason everyone wants the new thingamajiggy is because this is the hottest thingamjiggy of the season!"

I know this abuse is becoming more common, and, given the on-rushing Great American Dumbdown, is likely inevitable, but perhaps it can be squashed before it completely destroys its original, unreplaceable, use of "to beg the question".

3. LIKE, YOU KNOW, GOES, I MEAN, AND OTHER VERBAL TICS.

"Sam? Hi. Oh wow, hey, like it's really great to really meet you. I've got a question maybe you can like help me and stuff. (She plops down on my bed.). I'm at lunch today and Cindy Barry? she goes, "You off your diet these days?" I mean, hello? I mean like I'm standing there with my 50 calorie no-fat Yoplait yogurt and like that's all for lunch, and she goes am I off my diet? So I go nooooo and I walk away, like I have to take stuff from the last living virgin at seventeen? But I like head right down to the bathroom and check myself for the fortieth time and Omigod, like she's right. My face is like fat. Don't you think it's fat? I mean like, a little fat and everything? I mean like not really fat, but it's kinda like it's weird and all? I mean like under my eyes, and under this bone? (She pokes at her zygoma.) Of course Cindy is like slime, but I'm just like omigod, she's really right. I mean not right about the diet, like I also do 300 situps and smoke two packs a day and that kind of stuff, you know, whatever? But like, look at this tons of stuff her under my arms, like when I wave them around? Shouldn't that be tighter? And like my abs are great and stuff, but look at this. (She grabs her right butt, and wiggles it manually around.) Know what I mean?" "Um," I say. "It's just like omigod," she explains. "So I run to find Gabe, he's like my boyfriend? and he's incredibly deep, considering his brain doesn't really work anymore, know what I mean? And Gabe goes 'I think you look pretty nice,' and I'm like 'Pretty nice? You mean like sometimes in the right light on alternate bank holidays? I mean like wow, you want me to take off my shirt or my pants first? Know what I mean? (She rolls her eyes.) "Unh-huh," I

say. "So like here's my question. I mean like I can work on my triceps and glutes and all, but what do I do about my face? I mean I can't like work my face and all. (She opens and closes her mouth.) I mean like that's not going to do anything to this fat, right?"
(from my novel, *When the Gods Come Home to Roost)*

Running Out of Bookshelf Space

Why a Home Library

Written before having access to the infinite shelves of the internet. I am now trying to get rid of my books. My children and grandchildren don't want them. No one wants them. It's hard to throw Kant, Glenn Gould and Virginia Woolf into the trash.

My house is packed with books — upstairs, downstairs, in my lady's chamber. But my shelves are far more than space for "collecting". My library is neither an addiction nor a compulsion, but rather a gathering of my friends, a kind of social networking *avant la lettre*.

I am a writer, a novelist. When I stall in my inspiration I have two choices — to look for a word in the refrigerator (it's usually not there, but other, more fattening things are), or to stroll around my rooms, visiting with the spines of my companions, and sometimes with their pages. It's a lot more interesting than Facebook to find out what Flaubert is thinking at the moment, or where Dostoevsky intends to go tonight.

It is not only chiropractors to whom spines talk. My older volumes are like snapshots in my school yearbooks. I remember exactly what they look like, their color, their size, their smell — the messages they scrawled in my own, or even those scrawled by previous owners in their margins. Or I remember that I wish I had known them better, and pull a volume off the shelf to join the pile next to my bed to accompany my insomnia.

Why not go to the library? There's no goddamn parking up at the university, and the public library is not deep enough. Yes, shelf-browsing is rich, but shelf-browsing at home can be even richer.

Getting Rid of a Home Library

The First Stage of Death

We recently got rid of five or six hundred books in a section called THINKERS. Adorno to Zinn. Facing my desk are two blank walls instead. Some philosophy professor heard we were trying to disperse our things as our bodies were getting ready "to rejoin the universe", as my acupuncturist says. Came by and swooped up two floor to ceiling walls of books. I thought it was going to be easy since almost everything is available on line. Turns out the content of those shelves are not at all available on line. What's online are articles about their authors, with occasional references to what's in those books. What's also not available online is my years of notes and underlines. But what's the most not on line is the very existence of them. I can point to the exact spot on the blank wall where the words and thoughts I am looking for would have been. I often start to walk over there, until I realize there's no there there anymore. Just the titles, the book spines of familiar books can set me on the right thinking track. But there have been mass and multiple spinectomys. The area now smells only like white paint.

Once you get into your seventies or eighties, people are dying around you. Sometimes you pick up an obituary, but mostly not. You just don't see them anymore. What's with Stephen? And Fran? Are they still with us? Dunno. People just disappear. Strangely, they are not as persistent as the collection of spines on a bookshelf on a wall. Though the books are gone, I remember every one, and know where it was, and where its ghost now haunts. People not so much. Strange, eh?

Submitting Gregor

Beginning my Writing: Out From Under the Couch

Back around the turn of the century, I submitted a 900-page manuscript called *Gregor Samsa: A Life*, to a new Penguin Putnam imprint, BlueHen, suggested by my then agent. I got back from editor Fred the following gnomic message: "We love your ms, but we are not going to publish it." Something very like that. When I asked why, Fred wrote, "Because you are not going to want to make the changes we want you to make." Perhaps this was a phone conversation.

So here I am sitting at my desk, an unpublished writer, not yet *deeply* frustrated because still a newbie, and this is my first significant contact with a real editor from a real press. What to do?

I figured thus: "What do I have to lose? I'll let him make the changes he wants, and if I don't like the result, I don't have to sign the contract." What did I know? We tromped off together on the conversion of

Gregor Samsa: A Life

into

Insect Dreams: the Half Life of Gregor Samsa.

(That title, BTW, was arrived at in actual committee, giving the lie to the truth that committees can never come up with anything snazzy.) And on the way, the manuscript lost 300 of its 900 pages. My first experience with editing.

The contents of *Insect Dreams*, Fred's version of my original, catapulted me, at least for a moment, into the what? big time? not quite, but way beyond my previous punching weight. I was the only debut author ever to be interviewed on Michael Silverblatt's *Bookworm*, and was even put on a plane to LA to do it. I was offered a Jr.-faculty slot at Breadloaf, and a similar appointment "teaching writing" (ha ha) at the

Wesleyan Writer's Workshop. The book was chosen as one of the 25 Best Books of the Year by the New York Public Library, complete with banquet dinner which I couldn't make. Anyway, my book in Fred's edit did very well, as it should have. It's a terrific book, and my first comic raid on America's Faustian bargain and consequent fate.

However — it was a book quite different from the one I had written, not just in the number of its pages, but also in its general feeling. My original model had been Thomas Mann's *Doctor Faustus*, "the life of XXX, as told by a friend." My XXX was not Adrian Leverkühn, the demon-afflicted composer, but Gregor Samsa, the cockroach, also inexplicably poisoned. The brilliance of Mann's book lives in the contrast between the narrator, a mild-mannered academic, and his in-all-ways contrasting friend, the manic, driven, tortured composer, that dialectic being also a deep, extended metaphor for Germany, the land of genius and satanic savagery.

For various reasons, developed in our dialogue below, Fred thought it best to convert my biography into a "novel", told not by a friend, but by an omniscient narrator. Much of the same historical and characterological content remains in there, but the narrator was skillfully extracted, the tone of the book changed, and it was that book found which created the success we both thought it deserved.

But over the years, I kept missing the original book, partly for its warmth and partly for the chapters that were no longer in there. So? Big deal. The book's success wasn't enough for you? Yes, it was, it surely was, but still, there was an old friend missing, perhaps the way one's children are missing once they grow up. You just accept it, often bittersweet.

Then, along came Fomite Press, Donna's and my creation, and we could publish whatever we liked. For four years, we never thought of publishing one of my books because we didn't want Fomite to seem like a self-publishing vehicle for me. But after having published seventy or so books, that didn't seem like an issue anymore. So, OK — what should I publish with Fomite?

How about the original Gregor Samsa book, the one I've been missing for a dozen years? My initial thought was that Fred, my by-now longstanding friend, intellectual buddy and partner-in-crime, would be upset. After a few months I worked up the courage to float the possibility with him to see what he might think.

Not only was he not shocked and horrified, not only did he not see it as a repudiation of his and our work, but he thought it a most interesting proposal, and encouraged me to go ahead.

What I didn't really understand was the meaning of a *Kafka's Roach/Insect Dreams* duopoly going public, and what it might expose him to in the writing and editing community. These dialogues (initiated by Fred) are the discussion that followed.

They consist of a series of back and forth emails responding to each other, and our shared sense of the issues involved — not only my publication of *KR*, but in the more generalized scenario of self-publishing authors eschewing editors, editorial surveillance, and editorial intrusion on the text.

The Annotated Nose

A short interview of me by Ben Mirov, Brooklyn Rail, Nov 19, 2008

According to his website, Marc Estrin is "a writer, cellist, and activist living in Burlington, Vermont." However, in a secondary biographical note, he calls himself a "Biologist, theatre director, EMT, Unitarian Minister, physician assistant, puppeteer, political activist, college professor, cellist and conductor... baffling, even unto himself." Or, in a third, alternative note, "...was hired to teach theatre at Goddard College, but in his departmentless utopia, wound up also teaching music, writing, *Finnegans Wake*, math, physics, medical self-help and 'crazy courses' like Philosophy for Dishwashers, an audio—based lecture/discussion series to sweeten the life of cafeteria volunteers." There is an even longer, fourth biographical statement that mentions growing up in "a small apartment so full of books you had to walk sideways in the hall," giving up "literary virginity to Franz Kafka" at the age of 16, and reaching "back into a past life to study and practice medicine." Much like his newest book, *The Annotated Nose* (Unbridled Books, 2008), Estrin is a composite of raconteur-like embellishments and factual fictions, who challenges the idea of being hemmed in by terse description.

Estrin is the author of four previous novels: *Insect Dreams: The Half Life of Gregor Samsa* (2002), *The Education of Arnold Hitler* (2005), *Golem Song* (2006), and *The Lamentations of Julius Marantz* (2007). *The Annotated Nose* continues in a similar vein as his previous work, blending elements of fiction, non-fiction, and biography into a humorous novel that doesn't shy away from incisive political or social critique. According to its cover, *The Annotated Nose* is based on a cult classic called "The Nose," a biography written by William Hundwasser about the strange life of a man named Alexei Pigov. Estrin's annotated edition includes Hundwasser's original biographical text, Alexei Pigov's corresponding critical notes, illustrations by Delia Robinson, and an editorial introduction and appendix by Estrin. I contacted Mr. Estrin via email to ask him a few questions about *The Annotated Nose*:

Rail: On the back of *The Annotated Nose*, there's a list of authors: Jonathan Swift, Laurence Sterne, Franz Kafka, Bruno Schulz, William S. Burroughs. Included in this list is William Hundwasser, the original author of "The Nose." Many of those authors fall within a tradition of alternative/experimental writing. Is *The Annotated Nose* a part of a particular alternative and/or experimental tradition?

Estrin: I was not the author of that list, nor did I suggest it as text for the back cover. Nevertheless, I do tend to enjoy very much authors who are in your face AS AUTHORS. Not everyone on the list writes that way, but Swift and Sterne certainly (add Fielding), and I would add even unlisted authorial discourses such as those found in Thomas Mann. But all those folks are found on my shelves, and I enjoy them for reasons as various as they are. I don't tend to think of them as alternative or experimental since I consider the novel itself as an ongoing experiment since Cervantes, alternative only to itself as it varies and evolves. Fred Ramey, my editor, knows that this is a collection of "my guys" (since we at one time or another have discussed them between us), and he is good-naturedly tweaking me (us) by putting the fictive Hundwasser among them.

Rail: Your book makes use of footnotes, illustrations, differing typefaces and blank space to create a somewhat labyrinthine atmosphere. Did you set out to write a book that would have this quality, or did it come about as a result of your work?

Estrin: I actually don't see it as labyrinthine at all. It is simply two novels, one third person, and the other first person (in the form of notes) facing one another on left and right pages. Stay in your place. No mixing, even of presentational styles. The illustrations, all except two, belong to the original edition of Hundwasser's book on the left, while Alexei just writes text on the right. The typefaces are used only for chapter headings, as in any book. The complexity simply results from the fact that the two novels contradict one another in certain key parts of the story. The reader is left with the sense of two unreliable narrators, and must decide what is more likely to have actually gone on. Don't ask me. I don't know. I just edited the fight. The one other complexity, internal to Hundwasser, is that Delia Robinson is both the illustrator of and a character in "The Nose." But she is also the illustrator of *The Annotated Nose*. But not of its dust cover. What the...? Even Fred and I can't figure this one out. Delia is a very foxy person, diegetically speaking.

Rail: In *Tristram Shandy*, by Laurence Sterne, a person's nose figures greatly in the unraveling of their destiny. Your novel is also nose-centric, but in subtly different ways. Can you tell me a little about the importance of noses in *The Annotated Nose*?

Estrin: Gogol's "The Nose" played a crucial part in my giving myself permission to write my first novel, *Insect Dreams*. I figured that if he could have a nose walking around the streets and praying in church, I could have a six-foot, talking cockroach as my hero. As Gogol says, excusing his story, "It doesn't happen often, but it happens." With that warm and fuzzy (for me) permission always permitting, a gift that keeps giving, I simply seized upon nose-masks as characterizing a hero beyond his particulars—a character who has been trapped in a novel, and whose life has been pigeonholed thereby, a character distrusting and hating his author. (I have a good friend who was involved in that kind of a situation, and I thought I'd write about it in terms other than his.) I used to have a string quartet, The Flying Flonzaleys, and we wore Groucho nose glasses when we played wedding gigs. So the Groucho mask came up first, and brought forth the Alexei strategy of making things better by making them worse. Physically, his masks have longer and longer noses, and each takes over his personality more and more. I also know a guy, an accordion player, actually, who has been trying unsuccessfully for fifty years to get a girlfriend. So he crept in there too with very bad pickup lines. But the nose in "The Nose" was pretty accidental to the larger conception, the nose who came to dinner.

Rail: The novel's central character, Alexei Pigov, goes through a series of masks or disguises throughout the course of the novel. Could you talk about what this progression means in terms of Pigov's character?

Estrin: They generally follow Alexei's situation—his becoming Max Schreck, the monster, when he feels angry at one girl, or coming accidentally upon Scaramouche in the park, and transforming Scaramouche into Pantalone, when he feels tired, or hawking crazily on the street as St. Punch when he needs work. The only crucial formulation is Hundwasser's scheme that Alexei become a plague doctor—the longest nose yet. While Hundwasser comes to this image only as potentially good merchandising, Alexei takes his transformation into a plague doctor quite seriously—at last he has found his authentic role in life, diagnosing and organizing against the contemporary plague. This is yet another fight between character and author—one is serious, and the other is in it for the bucks.

Rail: You write yourself into the novel as the editor of *The Annotated Nose*, so that the work inhabits the realms of fiction, biography, criticism, and nonfiction. Was this your intent in including yourself?

Estrin: Once I conceived the annotated book format—text and notes—I realized that annotated books must have editors who make editorial comments. Because Alexei chose the texts he would annotate or dispute, and wrote the disputations, he didn't leave me much room for those editorial functions. But to earn my keep, and to contextualize the annotated edition for the reader, I added a regular introduction at the beginning, and tried to fill out the end, after Alexei abandoned the project.

Rail: By the end of the novel Pigov has transformed into Paphnutius, the plague doctor, covering himself in a medieval suit and mask meant to protect its wearer from the black plague. To some extent the suit is a comment on discourses of power; the power of the biographer over his subject, the power of government over its citizens. Do you think *The Annotated Nose* is ultimately a political book with a political message?

Estrin: Absolutely! All my books, though they have their comic aspects, have political thrusts, commentary and analysis of the nightmare our culture is going through and heading toward. Alexei says the contemporary plague is having your text written for you by someone else—like we are all characters, whether we like it or not, in Bush & Co.'s little world-play. Or all of us playing consumers in the marketed media marketplace. Or closeted into stupid gender roles of pursuit and submission. The trick—and this is something Fred and I toss about all the time—is how to make something political generalizable beyond place and time. How to make my books relevant years from now—as are the books listed on the back cover. (Not to compare myself (or Hundwasser!) to that collection of geniuses.) I have no talent for "political thrillers." So then what? "Then what" turns out to be the kinds of books I have found myself writing about the ongoing problems of Western culture. The next two books I have (one written, the other planned), may be the first which are not comedies. I don't know if that is a step forward or backward for me, or just reflects my being that much closer to the grave.

Rail: It's good to know there are authors out there like Mr. Estrin, authors who, as he put it, "...consider the novel itself as an ongoing experiment since Cervantes, alternative only to itself as it varies and evolves." Whether his next book is funny or not, it's a safe bet it will be a mind-bending, unruly, highly enjoyable piece of writing.

What first got you interested in writing?

I had always been a decent writer — school essays, and later, press releases, and as a minister, sermons. But my first really substantial writing bloomed when my 70-something aunt wrote me that she was taking a seminar on feminism, and that she "couldn't make heads or tails out of postmodernism." So I promised her I'd write her a 'Postmodernism for Beginners'. I had in mind a comic book format like the ones Andre Schiffrin pioneered for Pantheon.

I started writing, immediately over-ran the format, and wound up with an interesting full-length book called *Postmodernism: A Guide for the Perplexed*. Because I had discovered Baudrillard while doing it, I sent it to Jim Fleming at Semiotext(e)/Autonomedia, Baudrillard's US publisher. He loved it, and said they wanted to do it. But the project got so bolluxed in it's complex graphical design it never happened. So it sits on my shelf, and I think my aunt still doesn't understand postmodernism since she didn't read the ms I sent.

This was the first 'real' writing I ever did. I knew it was 'real' because it had more than 100 pages. 300 in fact.

My first fiction was *Golem Song*, written, as you note, after someone called asking me to send him a gun to kill blacks in the upcoming war between blacks and Jews in NYC.

Who or what particularly influences your work?

My reading, primarily, and also my music. I think in musical terms and forms and try to use them to structure my longer works. I also enjoy trying to write <u>about</u> music, and have scenes concerning classical music in each of my works. Hommage to Thomas Mann, who, after high school, turned me on to so many things. His description of Beethoven's last piano sonata in *Doktor Faustus*, or of Hanno's improvisations in *Buddenbrooks*, remain inspirations and unreached goals for me.

Looking over my work to this point I seem to have come down unintentionally as a writer of comic novels with serious themes. What gave me "permission" to write Insect Dreams was Gogol's short story, "The Nose". If a nose can go walking around the street, dressed in a general's uniform, well, hey, then a six-foot talking cockroach can become the risk management consultant to the Manhattan Project — no? As Gogol says, these things don't happen often, but they do happen.

In service to the comic level of my work, I bring into play the many lovely (and unlovely) maniacs I have known that seem to be attracted to my stodginess, yin to my yang. They generate events simply by walking down the street.

Describe your writing process.

I don't write on a regular schedule. It's more a process of inbreath and outbreath. An idea begins to pester me — often something that came up and was unaddressed in a previous book. I think about it, do some reading, do some research online or at my university library, and then it either roots or it doesn't. I then might start writing something, and will soon intuit if "this will work out" or not. If it's a "go", I'll plunge into more directed research, if necessary, and after a while, I start waking up a 3 AM, needing turn on the light to jot down phrases or notes. That's when I know it's time for outbreath. My sleeping wife, too. Sometimes I'll make an outline, but more often, things just follow, page to page, chapter to chapter. I'm not one of those who writes an inspired scene, then uses it where it is best placed. I have to write consecutively or I don't know what happened before, and have nothing to go on.

What is the most surprising thing you have learned as a writer?

Early in my writing career someone labeled me a "new Jewish writer." Hmm. I never though of myself that way before. I grew up a red-diaper baby of non-religious parents. I was the only kid on the block who wasn't bar mitzvahed. I (alas!) never learned Hebrew, or even the Yiddish my parents spoke when they wanted to keep secrets. So how come I was a "Jewish writer"?

Nevertheless, it seemed to be true, dammit! I did a lot of reading about what makes for a Jew. Much of it went into Arnold Hitler's explorations of possible conversion. I fit every pattern, especially my sense of humor. I realized that although my family was not officially Jewish, my neighborhood, my ghetto, was intensely so. And so I can effectively call on neighborhood types and themes when I choose to go there, as I did in *Golem Song*, and *Julius Marantz*. I'm trying to get away from this self-pigeonholing. *The Annotated Nose* has no obvious Jewish characters, and I just finished a manuscript set during the French Revolution, again without Jewish themes.

But it's true: the apple doesn't fall far from the tree, and I've just accepted an invitation from the Charlottesville Book Festival to be on a panel entitled "Good Jewish Boys Gone Wild." That may be me, after all.

Which of your books is your favorite and why?

I think of *Insect Dreams* as being the most significant, if only because its theme is world historical: the Trinity test at Alamogordo in July of 1945 was a moment from which humans can never turn back, and which, in its further development, profoundly affects our current world, and not just with respect to nuclear weapons, but concening our relationship to nature and power.

Arnold Hitler is about the misuse of language, also a crucial current pathology, and *Golem Song* explores the fraught concepts of chosenness and superiority, again something the world is habitually subjected to. But both these books embody themselves in a particular character, and so feel smaller to me. *Insect Dreams*, on the other hand, is a contribution to a larger intellectual history in its accurate tracing of the trajectory of paranoia, xenophobia and racism pointing the world to suicide.

What kind of effect do you hope your books will have?

I write my books to share my intellectual, political, and cultural concerns, and also some of my favorite things with any who may read them. While every reader will be somewhat familiar with, say, the bomb, or the situation in the Middle East, I hope I've been able to introduce some of them to the uniqueness of Charles Ives, or the provocative strangeness of Edmund Jabès, or the implications of the often-excluded parts of the Passover Haggadah, or the pregnant idea of God going into hiding. Such things are my little embedded gems. I'd like to see them as gifts to the diligent reader. Sharing.

It would be madness to think that books such as mine can have any effect in changing the world for the better, especially in a culture which pays less and less attention to text. On the other hand, among the small groups that they affect, they have generated deepening discussion of the issues they raise. That is all I can ask.

I also write to have fun, and to justify my existence.

From My Contemporary Authors 2008 Listing

For Marc Estrin, writing is just another vocation, along with music, theater, science, and political activism. Indeed, his first novel came about almost without his intention, as he explained in an essay on the BookBrowse Web site: During a visit to Prague, "My wife and I, playing tourist, had visited Franz Kafka's grave, and I left the poor guy a note (along with all the other notes thrust into the gravel) inviting him to come visit if he got a chance. Three weeks later, there he was, or rather Gregor, his most famous emissary, with a complete story outline on a platter."

Insect Dreams: The Half Life of Gregor Samsa focuses on the main character from Kafka's well-known novella, *The Metamorphosis*, a man who awoke one day transformed into a cockroach. In his novel, Estrin transforms Samsa into a sort of emissary from a Europe slipping into horror to the naive United States. The book takes place in the first half of the twentieth century, and Samsa meets many of the notables of the time, including Albert Einstein, Ludwig Wittgenstein, and Franklin and Eleanor Roosevelt.

Susan Larson noted in a review for the *New Orleans Times-Picayune*: "Readers will devour this book, just to see what happens next, what famous figure of the 20th century will be drawn to make the acquaintance of or test wits with a five foot-six inch talking cockroach." He also views seminal events, such as the famous Scopes Monkey Trial that dealt with the teaching of evolution, the execution of alleged anarchists Sacco and Vanzetti, and the creation of the atomic bomb.

Throughout, Samsa brings his unique perspective and unfailing decency to bear on the questions of the day as Estrin weaves philosophy, science, and history into his tale. "Indeed, if *Insect Dreams* weren't so perpetually funny, its philosophical ruminations and its encyclopedia of cameo appearances would be downright intimidating," commented *Christian Science Monitor* contributor Ron Charles. For *Library Journal* contributor David A. Berona, the result is a "colossal book of characters and events that inspires tears of laughter and sadness in its rich blend of clever metaphor and unsettling facts."

Along with his other pursuits, Estrin is also a puppeteer. In his text for *Rehearsing with Gods: Photographs and Essays on the Bread & Puppet Theatre*, he recounts his work with one of New England's well-known puppet troupes. Founded by Peter Schumann in the early 1960s and still performing all over the world, the Bread & Puppet Theatre features enormous puppets made from straw, clay, and, oddly, beer. [The writer means that the sculptures on which they are formed, are made from these materials. ME] They are also noted for spreading their "stage" over great distances, creating vast tableaus far different from the small spaces reserved for more conventional puppetry.

The book itself is divided into eight sections, reflecting the archetypal themes of the shows, including "Death," "Fiend," "World," and "Hope." While *Booklist* contributor Jack Helbig found Estrin's commentary too "subjective and self-consciously literary," a *Publishers Weekly* contributor commended him for making "the strong social activist component of the theatre clear, in tones that are by turns humorous and revealing." The collection of essays is enhanced by photography by Ronald T. Simon.

The author continues his satirical look at the world in his second novel titled *The Education of Arnold Hitler*. This time, the author tells the story of a Texas boy who ends up attending Harvard where he finds himself constantly facing the negativity associated with his name. The only people who seem to like his name are a group of right-wingers who plan to use him for their own purposes. The novel follows Arnold as he goes through his life dealing with his odious last name and, like Gregor in *Insect Dreams*, meets famous personages, including Al Gore, Noam Chomsky, and Leonard Bernstein.

Lawrence Rungrin, writing in the *Library Journal*, called *The Education of Arnold Hitler* a "wildly provocative tale of a young man who must learn to define himself." *Booklist* contributor Frank Sennett, noted that "this clever narrative package also makes plenty of room for literate explorations of Jewishness, [and] anti-Semitism."

Golem Song was called a "zany New York Jewish comic novel" by *Library Journal* contributor Molly Abramowitz. The story focuses on Alan Krieger, a repulsive, obese Jewish ER nurse who is also a genius and a self-styled savior of Jewish America, similar to the golem legend of Prague in the sixteenth century. Krieger sees antisemitism everywhere. However, Krieger's views are repulsive and loathsome, making him the most disturbing racist in the novel. In an interview with M.J. Rose on the *Backstory* website, the author revealed that he got the idea for his story from a real incident in which a Jewish acquaintance in New York called and asked him to buy and send him a high-powered rifle so he could shoot blacks in the upcoming race war between the Jews and the blacks. "Needless to say, I refused," Estrin told Rose. "He cussed me out, told me I didn't know anything about reality, that reality wasn't living in goddam beautiful Vermont, with my goddam beautiful wife and goddam beautiful children. Reality was New York City. The subway. At rush hour!"

Several reviewers praised Estrin's novel of a brilliant but delusional man who believes that his racist views are just. "Estrin gives Krieger's racism all the usual motivations," wrote Jason B. Jones on the *PopMatters* website, adding later in the same review: "What keeps this from dissolving into cliché is Estrin's vital sense of how easily smart people can delude themselves into thinking they are beyond bigotry." Donna Seaman, writing in *Booklist*, noted that the author's "mind-bending humor is at once intellectual and ribald."

Estrin followed up his novel *Tsim-tsum* — about God living on earth in a Hyundai while he checks in on his creation — with *The Lamentations of Julius Marantz*. Marantz is a physicist who has invented an anti-gravity machine he calls the "Doodad." The machine, which is able to whisk people into the Earth's atmosphere, is sought by several governments and eventually falls into the hands of a group of corporate lobbyists, religious right-wingers, and military people. The group, named GEKO, begin using the machine to get rid of anyone who opposes their plans. Meanwhile, Marantz finds himself on the run from GEKO while trying to figure out a way to get his machine back. As people witness other people flying from the Earth, the world goes into religious hysteria believing that the Biblical "Rapture" has finally arrived. Ron Jacobs, in a review on the *ZNet* website, wrote, "Estrin's manipulation of the language used by the Falwells, Robertsons, Swaggarts and their lesser brethren quietly exposes the vacuum behind the televangelists' revival circus."

A Writer's Eye: Interview

My Interest in 9/11

Kevin Quirk interviewed me for a book he is doing on 9/11 activists.

1) How and when did you first got involved in seeking the truth about 9/11?

I was immediately suspicious, and suspected foul play, when I saw the buildings fall. The event didn't correspond with any other physical incident I had ever experienced. But my initial thoughts were focused on the potentially catastrophic aftermath — just what the Bush administration would do with the occurrence. Later in the day, when I saw Building 7 come down, I was convinced all three buildings were brought down by controlled demolition, but had no way to follow up on this. In the succeeding weeks and months, my activist attention was detoured into the ominous response of our government. It was only when I read *The New Pearl Harbor* that I was able to begin putting the pieces together. I responded especially to Griffin's eight levels of possibility — from the administration simply taking advantage of the event to pursue a pre-existing agenda to the possibility of its active planning and execution. I've been able to use this scheme as a heuristic matrix to pursue my further investigations.

I reviewed the book for *Counterpunch*, and received a load of email which catapulted me into "the 9/11 truth movement". For quite a while I didn't like that term, feeling that "the 9/11 research community" would be more modest and realistic. But by now, I feel that we know enough to assert more than "unanswered questions".

2) What one piece ofevidence or one specific resource (DVD, book,

website, etc.) has been the most convincing to you in rejecting the "official" story of 9/11?

I've read so many books and seen so many films, I find it impossible to offer "one" as most crucial. Together, they all add up to an informational gestalt with a secure center and fuzzier edges. At a certain point investigation bleeds off into speculation — and that is valuable too, though it has to be understood for what it is. I do have to say that I am put off by the tone of Alex Jones's presentations, and, though they have some solid content, I don't feel that they are useful to show to beginners — at least any with an allergy to used car salesmen.

3) How has your search for 9/11 truth impacted your life?

It's been quite a burden, not only considering the time it has taken to read, watch, listen to, and study the material, but because of the depression it leaves behind, depression concerning the irrationality of most people's responses. Ignorance I can understand, when the MSM has so gotten behind the official story and obscured or pooh-poohed all else. But smart people, political people, lefties, people with an informed and developed criticism of the administration, and an understanding of the real history and politics of the United States, respected friends, co-workers and colleagues — most use the same gesture when I bring up the issues: the hands are thrown up, palms out, to face level, and the mouth says "I'm not going there." They all say the same sentence: "I'm not going there." They don't believe anything else Bush says, but they believe this whole, preposterous 9/11 story. I don't get it, I don't get it, I don't get it. One woman elaborated, "I don't want to live in a world where such things could be true." But they are, ma'am, they are.

And then there are the more stereotypical, but still confounding reactions of some folks-on-the-street. One would expect them to be as neutral about the 911 "issue" as they are about many other distant things in their lives. I say "some folks", and my experience has been that most people will listen if they have time, sign a petition for "a new, independent investigation" after hearing about the shortcomings of the official story and official reports, and accept a free DVD to watch at home. But there are a few who treat the idea of looking into the contradictions as some kind of thought-crime. The epithets vary, but the body language is the same — that of disgust, of anger, of having been polluted by the encounter, as if they needed to go right home to shower. These sorts of interactions are few, but always upsetting, no matter how cavalierly we try to brush them off.

The other side of this, however, has been meeting and joining up with a few like-minded, like-tactic-ed individuals with whom it's been a pleasure to share meetings, discussions and demonstrations, even if in the bubble of our own openmindedness and analyses.

The most basic downer, however is that the overall public response has undermined my faith, certainly in human rationality, but more deeply in the very possibilities of humanity. Sounds overblown, I know, but if ideological blinders are so thick, if folks are not capable of seeing what's in front of their eyes, what makes a coherent, reasonable story and what doesn't — then what hope is there for the survival of our species? And it's too easy to go from there to feeling that it's best if we acknowledge our civilization's downfall and give it all up in the least destructive way possible. Bad thoughts. Boo. What keeps me going? "Pessimism of the intellect; optimism of the will."

I persist with this subject matter because the stakes are so high. Even though the likelihood of mass consciousness change is so tiny, should it happen, should even 10% of it happen, it might very well be able — uniquely so — to bring down not only our corrupt political and governance systems, and preempt the possibility of the next "9/11 terrorist attack" with its inevitable martial law follow-up, but it might also change forever the way Americans understand history and government, and decimate the pathological exceptionalism we have so deeply imbibed. Were that to happen, the world would breathe more easily.

Old Jew Writer at the Young Men's Christian Association

Even If I Don't Look Like Any of the Photos on the Wall

How does the Y help your writing?

First of all, my daily Y workouts keep body and brain alive. Without them, I'd likely devolve into a lethargic ball of daily-napping lard. My particular occupational hazard is that I work many hours a day at home, seven steps from food. It's easy, in a difficult sentence, to go looking for words in the refrigerator. The funny thing is, they're often there — but so are the lipids. And the calories. The Y is my antidote.

Furthermore, the Y keeps my writing at a high level, since am a recovering illiterate. I grew up reading only comic books and, as a chemistry major and microbiology grad student, read very little fiction or poetry in school. So I use my workouts to fill in all the gaps in my education. I have a program called "treadmill reading" (which includes the stationary bikes) which started with Don Quixote, and continues with all the wonderful things I SHOULD have read, and now MUST read, if I'm going to be a writer. So my head is filled daily with the words and thoughts of the great authors, from Austin to Zola. All those insights, those story ideas, that glorious language! It does sustain and normalize a level to shoot for.

If my workouts sustain the reading, the reading also sustains my workouts. I come every day because I need to know what <u>happens</u> to Martin Chuzzlewit as he confronts the nauseating wiles of Mr. Pecksniff. No slacking off here.

Then too, there is the marvelous spiritual smorgasbord of the men's lockers. Fat-burning literary treadmills are available elsewhere, but the grand space and the unique gallery of characters which populate the Y's men's locker room have supplied me not only with new friends, but with amazing characters, un-inventable snips of dialogue, and glimpses into lives I'd never have come upon. That there seem to be no women chatting down there is, admittedly, a sad limitation.

Finally, there are the laps in the pool. No reading possible, alas, so I just have to meditate. A choicer word, a better way to construct a sentence, a new character who will add this or that — all pop up in that alpha-state of rhythmic monotony. The problem is to remember it past the showers, till I can get to my locker to write it down.

Absent the Y, vagueness and entropy increase. It is one of my essential tools, like Google and computer.

Happy Birthday, Happy Deathday

Review of *Améry's On Aging*

Apr 23, 2006 (Shakespeare's 442nd birthday)

Perhaps it's because I share my birthday with Adolf Hitler, born exactly fifty years earlier, but I've always had a doubtful attitude toward birthday celebrations, especially mine. Besides, I don't like getting birthday presents, or being the center of attention. And groups singing "Happy Birthday To You" (to anyone) give me the willies, out of tune ones, or worse, some of the choral groups I belong to, singing in "sophisticated" harmony.

In my forthcoming novel, *Golem Song* [2006], Alan Krieger tells his girlfriend, Debbie, about his attempt at a fix:

"I actually did write another, different birthday song. I sent it in to *Reader's Digest* hoping it would be adopted by the whole country, beginning with the semi-literate lower classes."

"What happened?"

"I've got the rejection slip in a cheap frame in the bedroom. Wanna hear it?"

"Sure. Do you think I should sit down first?"

"Yeah. Pull up a couch. Ready?

[Tune: Bach chorale O Haupt voll Blut und Wunden]
A semi-happy birthday
to you, ma'am (it could be "sir"), while you can,
for happiness is fleeting
and death does have his plan.
Though now you're able-bodied
and full of life and vim

your body will be sullied
and taken o'er by him—
Deb-bie. (You put the person's name in there.)"

"They didn't accept that? I'm shocked."

"Yeah. And the tune is even from the *St. Matthew Passion.* It's the chorale when Christ is up on the cross."

Birthdays. The number of years ahead is ever more miniscule compared to the number of years behind. And time passes ever more quickly. Memories become less detailed, reunions more frightening. Hair grows gray, skin scaly, trim turns thick.

Aging. We would do well to study up. I can recommend no better commentary than Jean Améry's *On Aging* (Indiana U. Press, 1994). This is not a book for the faint-hearted. Améry's forte is to pull no punches, but rather, in naming what is now happening, in depicting what's ahead, to equip us to better understand our universal plight.

Each of his five chapters confronts a different aspect of growing older, and finally, old. The first, "Existence and the Passage of Time", describes our changing sense of time, and the gradual shrinking of our space-in-the-world as we fill up with time. The second chapter, "Stranger to Oneself", considers the many ways that we become alienated from our own bodies, bearing them up now, instead of their bearing us. The third, "The Look of Others", develops the notion of social aging, the realization that it is no longer possible to live up to one's potential, but that one simply is — because one was. This chapter leads naturally into the fourth, "Not To Understand the World Anymore", a depiction of cultural aging, in which one tries, awkwardly at best, to understand the sign systems of the present through the understandings of the past, and thus becomes aware of being a stranger in the present world. The last chapter concerns our final chapter: "To Live With Dying". Aging, Améry asserts, is "the stretch of time in which we meet with the thought of death." Here, he challenges each of us to find our own uncompromised

313

combination of "revolt and resignation" — the subtitle of the book.

A serious reading of Améry's book generalizes out beyond the individual into the aging of a nation; the aging of the idea of a nation; the aging of the memory of a nation. July 4th, coming up.

Shades of the Comic Past

$$$ for The Beard Poster — The Fillmore and Me

February 19, 2006

As the future looms, here with its websites and podcasts, and out there in the hallways of fascism, the past occasionally arises, and often with a comic mask.

Today a friend sent a link to wolfgangsvault.com, which offers for sale "vintage t-shirts, rock posters..." etc. I was not the target of this message, simply a member of his "send interesting things" list. But I thought I'd look up a poster for a show I directed at the Fillmore Auditorium back in the sixties.

I found it. Imagine my surprise when I discovered that a small handbill for that event was selling for $408. To avoid excess, I'll spare you the purple ink version, which is going for $3,028.

Jeez, I once had 500 of these things in the back of my car. That's more than $200,000 worth. I couldn't have sold an equal volume of drugs for that much — and those were the high old days. It just goes to show, though what it goes to show is beyond me.

Well, should we speak of wagging the dog, here's one thing it goes to show:

In the early sixties, Bill Graham was working as the publicity guy for the San Francisco Mime Troupe, and was not getting on well with Ronnie Davis, its director. I was at the time directing at the San Francisco Actor's Workshop, doing experimental plays at the tiny Encore theater, while John Hancock, the artistic director did the mainstage productions. Bill wanted me to leave the Actor's Workshop,

315

and start a new theater with him. With a new baby girl, I wasn't very interested in seeking iffy new work, and giving up my excellent position. But Bill was an interesting character, and I thought I'd at least go for a ride with him one afternoon to see an empty building he had found.

The building was the Fillmore Auditorium, locked and shuttered. Bill let us in with a key he'd borrowed from the realtor, and we walked through the building, illuminating our way with matches. (Bill, as I recall, was a chain smoker.) The place was haunted by ancient elegance, and as spookily cobwebbed as Miss Havisham's wedding hall. I don't know how long it had been abandoned. We stood in the middle of the great central room, and Bill outlined to me his plan:

We would build a theater here, The American Theater, and would finance the whole operation by staging rock concerts — a new phenomenon at the time. Bill would be the impresario to engage the bands and advertise them, and I would direct the shows. Then we could afford to do new American plays no one else would do, and advance the cause of American theater.

I think *The Beard* was the only play ever headlined — perhaps ever performed — at the Fillmore. I had directed the show to some acclaim at the Encore, it had moved from there to be busted by the vice squad at The Committee, a North Beach theater venue, and by that time was pretty well known in town. So it was a good bet. But it's an intimate show in all ways, and going from a 200 seat theater to a 2,000 seat one was an intriguing challenge.

The rest is history — not of me and the Beard, but of Bill and the Fillmore. The theater plans were left behind, and the tail not only wagged the dog, but became the dog in toto — and a whole crucial chapter of American history and culture was born.

The ironic part is that having been present at the creation, I had almost nothing to do with what ensued. I never went to an event at the Fillmore other than my own — too loud! All the rock music of the sixties, seventies, eighties and nineties passed me by. I spent my music time playing Beethoven quartets and orchestral works right through the Vietnam war and beyond. I don't think I've ever heard Elvis. The only group I might be able to recognize is the Beatles. When I wrote a Greatful Dead chapter for *SKULK*, I had to ask a friend make a tape for me of songs he thought might be relevant.

Pathetic, huh? But you can't do everything, and I do know a helluva lot of early, baroque, classical, romantic and modern music. I just don't know any of the bands that played at the Fillmore.

Bar Mitzvah

How I Learned I Was a Jewish Writer

May 4, 2005

It's amazing how dumb we can be about ourselves. Or at least how dumb I can be. It took a reviewer of my debut novel, *Insect Dreams*, to point out to me that I was a Jewish writer. And yet my first novel, *Golem Song*, still unpublished, had already been on frankly Jewish themes. I'd thought it was just about some crazy guy.

I'd already conceived *The Lamentations of Julius Marantz* (between us, "Orange Julius" in Yiddish) about a Jewish kid growing up in Coney Island, seduced by the roller coaster and parachute jump into becoming a physicist. And still I didn't realize I was a Jewish writer. But then some reviewer said so. And then the National Yiddish Book Center invited me to read in their "Jewish Writers Live!" series. That clinched it. I realized I must be a Jewish writer!

But only after they told me. Dumb.

By now, I've written a short novel, *Tsim-Tsum*, about God — YHWH — who lives in a '96 Hyundai, and is thinking about how to fix creation according to tricks in the Lurianic Kaballah. And my current novel, *The Education of Arnold Hitler*, is heavily concerned with one young man's struggle to understand his Jewish heritage.

But in that novel, Edmund Jabès, the great Egyptian-French Jewish poet, instructs Arnold — and me— in the complexity of being a Jewish anything.

To become Jewish, Jabès says,

> *...you must not become Jewish. One must not*

enter the Promised Land, never accomplish the task. One must remain exiled — forever, for being Jewish is an expression in the conditional. The distance that separates Jew from the Promised Land is not only exile from the land itself, but exile even from the call — in order to be what is called. It means no rest — ever. It means swimming, swimming, swimming toward a nonexistent end, in order not to sink. Your questions are not to be linked to any answer, but to a vital, gaping breach forever there between the question and the answer.

Into the Blog

On Starting to Write at 57

I didn't want to get involved online. I had other work to do — like writing novels. Real work. But my publisher wanted me to have "an online presence", and being an eternally good boy, I obeyed. Makes me wonder what I would have done as a Jew in Warsaw in the Hitlertimes. Anyway, here is my first blog posting. I'm back to not being online anymore except for rare, special occasions.

February 18, 2005

Blog. The word alone makes me want to don a wet-suit and a self-contained breathing apparatus. Eschewing the arachno-gaian beauty of "web" and the theo-linguistic reach of "logos", it evokes for me only the dark muck of bogs and the visceral reaction, "Bleccch!"

But "blog" it seems to be—by the immediate embrace of computerland, and who am I to fight this City Hall? Hell, I wouldn't even have been asked by my publisher to write one sans computerland, and I wouldn't have a publisher because I would never have written anything.

I began writing only at 57 because I never wanted to retype a page. So much for re-writing and editing. And of course I'd never ask or hire anyone to type anything for me. Wrong side of the class struggle.

But back in the early 80s I was gathering signatures for a nuclear freeze in the mocking minus temperatures of a Vermont winter. My fingers were frozen, the pen wouldn't work, and there were very few customers crazy enough to be out. Across the street, the Capitol Theater was playing *The China Syndrome*, and I thought, "This is nuts. Instead of standing out here, I should just write a film, have it produced, and not have to freeze my ass off for a couple of names on a petition."

There followed a long and interesting story of stupid-naive-meets-the-real-world-of-publishing-and production, but early on, an inspired proto-geek told me I should have a better looking manuscript if I wanted anyone to take it seriously. He said he'd work with me on the computer he had built from spare parts.

It's hard to imagine today—typing into a Rube Goldberg machine with wires attached by alligator clips to an oscilloscope CRT. I think there were even some radio tubes involved. But there it was—my "Einstein Weeps" manuscript glowing green in the computer's memory, and no way to get it out but to print it, since there were no floppies I think, even floppy ones. I don't remember how the printer was rigged—perhaps there were already neonate dot-matrix printers, perhaps Sam had made wirey love to an IBM Selectric, but before we printed out, he noticed I had spelled Charley Brown (a character) wrong throughout the manuscript. I was about to go through (no pages to retype!) and fix each occurrence, when Sam said "Wait. I'll show you something neat." He had programmed in a find and replace function: when he typed in "Charley", then typed in "Charlie", his little machine whirred for some seconds, and then said "Peep!" That's what it said—a machine talking to me: "Peep!" And in case I didn't speaka da language, it put up on screen "Done."

"Peep!" "Done." That was it. My heart went out, and I was computerized forever. And also freed up to write more than press releases.

These were the days of the *Whole Earth Catalogue*, the first editions of which were written and composed on a Kaypro CPM computer. I bought one used for 50 bucks, a sweet grey and blue metal suitcase-y thing whose face detached to become a keyboard which spoke to a 6" screen. I wrote all my sermons on it when I went off to UU seminary. And then I got twice fired for being "too political" for my congregations, and wound up working at the University of Vermont, where I had a real computer on my desk. By the time I was downsized, I had computer, internet, and typing skills, and could get serious about writing. *Insect Dreams*, my debut novel, followed soon after.

So, having been seduced by "Peep!", who am I to object to "blog"? Especially if I don't have to retype a page.

Using Wolfgang's Book

A Mentor for Madness

I am a writer of comico-philosophico-politico-sometimes-historical novels. At the left of my writing desk sit shelves of reference books, dictionaries in seven languages, almanacs, guides to this and that — Marxist thought, contemporary thinkers, a *Dictionary of Theories*, an *Encyclopedia of Human Behavior*, a *Book of Days*. On my right, and upstairs, multivolume sets: the Britannica, the OED, the *Interpreter's Bible*.

I use none of them anymore. Who needs all that dust, small print, looking up, and thumbing through when you have old www. at your fingertips?

Only two volumes remain directly at hand, dust free, slipping easily out of and back into their slots: one is Bryan Garner's *Dictionary of Modern American Usage* (so brilliantly brought to my attention by David Foster Wallace's famous review, *q.v.*). The other is Wolfgang Mieder's *Encyclopedia of World Proverbs*.

The use of the first is obvious for any writer or editor shaky on the difference between "which" and "that", or the contemporary use of diacritical marks. But Wolfgang's book serves a much deeper function.

Exempli gratia:
I am now writing a novel about a dying patient and his doctor. The poor guy is afflicted with ALS, amyotrophic lateral sclerosis, Lou Gehrig's disease. You don't want to have it. Little by little, your muscle function decays until you can no longer move. But alas, your sensory and intellectual functions remain intact, even sharpened. You can itch like crazy, but can't scratch. And then you lie there *thinking* about that.

Your tongue and jaw muscles go, so you can't speak. Because you can't swallow, you have to be fed by naso-gastric tube. When your diaphragm stops working, you can't breathe. You have to *be* breathed by a mechanical respirator. Needless to say, you think a lot about your inevitable death. But what do you think? What does my character think?

I myself am constricted by my own pre-deceased imagination, my limited experiences of death, and my own culture's don't-think-about-death-iness. So what can I put in my character's mind as he lies there unmoving day and night — thoughts I don't have to give to him?

For a wide-range of possible things such a human being might be thinking, it is always a good idea to consult Mieder.

Perhaps my ex-potter wonders why him:
No death without a cause. (Maltese)
What have I karmically done? he worries.

Perhaps he is afraid of what will come to pass:
Death deals doubtfully. (English)
I wish I could make the choices, he longs.
Death is the revealer of secrets. (African) (Hausa)
What will they find out? he wonders.
Death will come uninvited. (Lithuanian)
There is plenty of time, plenty of treatment still to go, he reassures.

Perhaps he is longing for comfort:
Death answers before it is asked. (Russian)
Death is concise like good proverb. (Russian)
Death never comes too late. (Irish)
When death is there, dying is over. (Russian)
Look upon death as a going home. Chinese)
He feels better, more confident.

Perhaps he is longing for death:
Until death there is no knowing what may happen. (Italian)

So let's get it on, he thinks.

After death one becomes important. (Yiddish)

At last!

Perhaps he is considering suicide:

Better death than long sickness. (Welsh)

One cannot die before one's death. (Russian)

Yes, go for it.

Perhaps he is full of self-doubt:

Staying and staring is the death of the buck. (Ovambo)

Staying and staring — that's me, the old buck.

The death of the Wolf is the health of the sheep. (English)

Who will be my sheep?

Perhaps he feels his death should be punished:

Death pulls at a long rope who desires another's death. (French)

How can I get back at her — my doctor lover — for doing all this to me?

Perhaps he is confronted by mysterious images:

When death comes, the dog presses up to the wall of the mosque. (Turkish)

My poor invalid might not "know" any of these proverbs per se, but surely he could be thinking their themes.

You can easily see how mind-loosening a trip to Mieder can be, how stimulating of the imagination, how indicative of narrative roads-not-yet-taken, of unimagined character details.

I, at my desk, am only one person with my one person's thoughts. But the whole world and its thought possibilities are only twenty inches to my left.

Thank you, Wolfgang.

Marceau and the Bomb

Flying and Crashing Among the Great

Sometime back in the winter of 1979, I was standing, freezing, on State Street, the capitol of Montpelier, Vermont, trying to get signatures on a petition calling on both the United States and the Soviet Union to freeze all arms testing, production and deployment. It was so cold that there were few people on the street, and those who were out were so wrapped up in coats, hats and scarves, and so determined to get briskly to wherever they were going, that they were barely aware of me and my clipboard, and not likely to want to stop, listen to my pitch, "Would you like to sign a petition for a mutually agreed arms freeze?", etc., take off their insulated gloves, and sign their names on a piece of paper likely to be ignored by whoever it was addressed to. To top it off my ball point pen became semi-frozen by the time it was offered and delivered scarcely readable signatures. It was 11 in the morning. I'd been out for two hours, had only half a dozen signatures, and was shivering. An hour to go before the lunch hour crew would arrive to relieve me. This was ridiculous.

I looked across the street at the marquee of the State Theater: THE CHINA SYNDROME. I hadn't seen it, but knew it was about the possible meltdown of a nuclear power plant, and had been effective at making the public nervous about our own recently built nuclear plant, less than two hours south, at the bottom of the state. The following brainfart reasoning occurred:

"What the hell am doing standing out here, freezing my ass off, not getting any signatures anyway? I should go home and write a film, and it will play across the street and nationwide, and it will get everyone on our side around nuclear weapons and energy. Oh, and it should be about Einstein. Everybody loves Einstein, and he hated the bomb, and he was pretty smart…."

The gap between writing a film and having it play nationwide did not occur. The fact that I had no idea how to write a film did not occur. Nor did the fact that I did not know all that much about Einstein. I went home and "wrote a film" — completely unfilmable, something that would be circular-filed after the first page by anyone in the business…what did I know? I "wrote a film" about Einstein and the bomb, xeroxed several copies (@$1.37), and clutching my several copies, each in their manila envelope, now what? It occurred to me that I didn't know what I was doing.

One thing about the "film", though. Because I was determined to make it completely truthful, a documentary play completely documented, every word spoken by every character had to have been an actual quote, every speaker doing what he really had done, where he did it. (They were all hes, those bomb and government guys.) Because Einstein was such an uncontrollable blabbermouth, a fervent believer in universal, international science, he was kept far away from the goings-on in Los Alamos, Hanford, and Oak Ridge. But because I wanted his spirit to be present at counterfactual places and conversations, I included a figure called "Einstein Mime", a white-faced, long-haired figure, mute, identically dressed, who would be a silent presence at significant meetings and moments of the play. I hadn't thought of Marcel Marceau in his classic, eternal character of Bip, just of a mute Einstein replica whose existence wouldn't break the documentary rules I had set up for myself. Here is the opening:

THE PASSION OF A.E.
A film treatment

1. EINSTEIN-MIME plays solo violin in Bach's orchestra, 1730.
The BOY WITH THE CAT, watcher, pointer, judge, is in the room.

2. The H-bomb explodes at Eniwetok, 1952.

3. *The Little Boy's Dance with the Compass, Ulm, 1884. Einstein's FATHER presents a gift that changes a life.*

4. *PROFESSOR RATH (Emil Ludwig in Der blaue Engle) passes judgement.*
"He'll never make a success of anything."
1889
(Einstein:: The Life and Times by Ronald W. Clark p.27, attributed to one of young Einstein's headmasters)

5. *Los Alamos, 1945. Enrico FERMI enunciates priorities:*
"Don't bother me with your conscientious scruples! After all, the thing's superb physics!
(Brighter than a Thousand Suns, Robert Jungk, 1958, James Cleugh, trans. P 202.)

6. *FERMI Biography*

7. *In the beginning was the end: $E = mc^2$*

8. *War explodes. 1914.*
Voice over: Ernst Rutherford, "I have been engaged in experiments which suggest that the atom can be artificially disintegrated. If it is true, it is of greater importance than a war." (1919) (Junck, 1958)

9. *9 November 1918: The Kaiser renounces the throne. The Weimar Republic. The violence of Left vs. Right*
Alfred Döblin:
Die entscheidenden Angriffe auf die Menschheit gehen jetzt von den Reißbrettern und den Labors aus." Berge Meere und Giganten (1924)
"The decisive attacks upon mankind now come from the drawing boards and the laboratories."

10. *Overture. Totentanz.*
Inflation.

"Things cannot go on like this."
Mountains of money
  "Things cannot go on like this."
Eating dead horses off the streets.
  "Things cannot go on like this."
Women strip for pennies thrown.
  "Things cannot go on like this."
Adolf Hitler.
WALTER BENJAMIN sees it all: voice over:
Die Erwartung, daß es nicht mehr so weitergehen könne, eines Tages sich darüber belehrt finden, dass es für das Leiden des einzelnen wie der Gemeinschaften nur eine Grenze, über die hinaus es nicht mehr weiter geht, gibt: die Vernichtung. II. (Walter Benjamin, Gesammelte Schriften: IV, I
Herausgegeben von Tillman Rexroth, Suhrkamp, 1991)
The expectation that things cannot go on like this will one day be apprised of the fact that there is only one limit to the suffering of individuals and communities, beyond which it cannot go any further: annihilation.

11. Street interview, Vermont, 1982:
"War is good for technology."
The BOY in the background.

12. Cambridge, 1932.
The key is found to the final door in Bluebeard's
Castle: CHADWICK discovers the neutron

13. E-MIME throws a ball against a wall. The Berlin apartment house transforms for one throw into the Berlin Wall. Then back again.
EINSTEIN voice over:
"The armaments race between the US and the USSR assumes a hysterical character. On both sides, the means to mass destruction are perfected with feverish haste behind respective walls of secrecy. The ghostlike character of this development lies in its apparently compulsory trend. Every step appears as the unavoidable consequence of the preceding one. In the

end there beckons more and more clearly general annihilation." Speech: "Peace in the Atomic Era", February 19, 1950
The ball breaks an outraged window. E-MIME slinks away. The BOY watches.

14. PROFESSOR RATH predicts the future:
"He'll never make a success of anything."

And so forth. It turns out Einstein had a little bit more to do with the war than he cared to admit to himself.

After much to-do concerning science and politics in the age of Ronald Reagan, it ended thus:

123. Einstein Weeps.
EINSTEIN walks slowly into Bach's room, the room of the opening scene, now disheveled and empty. On the writing desk he finds Bach's last, unfinished, manuscript page — a fugue on the subject B-A-C-H.
The background music stops. Silence. A single tear drops from EINSTEIN's eye, making a small sound as it hits the manuscript. The camera watches an ink blot spread. It looks like an explosion.
FINIS

Over the credits at the end, voice-over:

EINSTEIN ANGEL:
"I am an old man mainly known as a crank who doesn't wear socks. But I am working at a more fantastic rate than ever, and I still hope to solve my pet problem of the unified physical field. I feel as if I were flying in an airplane high in the sky without quite knowing how I will ever reach the ground..."

Anyway, having spent $1.37 in xeroxing, plus the cost of five manila envelopes, I had to do something with them. Turns out that the very evening I had packed and sealed the unaddressed envelopes, Marcel Marceau was doing a show at the big Flynn theater up in Burlington. Though I loved what I'd see of Marceau on TV, at something like eight bucks a ticket, it was out of my range, even conceptually. So I handed one of my five envelopes to a friend who I knew was going, and asked him to leave it at the box office for MM. Two bucks down the drain, but what the hell else was I going to do with any of those envelopes? Who has ever made contact with a world-famous celebrity, by leaving an envelope at the box office, "Please deliver to Marcel Marceau"? What would happen? Nothing, of course. And that's what happened.

But three weeks later, I'm sitting in my room a few blocks away from the petitioning, when the phone rings.

"Allo. Marc Estran"?

"Yes."

"Zis is Marcel Marceau. You have made a masterpiece here. We must do it. You come see me in BosTON, and we talk more about it. I am at ze Park Plaza. It is time for Marceau to speak! You come tomorrow afternoon at two, and we talk, OK? OK. Goodbye."

I am not making this up. You just have to imagine the very thick French accent. The only trouble was "tomorrow" was threatening a huge, stay-off-the-roads, snowstorm, the kind where you can't see more than six feet in front of you, the road lines and signs are covered in snow, and every second is white-knuckle driving. Well, I'm alive to be writing this, so I must have gotten there, but never again will I do something so death-courting and stupid.

It turned out that MM had always wanted to play Einstein. He thought of his position in his performer's world as equivalent to Einstein's position in the world of physics. His family was Jewish. His father had died at Auschwitz, while his mother survived. Along with his brother, he had joined the resistance, helping Jewish children escape capture, using mime to keep them quiet while escaping to Switzerland. That's how he began his "art of silence". Who knew?

Now, using his many talented students at his École Internationale de Mime, he wanted to make large group shows, "mimodrame" he called it, and would like to develop my "film" into such a theater piece.

His instruction to me: "You go home and make it more zany, ok? Then you bring it to show me when I am in New York."

More "zany"? Who knows what that might mean to a Frenchman? "Zany" is not exactly "documentary". Well, "zany" brought up Harpo Marx crawling all over the place doing unexpected things, and then a stage setting (which I did know something about, having a Master from UCLA in Theater) involving the flies and the pit as well as the main stage. It was getting pretty zany.

When I met Marceau after an evening performance a few months later in New York, he was very rushed, and did not really have time to work with me, so he invited me to come work with him for a couple of weeks at his house outside of Paris. He sent me plane tickets, and had a student pick me up at Orly.

The funny thing is that he wasn't much less busy there, and I rarely saw him, except when accompanying him to teach his classes in Paris. (A master-teacher if ever there was one, sitting on a backwards chair in his studio, as his brilliant students performed for him, while he corrected them. The slightest change would make a huge difference, and he nailed it every time.) We did make some progress, but the play was never finished finished, or put into production. He'd gotten sick. I'd get a postcard every few months. His last said, "Do not worry. Einstein is eternal."

Then the project dropped through the cracks, and I never heard from him again. Next I heard from him, 28 years after our first phone call, he was dead at 84.

The following play, EINSTEIN WEEPS, is the product of those last weeks in Paris, plus some stagecraft thinking by the late Dennis Livingston, a former partner in crime.

It lacks the intense prosecutorial scenes in which Einstein flees the testimonial evidence of his peripheral participation in the war effort.

But thanks to Marcel Marceau, it is more zany than its homunculus predecessor.

The Golem Olympics

Jewish Museum Golem Exhibit

In Feb, 2016, I was asked by the Jewish Museum Berlin to contribute a catalogue comment on some item in a major show on the history of the Golem — a huge clay figure brought to life by Rabbi Löwe's kabbalistic magic in order to protect Prague Jews from a gathering pogrom. This story does not have a happy end.

I chose a painting from 1916, Fritz Ascher's "The Golem".

I warned the museum about what I might write. They said, "Write anything you want." This is what I wrote:

> Oh, Rabbi Löwe, [the rabbi who made the Golem
> out of clay and brought it to life] be careful what you
> wish for, and Victor Frankenstein, beware. And you,

Herr Doktor Faust, don't count on a second salvation.

Storytellers and artists foresee, but the world plays things out. Einstein nailed it: "Three great forces rule the world," he said, "stupidity, fear and greed."

Fritz Ascher captured those forces in 1916. His foreground translates Einstein's trio into the hands and faces of

— terminal Fear,
— expiring Wisdom,
— and desperately grasping Greed.

And rising above them, looming over the toxic miasma, their collective Golem.

"Thou shalt not pass!" say its arms, "I will kill!" say its eyes, and "darkest night" says its cloak, "No moon or stars for you. Only Nacht und Nebel."

Behind this apocalyptic gang of four stands their salient element: a wall, a fortress — or shall we call it a "separation fence"? — perhaps the most iconically prescient part of Ascher's vision. And stupidity, fear and greed have different faces now, smoother, white-haired, silver-tongued. But Ascher's wall still evokes… the wall.

Benjamin Netanyahu: "Will we surround all of the State of Israel with fences and barriers? The answer is yes. In the area that we live in, we must defend ourselves against the wild beasts."

Hear O Israel: hear this latest misguided, misguiding, misstepping "rabbi" protecting his community unto its death.

Will Judaism survive its current Golem? Will the snaking, apartheid wall protect — or imprison the wall-builders in suffocating isolation? Will their Zyklon breath kill not only the purported beasts beyond the barriers, but also the gassers?

I wondered if they would permit it.

In March, I received I received the following response (the Hebrew in the text means "Shoah") from the Museum's Deputy Director:

> "We are not going to include your text because we feel that your insinuation to compare the political situation in Israel with the האוש (fog and night / Giftgas) will be thoroughly misunderstood in Germany.
>
> What could be possibly expressed in Israel to underline the political and moral problem inherent in the governments dealings with the Palestinians will not necessarily be understood the same way in Germany. Being critical about Israeli politics ourselves, we also fight in Germany against resentful and ignorant attitudes against Israel which are based on no knowledge of the conflict in the Middle East and are mere projections on the background of German history. We deal with widespread groups of people who like to deny German responsibility for the האוש by accusing Israeli politicians of trying to annihilate Palestinians in the style of Nazi-Germany."

I responded as follows:

> Upon receiving your invitation to contribute to your Golem catalogue, I wrote a warning that I would be referencing Israel in my text. I was told to write whatever I wanted, and not that it would be subject to "approval".
>
> Understanding that there could be cultural differences in reception, I sent the text to some German friends, one a theater director, and one the chairman of a literature department at a German university that has hosted me as poet in residence. Both thought the text to be acceptable, appropriate both to the painting and to the current understanding of the Palestinian situation in Germany.
>
> So I sent it on to you.
>
> Without getting into the subject, I will simply say that it is standard Israeli hasbara to delegitimize any

comparison of Israeli behavior with that of the Nazis. Yet the comparisons are obvious and horrifyingly ironic. Especially to an old Jew like me.

I assume I was invited to contribute to the catalogue because of my novel, Golem Song. That work, while a comic novel, was explicitly about the pathology of thinking oneself and one's "race" "chosen". It had a good reception in the Jewish community, including a positive review in the Forward, and expense-paid readings in Omaha and Virginia.

Speaking openly about Israeli atrocities, —

— settlements as Lebensraum activities;

— restrictions of Palestinians from travel, work, building or reconstruction as comparable to race laws;

— widespread destruction of homes and agriculture as Kristallnacht without the glass;

— attacks on children (Ayelet Shaked's "little snakes") [https://electronicintifada.net/blogs/ali-abunimah/israeli-lawmakers-call-genocide-palestinians-gets-thousands-facebook-likes], their schools and their health as intentional genocide of an upcoming generation

— has become more common among Americans.

I am therefore surprised and disappointed that an institution as radical in form and content as the JMB would be so far behind the general understanding of Israeli government practices among the nations of the world, as demonstrated by annual UN General Assembly votes.

Should you reconsider, and decide to use my contribution (perhaps using gas without the Gift, and night without the Nebel), you can pay me the promised honorarium. Otherwise, please send it as your and my contribution to the next Free Gaza Flotilla, and let me know you have done that.

Thank you.

The Museum ignored my request to send my honorarium to the Women's Flotilla, but after some interesting back and forth about the continuing sensitivity to Nazi language on the part of contemporary Germans, the museum accepted a slightly expurgated version of my text, and sent me the honorarium. That honorarium (along with its story) was sent to the Women's Boat to Gaza — the next flotilla attempt to break Israel's cruel and illegal siege on the (occupied) territory.
I'd suggest you look into what these brave women are up to, and support them however you can. [https://freedomflotilla.org/]

The Golem exhibit opened on September 23, 2016, and ran for four months.

ESSAYS POLITICAL

F35

The F-35 As Golden Calf

Tearing open the sky

Below is a 2016 commentary I wrote for Vermont Digger concerning a piece by Air Force Col. Rosanne Greco, that attacked the F-35 as a colossal political boondoggle.

For those who have never experienced it, the F35 is the latest experimental jet bomber, with nuclear capability. It has three models, one for the Army, one for the Navy, one for the Marines. Each plane costs approximately $10 million, costs $27,000/hour in fuel to fly, and for some reason, a training wing is based, not out in the desert somewhere, but right in Vermont's largest city.

There are now 20 of them, taking off four or five in a row. The take off and landing approach noise (right over an airport-neighboring elementary school) has been measured at 115 decibels — not just intolerably loud, but of a barbaric quality, deeply penetrating bones and being. Almost all in its vicinity want the program stopped, except those whose cars sport a bumper sticker reading "F35 (graphic of plane) — the Sound of Freedom".

Rosanne Greco's equation of the F-35 with the golden calf of the Hebrews is a challenging read which becomes only deeper with further consideration.

Assuming only the symbolic, not historical, nature of the tale, we have to ask whether Moses' people were just "primitive", stupid, "worshipping" an object they had watched Aaron melt down and sculpt from their own jewelry. Clearly something else is going on in this Exodus story.

Moses had been commanded by YHWH to climb the Sinai mountain — alone — so that he may hear the truth, from the horse's mouth as it were, about what being "the chosen people" would require. We might compare our being the "indispensable nation".

But Moses had been gone almost 40 days and nights, and the people feared that he, and any further understanding of the great and only God they were to serve was hopeless. That God, he told them, was invisible, unimaginable — so what could they know, how were they to behave?

So while his brother was gone, perhaps forever, Aaron built the people a SYMBOL for their own desire for an imaginable, possibly knowable god, an object to temporarily lift their morale until Moses' return. The statue was not that of a powerful bull, but of a calf, something the people knew how to nourish and care for, a "godlet" that reminded the wanderers of themselves, a this-world representation of something valuable, and far greater which might soon be known.

Error! We know what happened. Moses spent the next 39 years trying to convince his people to take on the real demands of the inscrutable. That is the symbolic meaning — still relevant — of the story.

So back to Col. Greco: if the F-35 is a "golden calf", falsely worshipped because visible, understandable, then what is the misunderstood YHWH-object for which it stands? It may take more than another 39 years for America to understand its marching orders, even though it professes deep connection with the Christ that came to ease and simplify the 617 Commandments. ("His yoke is easy, his burthen is light.")

Whatever it is that is out there to be realized by us, the chosen people, the indispensable nation, it might have something to do with love (caritas) among people, and not with gold, cute-techiness, or violence.

Noiseless

Most of the noise concerning the F35 issues is about NOISE — and rightly so, as many Vermonters will be hurt, their lives and homes devalued and in some cases destroyed.

But let's not forget another aspect, at the moment relatively noiseless, but in the long run, equally worthy of note: the military's push for the F-35 is intimately connected with Obama's plan to upgrade the US's nuclear strike capability. The current F-16 fleet is incapable of carrying and delivering the newly-designed "smart" nuclear bombs. The F-35 has been designed to do just that.

By supporting the development of the F-35, in Burlington or not, Vermonters are willy-nilly upholding the US's evasion of the Nuclear Non-Proliferation Treaty — to which it is a signatory — which contains a pledge to slowly lower nuclear strike capacity to zero.

The anti-F-35 movement itself has bracketed this issue, in part because the local, clearly predictable effects will be so severe, but partly out of wariness about being seen as "unpatriotic". What I think is unpatriotic is to allow one's own country to be the linchpin and supplier of WMDs beyond any local nightmare.

Let this remain an undertone at least in the current symphony of noise

The Sound Of Freedom

A common assertion among F-35 proponents is that noise from military aircraft is perceived as "the sound of freedom." This seems odd.

Freedom is complex. But for simplicity, let's examine a most American summary — that of FDR's "four freedoms", a proposal for four fundamental freedoms everyone should enjoy: freedom of speech, freedom of worship, freedom from want, and freedom from fear.

What do our military aircraft, noise aside, have to do with providing them?

Do these planes provide freedom of speech? No, the First Amendment gives us that.

Freedom of worship? Again, no. Again, the Constitution.

Freedom from want? Here, certainly not, and rather the opposite, as the enormous sums to develop, build, and support them drain the treasury for domestic needs.

Ah, fear. Surely they make us less afraid of "the enemy" — whoever that might be. But what enemy has the air or missile capability to attack us? None on the horizon. And our overseas attacks to pre-empt any capability seem to be creating more, not fewer, enemies, enemies whose tools are not targets for such aircraft. Our fear, if anything, should be increased.

To me, freedom comes not from our warplanes, but from collaboration with nature and humans trying to be healed.

Sound of Freedom? Tell it to the good people of Russia, Iran, China, Venezuela, anywhere but here. They would not hear the roar of our planes in the air as the sound of freedom.

How Beautiful Is Death!

Reactions to the F35s

As I sit at my computer, the F35 fighter jets are roaring low overhead, tearing open the sky several times a minute. No, this is not Iraq or Palestine or Lebanon, though the aircraft are the same. It is Burlington, Vermont, the People's Republic, home of the University of Vermont, "Groovy U-V", the only "city" in the state.

This weekend we are suffering through the Vermont National Guard Air Show, with its world-famous Pentagon guests, some crack flight team, the Blue Angels or the Air Force Thunderbirds or something. Angels they are not. Nor are they sacred servants of the great spirit. Still, 40,000 Vermonters are expected to come out, cheer religiously, and bring the kids.

Very few of us support mass murder, yet I had an interesting conversation recently with an intelligent woman, highly critical of the war, who was all excited about this air show.

"I know I shouldn't really love it," she said, "but it's so exciting. Those planes are so beautiful, the pilots' skill is so impressive. It triggers off some visceral reaction..."

"Would you be excited to see someone beheaded, or perhaps burned at the stake?" I asked. "No!" she averred, "But nobody gets killed at the air show."

What was amazing to me was the screeching to a halt of thought. No, short of a crash, these planes will not kill anyone today. But they are the meanest and most vicious of killing machines, designed to bring fiery death to any persons or structures in their cross-hairs. They are "smart", these machines, and their pilots are smart, well-trained, and their bombs are "smart", and we never intentionally kill innocent civilians. Yet somehow, there is always "collateral damage". We've just seen their handiwork on the entire country of Lebanon. "No one gets killed at the air show." Only everywhere else these machines perform.

Yesterday, when they buzzed ear-shatteringly over Burlington, praciticing, I wanted to call someone up to complain. Could the police have investigated a noise complaint? The mayor's office? The governor's? No. We are simply supposed to admire — or tolerate it in the name of...of what?

Back in February, Ed Shamy wrote a column in the *Burlington Free Press* entitled "Cause It's Cool, Let Airshow Roar" : "C'mon guys," he wrote. "all you 'waterfront zealots, anti-war movers and shakers, environmental sorts. Can't you just get off your high horses for a day, stop being so stuffy, and, like, just have some fun watching the boys play with their toys? 'Cause it's cool, man. Don't get your undies in a knot. Hey, even the Make-A-Wish Foundation loves it. [The foundation will receive a charitable donation from the proceeds.] Are you against dying kids? Meanies." Shamey advises the peace-freaks to just "close their eyes and imagine that the jets torching along at 500 mph are on a peace mission promoting sustainable global tranquility."

But these jets, and the other Air Show events, are <u>not</u> promoting global tranquility. They are polluting the air, and the soundscape, and burning up many taxpayer dollars — almost 200,000 of them. But worst of all, they are promoting military macho, and by implication approving the world-wide death and suffering it creates. They are promoting killing kids who have no Make-A-Wish foundation, and whose only wish is that the wars around them would end. And not least, they are enticing our own children to graduate from violent video games to doing the real thing when they grow up.

I know — I'm a priggish elitist meany with twisted undies for thinking such thoughts. Why can't I just be cool?

Ontological Permeability

Elsewhere in this book, you'll find:

Sound of Freedom? Tell it to the good people of Russia, Iran, China, Venezuela, anywhere but here. They would not hear the roar of our planes in the air as the sound of freedom.

Yesterday morning, I was interviewing a possible intern for Fomite Press, and mentioned to him that we were looking for English translations from Palestinian and Iranian authors, assuming he would understand our goal of trying to publish the creative, poetic, humane thoughts of our "enemies" to humanize and "de-enimify" them. But no — no indication of solidarity with, or even understanding such a project. "Too theoretical," I thought, not immediately obvious to "the kids."

And you'll find:

We have been doing that for many years, most recently in Grenada, Lebanon, Libya, El Salvador, Nicaragua, Iran, Panama, Iraq, Kuwait, Somalia, Bosnia, Sudan, Afghanistan, Yugoslavia, Colombia, Syria. Did I forget somewhere? More, bigger, better. Our presidents promise broad, sweeping and sustained campaigns, against terror (!), and you may be sure that neither the Pentagon nor the record books will lack for megatonnage when our troops run out. "Bomb 'em back to the stone age" is a directive one still hears on the streets. "Put up a parking lot."

"These are old phrases," I thought. But then, yesterday afternoon, as I went outside to clear the snow off the car, a fleet of F-35s (we have 20 at the Burlington airport) approached, and seemed to circle my house.

A bone-shattering, brain-curdling, soul-grinding violence filled the dome of the world (peaceful, lefty Vermont) for a (measured) four minutes. I realized that, for all my frothing about the F-35s, I'd never really experienced them outdoors, directly overhead — but only sitting at my desk, sometimes with the safety earmuffs ("protects against power tools") that hang beside my desk for such occasions, or driving in a car. This morning they returned, though for a briefer time, somewhat more distant, and I remarked to my wife that they must not have finished the genocide yesterday. Ha ha — when it wasn't so ha ha at that very moment over Gaza, only a few time zones to the east. Or as Israel begins bombing Iran, Lebanon and Yemen, there too.

And elsewhere in this book, you'll find:

To cross the wall, Palestinians must go through checkpoints, experiencing harassment, violence and death via Israeli soldiers suffering from vast indoctrination and incompletely developed frontal lobes. Yet while the world generally looks askance at this building project, no country has definitively said STOP!, and US taxpayers fund the Israeli occupation to the tune of several billion dollars a year, with an increase on the way to propitiate Netanyahu for the Iran deal. President Obama and all the presidential candidates without exception (Bernie included) insist on the obvious "Israel has the right to defend itself" without extending that notion to its victims. The Israeli army confronts no walls other than its own to limit its roundups, kidnappings, killings and house demolitions.

It's shocking and ironic that while I can think about it, have written about it, and have mentioned it to an intern applicant, to actually realize it's not just a publisher's literary event, but is happening for real — it — in real time. It takes experiencing a mere ghost of it in the here-and-now to shatter the wall, and have ontological potential manifest as ontological act.

We Each Play Our Milgram Roles

As the Generals Test Us

Milgram? Oh, yeah... At Yale...

In the control booth, the subject sits at a switchboard. An authority figure in a white lab coat stands at his side. Behind glass, in another room, a man sits strapped to a chair. He has made a mistake in a memory test. The authority figure gives the signal, the subject throws a switch, and the man twitches and lets out a little scream.

At his next memory mistake, the subject is instructed to turn up the rheostat, and give the man a slightly stronger shock. He is already in the rheostat section marked DANGEROUS. "Really?" he asks the authority figure, pointing at the yellow marking. "You have to," says the authority figure.

At each subsequent memory error, the man's twitching becomes grosser, and his screams louder. At each increase of voltage, the subject is more reluctant to throw the switch. Toward the end of the yellow section, just this side of the red marked FATAL, the man strapped to the chair begins to cry out "I don't want to be part of this experiment anymore!" and then "Let me out of here!", and then, "Stop! Stop! I can't stand it!" Each time, the authority figure calmly says, "You have to continue." And after a certain voltage, the man strapped to the chair falls limp, unresponsive to test-questions. Many subjects do not get that far, and refuse to go on with the shocking.

Stanley Milgram's question in 1961, just after the Eichmann trial in Jerusalem: how far will people go if they are ordered by authority figures to harm others? His findings were distressing.

Granted, no one was killed, or hurt at all in this experiment. The screaming victim was an actor, responding, as instructed, to the numbers flashed on his side of the glass. The authority figure in a white lab coat was part of Milgram's investigatory cast. The subject thought he was taking part in an experiment to determine the effect of negative stimuli in teaching and learning. But the findings were still distressing: 65% of participants continued to the highest level of 450 volts. All the participants continued to 300 volts.

I recalled the Milgram experiment after reading Grace Elletson's Digger article, *Panic attacks. Ringing ears. Shaking walls. Happy 1-year anniversary to the F-35s,* in the 9/27/20 issue. In it, the VTANG commander acknowledges wide community concerns about the overflights, but that his fleet had a job to do — to become a mission-ready wing of F-35s in the course of the next year — and that it was nevertheless important to meet the mission and training requirements.

Let us place this dialogue in the frame of the Milgram experiment. Who, here, is in the role of the screaming, afflicted man, being helped to learn via negative stimuli? That's clearly us, the suffering community. Except we are not pretending.

And who is in the role of the subject of Milgram's experiment, dialing up the rheostat, throwing the switches? VTANG, of course, the Vermont Air National Guard, bringing in plane after plane, increasing the numbers of flights during our waking hours, and even into bedtime and nights. Even into the claustrophobic condition of shutdowns.

But more, even *most* interesting: who is the authority figure in the white coat, calmly repeating, "You must continue"? Who says these lines? Where is the character who speaks? Offstage? But where?

It isn't the VTANG pilots or leadership at the airport. They are "only following orders". It isn't Leahy and Co. They have only invited and approved the goings-on. It isn't Trump, or his SECDEF, or his generals, who, unlike Milgram's whitecoats, are surely unaware of Winooski's agony as "mission training requirements" are "fulfilled".

But what is that mission, and how is it to be fulfilled?

One Winooski resident quoted in the Digger article says, "I love hearing our very own Green Mountain Boy pilots practicing their craft…My newborn sleeps right through it but I hope one day when she's older, she gets to appreciate the sound as well." Another resident thought the sound of the jets was "exciting". "I think they bring a sense of security, having them here…They bring economic growth, which you know, what city can't use that right now? I love watching them take off and land, I really do."

OK. Local pride, that's a mission also plugged by our politicians. A demonstration of high-level local craft, a new twist in the old Vermont craftsman tradition. The sound, often called "the sound of freedom", which brings "a sense of security" (though exactly how the planes would protect Vermont, and against whom or what, is never stated.)

But well beyond Winooski, who is the authority figure requiring US world domination, and the military might to enforce it? Who wears that white camo-ed coat?

And what exactly is the lesson we are being putatively taught? Obedience to authority? Toughening-up to adversity in the name of the greater good? The dominance of force, even if over our own lives?

What? Who? It's a very ghostly figure we seem to be collectively obeying, nowhere near as convincing as a man with a clipboard standing behind us in a control booth. There is some spectral teacher determined to help us learn, to teach us some enormous something. But what exactly is it? And what if under the white coat there is no one?

We should ponder more carefully the casting and goals of the Milgram experiment of which we currently seem to be a part.

ESSAYS POLITICAL

9/11

Spam Blocker On

Blocking out 9/11 as spam

March, 2005

Hoa Ngo, our excellent web engineer, informs me that the spam blocker is now in place, and he's free to open my blog for comments. There is a dark side to this.

The other day, when I told a friend I was working on a comic novel about 9/11, he pondered a bit, then said, "Hmmm, there must be a niche for that." We both laughed. But ruefully.

Back last May, I published a review of a crucially important book, David Ray Griffin's *The New Pearl Harbor*, a compilation and discussion of many of the unanswered questions concerning the 9/11 attacks. The review brought much email, including a short story narrated by a passenger on one of the doomed flights.

This got me thinking that perhaps the only way certain material can be presented for public consideration might be via fiction. The minute one tries to present any serious alternative to the official story, one is immediately classed as a "conspiracy theorist", i.e. a nut job (as if conspiracies never happen!), and so delegitimized, dismissed and disappeared. But if it's admittedly fiction—and comic fiction at that? So I decided to write a 9/11 work of my own. It's called *Skulk*.

Over the past months, I've brought up the 9/11 question with many smart, politically-informed people, and the reaction I encounter most often is some version of "I'm not going there." Our city attorney, a long-time activist for peace and justice, said exactly that.

"Why?"

"I just can't go there."

Spam-blocked. And a very high-level full professor of physics:

"I don't want to hear about it."

"But Dan, you're a scientist. Have you looked at the data? Seen the engineering analyses? Looked at the photos and videos?"

(He hadn't.)

"Too improbable."

"Will you read a couple of articles I'll send you?"

"No."

Spam-blocked. But what—in this case—is spam?

My feeling is that, though armored in jack-boots, the Bush administration still has an Achilles heel: their possible complicity in the events of 9/11. The public seems ready to dismiss two fraudulent, disastrous wars with more wars threatened, two electoral frauds, innumerable financial and ecological disasters charging on exacerbated and unattended to, and a yawning income gap—among other horrors. But my desperate hope is that people will not tolerate proof, or even widespread discussion, of their own government planning, executing, or simply stage-managing the 9/11 attacks.

I can hear the spam-blockers slamming shut already. But wait. Griffin is very good here. He does not accuse or even theorize about how 9/11 happened. He simply notes the contradictions and impossibilities of the official story, and then discusses eight possible levels of administration involvement from level one—simply taking advantage of the event to advance a pre-existing agenda (a widely held analysis)— to level eight, active planning and execution. Without assuming some level of complicity, the facts simply cannot be explained. He leaves it to the reader to demand the investigations which might resolve the enigmas.

I'm for questioning spam-blockers.

September Songs

Disturbing Questions

September 2005

Four years and many Bushogenic catastrophes later (including—but certainly not limited to—Afghanistan, Iraq, Guantanamo, Katrina, and all they encompass and stand for), we have still not begun to confront the contradictions and implications of "9/11".

Let's take only the single most obvious strangeness: Building Seven. At 5:30 in the afternoon of that fatal day, a 47-story, steel frame office building collapsed neatly, at almost free-fall speed, right over its footprint. Whoosh, plop. Building Seven had not been hit by any aircraft, had not been touched by flying debris, and had only two tiny office fires the NYFD did not want to bother with. Nevertheless—whoosh, plop. Curious? But somehow not so curious as to arouse general curiosity. You'd think folks might get the hint that something was up.

But talking with my intelligent, political, lefty, news-aware friends, I'd found that almost no one had ever heard of Building Seven. When I mentioned that it was a classical example of a well-done controlled demolition, I would almost always get the same response:

Gesture: Elbows bent, both hands up to shoulder level, palms out. Followed by

Sentence: "I'm not going there."

And that was just Building Seven. Any further talk of the explosion patterns of the towers, of critical temperatures concerning jet fuel and weakening of steel, of architectural history, engineering analysis, NORAD standdowns, photos and videos of early Pentagon destruction—all and any of this got those hands moving, flapping outward from the shoulders, go away, "I really don't want to go there."

Right. But many people have gone there. Engineers, physicists, architects, photo-frame analysts, and the occasional intrepid, dot-connecting reporter. And guess what…they're all—all— nuts, crazies, lunatic fringe conspiracy theorists! not worthy of media or political discussion.

It seems there is no way at present for the simple facts, photographs and videos which contradict the "official story" to circulate or provoke investigation, public discussion, or action concerning what went on on 9/11. We are beginning to see some of those questions asked concerning Katrina, and the Bush response has been "Let's not get into blaming." Such avoidance may not work here—let's hope. But it has worked brilliantly so far concerning 9/11, and our national tendency toward amnesia, our allergy to history or analysis, and our yellow-beribboned, redwhiteand-blue, it's-time-to-move-on-ism may be able to slam the memory hole trapdoor in time to avoid "9/11", per se, as an issue.

It was my frustration with "I'm not going there" that led me to attempt my own pathetic end-run around the censorship of "conspiracy theory" dismissal. What could I do to somehow, somehow, get legitimate questions raised? So I've written a comic novel, SKULK, in which the characters, while involved with a lot of other zaniness, talk about and act on this material. My hope would be that some of these questions might see the light, if only in the book review section of otherwise-avoiding papers. After all, it's only fiction. Comic fiction. No threat. But some readers might choose to check the websites noted, listen to those physicists and engineers, and see what there actually is to see. Me, the amoeba that roars. Whether the novel will ever be published is another question. As a wry friend of mine remarked, "A comic novel on 9/11? Hmm. There must be a niche for that."

SKULK or no SKULK, there are some serious books out there on the subject. One of my favorites, because one of the least speculative, is David Ray Griffin's *The New Pearl Harbor*. The book is simply a compendium of all the areas in which the official story does not fit or explain the facts. His conclusion is that we must have a serious investigation which addresses itself directly to these questions. In a subsequent book on the 9/11 Commission Report, he demonstrates how the Commission's investigation avoided each and every problem raised by the contradictions, and instead, redirected public thinking to "failures of intelligence". Failures of intelligence do not explain the problems. They do exculpate the Bush administration, the poor victim of such failures.

You may want to read a review I wrote of Griffin's book posted at https://www.counterpunch.org/2004/05/25/a-review-of-quot-the-new-pearl-harbor-quot/. The review itself is a good, short introduction to the field of "9/11 questions". On the other hand, you may not want to go there. But do ask yourselves why.

Letter Exchange on 9/11

Rebuttal to Seven Days Article

Aug 6, 2006 [Hiroshima Day]

DOUBTFUL DOINGS

Seven Days' story on the 911 Truth march on Church St. was remarkable for openness and absence of dismissive tone. But the 911 Truth movement knows a lot more than a reader might gather from the coverage. And the primary thing it knows is that there MUST have been some level of inside involvement in the planning and execution of the day's events. Consider only.

1. There are standard NORAD protocols for scrambling jets when aircraft go off course, protocols that have worked routinely over the years. Yet the apparatus seemed non-existent on that day. The World Trade Center and the Pentagon are in the most heavily protected air corridors in the world. A stand-down must have been effected, whether by specific order or by pre-planned diversion. No Islamic terrorist could bring off such a thing. Who did?

2. The late afternoon fall of WTC Building Seven at almost free-fall speed, and right over its own footprint was a classic example of a well-done controlled demolition. The building was not hit by aircraft or debris, and had only two small fires on lower floors. Larry Silverstein, the building owner, himself stated that the building was "pulled". Now pulling a building takes weeks, if not months of preparation — structural analysis, planting of explosives, etc. How is it that the building was ready to be pulled so beautifully on a few hours notice? Once one asks this question, many of the more complex features of the twin towers collapse fall into place. Eye-witness testimony about explosions

make sense. They too could only have been controlled demolitions. Again, no Islamic terrorists could have had such intimate preparatory access to the buildings. The steel was quickly trucked away and melted down, contravening all law concerning crime scenes.

3. The initial photos of the Pentagon, before the roof collapse, show only an 18' diameter hole, far too small to admit the body of a 757, and with no indication of the impact of wings or tail. Further, there was no strewn wreckage such as is normally found. Given the photographic and video evidence, the official story cannot possibly be true. Minutes after the event, all footage from video cameras outside and inside the Pentagon was confiscated by the FBI, and no footage showing a 757 has been released. Why not? If it was not a 757 which hit the Pentagon, what was it? And who beside the military has the kind of missiles that can penetrate that thickness of concrete?

These three events alone (among many, many others) indicate not only an alternate story, but one which MUST involve high-level, inside work. 19 men with boxcutters could not effect such things, nor could al-Qaeda effect such post-event handling. The cui bono question is easily answered.

That most people find this difficult to believe is understandable. But before dismissing the obvious implications, the contradictions must be otherwise explained: NORAD does not stand down for no reason. Steel buildings do not melt and collapse from (short-term and partial) kerosene-temperature fires. 757s do not fit in 18 foot holes.

The implications of government and military involvement in 9/11 are immense and frightening, but must be confronted to truly explore the underside of power, and to prepare for a desperate repetition.
Marc Estrin, Burlington

REBUTTING 9/11 THEORIES

Marc Estrin ["Letters," July 5] seems to have swallowed uncritically the smorgasbord of 9/11 suspicions laid out in the film *Loose Change*, second edition...[These] dwell on the World Trade Towers: Steel doesn't melt at the combustion temperature of jet fuel, and only deliberately sapped buildings fall inward. An engineer might argue otherwise: (1)

Steel is, after all, smelted by mere coal, and nowadays gas fires (heat can be concentrated). (2) Its strength fails long before it melts (steel buildings used to fall under the heat of their burning furniture and flooring). And (3) the Towers were designed to sway (several feet) in the wind, so weren't likely to topple (but, weakened by burning jet fuel, couldn't continue to bear their thousands of tons of mass.

Again, despite "hermetically sealed" elevators (and stairwells), dozens of miles of HAC ducts were wide open. The film seems to assume that all of a plane's fuel is in one tank (it's in the two wings), and that it all goes up, Whoosh! as in a movie. Rather, it burns like anything else, at its interface with oxygen. In a closed space, with the oxygen exhausted, the fire draws from outside, so it burns for a while. During which, hundreds of gallons of fuel are sloshing around and no doubt draining into the ducts, falling to explode here and there down stairs and, more seriously, escaping through burst ducts to explode in the structural cores.

This is speculation and doesn't address the rest of the film. But conspiranoia is speculation, anyway, and I think mine is reasonable enough to cast doubt on the film generally. It and Estrin's rehash seem to be fueled by suspicion of the Bush administration. An irreverent observer, though, could wonder whether any federal administration, let alone Bush's could engineer so complex a set of events so precisely...
Fred G. Hill, Burlington

REBUTTAL REBUTTAL

The case against the administration's "official story" concerning the events of 9/11 is far broader and deeper than that presented in *Loose Change*, though the film is useful as an introduction to the story's inconsistencies. Those interested in seeing the work of chemists, physicists, engineers, architects, photo analysts, and other 9/11 researchers might start at the website of Scholars for 9/11 Truth, st911.org, or Burlington's own vt911.org.

One can spend many hours on minutiae and possible explanations, but at least three things are clear to all who have put in the study time:

— that the official story is impossible to correlate with the physical evidence,

— that the administration's changing story and subsequent behavior is strongly indicative of a cover-up,

— and that much of the evidence can be explained ONLY by positing government and insider collaboration.

Fred Hill (letter, "Rebutting 9/11 Theories"] is entitled to his theory of the twin tower collapse, and this is not the place for a technical rebuttal. If he finds jet fuel confusing, I would simply ask him then to explain the fall of Building Seven, with no significant fires, or why he thinks a 757 might fit through an 18 foot hole, leaving no debris behind, or why NORAD was on that day unable to protect the crown jewels.

One of the more amazing aspects of the fierce resistance to further 9/11 investigation is that even people who see lies and secrecy deeply embedded in this administration are uniquely willing to believe its assertion that 19 Arab hijackers, using beginner pilots, could successfully conspire to bring off such events.

As to Fred's doubt that a Bush administration "could engineer so complex a set of events...", the fact is that it was all pretty ham-handed — or the 9/11 truth movement would not have so much to go on. Buildings that don't fall on time, steel inexplicably sliced in pieces convenient for quick disposal, investigations that must be resisted, then manipulated, videos that must be hidden, crashes without wreckage, inconvenient firefighter testimony, too-convenient "evidence" found... the list goes on and on, with each piece crying out for real investigation. The only thing the administration did get almost right was their assumption that the public would never believe there could be government involvement. There was laughing all the way to Iraq.

Marc Estrin, Burlington

Fighting Fiction with Fiction

2008

After seven years, the resistance to 9/11 truth studies continues to astound. Many very smart people, lefties, political activists - people who don't believe one word of what anyone in the Bush administration says — for some reason believe every word of the preposterous official version of 9/11. Unlike any other blather from Washington, this seems to be the story they want to believe. In any case, when I've tried to raise the subject, they will "not go there". "Not going there" always involves the same hand gestures — both arms raised from the elbows, palms out, slightly in front of the face, blocking passage to the ears.

What's going on? It's not as if these people have no political analysis, or hold worldviews which won't tolerate 9/11 truth investigation. A standard explanation is that some truths are so destructive the most common defense is total denial. When I tried to bring up the subject, one woman actually said to me, "I don't want to live in a world where such things could happen." Well, if openness to thinking about 9/11 necessitates suicide, I can understand her reaction.

But there are many kinds of suicide. In my case, there is the suicide envisioned for me as an author by publishers, and a possible secondary suicide of their publishing houses for associating themselves with an author who might be perceived as a tin-hatted conspiracy wacko. In the case of normal, mainstream, journalism, it seems again to be the editor protecting the writer from suicide, and, more importantly, keeping the publication safe from assault — as the owners protect the public from the need to think. In any case, fiction or nonfiction which explores alternative stories and explanations of 9/11 seems to be firmly censored in the womb with little protest from the pro-life crowd.

I first started thinking about 9/11 fiction after writing an early review of David Ray Griffin's first book, *The New Pearl Harbor*. http://counterpunch.org/estrin05252004.html. In 2004, there were still so many unanswered questions and so little evidence with which to construct answers. As in any investigation, the first step is speculation: who might have done it, how might it have happened? Forensic investigation is well left to experts, but speculation itself is often best done by creative writers. So while Griffin and other investigators pursued their work, why not ask my fellow fiction writers to think about some clues?

I put out a call to the small circle of writers I happen to know, angling for 9/11 short stories for a possible anthology. I was surprised to see so few come in, and of those few there were even fewer that, qualitywise, were likely to be publishable. So I abandoned the anthology project, and thought, "I'll just do it myself." Out came this novel, *Skulk*.

Skulk was a pleasure to write. It was fun actually having fun writing about 9/11! The book contained many of the playful/serious elements common in my writing:

— inventing an Ann Coulter-ish heroine

— a political attack on the concept of Santa Claus

— the difficulties of making a quill pen in contemporary America

— how to smuggle pot past Homeland Security

— a short history of Bleeding Kansas

— Jesus and political weirdness in Cullison, KS

— instructions on trailing, evading and bugging

— a Kansan Indian anthropologist on PC towards Indians, Kansas Indians, and a Norwegian story of the devil

— a Middle-East address attacked by yarmulka-ed clowns, and descending into melee, with lab experiments in the latest methods of crowd control

— some advanced writing on learning skydiving, based on AUTHOR EXPERIENCE!

— flight training software from Sadosoft, a pedagogical breakthrough.

...and I thought such a book might actually make an end run around the censorship on the topic.

I submitted it enthusiastically for publication and submitted it again, and again: no one would touch it except for John Leonard at Progressive Press (at the kind suggestion of Webster Tarpley). It will be for him an infrequent venture into fiction.

There remains the question of how to reach beyond the initiates who are already looking for the kind of books Progressive Press put out. This is a general problem beyond that of 9/11 truth fiction. As activists, we all have to find ways to reach beyond the choir. What about 9/11 truth? As Dick Cheney so pithily observed, "So?" So the government is tricking the people? What's new? So the American government has murdered its own citizens in pursuit of its goal of world domination? "I don't have a dog in that fight."

As my publisher, John Leonard, sees it, "It's the old problem of the Big Lie. They got plausible deniability by doing something so unbelievably outrageous that it really can't be believed by most people. A lot of us who could see through it hitched our wagon to 9/11, figuring that it was dynamite, the highest-powered door-opener around. After seven years, it looks like it's no silver bullet after all. We might have to start a bit further back with people — maybe all the way back with learning how conditioning works? I'm reprinting one classic on that subject, but mainly I'm branching out from 9/11 and trying to cover the whole conspiracy, bit by bit, to build up people's background information. Marc Estrin's approach is a very creative one on these lines — to look for side doors that may be open, instead of trying to drive another truck through the front gate. Maybe that's why he called it '*Skulk*' — it's a stealth approach to 9/11 Truth."

The problem seems to be that so many of us — most of us — are "embedded." We are embedded in a culture whose frame has expanded to include anything that happens. There is no longer anything "beyond the pale." Everything is normal, bipartisan, omnipartisan, cloaked in the magic power of "whatever."

I had thought that the one thing that the American public would not put up with would be the idea that its own government had attacked it on 9/11. That's still probably the case. But between that truth and its consequences stands The Great Wall of Denial. It seems one cannot simply argue people over the wall, or hand them a factual triptik to get there. So in *Skulk* I have tried another strategy: the characters simply believe in 9/11 truth, so they are incorporated, not debated, into the underlying structure of the novel. As would-be activists, Gronsky & Skulk, pursue their goal — our goal — of public enlightenment, they are totally frustrated. But the websites they publish in their Calls to the People are real. Any reader who decides to check them — as many readers will now do, having grown used to hyperlinks — will find him or herself bathing in the wealth of facts and ideas that real 9/11 researchers have come up. In this way, I hope to have brought the 9/11 material to a new cohort — that of readers of (comic) fiction who might not otherwise come in contact with them.

Since September 13, 2001, I have been standing every weekday from 5-5:30 at a busy Burlington intersection with a group of vigilers, each with his or her own sign, protesting the many things there are to protest. I have thought it best to use my own signs to simply inject an idea into public discourse. For several years before the word became common, my sign simply said IMPEACH. Impeach who? That was up to the viewer. Once the word "impeachment" became common in public discussion, I changed my sign to read "GOT FASCISM?", a concept we are not yet commonly talking about. I often get questions from passersby — "what is that — fascism?" Sometime the pronunciation is comical. It amazes me, but there are many people who have forgotten — or never knew.

In the same way, I would like *Skulk* to simply put the materials of the 9/11 truth movement into circulation for the fiction-reading crowd. *Skulk* does not argue, it does not prove, it assumes the reader knows all about it. And on some level, I believe that many denying Americans do know. It needs only to be brought into legitimate discussion. 9/11 fiction may be another, possibly successful, doorway to that discussion.

The Griffin Takes Wing

Griffin's Early 9/11 Books

August, 2006

Christian Faith and the Truth Behind 9/11 appears to be two books in one. The first, "Part I: Evidence That 9/11 Was A False-Flag Operation", is both an updated summary of government actions and physical facts which contradict the official 9/11 story, and a witness to Griffin's developing conviction that yes, elements of the Bush administration, the military and intelligence agencies must have been involved in 9/11's planning and execution.

In his earlier book, *The New Pearl Harbor: Disturbing Questions About the Bush Administration and 9/11*, Griffin assembled the evidence unaccounted for by the official story, and set up a framework in which to try to understand it. He imagined eight levels of possible administration complicity, from simply capitalizing on an unexpected, external event to advance a previously formed agenda, through intentionally allowing the expected attacks, to, finally, the possibility of active involvement in bringing them about. Disturbing questions indeed. He called for a genuine investigation.

In the subsequent *The 9/11 Commission Report: Omissions and Distortions*, Griffin, after studying the long-awaited report, decimated the Commission's claim to be, in the words of its chairman, "independent, impartial, thorough, and nonpartisan", and demonstrated its conscious attempt to misdirect public concern away from both the "disturbing questions" with their possible administration involvement, and toward the putative incompetence of the FAA and intelligence agencies which, according to the Commission, gave Bush the bad information he had acted upon. Griffin's reading of the report confirmed his original suspicions. Why would those in charge of the investigation need to so grossly mislead were they not trying to cover up some very high crimes and misdemeanors?

His newly published third book expresses Griffin's now even greater certainty that 9/11 must have been "an inside job": *Christian Faith and the Truth Behind 9/11* is a clear indictment of government entities for having planned and executed the events of 9/11, and orchestrated a coverup incompetent enough to enable the 9/11 research community to flourish, but brilliantly effective nonetheless — largely through the complicity of the mainstream media, and the practice of secrecy brought to its highest level by this administration.

While "terrorism" or "incompetence" might possibly be used to explain some of the events, only an assumption of government involvement can explain its key elements: the non-functioning of normal NORAD procedures, the controlled demolition of the WTC buildings (now conclusively demonstrated and agreed on by all members of the research community), and the missile or other military aircraft which perforated the Pentagon (again, it is generally agreed that it could not have been a 757 which did the damage.) Griffin concludes that no "terrorist hijacker" or Al-Qaida operation would have access to the preparation time or the materials to effect these actions, and that only high government or military officials could call for them.

Griffin's account of current 9/11 research is generally up-to-date, and concentrates on the evidence most clearly suggesting complicity. He begins by confronting the first and major hurdle that all "truthers" must confront: "I can't believe our government would do such a thing," a statement which often signals the end of any conversation.

In the chapter "9/11 and Prior False-Flag Operations", he traces the well-documented practice, first by other countries, then with respect to US support of false-flag operations of its allies, then initiation of its own wars, and finally with the recently discovered "Operation Northwoods", a Joint Chiefs of Staff proposal to kill American citizens, blame the deaths on Cuba, and thus gain public support for an attack on the island. Operation Northwoods was vetoed by JFK, but did make it, unhindered, all the way to his desk, as one legitimate way to proceed. The chapter ends with a consideration of 9/11, per se, as a false-flag operation,which blamed the event on an unlikely group of alleged hijackers, run by Osama bin Laden from his laptop in a cave. Griffin underlines the impossibilites involved and the blatantly planted "evidence".

His second and third chapters, "Explosive Testimony" and "The Destruction of the World Trade Center: Why the Official Account Cannot Be True", demonstrate conclusively, with extensive documentation from physicists, engineers, architects, and first-hand witnesses, that the three WTC buildings must have been, and were, brought down by well-executed controlled demolitions. Although he cites the work of physicist Steven Jones, he could not, because of the publication deadline, include Jones' later work: a chemical analysis of WTC debris samples used for memorials, each showing the presence of thermate, the agent used in demolition to melt steel and slice it up in sizes convenient for removal. Thermate-driven reactions also account for the molten steel found in the sub-basements of each building.

In the critique of the 9/11 Commission Report, Griffin spends 45 pages examining the timeline complexeties concerning why the U.S. military was unable to intercept any of the planes. Because those chapters involved so many details, and were hard for a reader to grasp, Griffin uses the fourth chapter of his current book, "Flights of Fancy: The 9/11 Commission's Incredible Tales of Flights 11, 175, 77, and 93", as a short précis of his earlier findings. He concludes that the Commission's story of FAA incompetence, and its exoneration of the military is most unlikely, and that the military, along with high-level administration figures, principally Dick Cheney, must have been in on the "stand-down".

But the obvious question "Who ordered a NORAD stand-down?", while essential, is too simple to really address the investigations by the 9/11 research community. Rather than a simple phone call being made, and a nationwide order being given, it seems that on the day of 9/11, there had been scheduled more than a dozen terrorism drills, each of which took aircraft out of the area, also inserting fictional radar signals sent to air traffic controllers as part of the exercise. "Is this a drill, or is this real?" one of them was recorded asking when deviant aircraft showed up on his screen. The net result was a seriously compromised defense and reigning confusion at critical moments. The question then becomes, "How was such a concatenation of drills arranged?" As in other areas, recorded voice tapes have been mysteriously lost, and paper records mistakenly shredded. While Griffin convincingly demonstrates that the official story is preposterous, he does not lead the reader into the emerging labyrinth of the drill strategy, one that is particularly important to note as more and more military exercises and Homeland Security drills are held. Drills "going live" remain a potent weapon of both action and paralysis.

In the chapter that concludes the first half of the book, "Bush Administration Responsibility for 9/11: From a Prima Facie to a Conclusive Case" Griffin summarizes his previous discussions, and adds one additional factor — the unusual, most suspicious purchase of "put options" in the week before the attacks, market bets that the stock of American and United Airlines would precipitously fall. Much money was made.

There are, of course, huge questions left unanswered here, questions that neither Griffin, nor the 9/11 research community feels competent to discuss, focused as researchers are on the hardest evidence. "What happened to the passengers?" "How might people involved be kept from whistle-blowing?" "Why do intelligent Americans who are most suspicious of the administration believe the 9/11 official story — of all its lies, the most crucial?" Answers to such questions would be merely speculative, and speculation — theorizing on the basis of little or no evidence — is exactly NOT what the 9/11 truth movement is about. The first part of Griffin's new book is an excellent 80-page primer of many evidence-based contradictions in the official story, and their far-most likely explanation — that of government planning and execution.

A Once and Future Griffin

In the second part of his book, David Ray Griffin emerges, as if from a phone booth, in his birthright costume of theologian. For thirty years prior to his appearance as one of the chief critics of the 9/11 official story, he was a professor of theological studies, and the author or editor of several important books in the field, often focusing on the process philosophy of Whitehead and Hartshorne, and its application to the longstanding "problem of evil". "Part Two: A Christian Critique of 9/11 and American Imperialism" directs the reader's attention to that dimension of what might otherwise seem to be a purely secular problem. His 5-chapter argument is this briefly this:

His opening move is to establish the US's "imperial motives for 'a new Pearl Harbor'", and the fact that the government had both the means and the opportunity to plan and execute the events of the attacks.] In his history and critique of the neocons, he shows that 9/11 can surely be understood as a means to turn their agenda into policy.

Griffin then shifts focus to examine Jesus' revolutionary relationship to the Roman Empire as a model for authentic Christianity today. He introduces the theologically crucial notion of "the demonic" in a "non-mythological" form" — i.e., not anthropomorphized as "the devil" or "Satan". His view is that the demonic is "a real power with genuine autonomy, that is driving the world in a direction that is diametrically opposed to divine purposes." How is such a power possible in a universe created by an omnipotent, all-knowing, beneficent god? Ah — the "problem of evil" arises.

Griffin's answer centers on a reading of Genesis which postulates not God's creation of the universe from nothing, but rather God's shaping of a pre-existing chaos, a material with its own properties, some of which are resistant to divine values, and capable of developing, in its multi-billion-year evolution, the capacity to threaten divine purpose. Thus, he arrives at the idea of two opposing forces — not the standard, simplistic "good and evil", but rather a divine force and — with the emergence of a human civilization capable of becoming demonic. The question then arises: To which force is our contemporary western culture, and its most force-filled representative, the US, committed? Griffin demonstrates in no uncertain terms that America must be seen as "the chief embodiment of demonic power", acting in almost every arena in ways completely at odds with the divine teachings of the Christ.

The implication for a Christ-inspired church is clear: the church must take the lead in an attempt to break free from our gathering, planetary catastrophe, to teach and preach the disparity between America's actions and Christian goals, using the 9/11attacks on its own people as the most instructive example of the demonic in action.

Separation of Church and...?

Secular thinkers and activists may find the second part of Griffin's book at best irrelevant and at worst, delegitimizing of the 9/11 research movement. There is, they might say, already enough religious language out there clouding the grossly military-political activities of the country and its allies, and inviting the world into a crusade of religious war. Whatever one's private religious beliefs or traditions, 9/11 truthwork is best kept secular. And if this book is to be called anything, it should be titled The Truth Behind 9/11 and Christian Faith, rather than the other way around, since that is the order in which the material is presented, and the order of its practical usefulness. In fact, why not publish it as two separate books, since "Christian Faith" at the head of the title may keep many from picking it up at all? Let the general public buy the 9/11 truth book, and the Christians buy the Christian faith one. This is what many may say.

But Griffin has a savvy tactic here, titling the book the way he does, publishing it with a major Presbyterian publisher in a "political/religious" market niche. Not only does such reflect his long-held, and deeply-developed personal beliefs, but this strategy wants to, and may, open up a powerful new ally for the secular activist attempt to change our political trajectory. The various Christian church denominations include hundreds of millions of people who might be brought to see the tension between governmental action and the core beliefs to which they subscribe. In the eighties, the churches were in the forefront in Latin American, anti-imperialist battles. Liberation theology, the preferential option for the poor — remember those? Politically, Griffin is hoping to encourage a reemergence of an activist church by framing the current struggles in church-crucial terms. Regardless of what secularists might think of the ultimate "truth-value" of such framing (if there is no God who made the world... etc.) the mobilization of mainline churches in political struggle, in the potentially tranformative 9/11 truth movement, is likely to be an important, positive addition, especially as a contrast to the fundamentalist movements seeking to hasten the apocalypse. Nietzsche once observed that "the last Christian died on the cross." If that has been too-much the case till now, Griffin would change it by using this book to challenge mainline churches to engage full-tilt on the side of their professed values.

The griffin was a beast with the front of an eagle and the hindquarters of a lion, depicted in medieval iconography as a guardian of the road to salvation. Though long extinct in the imagination, I'm hoping this particular reincarnation may fly — at least as well as a 757.

Again, after works like Griffin's, how is it still possible that even politically astute Americans refuse to acknowledge the implications of 9/11 research. Every European, Canadian, Latin American, and Asian we have had stay with us has thought 9/11 Truth conclusions obvious. Can reflex "patriotism" override mind, even among the mindful and otherwise not-so-patriotic? This is the most perplexing puzzlement in my adult life.

ESSAYS POLITICAL

War and Peace, but Mostly War

Mein Kampf, Dein Kampf

The News from World War II

Gregor the cockroach, now living in the White House as assistant to Secretary of Agriculture, Henry Wallace, attends one of FDR's annual readings of A Christmas Carol. *On the way upstairs to FDR's bedroom, he snatches an package addressed to him from the postal desk, and carries it with him to his seat under a couch. It is from his old Vienna friend, Amadeus Hoffnung, catching him up with the latest situation.*

Christmas Eve, 1935.

Gregor had been invited to the president's reading of *A Christmas Carol* — an annual event anticipated with pleasure by the large, and ever-expanding presidential family.

This was not some species of flattering the king, for truly FDR's was a classic performance, complete with stage voices, props, and dramatic business that kept the smaller children on the edge of their seats, squealing with fear and joy. Harry Hopkins, a first-time guest, commented, "The President reads aloud better than anyone I know — he takes infinite pains with each word and phrase — placing the emphasis just right — and withal reading with such obvious pleasure. And you laughed when he said 'humbug' in a loud voice and 'good afternoon' even louder...The president had read this story to his children every Christmas for many years — and the little book is one of his priceless possessions."

And indeed, as in the earliest days of his parenthood, the performance was held in the presidential bedroom, with the smallest children piled on the bed, the larger ones on drawn-up couches and chairs, and the parents and guests sitting and standing against the walls. It was a happening mirrored perhaps in other households around the country, but here achieving a perfection of technique and good feeling that must have been rare.

The Assistant to the Assistant Secretary of Agriculture left his room at 6:25 that Tuesday evening, and climbed the circular stairs to the first floor, where he checked his cubby for late-arriving Christmas mail. Along with a Christmas card from the People's Bank, and a candy-cane wrapped with pipe-cleaner to resemble a thin, red-striped reindeer (cute), he pulled out a small package, brown paper, wrapped with string. There was no return address, and since the hour was getting late, he just stuck the items in his pocket, and made his way upstairs to the west wing.

The Christmas Eve reading was perhaps the only punctual time in the Roosevelt year. This was a long story, and by the end, the smallest audience members were just about gone. Some simply fell asleep, but others would begin to fidget and whine, so 6:30 — and no later — seemed the right time to start. Gregor entered an already crowded room, and found a good place for himself under a couch on the north wall. Under-a-couch brought back mixed emotions, and memories of a confusing time in Prague, but it was the only empty space in an over-packed room.

Eleanor Roosevelt, her usual charming self, called the event to order: "Friends, and wonderful family, we're so happy you can join us tonight — some for the first time, and welcome! — to hear this marvelous tale, so relevant in this time of hardship, when meanness often rules, and generosity goes begging. Have a cup of tea or milk or juice — there's post-prohibition egg-nog for the grownups — and settle in for what? the 30th? 31st? annual reading of..." and here she cued the audience who all chimed in,

"Charles Dickens' A Christmas Carol'!"

She took her seat, and out from the master closet came the President, in striped pajama pants, ascot and dressing gown, his "precious book" clasped, with crutch, in his right hand, doing his best imitation of John Barrymore for the applauding crowd. He sat down on the bed, scooted the littlest ones over, covered his legs with the comforter, and began his tale.

I have endeavoured, in this Ghostly little book, to raise the Ghost of an Idea, which shall not put my readers out of humour with themselves, with each other, with the season, or with me. May it haunt their houses pleasantly. Their faithful Friend and Servant, C. D., December, 1843.

Marley's Ghost

Marley was dead: to begin with. There is no doubt whatever about that....

Through the cage of dangling feet, Gregor could watch the children on the bed, and those sitting on the far side of the bed, and the grownups lined up on three walls. He could see the President's left profile and gesturing hand.

Mind! I don't mean to say that I know, of my own knowledge, what there is particularly dead about a door-nail. I might have been inclined, myself, to regard a coffin-nail as the deadest piece of ironmongery in the trade. But the wisdom of our ancestors is in the simile; and my unhallowed hands shall not disturb it, or the Country's done for. You will therefore permit me to repeat, emphatically, that Marley was as dead as a door-nail.

This was good! Gregor was expecting some treacly tripe, served up by Sentimentality, Inc., the thriving, leading corporation in depression America. Relieved, he settled in for a good time. But rolling on his right side, he felt the package in his pocket digging into his tegmen, and after a minute decided he'd better move it, perhaps take it out of his pocket all together.

Scrooge! a squeezing, wrenching, grasping, scraping, clutching, covetous, old sinner! Hard and sharp as flint, from which no steel had ever struck out generous fire; secret, and self-contained, and solitary as an oyster. The cold within him froze his old features, nipped his pointed nose, shrivelled his cheek, stiffened his gait; made his eyes red, his thin lips blue; and spoke out shrewdly in his grating voice. A frosty rime was on his head, and on his eyebrows, and his wiry chin. He carried his own low temperature always about with him; he iced his office in the dogdays; and didn't thaw it one degree at Christmas.

It was hard to extract package from pocket in the tight space under the couch, and as he pulled it round, it made an embarrassing crinkling, causing a child's face to appear upside down from the couch above, wondering what was going on. G gave him a conspiratorial hush sign, and the face disappeared. He continued his move more carefully.

The fog came pouring in at every chink and keyhole, and was so dense without, that although the court was of the narrowest, the houses opposite were mere phantoms. To see the dingy cloud come drooping down, obscuring everything, one might have thought that Nature lived hard by, and was brewing...

There! Free at last! That feels better. Gregor looked for a moment at the rectangular solid, and though there was no return address, he noticed that the original handwriting was decidedly European. The package had been sent to E.P. Dutton, his publisher, and forwarded to Ives & Myrick, probably the last address Dutton had for him. G recognized Mrs. Verplanck's handwriting forwarding it on to the White House. His curiosity was piqued. *I can listen to the story and open this quietly,* he thought. *I'll just see who it's from, then deal with it later.*

'Bah!' said Scrooge, 'Humbug!

All the children began to laugh, just as Hopkins had mentioned, so fierce was the President's line reading. Gregor used the commotion in the room to bite through the string, and slip the contents from the wrapping. A book and a long letter...from? It didn't say, at least not on the first page. Berlin. Who did he know in Berlin? And the book

...*Mein Kampf*. Oh yes, Mein Kampf. He'd never read it. Heard about it, of course, but.... He shuffled one-clawed through nine sheets of the long communication. Who would have the time to write such a thing?

'What right have you to be merry? What reason have you to be merry? You're poor enough.'

On and on. Last page...Amadeus Ernst Hoffnung! Amadeus! Oh, how wonderful to hear from you. I thought you might be gone by now. Those empty spaces on the mirror...Amadeus!

'What else can I be,' returned the uncle, 'when I live in such a world of fools as this? Merry Christmas! Out upon merry Christmas! What's Christmas to you but a time for paying bills without money; a time for finding yourself a year older, but not an hour richer; a time for balancing your books—and having every item in 'em presented dead against you?

What to do? He wanted to listen to the President's story, but Amadeus, Amadeus had written! All those pages. It must be important. And so he did what any of us might have done in such a predicament: he tried to take in both, to be mostly present for the reading, but also to get a preview of the news he would devour later in his closet.

> Berlin
> September 1935
> Most Honorable Gregor Samsa,

...a kind, forgiving, charitable, pleasant time: the only time I know of, in the long calendar of the year, when men and women seem by one consent to open their shut-up hearts freely, and to think of people below them as if they really were fellow-passengers to the grave...

> I send this letter and Gift (observe the multilingual
> pun) like a note in a bottle from the Less-Than-Happy
> Isle of Ditchland. My copy of <u>Wo Sind Sie Jetzt?</u>

credits you with the important Principles and Practice of Risk Management, which the library of Humbled University Across The Street lists (without owning) as published by E.P. Dutton and Co., New York, which the New York City Phone Directory lists at 124 Madison Ave — and the trail leads no farther. Tot. Which I hope and assume you are not. So on this solstice, truly a time in which light turns to darkness, I once again utilize my ever-resourceful father to scheme letter and poison into the U.S. diplomatic pouch, to be trudged to you, via publisher, safely out of this once-great, now grating, country. The Gift is in the turgid original, so as to minimize inspection by your monolingual postal thieves, assuming you have any in the land of dreams. I hope all arrives intact.

...more than usually desirable that we should make some slight provision for the Poor and Destitute, who suffer greatly at the present time. Many thousands are in want of common necessaries; hundreds of thousands are in want of common comforts, sir. ' 'Are there no prisons?' asked Scrooge...

...stooped down at Scrooge's keyhole to regale him with a Christmas carol...

Gregor, this is no joke. I don't know that this letter will even reach you, but if it does, YOU MUST DO SOMETHING to alert the American structure of Power to the real situation in Germany.

If he could only know where I'm reading this!

It seems you've become an important author, a theoretician of risk. Surely your word will be listened to. I have been following the coverage of our events in American papers, and I assure you that you have absolutely no realistic information. Last week, at the annual Nuremberg rally, Hitler announced the "Reich Citizenship Law" and the "Law for the Protection of German Blood and German Honor". So now we know who is "officially Jewish", that is, a member of the living dead, eliminated from any kind of civil or social existence. People who don't exist have a poor prognosis, especially here. The living dead may soon become the dead — period.

Darkness is cheap, and Scrooge liked it. But before he shut his heavy door...

Last Monday, the day after the Party orgy, graffiti denouncing the new laws was found on the Jungfernbruke, a few blocks from my apartment. The afternoon papers gave it lots of play, and that very evening I heard yelling in the street. Cat-curious, I went down to follow the crowd. Men and women, presumably Jewish — in any case, patronizing Jewish stores — were being rounded up and herded over to the bridge, where they were ordered to scrub off the graffiti using river water and their own clothing. When things got too dull, the SA boys borrowed whips from the cart-drivers gathered for the show, and added choreography to the Gesamtkunstwerk. You ought to see the Jews jump! Nijinsky would be jealous. One young girl lost an eye. The police kept order — that is, they kept the sightlines clear, and made sure no one disturbed the performance. In the middle of the cleansing, a car arrived carrying four old men, apparently grabbed at some ceremony of their own. They were made to polish the grimy metal with their prayer shawls — to great cheering and howling. The sacred garments, now ripped and filthy, were thrown into the Spree. Then the whole cleaning crew was marched, drill step, all the way to the Judischer Friedhof where,

I hear, they were forced to help with the difficult work of turning over gravestones. I have to admit I have a limited appetite for such entertainment. I went home from the bridge to vomit (I do this often) and to begin this letter to you.

Gregor didn't know if he could go on reading. Perhaps he should just calm down and listen to the story, then read the letter later.

The chain was long, and wound about him like a tail; and it was made (for Scrooge observed it closely) of cash-boxes, keys, padlocks, ledgers, deeds, and heavy purses wrought in steel. His body was transparent; so that...

The roach couldn't concentrate. His eyes went back to the pages on the floor in front of him.

Since God alone knows what you know (though you don't know what God knows), let me backtrack for the benefit of news-deprived Americans. Even before the Führer began to führen, there was "unofficial" boycotting of Jewish businesses, pushed by the bully-boys in brown shirts, who also punished anyone patronizing Jews in any way. So "because of Jews" "German citizens" had to suffer. Even talking to a Jew, having a conversation on the street, could get you accused of "race pollution" and "civic disloyalty", and lead to being paraded through town with a sign around your neck. The unofficial boycotts were peppered with equally unofficial violence. Naturally, there was the same kind of police protection.

With such "mandates" from the people, our governments began to act. A pastiche of wondrously creative local laws almost obviated the need for "unofficial" populist action. And now, after three years of this, Jews are no longer allowed in parks, in theaters, libraries, museums, on beaches, or into any club. They can't be guests in hotels, or get service at restaurants. One profession after another has un-licensed them. They can't open stores, or be allowed into workers' unions or any jobs they control. They can't be lawyers, they can't be tax consultants, can't be lifeguards, or actors, or salesmen, or stock brokers. They can't rent out park chairs, they can't distribute movies, or deal in art works, or currency. They can't be engineers, they can't sell guns. What have I forgotten? No Jew can be a detective, a guard, or an accountant. No Jew can be a guide, a peddler, an auctioneer, no Jew can manage anything — factory, house, estate, or land. Needless to say, all the new business and job opportunities have gone to Aryans, who are ever more grateful to the regime. You wouldn't like it here.

A slight disorder of the stomach makes them cheats. You may be an undigested bit of beef, a blot of mustard, a crumb of cheese...

G felt his stomach gurgle. He hadn't eaten dinner...

In areas where Jews are not yet banned, other ways are found to shut them down. Tax authorities won't deal with legitimate Jewish agents, so few property owners are interested in hiring them. Sugar has been cut off to Jewish bakers and candy-makers, destroying their businesses. Jewish newsstands can't get newspapers. Jewish businesses can't put ads in directories, in newspapers, on billboards or the radio. You don't read about these things in your papers. We don't need to read about them in ours.

It's true. I read more than most. The Times, the Tribune, the Post, the Worker... How come I don't know this? Terrible!

'You will be haunted,' resumed the Ghost, 'by Three Spirits.'

But not everything, dear Gregor, is bleak. Though many jobs are no longer available, at the same time, to balance things off, certain jobs have opened up for the children of Abraham and Isaac: cleaning public toilets, for instance, and sewage plants. Jobs at rag and bone works are considered possibly "suitable" for Jews. But outside of such work, they have to fend for themselves.

Ah, but what if they succeed — in fending? How could success be made less likely? Travel bans and invalidation of passports are obvious. But how about no parking for Jews, with special license plates to identify Jewish cars for special harassment? Ingenious. Original. In a few cities we now have prohibition of drivers licenses, and in Munchen, restriction from public transportation. It might be better to move. But Jews can't rent their homes, sublet, or sell them to come up with any cash. Retirement benefits and pension contracts have been cancelled, and all insurance policies.

Two years ago Jewish students were kept from taking finals, so couldn't complete their schooling — and their job prospects were already ... poor. All student loans had to be paid in two weeks, regardless of contract; those in default had engagements with the police, and they wasn't nice.

My God. Those poor...

And the stink! Yes, they smell, those Jews — when Jewish streets aren't cleaned, water is shut off, and no municipal services are available. The police, when present at all, are an occupying army, attacking at will. Many town centers are off-limits to Jews, and the remnants of Jewish culture are under siege: Jewish art and music is censored — "decadent", you know — and even your American jazz is assailed as "a barbarian invasion supported by Jews." Thorough. But not quite thorough enough.

...incoherent sounds of lamentation and regret; wailings inexpress-ibly sorrowful...

Because they are persona non grata, Hebrews need to be easily identified, and our rush-hour passengers are not about to put up with checking IDs. So in several cities, including my own, pretty yellow stars are required to be worn, with strict punishment for forgetting. I suspect this is the just the tip of a fashion alert. And names. Lots in a name. So Jews can no longer name their children with "Aryan sounding names" which might confuse us. They all have to adopt "Israel" or "Sarah" as middle names, and use them on all identification. Now you can tell all bruchs by their covers.

Gregor was breathing hard.

We German-speakers are of course addicted to Law and Order. So a few weeks after Herr Hitler became Chancellor, Herr Goering drafted 40,000 brown and black shirts into the police forces, with unlimited opportunity to indulge any pent-up sadism. I clipped the following marching orders from the horse's mouth:

"Police officers who make use of firearms in the execution of their duties will, without regard to the consequences of such use, benefit by my protection; those who, out of a misplaced regard for the consequences, fail in their duty will be punished in accordance with the regulations." Clear enough?

...found himself face to face with the unearthly visitor...

We now have 53 concentration camps around the country, centers for imprisonment and torture of anyone anyone thinks might oppose the regime. And something new — we have a certain GESTAPO — some post office employee's suggestion for a name — Geheime Staatspolizei — to run them. Since the Night of Long Knives — do you know about this? — guard duty is granted exclusively to Gestapo "Death's Head Units". You can imagine. Under the good old brown shirts, the camps were mainly there to give victims a hell of a beating, then ransom them to relatives or friends for as much as the traffic would bear. Comparative paradise. But now, under the black-shirted Totenkopfverbande — we shall see. I did clip the following for you from the new official camp rules: Article 11. The following offenders, considered as agitators, will be hanged:

Anyone who politicizes, holds inciting speeches and meetings, forms cliques, loiters around with others; who for the purpose of supplying the propaganda of the opposition with atrocity stories, collects true or false information about the concentration camp; receives such information, buries it, talks about it to others, smuggles it out of the camp into the hands of foreign visitors, etc.

Article 12. The following offenders, considered as mutineers, will be shot on the spot or later hanged: anyone attacking physically a guard or SS man, refusing to obey or to work while on detail, or bawling, shouting, inciting or holding speeches while marching or at work.

Caveat emptor.

"I am the Ghost of Christmas Past," the delighted audience chanted together with the reader.

Gregor looked out from his cavern, his attention momentarily diverted.

'Long Past?' inquired Scrooge: observant of its dwarfish stature. 'No. Your past.'

He drifted back to Amadeus, reluctant, but driven...

Oh, and in order to populate the camps (we want to get our tax dollars worth), there's the new SD, the Sicherheitsdienst. Security, Gregor, security. We now have 100,000 part-time, and 5,000 full-time informers directed to snoop on every citizen in the land and report the slightest suspicious remark or activity. You can imagine how many petty feuds are being settled. No one can say or do anything without wondering how SD microphones or overhearing agents — your son, for instance, or your father, or your wife or best friend, or your boss, or your secretary — might interpret it.

One of the fascinating, if lesser, tasks of the SD is to identify who votes "No" in the Führer's plebiscites, which at this point, garner only 98% approval. Members of the election committee number all ballots, and the SD makes up a voters' list. Since the secret ballots are handed out in numerical order, it's easy to identify the dissidents. There is some debate about whether this would be more effective overt or covert, but at the moment, they seem more interested in identifying nay-sayers.

It's all legal, of course. Law and Order, natürlich. Did your papers report "The Enabling Act" last March? If so, I missed it. It gives Hitler exclusive legislative powers for four years. Exclusive. The German Parliament turns over its constitutional functions, and takes a long vacation. But since this "Law for Taking Away the Distress of People and Reich" required a change in the Constitution, Hitler needed a 2/3 vote. It's hard to get 2/3s of legislators to slit their own throats. What to do? Part of the problem was solved by the "absence" of the 81 Communist deputies: they were all "outlawed" and sent to concentrations camps. Goering felt sure the rest of the problem could easily be dealt with "by refusing admittance to a few Social Democrats," and since Hitler was allowed to arrest as many of the opposition as "necessary", he got his 2/3 majority — though the Nazis had won only 44% of the previous election. Mathematics can be truly...

There goes Friday, running for his life to the little creek. Halloa. Hoop. Hallo.'

The President gave such a whoop, cried out so effectively, both voice and echo, that Gregor looked up sharply, and out through the barricade of legs.

'I wish,' Scrooge muttered, [the President's voice caught up with sobs] putting his hand in his pocket, and looking about him, after drying his eyes with his cuff: 'but it's too late now. '

Gregor was truly moved by FDR's performance. His heart went out to Scrooge, trying to break out of his shell. But the metamorphosis was incomplete. And the sheets of paper were burning in his claw.

Mathematics can be truly amazing.

So now we have a perfectly legal dictator, who, with no higher authority to limit him, has taken the country completely into his own mad hands. All other political parties and all trade unions have been abolished. The Reichstag does meet occasionally to be harangued, but its members have been hand-picked by the Party, selected on the basis of how loud they can cheer. Hence, real elections are a thing of the past. But even if we had them, we would never know what we were voting about. I criticize the American press. Oh, mote, oh beam! Our news is handled by Dr. Goebbels, "Minister of Propaganda and Public Enlightenment". Need I say more?

Germany, Eternal Land of Law and Order — if you are German. But Jews can't use the justice system to protect themselves should the government onslaughts get a tiny bit illegal. All our courts are now packed to enforce policy, not judge it. The object of the law is to protect the state, not the citizen. Our Commissioner of Justice opines that the law and the Führer's will are the same. Last week, he advised a group of judges to "say to yourselves at every decision: 'How would the Führer decide in my place?'" If Jews are a menace to the state, then all laws oppressing them are legal — and just. It's logical. Last year Goering complained about defendants still having so many rights that convictions were impeded. So Jewish lawyers were barred, and since Aryan lawyers can't serve Jews, Jews now have to represent themselves against highly trained adversaries. Schlau.

But to be fair, not only Jews suffer this way. We now have "Peoples' Courts" with jurisdiction over all political crimes. Two professional judges and five others chosen from among Party officials, the SS and the Armed Forces. All proceedings are closed, and there is no appeal from decisions or sentences — which usually involve executions. Who would dare testify for the defense of anyone accused of "treason"? After the murder of her husband on the Night of Long Knives, Erich Klausener's widow tried to sue the State for damages. Her lawyers were whisked off to Sachsenhausen concentration camp, until they formally withdrew the action. Dr. Erich Klausener — the leader of Catholic Action!

G had to take a break. He stared blankly out in front of him, then drifted slowly into the here and now, the here and then, of Dickens.

Scrooge was older now; a man in the prime of life. His face had not the harsh and rigid lines of later years; but it had begun to wear the signs of care and avarice. There was an eager, greedy, restless motion in the eye, which showed the passion that had taken root, and where the shadow of the growing tree would fall.

Gregor, too, was older. Chitin does not age as obviously as skin, but from the inside he could feel a subtle cracking, a reticulation of scar tissue at once deadeningly sullen and incisively inscribed. The pattern approximated the look of roots, but where would such roots be nourished? His eyes dropped again to the papers.

The Night of Long Knives again.

Yes, the Night of Long Knives. I can't recall...

...have seen your nobler aspirations fall off one by one, until the master-passion, Gain, engrosses you...'

Was this reported? Read through *Mein Kampf.* Begin anywhere — it's all of a piece. You may be tempted to dismiss it as the ravings of a paranoid schizophrenic with barely enough education to make a difference. But last June 30th such dismissals went to unquiet graves — along with several hundred of Hitler's former collaborators.

"Not like our good children here," Eleanor commented into the middle of the reading. She was referring to the tumult of "every child conducting itself like forty".

There had been some criticism of the regime, even from the conservative Right. The revolution, some thought, should slow down, the arbitrary arrests stop; the persecution of the Jews, the attacks against churches, and especially the arrogant behavior of the

390

storm troopers had gone too far. An environment of general terror was not good for business. But Hitler, Goering and Himmler did not take kindly to criticism. They needed to purge any SA moderates — and to liquidate all other opponents, Left or Right. So on that Saturday night, a coordinated series of bald-faced murders took place. In Munich, Ernst Roehm, Minister of the Reich, one of the founders of the Nazi Party, Chief of Staff of the SA, was taken off and shot in the head. Seven out of thirteen commanders of the SA were similarly killed. The SA! Had not these Brown Shirts and their leader helped seize power, and did they not even now control the streets? What daring to take on this group and their leaders!

The immense relief of finding this a false alarm. The joy, and gratitude, and ecstasy...

Simultaneously in Berlin, von Schleicher, former Chancellor of the Reich, General Kurt von Schleicher, was murdered in front of his house. Klausener was killed in his office at the Ministry of Communications. Gregor Strasser was killed in the street. All were murdered without explanation by ruthless gangs, mechanical death robots, killed out in the open, in front of witnesses. To whom would a witness complain? Bodies were left where they fell — in ministerial offices, in alleys, cellars, bedrooms and bars, slumped in cars, or floating in swampwater. After a few hours, police would come and take the corpses away. The Night of Long Knives.

"I am the Ghost of Christmas Present", the audience chimed in again. Gregor realized he was barely taking in the Christmas plot.

Hitler was secure enough to claim responsibility in an outrageous Reichstag speech:"It was no secret that this time the revolution would have to be bloody; when we spoke of it, we called it The Night of Long

Knives". He not only claimed the actions as his own, but laid down his right to repeat them:

"I was responsible for the German nation; consequently, it was I alone who, during those 24 hours, was the Supreme Court of Justice of the German People. In every time and place, rebels have been killed. I ordered the leaders of the guilty shot. I also ordered the abcesses caused by our internal and external poisons cauterized until the living flesh was burned."

The Reichstag deputies rose as one and cheered. The next day, they legalized the absolute monopoly of the Nazi Party.

And now these Nuremberg Laws. Gregor, I tell you there is gathering death energy such as has never been seen before, energy without any control. There are no voices left to speak against it — all rational people have fled, and their writings have been banned. Last year, at the Opernplatz just outside my window, Goebbels ordered a ritual burning of "immoral and destructive" documents and books. Your favorite authors, Gregor, and mine, were deemed too left-wing, too Jewish, or just too un-German to continue living and breathing. Up in flames went Thomas Mann, Rainier Rilke, Albert Einstein, Sigmund Freud — a fiery show specifically designed to enlighten the liberals of Humbled University. Heine wrote that those who begin by burning books end by burning people. His works, of course, went to the flames. Old man Spengler, I believed, survived, but I'm sure he's less than pleased with the conflagration.

mince-pies, plum-puddings, barrels of oysters, red-hot chestnuts, cherry-cheeked apples, juicy oranges, luscious pears, immense twelfth-cakes, and seething bowls of punch, that made the chamber dim with their delicious steam. In easy state upon this couch, there sat a jolly Giant, glorious to see, who bore a glowing torch, in shape not unlike...

His stomach began to hurt as never before. Was it an ulcer?

392

Gregor, I must repeat: there is only one power in the world that can stop this insanity — the United States of America. There will be a war — of this I am sure.

...for Tiny Tim, he bore a little crutch, and had his limbs supported by an iron frame.

"Just like yours, Grandpa, shouted little Katie, she of Heracles' smoke. Everyone, including the President, laughed. Everyone but Gregor.

Only the United States has the economic strength and the untested arrogance to call Hitler's bluff. I don't know how you are to do it, but someone has to alert the American government. Your President Roosevelt may be able to understand the dynamics. You must get to him somehow, make him listen — show him this letter if nothing else. Make him read Mein Kampf. Make him to know that Herr Führer means every word in it. He must understand that. He must understand that, just as in '17, America will have to go to war.

You must begin now, building up material and moral force for a quick, overwhelming victory — or all is doomed. Things can't wait until Hitler has overwhelmed all of hollow Europe — which he will. I don't know what to say. It sounds ironic and preposterous, but maybe the continuation of human, humane culture is up to you, poor thing.

He told me, coming home, that he hoped the people saw him in the church, because he was a cripple, and it might be pleasant to them to remember upon Christmas Day, who made lame beggars walk, and blind men see.

Look around: all the values and institutions of liberal civilization are collapsing. People no longer distrust dictatorship; there's no longer a widespread, clear commitment to constitutional, elected government under the rule of law. Security seems more important to people than rights or liberties, their freedom of speech, freedom of publication, assembly. We're not committed to reason any more, to public debate, to education, science, or even to the improvability of the human condition.

If Hitler Germany triumphs — and I assure you only the US can prevent it — Fascism will be the tidal wave of the future, hostile to any progressive politics, encouraging military and police as the only way to subvert subversion. Flag-waving will be the royal road to electoral success. Women will stay at home and bear children for armies, artists will be liquidated as degenerates. A lunatic set of beliefs will ride on the latest technologies....

If these shadows remain unaltered by the Future, the child will die. 'No, no' said Scrooge. 'Oh, no, kind Spirit, say he will be spared.' 'If these shadows remain unaltered by the Future, what then? If he be like to die, he had better do it, and decrease the surplus population.' Scrooge hung his head to hear his own words...

The activists will be those veterans for whom the war was a peak of personal achievement — simple inspiration or glory in brutality, men for whom uniform and discipline, sacrifice, blood, arms and power are what make masculine life worth living, men with a sense of savage superiority, not least to women and those who had not fought. These men will oppose all social transformation, all working-class movements, all foreigners, all sub-humans who might contaminate or pollute the world. These will be the men opposing us.

Do you think we can win against the hysterically nationalist and xenophobic, those who idealize war and violence, anti-liberal, anti-democratic, anti-proletarian, anti-socialist and anti-rationalist, those dreaming of blood and soil and a return to the values modernity destroys? Do you think we can win against those who can make the trains run on time?

'A place where Miners live, who labour in the bowels of the earth, ' returned the Spirit...

Gregor was not sure he could stand up against such force. He was not sure he could stand up at all, not sure he could make any difference in this deadly, vicious undertow of history. His heart was thumping fiercely.

...he saw the last of the land, a frightful range of rocks; and his ears were deafened by the thundering of water, as it rolled and roared, and raged among the dreadful caverns it had worn, and fiercely tried to undermine the earth. Built upon a dismal reef of sunken rocks, some league or so from shore, on which the waters chafed and dashed the wild year through, there stood a solitary lighthouse...

And let me return to one final dimension, Mr. Jewish Cockroach. A glance at any page of Mein Kakampf will demonstrate the centrality of antisemitism. You, Mr. Jew, are everywhere, a convenient symbol for everything hateful in an unfair world — not least its commitment to the ideas of the Enlightenment and the French Revolution which emancipated you, and made you so much more visible. You symbolize every conceivable villain: the hated capitalist financier, the revolutionary agitator, the rootless intellectual, every aspect of "the competition". You're too damn smart. You take a disproportionate share of professional jobs. You're a foreigner, a loathsome insect. Besides which,

you killed Christ. Do you think you and yours are
going to get out of this alive?

*...he was thinking of an animal, a live animal, rather a disagreeable
animal, a savage animal, an animal that growled and grunted sometimes, and talked sometimes, and lived in London, and walked about
the streets, and wasn't made a show of, and wasn't led by anybody, and
didn't live in a menagerie, and was never killed in a market, and was not
a horse, or an ass, or a cow, or a bull, or a tiger, or a dog, or a pig, or a
cat, or a bear. At every fresh question that was put to him, this nephew
burst into a fresh roar of laughter; and was so inexpressibly tickled, that
he was obliged to get up off the sofa and stamp. At last the plump sister,
falling into a similar state, cried out: 'I have found it out. I know what it
is, Fred. I know what it is.'*

Do you think you and yours are going to get out
of this alive? Not without help, Gregor, not without
big help. I urge you, with this, my dying breath, to
somehow get to the President. This ancient pullet
does not cry wolf. The sky is falling. Cluck, cluck.
Bawk, bawk, bawk, bawk, bawk, bawk, bawk, bawk,
bawk! Sssssssssss.

I suppose I owe you a few words about my condition. I send this package without risk: my life is
already forfeit. I have at last played out a "typical" role:
the average age of death in Werner's Syndrome is forty
years. I am now exactly forty, the scene of a grotesque
race to the bottom. Which contestant will have the
honor of bringing down the beast? Forty years old, and
ancient as Corruption, a boy within a corpse. My skin
is atrophic and sclero-dermatic — that is, I look like
a cross between an elephant, and the drought-cracked
lands of your midwest. Continuing the American
tour, my nose is dark and bubbled, somewhat like the
black, volcanic rocks of the Moon Craters Monument.
My face is the penultimate version of the picture of

Dorian Gray, except that I am now completely bald, the better to see the misshapen skull, my dear. General calcification is turning me into one big bone, though not even the dog seems interested. Cataracts keep me from seeing clearly except in the strongest light — such as I am now shining on this paper; I know what it's like to look fuzzily out of a mosaic eye. Perhaps we are converging: my leg and foot ulcers remind me of your wound, also unhealing.

But every cloud has its sulfur lining: I can hardly walk around for the pain, and this, you see, is good, since last year I broke my osteoporotic right hip exercising my right to exercise. Ewing's sarcoma, I have discovered, is a lovely little cancer of the tissue around my left femur. Dr. Werner, the glad-hand, tells me it's better to have this than meningioma. Thank God for little blessings. My scleroderma is lately rejoicing in the company of sclerotic arteries, though I can't say my heart is as happy, especially at the insufficient trough of the anterior descending coronary, now almost completely occluded. My kidneys, not to be left behind, are trying out their new act; "End-Stage Renal Disease". Catchy title. The good doctor Werner-San is proposing I become a human guinea pig for a new machine which will suck out my blood, launder it, and give it back, presumably cleaner and unharmed. I think I will pass. The good news is that my central nervous system has been totally spared, the better to appreciate and reflect on life's gifts. In short, my friend, I am a one-man Museum of Pathology, soon to be closed to the public. How poetic is Justice!

No need to write back. I enclose no address. The dead are not known to be avid readers.

Remember me!

Amadeus Ernst Hoffnung.

Gregor was in tears. Through his own silent moan he heard the distant voice of the most powerful man in the world. He listened as if hypnotized.

...a boy and a girl. Yellow, meagre, ragged, scowling, wolfish; but prostrate, too, in their humility. Where graceful youth should have filled their features out, and touched them with its freshest tints, a stale and shriveled hand, like that of age, had pinched, and twisted them, and pulled them into shreds. Where angels might have sat enthroned, devils lurked, and glared out menacing. No change, no degradation, no perversion of humanity, in any grade, through all the mysteries of wonderful creation, has monsters half so horrible and dread. Scrooge started back, appalled. He tried to say they were fine children, but the words choked themselves, rather than be parties to a lie of such enormous magnitude. 'They are Man's', said the Spirit, looking down upon them. 'This boy is Ignorance. This girl is Want. Beware them both, and all of their degree, but most of all beware this boy, for on his brow I see that written which is Doom, unless the writing be erased...'

Cocky Doody Politics And World Affairs

Childish Dealing with Atomic Threats

September, 2016

Reading through Oliver Stone and Peter Kuznick's minutely sourced and annotated book, *The Untold History of the United States*, I was struck by the language and thought-structures enunciated by our leaders concerning issues impinging on them.

Truman, for instance, on civil rights: "I think one man is as good as another so long as he's honest and decent and not a nigger or a Chinaman." (He regularly referred to Jews as kikes, to Mexicans as greasers.)

When Oppenheimer expressed to Truman his misgivings about having developed the atomic bombs, the president told his chief of staff, "I don't want to see that son of a bitch in this office ever again." He later called Oppenheimer a "crybaby scientist".

When Elliot Roosevelt, FDR's son, once spoke out against one of his policies, Truman characterized him as the "product of a piss-erection", and chided the "damned fool congressmen crying like a bunch of women" over "nothing but a bunch of bullshit."

This was the man whose finger did press the button.

JFK. the Hahvad aristocrat with his royal wife? When he found that Khrushchev had declared he would resume nuclear testing JFK erupted, "Fucked again!" His advisors urged him to hold off responding in kind so that they could score a propaganda victory, but Kennedy brushed them off, exclaiming "What are you? Peaceniks? They just kicked me in the nuts. I'm supposed to say that's okay?"

When the President invited the Chiefs of Staff in to thank them for their support during the Cuban missile crisis, there was (McNamara reporting) "one hell of a scene." Curtis LeMay came out saying, "We lost. We ought to just go in there today and knock them off!" But Kennedy viewed the outcome differently. He privately boasted that he had cut Khrushchev's balls off.

LBJ? Well, we know about him. Still, some of his locutions are worth meditating on. Concerning the Communists: "If you let a bully come in your front yard, be on your porch the next day and the day after that he'll rape your wife in your own bed."

Concerning his own intelligence operatives: "Let me tell you about these intelligence guys. When I was growing up in Texas, we had a cow named Bessie. I get her in the stanchion, seat myself and squeeze out a pail of fresh milk. One day I'd worked hard and gotten at full pail of milk, but I wasn't paying attention and old Bessie swung her shit-smeared tail through that bucket of milk. Now, you know, that's what these intelligence guys do. You work hard and get a good program policy going, and they swing a shit-smeared tail through it."

When the Joint Chiefs recommended mining Hai Fong harbor, Johnson started screaming, "You goddamn fucking assholes. You're trying to get me to start World War III with your idiotic bullshit — your 'military wisdom.'" He insulted each of them individually. "You dumb shit. Do you expect me to believe that kind of crap? I've got the weight of the free world on my shoulders and you want me to start World War III?" He called them shitheads and pompous assholes and use the F-word more freely than a Marine in boot camp, really degrading and cursing at them. So reported a military man in attendance.

When Sen. George McGovern warned that the bombing might provoke strong responses by both the Chinese and the North Vietnamese, Johnson responded, "I'm watching that very closely. I'm going up for leg an inch at a time…I'll get to the snatch before they know what's happening."

Johnson would not stand insubordination. "I don't want loyalty. I want LOYALTY!," he said of one aide. "I want him to kiss my ass in Macy's window at high noon and tell me it smells like roses. I want his pecker in my pocket."

Good one. Onward in statecraft:

Nixon and Kissinger decided to bypass the "impossible fags" in the State Department and run foreign policy out of the White House. He advised Kissinger to disregard Africa. "Henry," he said, "let's leave the niggers to Bill Rogers and we if the memory of thingswill take care of the rest of the world." He assured Chilean Ambassador Edward Korry that he was going to "smash that son of a bitch Allende."

And of course the Yalie in the cohort, George W, who popped unexpectedly into a meeting between Condoleeza Rice and a bipartisan group of senators and exclaimed, "Fuck Saddam. We're taking him out." He told press secretary Ari Fleischer, "I'm going to kick his sorry motherfucking ass all over the mid-East."

I guess he did.

As one might expect, Obama's potty-mouth is more Harvard educated, but equally spewing of shit.

Announcing the "end" of the Iraq war in 2011, he declared,

"We're leaving behind a sovereign, stable and self-reliant Iraq, with a representative government that was elected by its people," he told the troops at Ft. Bragg, praising their "extraordinary achievement." The "most important lesson," he declared, was "about our national character... that there's nothing we Americans can't do when we stick together....And that's why the United States military is the most respected institution in our land." He commended their willingness to sacrifice "so much for a people that you had never met," which, he insisted, was "part of what makes us special as Americans. Unlike the old empires, we don't make these sacrifices for territory or for resources. We do it because it's right. There can be no fuller expression of America's support for self-determination than our leaving Iraq to its people. That says something about who we are."

Surely that speech does.

And we freak out at presidential primary talk about the size of Donald Trump's hands, or the fictive throwing of a chair. Trump wants to kill Syrians. Bernie wants the Saudis to do it.

In 1946, Lewis Mumford wrote:

"Soberly, day after day, the madmen continue to go through the undeviating motions of madness: motions so stereotyped, so commonplace, that they seem the normal motions of normal men, not the mass compulsions of people bent on total death. Without a public mandate of any kind, the madmen have taken it upon themselves to lead us by gradual stages to that final act of madness which will corrupt the face of the earth and blot out the nations of men, possibly put an end to all life on the planet itself. ....

"Why do we let the madmen go on with their game without raising our voices? Why do we keep our glassy calm in the face of this danger? There is a reason: we are madmen too. We view the madness of our leaders as if it expressed a traditional wisdom and common sense: we view them placidly, as a doped policeman might view with a blank tolerant leer the robbery of a bank or the barehanded killing of a child or the setting of an infernal machine in a railroad station. Our failure to act is the measure of our madness. We look at the madmen and pass by."

Small Beginnings with Big Boom Ends

Roentgen's Ring Around Bones

On a dark November afternoon, 24 years earlier, a younger Wilhelm Conrad Roentgen had been working in his laboratory at the Physical Institute of the University of Wurzburg. Along with many others, he was exploring the properties of the newly discovered cathode rays — streams of energy which emanated from excited wires in semi-vacuum tubes known as Crookes tubes, named after their inventor, English physicist William Crookes. Bendable by magnetic fields, they seemed to be made up of electrons jumping off the metal, penetrating through glass and a few centimeters through the air.

On the afternoon of November 8, 1895, the slim, elegant, bearded professor had placed such a tube in a light-tight, black cardboard box, to contain its glow and better concentrate its energy and effects. When he activated the current, he noticed a faint purple-green glow in the pitch darkness of the room. Thinking there might be a leak, he turned on the lights, and checked the integrity of the box. Satisfied it was flawless, he darkened the room again, and flipped the switch. Again the glow, on a paper screen covered with barium platino-cyanide, a material which fluoresces — gives off light — when struck by various energy sources. What was exciting such fluorescence? Could it be the cathode rays? But the paper was several feet away from the tube, much farther than cathode rays were able to travel through air. He couldn't move the glow with a powerful magnet, so the rays did not consist of charged particles. What was going on? He didn't come home for supper.

The next weeks were spent exploring the properties of this odd radiation. He found the rays could create fluorescence up to six feet away. And most unsettling of all, he found they penetrated most opaque material. He knew they penetrated black cardboard. He tried to block them with a deck of cards: no go. He placed a thousand page physics text between the tube and the screen. It was as if the book were not there — merely a weak shadow. The rays went through a wooden plank, and various thicknesses of aluminum. He finally discovered something that would stop them: lead. They could not penetrate even a thin sheet.

Then came the moment that changed the history of the world. Roentgen was fairly sure that he was dealing with a particle stream: it seemed to travel in a straight line and cast a sharp, regular shadow around the lead sheet. To further examine the nature of the shadow, he cut out a small lead disc, and holding it carefully between his index finger and thumb, he positioned it between the Crookes tube and the fluorescent screen. To his amazement, he saw not only the sharp shadow of the the disc, but also the distinct outline of the bones of his hand. He shut off the current.

Roentgen was — as we would say now — spooked. It was a horrifying sight to this somewhat straight-laced man, his own skeleton encased in living flesh, a sight never before seen except under traumatic or surgical conditions. Accompanying his sense of awe were grave doubts about what it might mean for his career, should he tell the world. He could be snarled in controversy, ostracized from the world of respectable physics, all of his previous work discredited.

Paranoid, you may say, how could that be? This was a great discovery, why not trumpet it out? But we, in the world of Oprah and Geraldo, have entirely lost contact with the decisive force of bourgeoise "respectability" in the days when professors wore black frock coats and top hats: this was a real issue for Roentgen. Scientist that he was, he continued his work — but in strictest privacy, keeping all his observations perfectly secret. Replacing the screen with a photographic plate, he meticulously imaged every possible variation of penetration and shadowing. He photographed a box of lead weights: the weights were visible right through the wood. He made studies of his wife's hand: the gold wedding ring hung eerily around the bone. After assuring her he meant no harm, he brought his shotgun into the lab and photographed it ~ and was able to see the lead shot right through the barrels.

Finally, convinced that he had reproducible results, he submitted his researches to the Physical-Medical Society Journal for publication. The paper, "A New Kind of Ray, by Dr. W. Roentgen" is a model of clarity and humility. It is still worth reading, a classic example of 19th century science, and is contained as an appendix in the several biographies of its author. Buried in the text, almost as an aside, is the single sentence, "If one holds a hand between the discharge apparatus and the screen, one sees the darker shadow of the bones within the slightly fainter shadow image of the hand itself."

How To Make An Atomic Bomb. In Fact, Two.

Story of the Two Bombs

August 9

For Nagasaki Day, I want to tell you the story of the Manhattan Project, the grand scheme, as it were, the event terrain which has so affected our lives. Like all grand schemes, it began with an insight, and an insight about that insight.

The light—which grew to be "brighter than a thousand suns"—first dawned in Leo Szilard's brain, in 1939, at a street crossing in London. If there were an element, he reasoned, which would fission when struck by a neutron, and which, in fissioning, would release more neutrons—then a "chain reaction" was possible.

Imagining such a chain, I always think back to the story (clearly apocryphal) my father told me when he was teaching me chess. The putative king of some foreign country was so pleased by his subject, the putative inventor of chess, that he offered him any reward he pleased. The wily strategist played humble, and said, "I have few desires. But if you would put a grain of wheat on the first square, and two on the second, and four on the third, and so on, I would much appreciate it." "Nothing easier," said the innumerate king, and ordered his steward to attend to it. Point implicitly made, the story deteriorates rapidly, as the computation of 2^{64} is indicated, and the immoderacy of the consequences ensue: "more wheat than exists on earth," "more wheat than stars in the sky", and so forth—an accumulation even William Gates might turn down.

But in a chain reaction situation, rapid multiplication of neutrons is a fact, two producing four, four eight, until, in a rather small space, in microseconds of time, unthinkable neutron densities can occur. And when each of these neutrons is capable of splitting some special, neutron-sensitive atomic nuclei, a lot of action can ensue.

It turns out that when these extraordinary elements split, the masses of their products do not add up to the original mass, but come out slightly smaller. Enter Einstein, thirty-five years earlier. 1905, the famous $E = mc^2$. Here is another profligacy of number, the speed of light being so great, and the squaring of that speed so extravagant. Numbers aside, Einstein's equation says, simply, "even a very small amount of mass can be turned into a colossal amount of energy." The trick is to do it.

In 1938 Otto Hahn and Fritz Strassman demonstrated that uranium had split into lighter atoms under neutron bombardment, and physicists ran back to their labs to bombard uranium with everything they could throw at it. In 1939 Lise Meitner and Otto Frisch figured out an explanation of the process, which they named "nuclear fission". It seemed uranium might provide a real-world demo for Einstein's equation. In 1940, Glenn Seaborg detected something strange while bombarding uranium in his Berkeley cyclotron. The unexpected guest was not a lighter fission product, but a heavier new element, never before seen on earth, plutonium, the result of neutron capture—without fission—by uranium. It turned out that plutonium, too, was able to fission under neutron bombardment.

Two heavy elements — uranium and plutonium—both capable of splitting under neutron bombardment, and releasing excess neutrons and Einsteinian energy. One might think uranium the preferable beast, since it was relatively plentiful. But it turned out that the actually performing uranium was U235 —a "contaminant", 0.7%, of U238 metal from the mines. Because they were isotopes of the same element, the two could not be separated chemically. Because they were so similar in weight, it was only with great difficulty that they could be separated physically. And without separation, the mix was pretty bland, explosion-wise. But the path was clear: if U235 could be isolated and stockpiled, or if enough Pu239 could be produced, either of them might be used to tickle the Einstein equation to climax.

Szilard had one other key insight, (one wonders if there is something in Hungarian water)—the notion of critical mass. The reason all the uranium on the planet does not set itself off and explode is that it is too dilute: should a stray neutron split a uranium atom the secondary neutrons produced would fizzle out before they could enter and split another atom: no chain reaction would occur. Same with plutonium. But—what if those atoms were concentrated—brought together in a small space? Then, secondary neutrons might penetrate their close neighbors, and tertiary neutrons theirs, and the chain would begin to rattle. Szilard called this "critical mass". How much uranium, how much plutonium would you have to pack into how much space for critical mass? That was unknown.

Enrico Fermi decided to find out. In 1942, there was only unseparated uranium to play with, and that is what he did. Where do you play? In a stadium. In a squash court under the west stands at Stagg Field at the University of Chicago. On December 2, 1942 at three in the afternoon, the consequences of piling up enough uranium in one place became clear: embedded in 771,000 pounds of graphite, piled brick by brick, 80,590 pounds of uranium oxide and 12,400 pounds of uranium metal "went critical", and began to produce a potentially enormous flux of neutrons—till Fermi dropped the neutron-absorbing control rods into the pile. The wily Italian, using Szilard's original notions, had invented a nuclear reactor. The afternoon did more than demonstrate the truth of theory: one of the byproducts of pile reaction was plutonium. Fermi had also invented a "breeder". On December 2, 1942, the nuclear age had begun. Today, a Henry Moore sculpture sits commemoratively on the site. Could Fermi have blown up the entire city of Chicago? Possible, but unlikely—according to his 6" slide rule. Since word was that "Fermi never makes a mistake," breath-holding physicists hung out on the balcony and watched. And Chicago didn't know anything about it.

Neutron sources, nuclear fission, uranium, plutonium, the idea of critical mass. Everything material and intellectual was in place to make a bomb. Still needed was the catalyst of will.

It is no accident that European scientists were the first to imagine that Germany had already begun developing a bomb. German thought, German art, German philosophy, German science monopolized peak after peak in their cultural heritage. Consider: the atomic bomb is the ironic legacy of Beethoven. And Goethe, Kant, Schopenhauer, Einstein and Mann. If German Geist could consistently produce such giants of the mind, then surely Germany—even Nazi Germany—must be well on her way to exploiting original discoveries made by German scientists on German soil. That America must play catch-up to an already advanced German bomb project was the most universal, most powerful assumption, practically a certainty, the catalyst for the gargantuan striving of the Manhattan Project. No matter that many top Jewish scientists had been exiled. Planck was there. Von Laue was there, Hahn was there, Weiszäcker was there—Heisenberg was there. All you needed was one Heisenberg.

The Europeans were motivated, but Roosevelt had been sitting on Uranium Committee reports for almost a year. The British, however, their senses sharpened by a rain of German bombs, were not so nonchalant. In July of '41, a group of British scientists visited the States to try to provoke more urgent activity. Important research had been done for a year, both on the design of a weapon, and on the separation of uranium isotopes. But with bombs falling, and the country stretched to its limits, Britain could simply not move on to the massive manufacturing necessary to bring about a weapon before the end of the war. Persuaded by some high-level scientific politicking, on October 9, 1941, FDR agreed to put all possible resources into the expeditious development of a nuclear bomb. The Manhattan Project was born.

This was a double race, both with Germany, and between the two known fissionable metals. Which would be ready faster—a uranium bomb or a plutonium one? There was no telling, so both would be simultaneously pursued. Two huge secret cities were created, employing tens of thousands of workers, none of whom had any idea what they were working on. Oak Ridge, Tennessee was charged with separating out U235, and Hanford, Washington with the creation of plutonium. These astonishing industrial operations were to feed their products into the brain of the operation—Site Y at Los Alamos.

There, on the New Mexican mesa, physicists, chemists, metallurgists and ordnance experts worked together to design and produce a weapon that could be carried in an aircraft, and, when dropped, might actually explode.

Once the theoreticians had determined the likely critical masses involved, the initial design plans were fairly straightforward. A large gun would be built inside a bomb case. Using well-understood engineering, a sub-critical bullet of uranium or plutonium would be fired into a sub-critical target of same, and the two, coming quickly together, would form a critical mass, a neutron flood, a consequent explosion. The only problem was that, for almost a year, there was not enough U235 to work with, and almost no plutonium at all. Oak Ridge's progress was slow—uranium would probably work well, but not enough separated U235 could be produced out to make more than one weapon during the likely duration of the war. Hanford began at essentially zero—by the fall of '43, there were only milligram quantities of Pu available: all the plutonium on earth could be placed on the head of a pin. Still, as the reactor technology pioneered by Fermi matured, it looked as if quantity production of plutonium would be less problematical in the long run than uranium separation. The health risks were larger, as we will see, but plutonium seemed the more likely basis for a substantial nuclear arsenal.

All great enterprises have their crises. In July of '44, there were finally gram quantities of plutonium to work with, and it was discovered by Emilio Segrè that the metal available from the reactors was actually a mixture of isotopes. One of them, Pu240, was an alpha emitter, and source of "background" neutrons, creating a million and a half spontaneous fissions each hour. With such pollution, the gun design would simply fail: that thin hail of unwanted neutrons would condemn any plutonium gun to fizzling pre-detonation. Separating plutonium isotopes would be even more difficult—and much more dangerous—than separating uranium. That tack was out of the question. The race seemed lost, the project hopeless.

Oppenheimer was devastated, and considered resigning as Lab Director. But Seth Neddermeyer came to the rescue, and was able to salvage the plutonium bomb with a new design. The "implosion bomb" replaced the gun model: only implosion could develop critical mass quickly enough to avoid pre-detonation. It was Neddermeyer's implosion idea that was tested at Trinity in July of '45. It was his implosion idea that destroyed Nagasaki in August.

Implosion design was far trickier than the familiar ballistics of cannons. A ball of sub-critical plutonium had to be compressed in microseconds, absolutely symmetrically, in order not to fizzle. (Fizzling, by the way, meant exploding with the force of five or six tons of TNT, rather than fifty or a hundred.) Achieving this almost instantaneous spherical compression provided the drama of the last phase of the work. Explosive lenses had to be developed, shaped charges of various materials which would focus the otherwise unpredictable shock waves. A tampering container was needed to reflect escaping neutrons back into the fission. A timing circuit and detonating system had to be invented which could trigger the jacket of lenses with fantastic accuracy so that pressure waves from all directions would converge in step towards their target. An internal initiator was needed at the center of the plutonium core to provide an exquisitely timed burst of neutrons to initiate the process. And finally, diagnostics had to be developed, ways of measuring all these processes—wave profiles, neutron flux, materials stress: super-high speed cameras, new x-ray devices, magnetic sensors, radiation detectors—all this without being able to test the crucial materials in full-scale assembly.

Hiroshima, Notre Amour

Truman's False Stories of the Need to Bomb

On August 6th-9th, the world observes the anniversary of the atomic bombing of Hiroshima and Nagasaki. These activities always call forth responses asserting that the bombings ended the war, and saved an invasion of Japan and a million lives.

So much rides on the outcome, that discussing this is always a delicate matter. Still, at some point, even the most patriotic must face up to the many statements, memoirs, diaries and documents revealed over the past 70+ years which tell a story quite different from the official one. Presidents, as we know, do lie, and their stories are often self-serving. Such has been the case with the "history" of Truman's decision to drop the bomb, as anyone will easily discover by consulting the vast literature on the topic. Here is the gist of the matter.

It is certainly true that plans for an invasion were being worked on by each of the armed services. The model was for an initial, preliminary landing to be made on the island of Kyushu on November 1st, and for a full invasion to begin, should it still be necessary, in the spring of 1946. A prudent military plans thoroughly. But no order for such invasion had yet been given.

Although Truman repeatedly asserted that "The dropping of the bombs stopped the war, saving millions of lives," there is little evidence that he believed an invasion would be called for. The question is not whether the atomic bombing ended the war (the war did end right afterwards), but whether from a military point of view, the use of the atomic bombs was NECESSARY to end the war without an invasion. The evidence indicates otherwise.

Shortly after the War, the official US Strategic Bombing Survey concluded that "certainly prior to 31 December 1945 [i.e., before the general invasion], and in all probability prior to 1 November 1945 [i.e., before any preliminary landing], Japan would have surrendered—even if the atomic bombs had not been dropped, even if Russia had not entered the war, and even if no invasion had been planned or contemplated."

Russia? By agreement among the Allies (remember Russia was our ally), the Soviet Union was scheduled to enter the Pacific war on August 15. Truman's own estimation of the effects of this major new factor was clearly stated in his diary: "[Russia]'ll be in the Jap War on August 15th. Fini Japs when that comes about." Why "fini"? Because Truman knew, as did most of his advisors, that Japan was already suing for peace, with only the status of the Emperor to be bargained over. The US had cracked Japanese codes, and was fully aware of international diplomatic traffic around this issue. Indeed, Secretary of War Stimson remarked at a cabinet meeting on August 10th, that "the Japanese had broadcast their offer of surrender through every country in the world." (Diary), and our own intelligence services had provided voluminous data to back up this assertion.

Moreover, Truman's own military and political advisers (with the exception of Secretary of State Byrnes, who had his own political agenda) were not of the opinion that the bombs were necessary to win the war or avoid invasion. Eisenhower, when informed of Truman's plans to use the bombs voiced his "grave misgivings, first on the basis of my belief that Japan was already defeated and that dropping the bomb was completely unnecessary, and secondly because I thought that our country should avoid shocking world opinion by the use of a weapon whose employment was, I thought, no longer mandatory as a measure to save American lives."

Truman's head of the Joint Chiefs, Admiral William Leahy, agreed: "It is my opinion that the use of this barbarous weapon at Hiroshima and Nagasaki was of no material assistance in our war against Japan. The Japanese were already defeated and ready to surrender because of the effective sea blockade and the successful bombing with conventional weapons....My own feeling is that in being the first to use it, we had adopted an ethical standard common to the barbarians of the Dark Ages."

And even the aggressive General Curtis LeMay, subsequently head of the Strategic Air Command, thought that the atomic bomb "had nothing to do with the end of the war." As early as April, LeMay had argued that the war could be ended by September or October without an invasion. And even Winston Churchill insisted, "It would be a mistake to suppose that the fate of Japan was settled by the atomic bomb. Her defeat was certain before the first bomb fell." (*Triumph and Tragedy*, p. 646.)

On the basis of much historical evidence, it is surely fair to say that Hiroshima and Nagasaki were NOT bombed in order to end the war and spare lives from an invasion. The end of the war was within reach, and an invasion, though planned for the following year, was no longer considered necessary by the end of June, 1945. The story to which so many Americans cling is just that—a story, easy to tell, and easy to accept. But it was not—and is not—the truth.

Why, finally, the bombs were dropped remains a matter of historical speculation, since the "official" reasons do not account for the facts. But with increasing access to documentary materials (see Gar Alperowitz, *The Decision to Use the Atomic Bomb*), the most likely hypothesis is that Truman wanted to use an atomic attack as a means of ending the Pacific war BEFORE Russia entered it, and thus position the US as the unchallenged post-war world leader. The Cold War was born even in the victory of the hot one.

The Nagasaki bomb, entirely unnecessary, since the "point" (if there was one) had already been made to the Japanese, was dropped because the complex design of that plutonium bomb wanted testing in combat conditions. Hiroshima had used a simple, untested, uranium design, but it was plutonium, available in ever-increasing quantities, that would have to be the basis for an American nuclear arsenal. The Manhattan Project's plutonium effort had to be evaluated.

Such facts are disturbing, I know, and may seem insensitive to those whose lives and loyalties are tied to the official story. But they ARE the case, and arguments, if any, to justify the use of the bomb must be made in their context.

Awesome Days of Awe

Proposal for a New Holy Day

August 6th: Hiroshima. August 9th: Nagasaki. Three days in between.

The days between close-set giant pillars take on special significance. Whatever the current behavior of the state of Israel, most Jews know such spaces well.

The ten days between Rosh Hashanah, the beginning of the year, and Yom Kippur, the day of atonement, are not actually holidays, but mark a special period of time — what are called the Days of Awe. They are a kind of spring cleaning in fall, a purification of one's world and soul so that on Yom Kippur the Jew can faced the Eternal with all worldly issues in place. And what is the main strategy for this cleaning? It may surprise you. Asking and giving forgiveness.

The tradition of the *shtetels* — those small eastern European Jewish communities depicted in *Fiddler on the Roof* — was that in the ten days between Rosh Hashanah and Yom Kippur people would ask forgiveness of everyone they had wronged that year. All the little, and sometimes the big, wrongs that had been done in the community were brought out into the open, confessed, made good if possible, and forgiven. The entire community felt cleansed and pure. Perhaps not everyone was that honest. Like folks everywhere, not all Jews had the courage to beg someone's pardon or, when they themselves were asked, to give pardon with a full heart. But they found it a lot easier to do than we would today. While we have much more information now than they did, we don't know as well how to say "I'm sorry." But in those simple villages, to avoid a world full of hate, people often took the ten days and went knocking on the doors of any estranged friends, and cleared their personal paths, and those of the community. The world was cleansed for Yom Kippur — the "Day of Atonement".

And on that day the naked human being was scheduled to go mano a mano, godwrestling with the Eternal. Tradition has it that on Rosh Hashanah, God inscribed your name in either the Book of Life or the Book of Death. That's why the concern for measuring up. But the verdict on Rosh Hashanah was not final. You had the ten days in between, and especially Yom Kippur, to change the Judgement. But at the end of Yom Kippur, the Books were closed.

And so it is understandable that Yom Kippur be a full day of prayer without food. Five separate services take place during 25 hours — like Muslim practice — but with little or no pause between them. The idea of the fast is this: when the human body has paused from its natural acts of life, and history has suspended its normal ups and downs, the spirit can be utterly reborn. We don't really do fasts in America. We're better at pig-outs.

And sin — or evil, for that matter — is not a very popular concept in the contemporary American heartmind. Yet some concept of estrangement from the Truth has been common to most religious world views. The acknowledgment of sin is a crucial part of the Yom Kippur service.

"The Cloud Over The Culture" is the punning title of an extraordinary article by Paul Boyer (1985) which appeared on the fortieth anniversary of dropping the bombs. In it, he asserts, as do I, that although "Hiroshima" and "Nagasaki" are such familiar words — banal even — the United States "has yet to assimilate fully what those words represent in its political, cultural or moral history."

He quotes the American Catholic Bishops' 1983 Statement on Nuclear War:

416

After the passage of nearly four decades and a concomitant growth in our understanding of the ever-growing horror of nuclear war, we must shape the climate of opinion which will make it possible for our country to express profound sorrow over the atomic bombing in 1945. *Without that sorrow, there is no possibility of finding a way to repudiate future use of nuclear weapons.* (My emphasis)

Sorrow. Remorse. It sounds Days of Awe-like. How very, very strange it is that we — as a nation — have *never* done that. Not once, in now sixty-five years. Not even the teensiest bit. Un-Amerkin.

We have consistently refused — and still, even now, refuse — an absolute and explicit "no first use" nuclear weapons policy. One of the physicists who worked on the Manhattan Project observed that

If the memory of things is to deter, where is that memory? Hiroshima has been taken out of the American conscience, eviscerated, extirpated.

1945 seems so long ago. We were a nation in genuine and legitimate relief from a dreadful war. But what tenacity there is in the myth of American innocence, the belief that we are somehow set apart from the world, our motives higher, our methods purer.

It is this constant myth that prevents us from having any national Days of Awe, that keeps us from expressing sorrow over the event. And, as the Catholic Bishops so insightfully express, without that sorrow, we cannot go on, we cannot build a world safe — from ourselves.

New National Holydays
Let me therefore beat the drum for some pre-Labor Day labor. Down with innocence! Up with memory, confession, sorrow, apology, healing!

I hereby propose a new national holiday, modeled on the Days of Awe, but occurring in August, between Hiroshima and Nagasaki. Like the Days of Awe, they would be bounded by two momentous events, would celebrate those events with appropriate ritual, and would feature redemptive tasks to be done in between.

"It could never happen," you say, "too serious. It runs against the American grain to do that kind of self-criticism."

Maybe, maybe not. We have our solemn holidays, in places still solemnly kept. And besides, we may be growing up as a nation. Engaged in five current wars, with Iran coming up, the peach fuzz is off our cheeks. Obama's fairytales notwithstanding, we know we're not in Kansas anymore.

The vast majority of people realize we can't go on as we are — exporting jobs, exploiting foreign workers, making wars, eviscerating and polluting the planet. "Change" has become the buzzword to win elections.

The Christians have taught the world to acknowledge a December season of Peace. Is it too much to imagine that churches and synagogues, national organizations and neighborhood groups, schools and universities could slowly grow a late summer holiday to express the profound sorrow the Catholic Bishops recommend — a mindful holiday to witness and grieve, to assimilate a painful part of the past, to dissipate the cloud over the culture, to ask and give forgiveness, to sing in chorus "Hiroshima, Nagasaki. Never Again", and to be able to go on, safer from ourselves?

The religious historian Mircea Eliade has made a distinction between sacred and profane time. In sacred time, historical events gradually come to partake of the permanence of myth, while in profane time they gradually lose their grip on people and become merely material for historians and the technicians at Disney World. I am calling for a holiday that would change Hiroshima and Nagasaki into universal myths, deeply grounded in sacred time, permanent stop signs on the road to destruction. Four new holydays, making things whole, healing.

Here's how it might go. On August 5th, supper is a Japanese meal, which Americans would learn to make as beautifully as we do a turkey dinner. The event would have a ritual component like a Seder, in which symbolic foods are eaten, and history is thoughtfully reviewed. Each family, each congregation, each school would develop its own texts until some key themes and treatments became solidified.

The morning and afternoon of the 6th — Hiroshima Day — would be a time for fasting, or some special breakfast, with a ritual observance at 8:15 AM. During the 6th, 7th and 8th — our three days of awe and repentance — individuals would consciously perform expiatory tasks, personal and interpersonal, as in the Jewish Days of Awe, but also social, holding teach-ins, attending peace events. If a weekend fell between Hiroshima and Nagasaki, there would be special services at churches, synagogues, mosques. Morning and afternoon of the 9th is again a special time of fasting. 11:02 is observed, and everyone gears up for a big celebration in the evening, at which international foods of all kinds would be prepared — a huge community festival.

What I'm describing is a full-blown, big holiday. Things don't begin that way, of course. We might just start by thinking about it for a few years, by recognizing that in fact something important did occur on these days. Then, who knows what would grow — in individual hearts, in individual families, in individual congregations and institutions. Were something like this to get underway, in ten years we'd have *Good Housekeeping* printing August peace recipes.

We postmoderns like to play with history. Now we can play in its real mudbath, and actually get dirty — a death-defying vital alternative to psychic numbing. Would the New Days of Awe change anything? I can't imagine otherwise. The power of confession has been known to the Catholic Church for centuries. If anything has sustained the even older Jewish community, it has been the inspiration of the High Holy Days. The Muslims make pilgrimage to Mecca. This stuff has both a track record and the power of newness-at-large. Like an exotic virus spreading in a vulnerable population, the power of guilt could quite transform postmodern American culture. Revelation through genuine memory, then *Teshuvah*, turning and *Tikkun*, healing.

Or shall we just go on making wars?

Body Parts in Paradise

A Mill Valley Art Sale

In 1972, I had taken a dozen Goddard students for an off-campus semester in San Francisco. The College had rented for us a nice house and backyard just across the Golden Gate Bridge in Mill Valley, a gorgeous suburb at the foot of Mt Tamalpias. Each morning, we would examine the SF Chronicle for ideas for a theater event.

In the early 70s, our young men and women in uniform had taken to posing — as if post-safari — with one boot on top of Vietnamese they had shot, and then sometimes cutting off body parts as boasting souvenirs. The few photos published in the national press were not seen as "cute" but as extremely disturbing.

So our Goddard commune spent a night forming fingers, noses, penises, ears, out of clay (real donated pubic hair as needed), and the next day showed up with a table full of them for sale in a lovely Mill Valley park holding a community art show and sale. Redwood shade, pine needle floor. Our prices were low ($1.25-$3.99) to denote the small value of the objects.

The display was truly outrageous, but no one was arrested, and the "art" must have been on display for several hours before some reasonably civilized cops found out about us, asked us if we had a sales permit, and hearing that we didn't, politely told us that we'd have to move on. That's the normal relation between Mill Valley police and the usually white, rich people they protect and serve. Had it been the SFPD, and had we all been black, this report would no doubt have had a different ending.

Suicide Bombing, Anyone?

Americans, Too, Know Suicide Bombing

(October 26, 2005)

Many suicide bombers in Iraq and Israel. There showed up on my computer screen an article by a Palestinian writer entitled "Why We Have Become Suicide Bombers", which feelingly narrated a long history of oppression and frustration leading some Palestinians to ultimate despair. It strikes me that an article with the same title might now be written by an American.

So—before the "why", the "that": We, US, are currently slaughtering many innocent civilians. More than a million direct war deaths as of 2021 according to Brown University's Costs of War Project — and that does not include indirect deaths, namely those caused by loss of access to food, water, and/or infrastructure, war-related disease, etc. Plus we bomb their crops, their water supplies, bridges, roads and communications.

We have been doing that for many years, most recently in Grenada, Lebanon, Libya, El Salvador, Nicaragua, Iran, Panama, Iraq, Kuwait, Somalia, Bosnia, Sudan, Afghanistan, Yugoslavia, Colombia, Syria, Iraq. Did I forget somewhere? More, bigger, better. Our presidents promise broad, sweeping and sustained campaigns, against terror (!), and you may be sure that neither the Pentagon nor the record books will lack for megatonnage when our troops run out. "Bomb 'em back to the stone age" is a directive one still hears on the streets. "Put up a parking lot."

That these past and current bombings, and the bombings to be done, are suicide bombings is equally clear. Ours is a slow-ish suicide, a suicide-by-parts, but a suicide nonetheless. Death accrues by misallocation of resources, and the domestic despair and mistrust that result. It seeps in with the poisoning of our environment, both by toxic wastes produced, and those we can "not afford" to clean up—not to mention the ideological poisoning which will cause the upcoming global deaths, and the celebration of them here at home. And most dramatically, our past, present and future actions are a certain investment in more acts against Americans. One by one, or ten thousand at a blow, we are asking for it. All the king's horses and all the king's men…

All right—we are suicide bombers. But why? What drives a people to such despair that they feel forced to strike out against innocents and themselves? Einstein once commented: "Three great forces rule the world: stupidity, fear and greed." That's a good place to start.

America's stupidity is not a natural one, but has been carefully cultivated, especially over the last century. We are taught little history or geography; we speak few foreign languages, our information has become infotainment. All this pays off grandly in creating a nation filled with contented consumers, satisfied with the status quo, and unlikely to practice any "excess of democracy" such as aggressive voting, or turning out a government-in-question.

Greed, too, has been well-taught by a complex history of open land, "manifest destiny", racism and a sense of exceptionality: If stupidity clouds the realms of feedback, there is no natural check on self-aggrandizement.

Fear, is a natural consequence of even a glancing sense of unbalance. THEY want to take away our goodies. We'd better spend more on defense than the rest of the world combined. Oh, and missile defense, too. And weaponize space, just in case.

Stupidity, fear and greed—combined with great wealth and power—must ultimately lead to the semi-conscious despair we are now experiencing. Our children are shooting one another. They no longer believe they will have jobs. They are taking to the streets to be gassed and shot at. Their parents just want to "get through this, and leave the problems to them," as I heard one suit say to another. Suicide bombing, why not?

Like all apocalyptic action, this has its religious dimension. Our leaders intone the credo: we will rid the world of evil, of the Great Satan—them. Our fresh-faced bombers—alive and dead—are the heroes and martyrs praised in the bunkers of elders and priests, ecumenically, in the names of God and Mammon. Now over 7,000 just since 9/11.

On The Need Not to Know

Stealing of Porch Signs, No 9/11 Thanks

December 2005

A large sign was recently stolen from our front porch, where it had hung for ten months, toting up Iraqi casualties. The theft may have been simply an alcohol-related whim. But the sign had already been defaced with the following message: "So you can put up this sign. If you don't like it here, why don't you move to Iraq!" There was no drunken noise on the porch during the theft, four holding devices had to be unhooked, and I can only assume this was an act of stealth—a political one.

The sign was a terse accounting, updated several times a day as the numbers came down from the Pentagon. One would think that even patriots—especially hand-over-heart ones—would treat such information with respect. Even the logic of the inscribed graffiti would mitigate against its theft: American kids are dying in Iraq so we'd have the freedom to display such a sign. So why steal it?

This was likely the act of a single individual. Yet it corresponds to a larger pattern of censorship epidemic in our society. The White House bans photos of the coffins of these very subjects. Television may not show their deaths. So much else goes unreported—like the views of the underclass, or the huge votes against US policies in the UN General Assembly.

One might expect criminals to want to cover up their footsteps, and at this the White House has been a master. But how are we to understand the complicity of the media in such covering up? And even more curious, how to explain the behavior of the victims who would rather not know they're being had?

Three huge areas of know-not-ism spring to mind. The first concerns the details of our current wars, and includes the very numbers that were censored off our porch. What we don't know here won't hurt us.

The second area concerns what most commentators feel is the festering seed of the wars and backlash around the globe: US support for Israel's cruel occupation of Palestine. Some of us hold a monthly vigil, walking through the Saturday crowd on Church Street. Our signs say END THE OCCUPATION, or TEAR DOWN THE WALL. The most common comments are "What occupation?" "What wall?" Whether reported in the media or not, this story is easily available at least for anyone online—the majority of American households. It is the curiosity that is lacking. Out of sight, out of mind.

But the major weirdness concerns 9/11. [Two decades] and many US-fueled catastrophes later, people still refuse to confront the contradicions and implications of that day.

Let's take only the single most obvious strangeness: Building Seven. At 5:30 in the afternoon of that fatal day, a 47-story, steel frame office building collapsed neatly, at almost free-fall speed, right over its footprint. Whoosh, plop. Building Seven had not been hit by any aircraft, had not been touched by flying debris, and had only two small office fires the NYFD did not want to bother with. Curious? But somehow not so curious as to arouse curiosity. You'd think folks might get the hint that something was up.

But talking with many news-aware friends, I'd found that almost no one had ever heard of Building Seven. When I mentioned it was a classical example of a controlled demolition, I would almost always get the same response:

Gesture: Elbows bent, both hands up to shoulder level, palms out. Followed by

Sentence: "I'm not going there."

A few people added: "I don't want to live in a world where such a thing is possible."

Any further talk of the explosion patterns of the towers, of critical temperatures concerning jet fuel and weakening of steel, of architectural history, engineering analysis, NORAD standdowns, photos and videos of early Pentagon destruction—all and any of this got those hands moving, flapping outward from the shoulders, go away, "I really don't want to go there."

But many people have gone there. Engineers, physicists, architects, photo-frame analysts, and the occasional intrepid, dot-connecting reporter. And guess what...they're all—all— nuts, crazies, lunatic fringe conspiracy theorists! not worthy of media or political discussion. The need-not-to-know.

Albert Einstein once noted that "Three great forces rule the world: stupidity, fear and greed." Interesting observation. This trio may go partway toward explaining the need of not-knowing.

The economics of "free trade"? "Too complicated." When you put that sort of thing together with not knowing much about history, or geography, or math or science, it does add up to a semi-dysfunctional stupidity endemic in the population, annually measured and bewailed. But as Chomsky points out, this is not native stupidity, but a stupidity engineered by the system. People are plenty smart on the street, or concerning the statistics of sports. But intelligence about history, etc. is not encouraged. The attitude is introjected: "I can't understand." "I do not need to know." "Best to trust the experts."

The fear factor is obvious, a major tactic of all authoritarian institutions, from elementary school to Guantanamo. The more I know, the more there is to be afraid of. Like possible administration complicity in 9/11? Best not to know.

Greed may be what drives it all. Why are we afraid? In large part because we've got it and they want it. Share more equitably with the world? Forget it. The best way to avoid guilt around this moral weaseling is not to know—not to know other languages, world geography, international dynamics, the ecological state of affairs. Not to know the misery our greed creates. Our need not-to-know is urgent. Steal the signs.

ESSAYS POLITICAL

Israel/Palestine

Prophetic Visions

Protesting Photos No One Has Seen
Because of the Word "Gaza"

Every September, Burlington hosts an annual "Art Hop", during which hundreds of businesses along one mile-long street, open their doors, and offer their walls and lawns to thousands of Vermont artists, some already famous, some not. In 2008, Peter Schumann of Bread & Puppet, mounted a large exhibit concerning a recent trip to Palestine — eight foot high drawings on brown butcher paper, with lettered narration, wrapping around the walls of an oily, stuffed-toilet, barred-windowed, dimly lit ex-garage basement. Although the room sounds ghastly, and unfit for art-display, its gestalt captured the impoverished surroundings in which may Palestinians are forced to live. In order to open at the official Art Hop opening, we had put paper up over the windows.

Meanwhile, because they couldn't see in, and because the word "Palestine" was use in the catalogue announcement, several Jews and Jewish organization, began warning the community about an "antisemitic" exhibit being shown at the Art Hop. Individuals and venues threatened to withdraw their monetary contributions, or decline the use of their spaces. Some did.

When the show did open on a Friday night, many of them were there — in yarmulkas and prayer shawls, wearing and carrying Israeli flags — to inspect. And lo, and behold, there was nothing problematical to be found, just some large, beautiful art and writing concerning a trip to Jerusalem.

But then there was the next day, Saturday, which featured an artist talk/fiddle lecture, which Peter titled "Birds in the Brain", and, with its Sprechstimme, singing, and ya-ya-ya-ing was incomprehensible to the evidence-gathering prosecutors. Also scheduled that afternoon was a talk by a friend, and sometime puppeteer, Joel Kovel, author of several books on philosophy and psycho-history, his last entitled *Overcoming Zionism: Creating a Single Democratic State in Israel/Palestine*, perhaps the first such book, and published by the most respectable University of California Press.

Once again, the Zionist troops arrived, all blue-and-white flagged up, ready to rumble. One artist among them asked me if he could put up a (beautifully drawn and designed) poster which announced "PUPPETS LYNCH JEWS". I told him no.

"Why not???"

"Because the message is contrafactual — puppets don't lynch Jews."

He stomped off to hand out his posters at the door. During Peter's fiddle lecture people walked in and out of the aisles of chairs, loudly demanded to ask questions, and thronged noisily at the doors, an unruly crowd. But once again, it was much ado about nothing. Peter finished his talk, Joel, his, warriors left without much war, and folks remained to examine the art.

I wrote a little piece about the affair:

Concerning the Hubbub at the Schumann Exhibit, and Why the Sponsorship and Speaker Were Appropriate.

The Art Hop is about art, and art is about life. Art teaches us to see, think, and feel life outside its strictly "artistic" borders. Art does not end at the picture frame, the last page, or the falling of the curtain.

This is especially true of political art, and more especially so of the art of Peter Schumann. His paintings routinely leap off their canvases onto stages, streets and fields around the world. His production produces puppeteers, here and abroad, and these puppeteers charge into the issues surrounding them. During the summer, the Bread & Puppet farm is visited by other theater groups, and evenings are devoted to activist speakers, poets and musicians. Peter's work does not end at the "Thank you" and bow closing most of the shows.

That Joel Kovel, an old puppeteer, a long-time friend of the theater's, a scholar and political activist, should be invited to extend the

432

content of Peter's Palestine show beyond the walls of 696 Pine St. is a completely logical and consistent emanation from Peter's work.

"This is politics," a loud contingent of the audience complained about Joel's talk. "It doesn't belong here." Which, of course, didn't stop that contingent from leafleting the audience, posting flyers on its door, and generally trying to disrupt Kovel's talk with aggressive muttering, badgering, shouting and flag-waving throughout, and starting a political campaign to get individuals and businesses to withdraw sponsorship from the Art Hop.

But political art is political by definition, that is, it addresses the polis about urgent issues affecting the life of people, and Israel/Palestine is an urgent issue. The back room of 696 is devoted for the month to a show of political art. That it should be accompanied by related speakers, films and community discussion — and even controversy — sharing its universe of discourse is a legitimate dimension to such work.

I hope the Art Hop will not be cowed in the future by the low-grade violence, economic and other threats of this particular group into disallowing the multi-dimensional existence of political art.

The Art Hop is about art, and art is about life.

****

I am proud to say that SEABA, the South End Arts & Business Association which organizes the Art Hop each year, made the following comment: "We do not, and will not, censor art."

****

The following year, our group, Vermonters for Justice in Palestine, sponsored an exhibit of photos by Aymen Mohyeldin, at the time, the courageous reporter for Al Jazeera, who, in helmet and flak jacket, stood for several days on the roof of a building in Gaza, reporting the Israeli air attack going on around him.

Once again, without having seen the exhibit, members of local Jewish communities were on a tear, writing essays and letters for the Burlington Free Press. Again I wrote a response, entitled

Art Does Not End At The Picture Frame

I write on Thursday, September 10th, the day before the Art Hop opens. No one (including myself) has yet seen the exhibit of photographs of Gaza at the FlynnDog Gallery. And yet, as a result of SEABA's promotion of the weekend's events, there have been two BFP essays concerning "hate speech" and "anti-semitism", garnering by today 42 comments.

I've followed these comments with interest to try to understand what — in the complete absence of any experience of the exhibit — people are doing with their hearts, their minds, and their invitation to public speech. Here are some patterns I've gleaned from the texts:

No one has seen the photos, so most of the "controversy" is necessarily abstract. In one of the two initial pieces, Mark Hage, one of the organizers of the exhibit remarks, "Art can liberate us from fear and ignorance". Which, quoted, called forth two comments: "It can also lie..." (elipsis by the commentator), and "So can an acorn squash," a comment quite mystical, but vaguely equating art-intelligence with that of a soulless fruit.

Concerning the first comment, though, the writer, in the context of a debate about the upcoming exhibit, implies the possibility that the photos of a photograher on the scene of the recent Gaza events, may "lie". Viewer, remember that. The images you see — like all art — may be lying.

"Propaganda labeled as art is still propaganda," another not-yet-viewer writes, warning the art hoppers that what they will be looking at is [not "may be"] propaganda. The writer would not close down the propaganda — "I don't advocate silencing him but he certainly seems to be out to lunch." — "out to lunch" implying, I gather, that the photographer, the host, and the organizers of the exhibit have gone off duty for the moment, no longer responsible this lunch hour to the public which they are supposed to serve.

The writer goes on to explicate his critique of contemporary art in general: "Art by nature, always seems to have to be a view of a tradgedy (sic) or something that will disgust the viewer. Some people believe the crucifix with Jesus peppered with dung is art? To me it seems that people use 'art' to make gross predjudice, ignorance and loose facts relevant." The not-yet-seen exhibit will likely, in his view, reflect the latter.

Name calling of the presenters aside ("PC", "moron liberals", "uneducated", "monster"), the comments I find most interesting are those dissociating themselves from the exhibit per se, but clearly offering *themselves* as a context in which any exhibit concerning Palestine must be viewed.

Floating over all is the threat of a second holocaust following "disparagement" of the Jewish people. "We Jews know the effect of such disparagement," one contributor writes, "the robbing our people of the legitimacy of our own existence." A slippery slope to an existential threat? The writer explains that "We know from harsh experience that verbal and visual expressions of hatred often lead to violence." Remember, this is in an essay about the upcoming South End Art Hop, an essay which calls for a "response to hate", such as happened with "the picketers from Kansas" or with Sweden's failure "to criticize an article in a major newspaper of Scandinavia that alleged that Jews killed Palestinians in Gaza to harvest their organs." (This is a rhetorical technique known as guilt by association.)

The writer is well aware of the over-application of the word "antisemitic" by some in the Jewish community. "Clearly," he writes, "not all criticism of the State of Israel is antisemitic. I have spoken publicly about my experience in East Jerusalem, standing beside Palestinians as their home was demolished for no good reason; harvesting olives outside of Nablus with Palestinians threatened by Israeli settlers. But the assertion through words, photographs, cartoons, or artistic suggestion that Israelis are Nazi-like, genocidal murderers is hate speech."

While he admits that he cannot comment on this year's exhibit on Gaza because he hasn't seen it, his comment above clearly implies that photographer involved may be artistically suggesting that Israelis are Nazi-like, genocidal murderers, and that the potential viewer had best be prepared to reject such assaults, which he, with Swedish writer and political leader Per Ahlmark, compares to those "most dangerous anti-Semites [...] who wanted to make the world Judenrein, 'free of Jews.' Today, the most dangerous anti-Semites might be those who want to make the world Judenstaatrein, 'free of a Jewish state.'"

That's a lot of associative projection onto a photographer, who was present during the Gaza events, and as many of us would, took photos of the most affecting scenes to present themselves.

As we take in the Art Hop this weekend, let us beware of seeing more than there is to see, and be open to what is actually there to be seen.

Two Jewish Walls

Something There Is That Doesn't Love a Wall. Or Does.

Something there is that doesn't love a wall. Something there is that does. People there are that do not love a wall. People there are that do.

One of them is Benjamin Netanyahu, the less-than-loveable Prime Minister of Israel, who in February of this year announced his intention to "surround all of Israel with a fence" to protect the country from infiltration by both Palestinians and the citizens of surrounding Arab states, whom he described as "wild beasts".

The entire route of the wall — between 423-441 miles (the first is a Ministry of Defense figure, the second B'Tselem's) is more than twice the length of the Green Line, Israel's recognized border with the West Bank (199 miles), part "separation fence" with its electric detection, cameras and barbed wire, and part concrete wall, 26 feet high, more than twice as high as the 12 foot Berlin Wall, and like it, studded with guard towers, with soldiers free to kill. The difference between the "fence"s length and that of Israel's borders is explained by the fact that 85% of the wall snakes around inside Palestinian territory, on Palestinian land, separating Palestinians from their loved ones, their farmlands, their places of work, and any acute medical care.

To cross the wall, Palestinians must go through checkpoints, experiencing harassment, violence and death via Israeli soldiers suffering from vast indoctrination and incompletely developed frontal lobes.

Yet while the world generally looks askance at this building project, no country has definitively said STOP!, and US taxpayers fund the Israeli occupation to the tune of several billion dollars a year, with an increase on the way to propitiate Netanyahu for the Iran deal. President Obama and all the presidential candidates without exception

437

(Bernie included) insist on the obvious "Israel has the right to defend itself" without extending that notion to its victims. The Israeli army confronts no walls other than its own to limit its roundups, kidnappings, and house demolitions.

One wonders why the gross imbalance of all things on either side of the "separation fence"/"apartheid wall" is allowed to persist. I thought I'd inquire of a particularly prophetic Jew, Franz Kafka, to see what he might have to say about Netanyahu's wall.

Many of Kafka's thoughts on walls, wall-builders, and wall-subjects are contained in his short story, "*Beim Bau der Chinesischen Mauer*", usually translated as "The Great Wall of China", a title which misses the central thought of the original: it is not the wall itself which is the subject of the story — it is barely mentioned as such — but rather the building of the wall — who builds walls and why, and in what manner, and with what result.

And of course, as with all things Kafka, the text narrates merely the surface of situations of great, often comical, but sometimes ghastly depths, situations in which all humanity is embedded in enduring perplexity. The Chinese Wall, our Chinese Wall, Kafka's Jewish Chinese Wall and especially Kafka's Israeli Chinese Wall are all in play here.

How can I talk of Kafka and Israel? The poor guy died of TB in 1924, a quarter century before Israel was established. But just as his imagined bureaucratic dystopias predicted the horrors shortly ahead, as his penal colonies predicted the Nazi's (two of his sisters were later killed in the camps), his thought of a land of builders, Jewish builders, swirled with his post-1911 religious concerns. Though indifferent to Judaism as an assimilated youth, from the age of 28 until his death, he was intensely involve with research on Jewish history, Jewish tradition, Jewish learning, and Jewish literature and myth. His engagement with the Jewish question included an interest in Zionism in the face of European antisemitism. Interested, but critical. Thinking about emigrating, he worried in his diaries about chauvinism, zionists who "have the Maccabees forever in their mouths and want to take after them."

However many things his 1917 Wall story is about, it is clearly and

438

centrally about religion, about the Church of Empire, with its mysterious founders of old. A major section of the story reports the writing of a book at the archaic time of the planning and beginning construction of the Wall, and its relationship with the biblical Tower of Babel:

In den Anfangszeiten des Baues ein Gelehrter ein Buch geschrieben hat, in welchem er diese Vergleiche sehr genau zog. Er suchte darin zu beweisen, daß der Turmbau zu Babel keineswegs aus den allgemein behaupteten Ursachen nicht zum Ziele geführt hat, oder daß wenigstens unter diesen bekannten Ursachen sich nicht die allerersten befinden.

At the time construction was beginning a scholar wrote a book in which he drew this comparison very precisely. In it he tried to show that the Tower of Babel had failed to attain its goal not at all for the reasons commonly asserted, or at least that the most important causes were not among these well-known ones.

The scholar maintained

daß der Bau an der Schwäche des Fundamentes scheiterte und scheitern mußte.

that the structure collapsed and had to collapse because of the weakness of its foundation.

And because people in his time knew much better how to build walls than those in Babel time, the new Chinese Wall would

zum erstenmal in der Menschenzeit ein sicheres Fundament für einen neuen Babelturm schaffen.

for the first time in the age of human beings create a secure foundation for a new Tower of Babel.

And then on top of that sturdy wall, a new Tower of Babel could be built, a skyscraper whose top would reach the heavens.

Also zuerst die Mauer und dann der Turm.

So first the wall and then the tower.

Kafka notes that such a wall, built incompletely by plan, and linear, not circular, could not provide the foundation for a tower, so that the assertion

konnte doch nur in geistiger Hinsicht gemeint sein.

could be meant only in a spiritual sense.

Hold that thought. The Tower of Babel in a spiritual sense.

A second illuminating comment is this

*Es gab — dieses Buch ist nur ein Beispiel — viel Verwirrung der
Köpfe damals, vielleicht gerade deshalb, weil sich so viele möglichst auf
einen Zweck hin zu sammeln suchten. Das menschliche Wesen, leichtfer-
tig in seinem Grund, von der Natur des auffliegenden Staubes, verträgt
keine Fesselung; fesselt es sich selbst, wird es bald wahnsinnig an den
Fesseln zu rütteln anfangen und Mauer, Kette und sich selbst in alle
Himmelsrichtungen zerreißen.*

There was a great deal of mental confusion at the time—this book is
only one example—perhaps for the simple reason that so many people
were trying as hard as they could to join together for a single purpose.
Human nature, which is fundamentally careless and by nature like
the whirling dust, endures no restraint. If it restricts itself, it will soon
begin to shake the restraints madly and tear up walls, chains, and even
itself in every direction.

This assertion is almost identical to that to the Passover command-
ment to remove every jot and tittle of leavening from a Jewish house.
What is all that about?

Yes, there was unleavened bread — matzoh, the "bread of afflic-
tion" — baked on the run, without time for dough to rise. But is that
enough to account for removing from one's house all cereals and
grains, all grain alcohol or vinegar, all canned or bottled or processed
foods containing cornstarch, or any cosmetics, inks, glues or toothpaste which may be leavened? Out? Nothing that has come in contact
with leavening may be spared. The house must be fiercely cleaned
so that no particle of yeast might hide among the dust; pots must be
boiled so that the water overflows the rim. Such behavior comes from
roots thicker than matzoh.

Leaven, Rabbi Arthur Waskow tells us, "is what lifts us up throughout the year — leads to our working harder, searching deeper, loving
more." It represents the yetzer, or rising-impulse of the soul. But allowed
to rise without limit, yetzer becomes yetzer ha-ra, the evil impulse which
"impels us not only to productivity, but to possessiveness; not only to
creativity, but to competitiveness; not only to love, but to jealousy and

lust. So once a year we must clean out even the uplifting impulse; we must eat the flat bread of a pressed-down people, we must clean out the pockets of pride that have grown big again."

That so many people would be working together on the infinitely huge project of the Great Wall, and then plan to pile on top of it a tower to the heavens (if in Israel with the latest elevator technology, paid for by the US) — that would be an offense unto God. How did He react the first time? Let's listen in to Genesis 11:

> 3 And they said, "Come, let us build ourselves a city, and a tower whose top is in the heavens; let us make a name for ourselves, lest we be scattered abroad over the face of the whole earth."
> 4 But the Lord came down to see the city and the tower which the sons of men had built.
> 5 And the Lord said, "Indeed the people are one and they all have one language, and this is what they begin to do; now nothing that they propose to do will be withheld from them.
> 6 Come, let Us go down and there confuse their language, that they may not understand one another's speech."
> 7 So the Lord scattered them abroad from there over the face of all the earth, and they ceased building the city.
> 8 Therefore its name is called Babel, because there the Lord confused the language of all the earth; and from there the Lord scattered them abroad over the face of all the earth.

Via this comparison, Kafka's Chinese God-puppet shakes the Babel stick. Building a Wall is a No-No. Don't even think about it.

But the Israelis do love walls. If one looks at post-1968 photos of crowds of worshippers at the Western Wall, the Wailing Wall, the sacred Wailing Wall, you will see a seven-foot white wall between worshippers with XY chromosomes and those with XX.

In 2013, after much violence from orthodox Jews asserting that the space before the wall is as sanctified as an orthodox synagogue, and objecting to mixed worship, the Jerusalem District Court ruled that as long as there was no other appropriate area for pluralistic prayer, prayer according to non-Orthodox custom should be allowed at the Wall. So now the Israelis are building a separate area at "Robinson's Arch" for female prayer and other non-orthodox worship. Such as by LGBT Jews.

In 2005, Banksy undertook a Palestinian summer project, decorating the walls in the occupied West Bank, drawing attention to their deeply inhumane existence and purpose. (Drawing western attention that is. Palestinians need no instruction.)

But you can't please everybody. On his website, Banksy reports a conversation with an old Palestinian man:

Old man: You paint the wall, you make it look beautiful.

Me: Thanks.

Old man: We don't want it to be beautiful, we hate this wall, go home.

The Old Enemy Within Wherever

Kafka and Israel

Jun 11, 2009

Historical parallels are messy matches — Venn diagrams overlapping in the center whose leaves flap independently in their own unique breezes. And parallels made via notions held in common are iffier still, language and context shifting to alter color, shape and meaning. Still, catchwords held in common resonate, sometimes ominously so: "The enemy within" is one of them.

At the end of his blog, "Prussia on the Mediterranean?" Roane Carey describes an Israel which "increasingly sees its Palestinian citizens as a menace, as the enemy within..." Political dissidents, they are, untermenschlich voters reproducing themselves at non-Jewish rates, genetically scheming to become a voting majority. Guns they may not have, or F-16s, but sedition lies in their hearts. Better, safer without them. And so —

National Socialist Strategy

Step 1. Define the enemy. Jewishness was clearly and legally defined as part of a problem. Thus the Jews were made "other" to the rest of the population.

Step 2. Eliminate the enemy from the economy. Jews were not allowed to work in state-affiliated institutions. Jewish stores were boycotted and vandalized. "Otherness" was thereby increased, as the Jews were forced from the normal productive economy, and were now an ever-increasing problem — and not just by definition.

Step 3. Ostracize by custom and law. Many other discriminatory laws were put into place.

Step 4. Remove from view. Ghettos were created to wall the problem off from the rest of the population. Jews thus became less visible. When they began to disappear, there was often little to notice. As intolerable conditions developed in the ghettos, inhuman measures were justified as humane. Jews were killed in "acts of mercy" — in order to "spare them the agony of famine". In deliberately intolerable conditions, the stage was set for even more radical steps.

Nazi Germany, of course (see Amadeus' letter to Gregor, above). But consider, too, the early French Revolution, from the overthrow of the Bastille in '89 to the beginning of the Terror four years later.

France's Great Fear

La Grand Peur normally refers to a period in the French countryside shortly after the storming of the Bastille in Paris.

"They're coming, they're coming!" "Who's coming?" "They!"

Out in the boonies, in the apprehensive weeks following the taking of the Bastille, "they" might have been anybody: British marines already landed; the Swedes gathered in the northeast led by Artois, or the thirty thousand Spanish troops gathered, perhaps, outside Bordeaux.

But the "they" most often feared were the enemy within — putative gangs of frightening "brigands," relishing rape, dismemberment, and the wholesale burning of houses, farms, and crops, starving peasant bands gathered to devour their own, financed by Artois and other aristocrats to take revenge on the French people for their theft of the National Assembly. "The brigands are coming!"

The tocsin is rung, village militias are gathered, armed with pitchforks and scythes. People are sent to warn the next village.

The children are hidden in haylofts and given bread, cheese, and milk for a multi day siege. The brigands, so they say, have already murdered all the men and boys two towns over. The mayhem never arrives. But the breathless band sent out to warn is seen itself as evidence of the approach of the brigands.

And then again: Nobles out to attack us? Let's fire the castles. The nobles, the landlords, the judges—they're always preying on us. Do they know what we're thinking? Do they think us incapable of thought? Do they even know we're here? We'll show them.

All over France, estate owners were attacked, their cellars and larders looted, their legal documents—those mysterious orders written by lawyers and enforced by the police—destroyed, and their chateaux burnt.

In fear of retribution, they, too, were coming, the landlords and their armies. They've been meeting. Soldiers have been seen. Cottagers drove their cattle in from the fields, shuttered their windows, and barred their doors. Townspeople armed themselves, locked the gates, manned their walls. Rumor was cheap—but decisive. "La grande peur.": the enemy within. As the illiterate and unpropertied majority rose up, paranoia reigned, and the countryside feared even itself in collective psychosis.

After a while, as reality failed to correspond with imagination, "the great fear" waned, and slept, until its grand, better-than-ever awakening.

The Terror

Historians call it The Terror, or The Reign of Terror, and generally date that period from the fall of 1793 to the late summer of the following year. But, for me, The Terror was yet another statement of La Grand Peur — of the Enemy Within.

With the formation of the Committee on Public Safety on September 6th, '73, the stage was set for the elimination of the enemies of the revolution. Vernichtung. And that stage became the scaffold, the viewing platform of Dr. Guillotin's humanitarian device for painless, instantaneous execution and intimidation of the enemy within — the scheming nobility wanting the return of their privileges, the avaricious clergy wanting the return of their domain, and above all, the vast sea of unidentified people who might want to keep (as Peter Weiss so admirably describes) a painting, a mistress, a horse, a garden, an estate, their factories, their shipyards...their king.

Dissenting political parties were closed down, and their leaders arrested: the Revolutionary Tribunal became a Revolutionary dictatorship, and the guillotines were fully booked. Robespierre called the shots: "The Terror is nothing other than prompt, severe, inflexible justice."

An arresting detail: back in December of 1792, Robespierre had given a long and passionate speech to the National Assembly against capital punishment as a policy for an enlightened new world. What happened to this "incorruptible" lawyer, who as a child rescued baby birds, and had dedicated his law practice to the poor?

What had happened was the Great Fear of the Enemy Within, an "existential fear" that the world-shaking project of revolutionary France would be suffocated in its cradle, pushed into the sea of human fallenness and greed. Robespierre and France turned from savior to mass murderer, as the new world sunk deep into old blood-threaded mud.

Prussia on the Mediterranean

Palestinians the problem. Ostracism. Ghettos. Walls. Removal from view. Work limitations. Economic strangulation. Travel restrictions. Legal justifications. Imprisonment of opposition lawmakers. Sadistic local regulations. Enabling acts. Mass arrests. Secret prisons. Torture.

Even given the looseness of historical parallels, that Israelis are so worried about "the enemy within" is a cause of great concern. We have already seen full-blown Israeli terror against innocent populations in Lebanon and Gaza. Who needs guillotines when one has F-16s, Merkavas, and white phosphorus? We continue to see Israeli terrorist behavior in the West Bank — settler violence against people, land, crops, animals; bulldozer violence against homes; checkpoint violence day in and day out; IDF shooting at children and peaceful demonstrators. The Great Fear of the anger of Untermenschen grows along with that anger in a devil's circle of violence and potential violence.

The world is witnessing a saber dance on very thin ice. If history provides at least a warning guide, Israel is dangerously close to falling into a cold Reign of Terror, even within its '67 borders.

A broken-jawed Robespierre ended up screaming in pain and

horror under the falling blade he so embraced. Germans have still not recovered psychically from the Third Reich.

Israelis? The Enemy Within is themselves.

Burning Tires

The Urgent Palestinian Smokescreen

"The terrorists! The snakes! The cockroaches! Burning tires to poison our brave men and women protecting us at the fence! And horrible, too, for the environment! But Hamas doesn't care..."

I've seen all these assertions in Israeli articles and comments since the Great March of Return began, and crowds gathered weekly at the Gazan fence. "What country would put up with this?" "What would *you* do if someone invaded *your* home?"

Well, ok, what would I do if a preannounced set of 100 snipers (not soldiers, mind you, but "snipers") were lined up behind and atop huge berms of earth for self-protection, and their scopes and rifles were pointed my way?

If I were clever enough, I'd try to become less visible to their shoot-to-kill-or-permanently-damage intentions. Hence the tactic of holding a celebration/demonstration behind a screen of smoke — not from high tech military chemists, but from the only available source — burning old tires. Brilliant. Daring (depending on wind or wind-lessness), cheap, camera-worthy.

The irony of Israelis objecting to a smokescreen is really too much to bear. Israel is one huge smokescreen. I'd put a smokescreen as the central image on their flag.

Consider:

— the whole "peace process" since Oslo, which simply disguised the creation of illegal settlements for half a million illegal settlers in the Palestinian territories.

— the whole "Israel has the right to defend ourselves" gambit, using that excuse to slaughter, starve, and control whole populations of Palestinians with small arms at most, or handmade resistance weapons against modern high tech weaponry supplied as needed by the US. Self-defense — a smokescreen more lethal and long-lasting than the Israeli tear gas and phosphorus in the skies.

— "they want to push us into the sea" smoke-canard. Who? How push? (no room given the Israeli nuclear submarines.) When was the last time you heard any Arab make such a statement?

— the Israeli policy of "non-declared" nuclear weapons. Such a smokescreen allows Israel to proceed with its weapons program without inspections, or responsibility to non-proliferation treaties, destroying the possibility of a nuclear weapons-free Middle East.

— the labeling of everyone killed by an Israeli bullet as a terrorist, or in the case of young children, as a potential terrorist or "human shield". But who are the victims? What were they doing? Can't see through the screen of label-smoke. "We will investigate. If necessary."

— interesting psychological smokescreens that go with all this: The most recent I've seen was the idea that killing a few at the fence was "good for the Palestinians". Why? Because it would keep down the possibility of some getting across the fence, and establishing a " terrorist beach head" in Israel — in which case far more slaughter would have to occur in order to wipe them out...

— ...even "mowing the lawn" — the regular massive attacks on the imprisoned Gaza population, whenever Israel feels the need for political or "defense" purposes. A huge smokescreen surrounds the whole business of having "withdrawn" from Gaza, so no longer an occupation — when in fact Israel takes sadistic pleasure in controlling export and imports, movement in and out, even for medical reasons, air space, sea space. Best to starve or cripple the next generation.

— less lethal smokescreens are white-coated, or colored green or pink. In 2006, Israeli foreign ministry officially launched the "Brand Israel" campaign, and with the help of US marketing executives, is currently pouring in enormous resources to "rebrand" Israel in a positive light upon the world, and at the same time to legally shut down any criticism or pro-Boycott Divestment and Sanctions activity at home and abroad, especially on US campuses.

As the smoke from burning Israeli tires continues to engorge the world, we must continue our efforts to disperse it.

Burlington Occupation

If Israel Ocuppied Vermont

In response to two op-eds justifying the Israeli treatment of Palestine, I'd like to step directly into the daily reality of life under Israeli occupation. Let's imagine a similar situation in Burlington:

Movement is severely restricted. Passports are required at the Main Street, Riverside Avenue, Route 7, and I89 checkpoints, and there are mile-long backups on all routes. Within city limits, all major east-west streets are restricted to permitted drivers and vehicles, and many businesses have been severely affected. To control movement in and out of a particularly troublesome area, razor-wire now surrounds the Old North End.

Life is hard in occupied Burlington. More than 400 homes have been bulldozed or claimed via eminent domain to be used for other purposes, leaving many homeless. All public schools are closed for use as detention centers. There have been sporadic reports of torture in these facilities, but no contact is allowed with families, so details are scarce. Burlingtonians out-of-city will not be allowed to return to their homes, as these dwellings are needed for a selected out-of-state population. Though schools are closed, no day care is available; many have lost jobs taking time off to care for their families. Running water and electric power are limited to 3 hours/day and all telephone service has been suspended. Police stand by as the more affluent attempt to appropriate goods and services by force from their less well-off neighbors. Those with extensive bank holdings have watched money and valuables taken from vaults by armed officials to support the expenses of the occupation and the construction of the South End hotel and government theme park complex.

Not surprisingly, public health has precipitously declined. All community and backyard gardens have been poisoned by occupiers and the Intervale shut down; a food emergency is fast approaching as City Market and Walgreens have closed, and the Food Shelf sees no more donations. Burlington water is being diverted to Shelburne and Williston.

Health care has not been able to keep up. At least 40 people have died at checkpoints in the last month, unable to reach UVM Medical Center. Both BFD and St. Mike's ambulances have been fired upon, and two EMTs have been killed insisting on getting their patients through checkpoints. Hospital supplies are running low, and the destruction of its water tower by F-35s has severely affected operations. Medicine is increasingly unavailable, and its importation into the city restricted. Unassisted home births have become the norm, with both Infant and maternal mortality much increased.

There is little hope for political relief. All Independent and Progressive city councilors have been arrested, and Council meetings are being held without them. Mayor Weinberger has been targeted for assassination if necessary. All city paychecks are on hold until further notice. The Peace & Justice Center has been shut down, its staff arrested, and all demonstrations have been met with violent responses from the authorities, using illegal gas and live ammunition. The curfew has been extended, and people on the street or at their windows have been shot. Landmines surround the lake to prevent escape by water. All calls from other state, national and foreign governments have been rebuffed, as authorities assert that this is not the time to discuss key issues. It is promised that some of these restrictions will be lifted, pending correct results of the next election.

An unimaginable dystopian fantasy for us, but a compendium of real experience for Palestinians, with all mechanics and ammunition funded by US tax dollars. Is this really how we want to spend our money and our moral and political capital?

ESSAYS POLITICAL

Death Penalty

Sitting in on the penalty phase of the 2000 Donald Fell murder case led to my standing, along with several others, holding an anti-death penalty sign at the busy intersection outside the Federal Courthouse, two blocks from my own home. Here, someone had just been condemned to death, potentially multiplying the number of victims, and all I could do was hold a stupid sign up to unimpressed drivers. Wondering what I could do to address the problem of death penalties more deeply, I decided to "write a book about it." But what book? There had been a spate of recent death-house biographies, and lawyerly books, and I wanted to do something different. So I chose to examine the invention of the guillotine, up to the first drop of its blade. I knew Citizen Doctor Guillotin thought of his machine as a contribution to revolutionary ethics, egalitarian across classes — same crime, same punishment — quick, painless, and certain. But its use quickly got out of hand. The story is told in The Good Doctor Guillotin. But none of those questions are at play in the current semi-enthusiasm for execution — to be pushed on our lefty state that itself has no death penalty. Bush II's feds had to step in to teach Vermont a lesson. Their weapon? Victim families.

The Hand on the Needle

Bush intervention in the Donny Fell trial

May 16, 2006

Ashes to ashes, the first being the ghostly hand of John Ashcroft, the second the ashes of a twenty-something Donald Fell who will be killed by that hand, unanimously approved by twelve Vermonters.

On June 16th, Federal District Court Judge William K. Sessions III, will officially (and I assume unwillingly) pronounce a sentence which has not been issued in Vermont since 1957 in a state which 30 years later officially abolished its death penalty.

Donald Fell, admitting to the murder of Terry King, had concluded a plea bargain with federal prosecutors — life imprisonment without possibility of parole in return for a guilty plea. But the Bush administration was not satisfied. Instead, prompted by the King family, Fell's became one of 12 plea bargains rejected by John Ashcroft — at the time Bush's Attorney General — in a pattern targeting abolitionist states by imposing death-penalty requirements upon them.

In September, 2002, Judge Sessions declared the Federal Death Penalty Act of 1994 unconstitutional, arguing that the measure deprived defendants of their rights under the Fifth and Sixth Amendments of the Constitution, a ruling later reversed by the US Court of Appeals and declined by the US Supreme Court for review. Score a big one for Bush and Ashcroft overruling their own prosecutors. And for Death.

The Bush administration's aggressive pursuit of federal capital punishment comes at a time when other government officials and society as a whole, are increasingly skeptical of its justice. Issues of racial disparity, incompetent representation, and execution methodology are all in the news, but the federal push goes on in a conscious attempt to normalize state killing. States like Vermont that do not have the death penalty cannot opt out of federal laws even if they oppose them.

Gene Primomo, a federal public defender for Fell, commented on the long and difficult death-penalty process. "It's an inside-the-Beltway exercise by the attorney general for political points." And prosecuting attorney Peter Hall noted that his office was obligated to pursue a capital case against Fell regardless of the earlier agreement. Justice Department officials said Ashcroft's review of plea agreements would help ensure that heinous cases would be punished by death.

Such interventions by the Bush administration are consistent with its larger agenda of maximum control by a "unitary executive", privileged to ignore what laws it will, controlling every branch of government. The death penalty now rules in Afghanistan and Iraq. And so it will here, once more, in the Green Mountains.

> *Dies irae, dies illa,*
> *Solvet saeclum in favilla...*

> That day, the day of wrath,
> Will turn the universe to ashes...

Both Victim and Executioner

The Donny Fell Trial

Vermont has no death penalty. Still, federal prosecutors demanded that Vermont hold a capital punishment trial in a recent federal murder case which crossed a state line. And a jury of twelve Vermonters delivered the first death sentence in 50 years — another step backward toward barbarism as the feds contrived to teach liberal Vermont a lesson. Accompanying that verdict, there is now a citizen and legislative push to bring capital punishment back at the state level.

There are two entrances to the Federal Building in Burlington. One is near the corner of a busy street; it is wrapped around that corner — for maximum visibility — that we held our weekly vigils against bringing the death penalty to Vermont.

Yet the press massed itself daily at the other entrance, a smaller, mid-block one, half-hidden by luxuriant trees. Why? Because it was there that "the family" emerged for lunch or dinner. It was there they could be exhaustively interviewed and photographed for their every response to the courtroom events.

In the courtroom itself, one whole side of the public seating was marked off as "reserved". For whom, the sign was tacit. But that was where the family and their friends sat, sparsely, compared to the larger public packed into an equal space on the other side. The empty seats around them were treated as sacred space, not for outsiders. It was a rare courtroom visitor who was clueless enough not to take the hint.

The family. Even the defense counsel in his summation, chose to praise the family, that very family whose insistence before the trial sought death for their client, and whose performance before the jury and in the media did much to condemn him. That family was extolled

457

as a prime example of what their client never had — a loving clan that could come together to support one another in hard times, and celebrate in good ones. A model family which had overcome its many hardships. A model family — something their client never had.

In a country where more than half of marriages end in divorce, where single-parent households are now in the majority, "Family" has taken on iconic, white-hat status. Elections are won on "family values". All our holidays feature "family fun". You want to be a bad guy? Target the family. Worse, turn them into victims.

The family played their media hand with skill. I am not suggesting that their pain over the murder was not authentic. I don't know what many things they were really feeling, or who was advising them on their strategies. Perhaps they were even played by the media more than they played it. But the overall effect was such as to achieve their goal — to get a death verdict from a Vermont jury for the first time in half a century. Perhaps they felt justice was served. Perhaps it was merely revenge. But what they said they wanted was "closure".

We found much support as we stood Wednesdays at noon against the death penalty. Yet there were still many passers-by who felt otherwise. "An eye for an eye," they would yell from their cars, or "They kill us—we kill them!"

While the rest of the western world has long put capital punishment behind it, the United States perversely bucks the trend. For years, Amnesty International has indicted the US for its killing of juveniles, killing the mentally ill, for the wide regional disparities in executions, for the arbitrariness of those selected for execution, the obvious role of race in those selections, the systematic exclusion of opponents of the death penalty from juries, the use of peremptory challenges to exclude blacks from sitting on capital trial juries, especially if the defendant is black, for the assignment of inexperienced, often incompetent counsel to indigent offenders, for a whole array of procedural bars to appeal, for the increasing unwillingness of federal courts to consider new constitutional questions, and for the very narrow view of the role of clemency taken by governors and pardon boards. All these, says Amnesty International, puts the US outside the norms of international behavior.

No technical or bureaucratic problems were present in the Fell trial. Fell's guilt was admitted, and his legal representation was competent and strong. The judge was attentive, and scrupulously fair. The drama was focused on one question only — would the jury unanimously ask for death? The answer was yes.

Whence the still strong American embrace of the death penalty? In addition to the merry brutalization of our culture discussed above, I suggest it also arises from two spurious needs, both of which have been normalized by a bizarre combination of collateral damage from our war-making and politically-correct "sensitivity". The first is obvious; the second less-so.

One of the hallmarks of our contemporary culture is its curious competition for victim status. In addition, since 9/11, our administration has actively flown the banner of the victimized, crucified, vengeful Christ. Now that we as a nation have suffered so, we have a right to judge and punish. The city on a hill. And our punishment is far from unholy: we kill in order to redeem.

As we continue to victimize others around the globe, it is most convenient to proclaim our American selves as victims. And national claims trickle down to groups and individuals. Whites claim victimization by affirmative action, males by feminism, Republicans by "the liberal media", the rich by "big government" — and so forth, a whole convenient upsidedownism whereby victimization is seen not only as a right, but as a claim on resources. The competition is fierce.

Think for a moment about the demands of the Victim's Rights Movement.

First of all, it is now unquestioned that more people are victimized by a murder than simply the murder victim. All friends and family are understood as affected by the crime, expanding the test of victimhood to the suffering of those left behind, whose emotional performances seem so persuasive to juries. A new spotlight for "the family".

For the most part these people insist on vengeance as the only possible "closure" for their distress, a word that has been recently taught them by the political culture and its media—as if the effects of a murder are ever "closed". Protecting the community via life without parole will simply not serve. Though it would achieve immediate closure of the case — no further appeals, no further media attention to open old wounds — still "real" closure concerning a murdered loved one is sold to us as requiring the death of the murderer. That psychiatry does not support such dynamics is neither here nor there. Life imprisonment just isn't satisfying.

Concerning the jurisprudence of sentencing, what the Victims' Rights Movement has done is to substitute private for public justice, normalizing a sense of entitlement to the death penalty. Only a satisfying personal experience will do, and this now becomes the only adequate gesture for the rest of the community. The goal of the Victims' Rights Movement is to repersonalize criminal justice so that the public — and potential juries — must declare an alliance with either the victim or the offender. Criminal sentencing thus becomes a test of loyalty to one's community — a dangerous new path which predisposes toward the punishing needs of the emotionally involved. Rehabilitative strategies are overlooked, rejected as not sufficiently reparative to the new class of victims. Capital punishment becomes the ultimate assertion of righteous indignation, *and* the highest form of public victim-recognition.

No less a legal figure than former Attorney General Janet Reno has raised victim status to absurd heights:

"I draw most of my strength from victims," she said, "for they represent America to me: people who will not be put down, people who will not be defeated, people who will rise again and stand again for what is right. You are my heroes and heroines. You are but little lower than the angels."

Is victimhood, then, not a goal worth striving for?

The elevation of extended victims to sub-angelic status has two major consequences. First of all it normalizes and legitimates revenge in place of retribution, opening society to suffer an unending chain of reciprocal act of vengeance. We see this result playing out overtly in the Middle East, and covertly in the consciousness of people of color in this country, and around the world. By creating victims, we become the new victims, and victims are beatified.

And in this beatification, legitimate questions of restorative justice are passed over:

— Just what are the real needs of those who have been harmed? What, on deeper questioning, is really important to them? On surveys and in interviews, victims have most often indicated that acknowledgement by the perpetrator of the damage he or she has done is crucial, and would go a long way to easing them. Quite often questions need answering which would otherwise gnaw: why?, how?, what were the details of the death? Imaginations haunt; facts set to rest.

— And what about the defendant's needs? Restorative justice belongs to all parties, before any situation can be in some measure "restored". Again, as surveyed, perpetrators most often need to acknowledge what has happened, and in some way make amends. They don't know how to do that, and the system does not help them. We are open to helping those soldiers psychologically wounded from killing Iraqi innocents, but not a civilian who has killed one of our own.

Aiding both victim and perpetrator would restore as best it could. Further killing restores very little.

A further social dimension of embracing the vengeful victim plays out in the political sphere: revenge killing by the state becomes part of a strategy of governance that makes us fearful and dependent on the illusion of state protection, that divides rather than unites, that promises simple solutions to complex problems. The number of men and women condemned to die grows each year, and we are treated to the spectacle of people running for public office on the basis of how many they are prepared to kill. Tough on crime, it's called.

Caught up in the contemporary cultural preoccupation with identifying and paying homage to "real" victims, the idea that criminals can be victims too all but disappears, and deeper sociological, political and cultural issues are ignored as the white hats simply execute the black ones. Any mature engagement in responding to society's most severe social problems is shouted down by victims' claims for lethal "closure". Constitutional guarantees of equal treatment under the law are overlooked. Our fragile democracy increasingly calls for strong symbols of public sovereignty, like expanding jails and capital punishment. The desire for victim status, and a fearful aversion to non-government violence lead to an apprehensive attitude toward others. Increasing fear and frustration mark the current American condition.

The focus on victims functions as a strategy of political legitimation. The centrality of crime to governing, especially in a democratic state, requires citizens who imagine themselves to be victims, potential victims or those responsible for the care of victims. As criminals are demonized, many ordinary citizens are enlisted as authorizing agents and appreciative, applauding audience for America's own brand of lethal violence. To be for capital punishment is to be a defender of traditional morality against permissivism and of the rights of the innocent over the rights of the guilty. Down with protesters. Up with the fall from grace, with no prospect for redemption. In the land of the free and the home of the brave, we are all victims.

And can the land of the free ever evolve to crawl out of such larger embracing muck? Let's examine the muck to determine its adhesiveness.

There is a concept in the Russian language known as *poshlost*. Speech or attitudes or states of soul that are *poshlost*-y embrace values that are almost, but not quite, kitsch, containing some level of authentic thought or emotion, but nevertheless, more — or less — subtly — trumped-up, false or phony. A quintessential example of *poshlost* appeal is contained in the defense plea to the jury for mercy. His speech is worth quoting in some detail:

> We see such devotion and love in [the victim's] family, that [it] is overwhelming. They have been here every day in support of Terry [the victim], because that's all they have left. That's — that's what they, that's where they have committed as a family and have come together. And, you know, and that doesn't, that never even came close, close to existing to what the childhood that Donny [the killer] had. And isn't it important? How — and that's what — that's what this mitigation is — our mitigation case is all about.
>
> Don't underestimate the power, the significance of, of a father figure, someone to care, someone to nurture,

someone to provide. Don't underestimate the power and significance of a mother's love for her children. Look, look at what it's done, what it's done for the King family. They will never — and it was poignant when Michael — the grandson's letter was read, and he said — and he compared it to 9/11, and it definitely — their family will never be the same, and America will never be the same. But America is not destroyed, and when you see their faces and heard their testimony about their love for Mrs. King, their family's not destroyed. It can't be because they have too much of those protective, nurturing factors that exist, that are what we all — that makes us who we are.

Surely, overwhelming love, devotion and commitment are worth rewarding. And yes, nurturing fathers are rare enough and nice. The comparison of a death in the family to the world-shaking 9/11 may have its metaphorical value. And while the assertion that "America is not destroyed" may be somewhat nearsighted, still the co-appeal of both prosecution and defense to the jury's patriotism (if for opposite purposes) is probably a universally-endorsed tactic of the times. The summary, however, bodes ill. For it seems there cannot be "too much of those protective, nurturing factors...that are what we all — that make(s) us what we are."

The Oprah-appeal of this language, this thinking; the culture that feeds on it, that somehow seems to need and support it; the implied be-all, end-all prioritization of untutored emotion which we see amply demonstrated in every facet of contemporary American culture — this is not a likely milieu to transcend the kind of selfish emotionalism with which victims demand harsh penalties "for closure". That a defense lawyer in a capital case — buoyed along by these normative phrases, and counting on the jury's receptivity to them — would lionize the very family asking for his client's death is a self-defeating notion, lethal, as it turned out, to the defendant. What was the defense inhaling? Only air polluted by ubiquitous *poshlost* could create such confusion.

Not once in my hearing were the non-*poshlost*-y dimensions

seriously presented to the jury as a challenge:

— that, if they disapproved of murder, should they really be willing to coolly, and premeditatively, murder someone?

— that there is no scientific psychological evidence for "closure" after demanding death. Indeed, that families and jury members often suffer after doing so.

— that the US stands alone among western nations in exacting the death penalty, and that they must question the reasons for such exceptionalism.

— that there were likely political reasons for retracting the government's previously agreed-upon plea bargain — and did they want to cooperate with this?

Instead, the defense strategy focused entirely on the *poshlost*-y dimensions of Fell's horrible childhood. Why? Because *poshlost* is the reigning language and currency of the land, the only dimension one can assume operative in a juror? Or in a voter? Or a consumer? Or a 17-year old wanting to "serve his country" and help "establish democracy and freedom across the world"?

As long as *poshlost* rules American culture and American hearts, and is offered up to juries, we may have a hard time joining the majority of the world in opposition to the death penalty. In this, we are truly victims.

ESSAYS POLITICAL

U-S-A, U-S-A!

A collection of some remarks on phenomena which — though themselves unrelated — seem to me to bizarrely characterize the US national scene.

A Tale of Two Courses of Human Events

A recent Rasmussen poll found that 70% of Americans "Still Agree with Declaration of Independence." If that is the case, it may be that they haven't recently read beneath the fold to the fine print.

There, among others, we find as reasons for revolution a government's

— refusing Assent to Laws,

— refusing to pass other Laws for the accommodation of large districts of people,

— invading the rights of the people,

— obstructing the Laws for Naturalization of Foreigners; refusing to pass others to encourage their migrations hither,

— obstructing the Administration of Justice,

— keeping among us, in times of peace, Standing Armies without the Consent of our legislatures.

— affecting to render the Military independent of and superior to the Civil Power,

— subjecting us to a jurisdiction foreign to our constitution, and unacknowledged by our laws,

— quartering large bodies of armed troops among us,

— protecting them, by a mock Trial from punishment for any Murders which they should commit,

— imposing Taxes on us without our Consent,

— cutting off our Trade with all parts of the world,

— depriving us in many cases, of the benefit of Trial by Jury,

— transporting us beyond Seas to be tried for pretended offences,

— taking away our Charters, abolishing our most valuable Laws and altering fundamentally the Forms of our Governments,

— transporting large Armies of foreign Mercenaries to compleat the works of death, desolation, and tyranny.

Because "In every stage of these Oppressions We have Petitioned for Redress in the most humble terms: Our repeated Petitions have been answered only by repeated injury," the writers and signers of the Declaration conclude that the government is "unfit to be the ruler of a free people."

In their case, they did something about it.

Thanksgiving According to R. Cobb

Sagittal Section

Who's the Turkey?

Class and Gender Wars at Thanksgiving

Moms and daughters in the kitchen, cleaning up; dads and sons in the living room around the tube, watching the game. Way to go! Yes! (Burp).

How did we get from 1621 to this? By continual re-invention of an American "tradition" with largely fictitious continuity with the past. The Pilgrims did have a harvest feast with their Indian neighbors to celebrate a year of (50%) survival in the New World. But the first holiday called "Thanksgiving" was not until two years later in '23? and it was not a feast, but a day of fasting, prayer, and somber reflection, as one might expect from a colony of Puritans who abjured all religious excess.

Thanksgiving's asceticism was the first tradition to be challenged, as the Eighteenth century came and went, and the Industrial Revolution created a society of rich and poor. For with the poor came an accompanying tradition of misrule? attending every celebration where alcohol flowed. Holidays (once holydays) were a merciful time out of the status quo, when the industrial clock stopped ticking, and those who could not afford turkeys resorted to unlicensed drunkenness, children begging in the streets, rowdy gangs of youth and men ridiculing authority, and "disturbing the peace" by going house to house, demanding treats from the wealthy. By the mid-19th century, there was a decided whiff of class war about the day, which smelled of industrial strikes, and marches of the poor. The more affluent public was becoming nervous.

It was time to counter events with a huge public endorsement of bourgeois, middle-class values. As a result of conscious strategy, Thanksgiving would become a demonstration of loving domesticity, and "the affectionate family": See? In the face of capitalist crime and grime, family values were still with us? at least the us who could afford them? and the media, especially women's magazines, and the politicians, began campaigns to domesticate the day into the homeiness with which we are familiar. Demonstrations by the poor were policed away. Thanksgiving became a holiday centered around women's work in the home, the one time in the year when their skills were featured and not assumed. Public compliments on mince pie went a long way to ameliorate blows from spouses over the timing or quality of other meals at other times. For this day at least, the female nurturing role was affirmed. No wonder women embraced it.

And politicians. Thanksgiving had a potentially useful "bring us together" face which some thought might prevent Civil War. In 1864, Lincoln decreed Thanksgiving a national holiday to create solidarity, a sense of Nationalism, celebrating the civil religion of our "spiritual mission" — America blessed by God for special purposes. The Great, All-Embracing National American Festival of Thanksgiving. The South didn't buy it.

As waves of immigration followed at the turn of the century, it was the teachers' turn to use Thanksgiving? via their pupils — to Americanize the newcomers. Classrooms were filled with Pilgrim and Turkey cut-outs; children were taught that America was a land of immigrants just like themselves, and that they should go home and convince their parents of the American myths which filled their schoolbooks. A turkey meal? with all the fixins — would be a good place to begin. But there was resistance: As one Jewish mother lectured her importuning son: "Turkey? Thanksgiving? What's the matter — we don't have enough holidays of our own?"

What American holiday has ever escaped commercialization? In 1924

Macy's seized upon Thanksgiving to extend the Christmas buying season back a month. In the first Macy's Thanksgiving Day Parade (or Macy's Day Parade, as I knew it in my youth), it was Santa who brought up the rear, blessing and inaugurating the buying season. In 1939, at the behest of insistent merchants, FDR changed the date of the official holiday from the 4th to the 3rd Thursday in November to extend the shopping season by one more week. Two years later he moved it back again; people didn't want big government playing with their traditions To this day, the day-after-Thanksgiving is the busiest shopping day of the year, though Santas now arrive at larger malls in helicopters.

Apparently, even one female-centered day was too much for American males. In a typical revaluation of values, football was added to the mix of family, food and thanks, providing masculine balance to a feminine affair. Today's Thanksgiving celebration ends with the scene above, women in the kitchen, and men watching football.

The Thanksgiving Day game has a relatively long history. At the end of the 19th century, the upper class, now protected from the threat of the poor, found an opportunity to continue the tradition of Thanksgiving misrule on their own turf? the collegiate football field. Before radio in the 20s, football was an out-of-home activity during which alcohol ("Gotta keep warm!") called the shots as (male) fans celebrated and debunked, and occasionally fought their rivals. Radio, and in the 50s TV, brought football indoors, and men were quick to dub it "a tradition." Macy's had a bit of a problem on their hands: a morning parade conflicted with church-going, while an afternoon parade conflicted with football. I leave it to you to guess which conflict was eventually endorsed.

So now we have our post-Thanksgiving scene: rampant gender segregation, men talking to men, women to women. Camped in the living room, men find solace in an all-male group after a female-centered pigout. True, the carving was theirs? man the armed hunter dishing out the prey. But now, in the bright green light of the Astroturf, male bonding comes to the fore as testosterone overcomes estrogenic sentimentality. Huge brutes, aggressive, violent and dangerous play out a substitute for war, and simultaneously demonstrate American fair play, teamwork and management. Way to go. Fans demonstrate American loyalty, and give college development staffs hope for large alumni gifts. The gladiators on the field show their American ability to withstand pain, while the sons in the room, watching with their fathers, are weaned away from their mothers, and learn the rules of male sociability in America. That the women in the kitchen are giving up their leisure to wash the dishes may vaguely occur to some, but it is a rare man who will miss a kickoff to go help.

Have a happy Thanksgiving.

Divided We Stand

Red Sates, Blue States, a Book Review

DIVIDED KINGDOM
Rupert Thomson
Knopf, 347 pp.
Reviewed by Marc Estrin

Red states, blue states; rich and poor; the values crowd vs. the degenerate; Palestine/Israel (the slash is a wall); Blair and Bush against the world: we do stand divided. In his new novel, Rupert Thomson assays the situation with a provocative thought-experiment:

What if our divisions were made permanent, institutionalized as political and cultural underline solutions for the disastrous Kingdom of the World? What if a clutch of secretive leaders effected a "Rearrangement" of society, forcing the humoral personality types — choleric, melancholic, phlegmatic and sanguine — to live in nations unrelieved by diversity, restricted to their own psychological affinities, the better to get along?

Would it work? Who, after all, is not more comfortable — and less combative — among those whose manner he shares, whose values are held in common?

In *Divided Kingdom*, Thomson brews up a son of *Gulliver's Travels*, in which his protagonist experiences — via various plot devices — four different quarters, each populated exclusively by one of the humoral types:

— The Red Quarter, his own, good-humored, optimistic, full of purpose,

— The Blue Quarter, driven by feeling, empathy, spirituality, but largely unequipped to deal with life,

— The Green Quarter, melancholic, morbid, introspective, sometimes suicidal,

— The Yellow Quarter, angry, aggressive, rash. Permanent road rage.

Although Thomson's exposition of humoral theory specifies that health — of person or state — requires a judicious balance of all the humors, the planners, much like our own, have created precisely an un-balance, one more easily controlled. That such a tack might end in four dystopias is a foregone conclusion. Yet here, as reader, I am ambivalent:

The Problem of Solidarity

I was particularly struck by an episode in the Yellow Quarter in which a group of dissidents burn huge puppets of the four totem animals of the System. The Master of the Conflagration exhorts the crowd to spurn "what we are not", establishing its superiority. One of the characters speaks of "the need for someone to despise." It is clear that Thomson disapproves. And yet, and yet...

Each year, up in Vermont, the Bread & Puppet Theater holds a similar, inspiring, ritual to frighten off their own figures of evil. Once, they invited the audience of 10,000 paint name-signs for a huge wooden monster to be burned. The words contributed were GREED, BUY, GINGIVITIS, MONOCULTURE, GIRDLES, MANUFACTURE OF CONSENT, PUNISHMENT, COMPLICATIONS, COUNTER-INTELLIGENCE, PLAN COLOMBIA, FRANKENFOODS, EXTRACTION, BAR-CODE, SHIN BET, ARTIFICIAL NATURE, POST-STRUCTURAL CAPITALISM, INCARCERATION, MASS PRODUCTION, GIGANTIC APPETITE, PSYCHOLOGICAL WARFARE, SLAVERY, NORMALITY, REALITY, STUPIDITY, COMPLIANCE, INNOCENCE. As the beast went up in flames, the cheering and embracing were deep, devoted, heartening. One can easily imagine a right-wing ritual which might give equal satisfaction to its participants.

What is one to make of such human solidarity? Positive? Useful? Or ultimately destructive? It is the function of fiction to make one wonder; one of the strengths of Thomson's book to force the contradictions.

But we're left wondering, through all the events, wise words and snide commentary, just where <u>Thomson</u> comes down. Is it at "Little Gidding?

> *We shall not cease from exploration*
> *And the end of all our exploring*
> *Will be to arrive where we started*
> *And know the place for the first time.*

For at one pivotal moment, our hero is transformed by an experience in The Bathysphere — a Magic Theater à la *Steppenwolf* — released from the psychological straight jacket of his past. Much of the movement through the colors is motivated by his thirst for more of that bluish event.

Yet in several ways, Thomson rejects this easy, perhaps tired, resolution. "I wanted it to last forever," the protagonist says, and with this formula, throws in our face the damnation of Faust. "Quack," says the duck, "you said the magic words. To hell with you." He does arrive "home" in the Red where he started, the quarter of contentment. But, as someone remarks, "Perhaps it's *too* perfect. Perhaps one craves a little discord...Perhaps, in the end, we tire of harmony."

Thomson rejects, too, the superficially attractive, new-agey Church of Heaven on Earth. Following a didactic sermon on its liberal values, the scene devolves into a farce out of *The Life of Brian*, in which our washed-ashore hero is celebrated as messenger and savior. "The Gourd! The Gourd! No, the Sandle, the Holy Sandle!" So much for utopia.

Jesus Saves?

What then <u>is</u> the author's implied recommendation, his solution to the discord of otherness? Here Thomson might well say, "If I wanted to send a message, I'd call Western Union." Nevertheless.

Lurking throughout the text are pointed indications, some hidden, some not-so-, of a Kierkegaardian answer to Thomson's Either/Or/Or/ Or. Read, please, Mark 3 — the origin of the title phrase. Add to it Titus 11:14, the oddly specific time (ah, Google!) at which Thomson stops the clocks, Hiroshima-like, during a terrorist attack. And then forgive, if you can, the rescue of our drowning hero by a large, floating crucifix. A little bald, that.

Yet many hints point to a need for some religious response to the world predicament — beyond the ethical, the aesthetic or the political. Only then, suggests the book — at least to me — might the crooked be made straight, and the rough places plain.

M'aidez! M'aidez!

May Day/Law Day

SOS was the Morse Code signal requesting aid. Mayday became the oral radio code, probably a corruption of the French *M'aidez*, "Help me". And "help me" was what political Mayday has traditionally been about — a day of international workers' solidarity. This notion was eventually too much for capitalist, fortress American, which don't need no help from nobody, and in 1961 (yes, under JFK), Congress passed a bill creating May 1st as "Law Day". That's right, as you watch all those nice blue flowers come up, you can let your mind drift to the men in blue who protect and serve — if you are white and middle or upper class.

A quick web search of "Law Day" sites shows an interesting evolution of the custom. Many are now maintained by lawyers' and law school organizations, and are dedicated to the notion that lawyers are essential to "freedom under the law". This may be, if you are rich enough to retain the right one. But there are enough people who remember the political origins of May Day to be using the calendrical energy to combat the oppression of corporate globalization and US imperialism.

It's a beautiful, sunny afternoon in early spring, and it thus occurs to me that there was once — and still is — more to Mayday than just politics. Or maybe not. Our Puritan forefathers spent much vituperation on Mayday — and Christmas — (see Hawthorne's great story "The Maypole of Merrymount") — which they felt to be superstitious and idolatrous. Here is Philip Stubbes in 1583 railing against a "stinking idol" of a Maypole:

Against Maie Day, Whitsunday, or some other time of the year, every parish, town, or village assemble themselves, both men, women and children; and either all together, or dividing themselves into companies, they goe some to the woods and groves, some to the hills and mountaines, some to one place, some to another, where they spend all the night in pleasant pastimes, and in the morning they return, bringing with them birche boughes and branches of trees to deck their assembles withal. But their chieftest jewel they bring from thence is the Maie-pole, which they bring home with great veneration, as thus — they have twentie or fourtie yoake of oxen, every oxe having a sweet nosegaie of flowers tied to the tip of his horns, and these oxen draw home the May-poale, their stinking idol rather, which they cover all over with flowers and herbes, bound round with strings from the top to the bottome, and sometimes it was painted with variable colours, having two or three hundred men, women, and children following it with great devotion. And thus equipped it was reared with handkerchiefs and flagges streaming on the top. They strawe the ground round about it, they bind green boughs about it, they set up summer halles, bowers and arbours hard by it and then fall they to banquetting and feasting, to leaping and dancing aboiut it, as the heathen people did at the dedication of their idols.

O, well. There is always incorruptible nature:

> *Im wunderschönen Monat Mai*
> In the wondrously lovely month of May
> *Als alle Knospen sprangen,*
> when all the buds sprang forth
> *Da ist in meinem Herzen*
> there, in my heart
> *Die Liebe aufgagangen.*
> Love also broke out.

Im wunderschönen Monat Mai
In the wondrously lovely month of May
Als alle Vögel sangen,
when all the birds were singing
Da hab' ich ihr gestanden
then I confessed to her
Mein Sehnen und Verlangen.
my longing and desire.
(Heinrich Heine/Robert Schumann)

These are also Laws.

Art Project Proposal

Gladwrapped Reichstag to Be Updated

After a decades-long struggle, the artist Christo, and his partner, Jeanne-Claude, obtained permission and raised enough money for materials and worker salaries to wrap the entire German Reichstag in polypropylene.
https://christojeanneclaude.net/artworks/wrapped-reichstag/

Appropriate analogues for current action are innumerable.

Wrapped *Reichsfamilie*

Lifesize Barron, Donald, Donald Jr., Eric, Melania, in alphabetical order, wrapped and hooded and displayed for two weeks in People's Park, Berkeley.

Project budget:
1 pkg (10ct) small black Glad™ garbage bags @$2.19
10 rolls 3" duct tape @ $3.40
Subtotal $36.19
State tax 6% $2.17
TOTAL $38.36

Notes For The Downwardly Mobile, Part I

Integration of Food, Clothing and Shelter

Now that the war on terror is chugging nicely along, the country as a whole can get back to planning for its domestic survival in the face of infrastructure decay, public school chaos, banking crisis, increasing militarization, unaffordable health care, rising unemployment and deepening recession.

Even readers of this book, though likely well-placed in the socio-economic spectrum, are vulnerable to the dangers facing other Americans. We have therefore undertaken to investigate survival techniques potentially useful to the literary classes. Over the past year, the homeless populations of four major cities have been surveyed; this is the first report of information gleaned from years of human experience in exceedingly trying circumstances. It is hoped that as political, social and economic circumstances deteriorate, you may be able to take advantage of some of these techniques.

Optimal Integration of Food, Clothing and Shelter

Multiple use of existing materials makes for economy in scarcity situations. Food, for instance, can serve for clothing, insulation, and even privacy. Consider for example the following not uncommon situation:

After a sleepless night in a public shelter or lavatory, exhausted by guarding your possessions, you will need a good daytime place to nap. In inclement weather, public libraries are ideal, especially for the well-educated. However, library policy has recently turned draconian, and anyone sleeping rather than reading is usually asked to leave.

Two slices of baloney can solve the problem. Choose a color as close to your skin tone as possible. In the center of each slice, cut an eye-shaped hole. Choose a good book or journal, *Tin House* perhaps, open it, sit well-propped in a chair, and place a slice of baloney over each eye. A cap or kerchief low on the forehead will improve the illusion. Then, off to the arms of Morpheus. It will take a sharp-eyed, highly motivated guard to catch you napping, and these are in ever rarer supply. After your nap, put the baloney away for further use.

Soft white bread, such as Wonder Bread or Tiptop is not only inexpensive, but is also an excellent insulator. Due to trapped air, its R rating is high, comparable to fiberglass or foam: a must investment, even with diminished funds. Slices can be stuffed in clothing, and in key body areas such as the small of the back or lower abdomen to maintain core temperature in hypothermic environments. Don't forget the head! — 70% of body heat escapes from the scalp. Wonder Bread fits nicely under any hat or cap, or can be trimmed for a custom fit.

Fast food restaurants invariably have packets of yellow mustard available for the taking. You'd be surprised at how well Grandma's recipe for cold still works! Simply smear yellow mustard over your chest and abdomen, and along your sides (get up under those arms!) for long-lasting, bio-chemical warmth. It's free — and it's good for you, too.

Forget Kleenex from now on, and don't keep a cold in your pocket with cloth hankies. Even the worst exposure-induced upper respiratory condition can be contained by blowing the nose into lettuce leaves, available free in great quantity in supermarket dumpsters. A day's supply can easily be carried in pocket or purse.

Now here's a trick: At the end of a long day, when the baloney is a bit soiled and the bread somewhat tamped, scrape a small amount of mustard from the small of your back, whip out a few lettuce leaves, lay meat eye-hiders to bread insulation, and voila — a perfect baloney sandwich — utilizing three of the four major food groups — for your evening meal. Well fed, you can re-pack for a nighttime of maximum insulation.

This is only one example of efficient multi-use of food materials. Please write *Tin House* with any ideas of your own.

Notes For The Downwardly Mobile, Part II

Other Food Possibilities; a Modest Proposal

It is an open secret among the poor that pet foods are perfectly fit for human consumption. Don't be embarrassed to survey the huge selection in your supermarket — no one will suspect you are shopping for yourself and not for Fido or Kitty. There are so many choices that it may take a while to discover your favorite brands and flavors. No need to restrict yourselves to "gourmet" varieties. The "gourmet" label is simply a marketing device targeted at upscale pet owners. The contents are virtually the same as that of cheaper brands. Dry dog or cat food travels well, and can be wetted down at public drinking fountains. It is also ecological, since there is no can to dispose of. For the more affluent, canned cat food is probably your best bet. 9-Lives remains the trend setter, though it is virtually indistinguishable from other canned varieties. For an occasional treat, this writer recommends Sheba Moist Tender Chunks: Salmon Entree.

There do seem to be gender difference in the choice of food types, with men preferring dog food, and women, food for cats. For you he-men out there, we can recommend Mighty Dog — Beef.

National Legislation

The Bush and Trump presidencies have already been marked by radical conservatism combined with a fearless approach to the future. It is therefore not surprising to note the beginnings of a movement hearkening back to institutions of the past, yet clearly attempting to deal with the problems which lie ahead.

Currently riding high in its war on terrorism, the Administration is now proposing humane domestic legislation to bring back an idea whose time has, in its opinion, come again. Slavery has gotten a bad name with the liberal press, yet an unprejudiced mind can easily see its many benefits. Who can deny that living in the homes of wealthy families — even without pay — is preferable to a life of hardship, disease and crime on cruel streets? Family values would be maintained and promoted as mammys took care of the children, aiding harried executive mothers. Cultural pluralism would prevail as the old songs of the Savannah were heard again, and mixed races and cultures would be seen once again in the more exclusive neighborhoods. This is compassionate conservatism at its best.

However, liberal opinion seems divided on the issue. It is clear that slavery would benefit people of color more than middle-class Caucasians. But given the advancing pauperization of the middle class, it is not hard to imagine a time in the near future when it, too, could benefit by such a system. On the other hand, those among us who remember once-prized abolitionist roots feel challenged by such an idea, uncertain about what may be politically correct. It will be worth following the upcoming congressional and social debate on this significant issue.

Essays Acted Out

Back in the late sixties and early seventies, just out of theater grad school, and bathed in the fierce opposite energies of Artaud and Brecht, I developed the idea of "Infiltrative Theater". Why should "a theatrical experience" be walled off from life by high ticket prices, comfortable seats, and the social niceties that surround "going out to the theater"? Why should we be able to watch King Lear in agony, and then go out for a late night cocktail with friends? Why can't theatrical events — Artaud-visceral or Brechtian teaching events — penetrate lived life and change its pH as reality daily does? So I got together a company of people to perpetrate some planned events on unplanned existence. Some of our "infiltrations" got pretty complicated, but I present here two simply told ones which demonstrate making essays, not writing them. Forgive the 60's "Hey, man" diction. That's the way we talked.

The Thirty-Second Flavor

Baskin & Robbins is a national chain, serving rather good ice cream, but for some reason, they will never let you in back to use the can. We decided to explore the dimensions and implications of this with the customers and store personnel, whence the following piece.

We drifted into the store until we made up about half the customers. Then big Ed approached the clerk:

ED, *whispering*: I gotta go to the John.

CLERK, *friendly*: there's a Standard Oil station two blocks down.

[United Fruit sends its customers to shit at Standard Oil.]

ED: look, I got diarrhea...

CLERK: I'm sorry, we can't allow customers in back.

ED: I can't make it two blocks, you dig?

CLERK, *less friendly*: Sorry, it's against the rules…

ONE OF US CUSTOMERS: Hey look, man. I know it's against the rules, but this guy's got a problem. I mean, fuck the rules, right?

At this point people in the store begin to get involved in the dispute, either speaking directly to the clerk, or among themselves. The three hip young clerks supported one another's assertions of "I only work here," "I'll lose my job," "I don't make the rules," "It's an insurance problem," etc. This gave us a chance to develop the themes of rigid laws versus human people, of job security, of individual responsibility.

Meanwhile, it is twisting around in a tight ass dance.

At one point I upped the ante with "Hey man", Don't listen to that guy. Just go in there and take a shit." The clerk was actually about to defend the crapper with his life. (Ed is 6'4", 270 pounds.)

A compromise was finally reached: we had to call the manager at home at 9:30 PM to get permission! After three or four minutes of harangue, he gave his OK, but instructed the clerk to stand outside the john while Ed was in there. Luckily, Ed came through with a good load.

The whole thing was quite an experience for all concerned. A few customers left in disgust, but most participated, actively or passively in the drama. Comments were generally directed to the rigidity of the rules. I spoke quite a bit to the clerks about individuals undermining bureaucracy. We'll see what the effect was there when we try again with a pregnant woman…

This piece is easily generalizable to many different settings: look for the rigidity, devise an emergency around it, make sure there are plenty of customers, clients, etc., then go.

The Costs of Cost Plus

Cost Plus is a mammoth import store on the San Francisco waterfront which caters to tourists and Bay Area bobos by supplying them with hand-wrought goods from around the world — from inexpensive mass-produced trinkets to costly one-of-a-kind curiosities. It is self-help, with no sales personnel on the floor. We began to wonder about the flow of goods that went through the store, and after getting some information from one of the buyers we came up with the following piece.

Five of us, looking as straight as possible, dispersed throughout the store as customer aides. We approached people who were inspecting possible purchases. A typical dialog went like this:

US: may I help you?

CUSTOMER, *generally unsuspicious*: No, thank you.

US, *waiting a bit, watching over customer's shoulder*: Isn't it amazing how we can bring you such an intricately carved box for only $4.99?

CUSTOMER: Why, yes it is.

US: Do you know how we can do it?

CUSTOMER: No.

US: Well, the man who carves this box —he's very good at it, he can do two a day—gets 50¢ a day for his work.

CUSTOMER: Oh?

US: Yes. You see, there's a lot of famine and disease in Bangladesh, and he has to work for whatever he can get.

CUSTOMER: Oh.

US: He has no choice.

CUSTOMER:...

US: And since we control the world economy, more or less, we can decide on the right price.

Silence.

US: Yes, and you have to realize that what you pay includes the markup for the buyer, the warehouse, the shipper, the import duty, and our own small overhead—so it's really an incredible bargain.

Thoughtful, nonhostile silence. This was usually a turning point: either the customer began reacting to what we were saying or else we carried it further.

US: I think it's right—don't you—that we in this country should be able to benefit from people's work around the world? After all, we give them a market. They'd starve without it. And we can have these really nice things. I mean Americans work really hard, right?

We have to put up with so much—like the war and everything—we deserve these kind of beautiful things. People who work hard should be rewarded. Don't you think so? And the natives? They're hard workers too, but I mean 50¢ a day is a lot for Bangladeshies, right? Did you know that although we're only 6% of the world's population, we consume 60% of its natural resources? That just shows—we're sort of 10 times ahead of everybody else because we're willing to work hard and bring home the bacon.

Etc., etc. Eventually these customers drifted away with an embarrassed "thank you." But none of them bought the items they had been looking at.

After an agreed upon two hours, we all met outside the store to trade stories. We were never caught, and the customers, too, would have their stories to tell.

Some Reflections on Manipulation

When I began publishing these little pieces in various theater journals, I was met with a storm of protesting letters concerning unethical "manipulation" of the bystanders. I wrote a piece in response describing what I thought to be a continuum of manipulations, from those which *decreased* understanding and degrees of freedom to those which *increased* them.

It might be good to look at such a continuum in the light of what is going on today. Let's start with the bad news:

An article by George Monbiot reports a training session organized by the right wing libertarian group, American Majority on "How to Manipulate the Medium":

"Here's what I do. I get on Amazon; I type in 'Liberal Books'. I go through and I say 'one star, one star, one star'. The flipside is you go to a conservative/ libertarian whatever, go to their products and give them five stars… If there's a place to comment, a place to rate, a place to share information, you have to do it. That's how you control the online dialogue and give our ideas a fighting chance."

On a wider scale, we have Israeli government support for a special undercover team of workers paid to surf the internet and spread positive news about Israel. (https://www.globalresearch.ca/internet-warfare-team-unveiled/14465)

The deputy director of the Foreign Ministry's hasbara ("public diplomacy", aka propaganda) department has admitted the team will be working undercover:

About 50,000 activists are reported to have downloaded a programme called Megaphone that sends an alert to their computers when an article critical of Israel is published. They are then supposed to bombard the site with comments supporting Israel. (http://en.wikipedia.org/wiki/Megaphone_desktop_tool)

A justification for much of this was shamelessly enunciated by our own government's Cass Sunstein — Obama's Harvard Law School bud, and, under Obama, appointed Administrator of the White House Office of Information and Regulatory Affairs. Writing in a scholarly journal, (J. Political Philosophy, 7 (2009), 202-227), Sunstein proposes the following:

> *"[W]e suggest a distinctive tactic for breaking up the hard core of extremists who supply conspiracy theories [by which he means questioning the official stories of 9/11, or the JFK assassinations]: cognitive infiltration of extremist groups, whereby government agents or their allies (acting either virtually or in real space, and either openly or anonymously) will undermine the crippled epistemology of believers by planting doubts about the theories and stylized facts that circulate within such groups, thereby introducing beneficial cognitive diversity."*

From cognitive infiltration of websites, groups and meetings, it is a short enough step to the entrapments by *agents provocateur* we read about so commonly today. The missteps of suckered individuals have enormous life consequences — for them, and for all of us — in the age of Patriot Act paranoia and power.

If these kind of infiltrations populate the bad end of the continuum, what is the other end — the "good" end?

The most obvious current example lies in the operation of Wikileaks and the brave individuals that feed it sequestered material. A person working in a dishonest, destructive organization has every right to transform him or herself into an infiltrator, making available to Wikileaks or other publicity groups secret material the organization would otherwise have hidden.

As Julian Assange wrote on the Wikileaks homepage, "The goal is justice; the method is transparency." It is paradoxical that it takes invisible infiltration to create public transparency, but there it is, and the effectiveness of this tactic can no longer be in question. Nor can the public good resulting.

While the theatrical infiltrations I describe above may be absurdly trivial compared to these larger examples, both good and bad, they do raise the question of whether all arts — Art itself — does not function as an infiltration.

One innocently goes to a bookstore to buy a book. But the contents of that book, if a good one, will infiltrate and infect one's heartmind. The infiltrating virus will lie within, creating biopsychical response, spiritual molecules unlabeled, unacknowledged, perhaps unknown, but potentially agents provocateur for new thinking and action.

It is with this infiltrating image in mind that my wife, Donna, and I began Fomite Press. A fomite is a medium capable of transmitting infectious organisms from one individual to another.

"*The activity of art is based on the capacity of people to be infected by the feelings of others.*" Tolstoy, What is Art?

Art, writing, music are the kinds of infiltrations which — if ethically and mindfully done — have the capacity to increase, not decrease, degrees of freedom.

Small Essays, Large Readership

1. *Defoliation for peace.* Remember how concentration camp prisonerss used to drop the dirt from tunnels they were digging? Try walking on a convenient lawn (like the Pentagon lawn) inconspicuously dropping

grass killer from your pocket (Plastic bag, plasic gloves.) Walk in a pattern which spells out in big letters the message you want to leave. Wait a week, and you've got it.

2. *Spray paint and stencil.* A nice example are STOP signs turned into STOP WAR signs. They take only a second to do, and reach many people before they're "corrected" (which, given the bureaucracy, can take a long time.)

3. *Bumper stickers in better places.* SHOOT LOOTERS stickers put on police cars in poor sections of town, or SUPPORT YOUR LOCAL POLICE stickers added to traffic signs such as NO LEFT TURN (Support your local police), RIGHT TURN ONLY (Support your local police), etc.

4. *Paint on your car or your house.* It's your own property. You can take your time and do a good job. There are no laws against it, except perhaps obscenity laws. But who needs obscenity? The state of things does it for you (and doesn't get ticketed). Our front porch has a sign that reads RADIX MALORUM EST CUPIDITAS. SMASH CAPITALISM. As well as a large and beautiful sign on driftwood listing the countries the US is currently bombing.

5. *Use chalk.* White chalk on soot-black buildings doesn't come off easily. Ask your kids for some.

6. *Graffiti in toilets*, or public transportation, on restaurant menus. Ask questions. You'll get answers. Start dialogues, and go back to tend them. I'm convinced many peoples' heads can be changed while they're sitting on the can.

"Art, if you want a definition of it, is criminal action. It conforms to no rules. Not even its own. Anyone who experiences a work of art is as guilty as the artist. It is not even a question of sharing the guilt. Each one of us gets all of it." John Cage.

FDR Assassination Attempt

True Story, and Sad

From Insect Dreams/Kafka's Roach. *In February, 1933, FDR was return-ing from a pre-inaugural fishing trip. On his return, passing through Miami, he rode along with the mayor of Chicago in an open car, from which he gave a short speech. An assassin got off several shots, which missed the president, but wounded the mayor, who died nineteen days later. Gregor was asked to visit with the imprisoned, would-be assassin to try to determine the motivation for the attack, and whether his was a lone attempt or a plot with others involved.*

People were hungry, marriage was rare, bank accounts were over-drawn. And on Roosevelt's 51st birthday, January 30, 1933, Adolf Hitler became Chancellor of Germany.

FDR, tanned and relaxed from a twelve day cruise, disembarked at Miami, the day after Valentine's, the day after all Michigan banks had been closed down by order of the governor. On the Ides of February, he rode in an open car to greet a crowd of 20,000 sup-porters at Bay Front Park. He rode in a light blue Buick convertible, along with Raymond Moley, who had come down to Miami to report on the Cabinet search, and with Gregor Samsa, who had been rewarded for his Herculean labors with a Caribbean cruise on the *Nourmahal*.

Gregor Samsa on Vincent Astor's yacht. Now there's an image to ponder! This child of the Jewish quarter of Prague, this circus freak, this erstwhile elevator boy and dumpster diver, this toiler in the innards of insurance. What a rise was there, my countrymen.

Seated in an open car, driving along a dark street on the way to the park, Moley remarked to his companions how easy an assassination would be. But FDR was fearless. "I remember T.R. telling me that the only real danger is from a man who does not fear losing his own life. Most of the crazy ones can be spotted first."

In the crowded, well-lit park, shortly after nine, Moley and Gregor hoisted the President-elect[1] up on top of the back seat, where he could be seen. Roosevelt spoke entertainingly for two minutes to much laughter and applause, then lowered himself into the seat of the car to greet Mayor Anton Cermak of Chicago, who was visiting his father in Miami.

Then, a popping in the air. Roosevelt thought it a firecracker, Moley a backfire. Gregor was the first to spot a short, swarthy man, standing on a rickety folding chair twenty feet away pointing a revolver in the direction of the President-to-be. After the first shot, a nearby woman grabbed his arm, and subsequent bullets made their wild ways through the crowd. The gunman was tackled and subdued by bystanders and Park Police while Secret Service men bulled their way toward the center of the violence. "I'm all right! I'm all right," Roosevelt yelled. But Mayor Cermak was not all right, nor were four others. The mayor's shirt was covered in red, and blood streamed from from lung to mouth. Secret Service shouted frantically for the car to evacuate, but FDR ordered the driver to stop so the mayor's body could be lifted into his, the first vehicle which would be free of the crowd. He tried to find a pulse as Cermak slumped forward. "I'm afraid he's not going to last," he whispered to G, as the car made for Jackson Memorial Hospital. The man from Hyde Park coached his friend from Chicago: "Tony, keep quiet — don't move. It won't hurt if you don't move." "I'm glad it was me and not you," the mayor gasped. It's true. Gregor was there. There is honor even among politicians.

In the ER waiting room, Moley approached Gregor. "I think it would be good for you to visit our would-be assassin. Find out if he

1   The Twentieth Amendment, moving the presidential inauguration back from March 4th to our current January 20th, did not go into effect until October 1933. Its intention was to reduce the amount of time the president may serve as a lame duck by six weeks. FDR's first inauguration was the last to be held on the older date.

acted alone or if there are others. Get back to the railroad car by 11:30."

Armed with a hand-written note from Roosevelt, G took a cab back to the park and made his way to the 21st floor of the Dade County Courthouse, overlooking the scene of the crime. There, surrounded by Secret Service, was an unemployed bricklayer, one Giuseppe Zangara, 33, come to the United States ten years earlier aboard the steamer *Martha Washington*. So much was Gregor told. He went into the cell, and asked to be left alone with the prisoner. Secret Service reluctantly retreated. G could repeat the conversation almost verbatim.

"Hello, Mr. Zangara. I am Gregor Samsa, a friend of Mr. Roosevelt."

"I am friend of nobody."

"Mr. Roosevelt wants you to know he is all right."

"Too bad. I am better kill him. Too crowded. Too much crowds."

"Why do you want to kill him?"

"Because rich people make me suffer and do this to me."

He lifted his shirt to show G a large, keloid scar on his flank and abdomen.

"Rich people make me to go out from school," he continued. "Two months I am in school and my father come and take me out and say 'You don't need no school. You need to work.' Six years old, he take me out of school. Lawyers ought to punish him — that's the trouble — he send me to school and I don't have this trouble. Government!"

"Do you hate the government?"

"Yes," he answered, through clenched teeth. "Because rich people make me suffer and do this stomach pain to me."

"The rich men make you suffer?"

"Yes, since they sent me to work in a big job." He clutched his abdomen and groaned.

"Your belly hurts?"

"Because when I did tile work it hurt me there. It all spoil my machinery, all my insides. Everything inside no good."

Zangara was barely five feet tall. At sixteen, he left home to carry a gun in the army. He had come to the conclusion that the real causes of exploitation — and of his constant stomach pain — were political leaders. He was going to kill King Victor Emmanuel, but he never got the chance. So he came with his uncle to America. He joined a union, and saved his money. In the prosperous twenties, he sometimes made $14 a day. Then his uncle decided to marry, and Giuseppe had to move out of the apartment they shared. From that time on, he lived in complete isolation, an angry hermit who took no part in the Italian community around him. A stranger to wine, women or song, his whole life revolved around his stomach pain.

When the depression struck, he took his savings and travelled from city to city with no clear goal. He wound up in Hackensack, N.J. where he lived in one $10-a-month room and rented the room next door to prevent anyone from living near him. For the winter he moved to Miami. By February, 1933, he had less than a hundred dollars to his name, and his stomach was pure agony. He decided he was going to get even, and kill Herbert Hoover.

"I kill that no good capitalist," he told Gregor. "He make the depression. He make unemployment and the soup lines. He make burning in my stomach."

"But Mr. Roosevelt works against Herbert Hoover. He is your friend."

"Hoover and Roosevelt — everybody the same. Hoover too far away. Washington too far. I have only 43 dollars."

"So Mr. Roosevelt came right to you, to Miami."

"I read in the paper he is coming, and I don't must go to Washington. I make Roosevelt suffer. I want to make it fifty-fifty since my stomach hurt I get even with capitalists by kill the President. My stomach hurt long time."

Gregor was dealing with a nut case. This man could only act alone. Who would act with him? G probed a possible insanity defense.

"Did you know what you were doing when you shot at Mr. Roosevelt?"

"Sure I know. You think I am crazy? I gonna kill president. I no care. I sick all time. I think maybe cops kill me if I kill President. I take picture of President in my pocket. I no want to shoot Cermak, just Roosevelt. I aim at him, I shoot him. But somebody move my arm. Every American people mistreats me. You give me electric chair. I'm no afraid that chair. You one of capitalists. You is crook man too. Put me in electric chair, I no care."

At the time of the interview, Zangara was charged only with four counts of assault with a deadly weapon. But three weeks later, when Mayor Cermak died, the charge was changed to first degree murder. Only thirty three days after the event, the wiry Italian got his wish. Strapped down in "Ol' Sparky" at the Florida State Penitentiary, he railed at the observers, "Lousy capitalists — go ahead, push the button." They did.

On the train, Gregor reported his interview to a much-relieved Brains Trust. The President-elect was quite moved to hear, "I no hate Mr. Roosevelt personally. I like him, but I hate all presidents, no matter from which country, and I hate all officials and everyone who is rich."

"Do you think this was a political act?" Moley asked the roach.

"He said he thought anarchism, socialism, communism and fascism were stupid. Also religion, God, Jesus, heaven, hell and any thought of soul. When I asked him if he believed anything he read, he said, "I don't believe in nothing. I don't believe in reading books because I don't think and I don't like it. I got everything in my mind.

"Did you get any sense about what he did believe?" Roosevelt asked.

"I asked him that. You know what he said?"

"What?"

"The land, the sky, the moon."

The men and the roach sat in silence. Beyond the ticking telegraph poles, the moon in the sky shown full on the land and the track back to Washington.

You Want Holocaust With That?

Holocaust Thinking in America

Progress. In place of Obama's *Change We Can Believe In*, we have Trump's *Make America Great Again*. And the rich, as usual, are to get richer, and the poor to get sick, become homeless, starve, or shatter in endless wars. The road map?

Though frowned upon as a thought-crime, the comparison of our current American trajectory with the tactics and strategy of Germany in the 1930s is striking. We would do well to study this era carefully for a possible glimpse of our own future. Those targeted are no longer just our dispossessed, reviled and outcast — our "Other", our "Jews" — but much of the American (and of course world) population.

The attempt to exterminate European Jewry during the Nazi era was, in many ways, as unique as Jewish culture asserts. Never before had an organized, industrial state targeted a population for complete annihilation, ruthlessly and efficiently pursued even within its "civil" codes and activities. But to think of the Holocaust as a completely unique act, restricted to 20th century German antisemitism, is to limit it unduly, to make it unavailable as evidence and warning about tendencies in our own place, our own time.

For it would seem that every major thought pattern, every cultural institution that fueled the Nazi holocaust is present and empowered in the United States today. Safeguards against catastrophic outcomes are few and weak. "It can't happen here"? Maybe. But with so many elements brewing together, and no visible controls to dampen the flux, there is no predicting in what direction the reaction will run.

In recent memory, a civilization as culturally advanced as our own underwent a society-wide suspension of morality. Jews were the target.

At present, the next set of domestic victims has already been chosen: the middle class, the foreign, the poor and unruly. Ready... aim...

The Once and Future Perpetrators

Much of the current political agenda is dominated by what is popularly known as the "extreme right". Clinton and Obama were instrumental in moving the Democratic Party in that direction, and now, the quantum leap of Trump. Tea Parties and religious fundamentalism nourish the "shift to the right" within the population at large.

Critics have unanimously deemed right wing motives as "greedy" and "mean-spirited", but such labels obscure the positive agenda involved — an agenda described in most detail by the Frankfurt School in its attempt to analyze the roots of German fascism. Then and now; the descriptions are eerily alike.

It is reasonable to assume that our leaders and their followers are nice enough folks who love their children and grandchildren, and hope to pass on to them a better world. What is it, then, that drives them to outlandish and seemingly heartless proposals concerning immigrants and "the 99%", including, sometimes, themselves?

The Authoritarian Personality

In each event — in the living act, the undoubted deed — there, some unknown but still reasoning thing puts forth the moulding of its features from behind the unreasoning mask.

Captain Ahab

While differing in detail, many right-wing positions are driven by belief systems characteristic of what The Frankfurt School called "the Authoritarian Personality", whose main characteristic is the urgent need for order. When ALLES IN ORDNUNG becomes the highest value, the consequences are predictable.

For the authoritarian personality:

1. *Powerful leaders* are needed to keep society in line and restrict it to conventional, middle-class values. Exaggerated assertions of

toughness and strength become the norm. Trickle-down theories are designed to protect the powerful — in the interest of all.

2. *Democracy becomes a threat* and must be limited. A need to control unpredictable "excess" democracy has guided foreign and economic policy throughout America's history. The pattern of supporting dictatorial strong-men is likely driven as much by rage for order and fear of chaos as by a selfish need to maximize profits. So great is the need for predictable order that maximal profits are sacrificed.

3. *Individualism becomes suspect,* a negative value to be stamped out. "Difference" means unpredictability, and fear of an unpredictable, uncontrollable "Other" spawns all the "isms" which rampage today: racism, sexism, classism, antisemitism, anti-immigrant, anti-Muslim rage, xenophobia. Nature itself becomes an uncertain enemy to be conquered and subdued.

4. The psycho-sexual chaos at the core of an authoritarian personality simultaneously fascinates and repels. *Rigid moralism* seems the most secure protection against anarchy and chaos. There is exaggerated concern with sexual "goings-on". At the same time, unconscious emotional impulses are projected outward, and the world is seen as a wild and dangerous place in which *worst-case scenarios abound.*

5. Fear and guilt about chaotic thoughts within and anarchy without is so potentially threatening that *psychic numbing* is a typical response, with emotional dissociation from the consequences of action. *Knee-jerk "patriotism"* in response to moral questions is an effective defense mechanism. "Support the Troops" blindfolds the eyes against mass incineration. Such defensive control of information minimizes compassion for victims.

6. A *culture of punishment* follows hard upon. Offenders against order must be strictly punished. The very same heartmind is both pro-life and pro-death penalty. But the sanctity of life is secondary: the important thing is punishment. Tender-mindedness is for "bleeding-heart liberals".

While no political leader or follower may display every characteristic above, they are all on fine collective display in the current Trumpian *Zeitgeist* — as they were in Nazi Germany.

Is it just that "people are no damn good", or is their behavior created by social conditions surrounding them?

The Milgram Evidence

In her study of Adolf Eichmann, Hannah Arendt noted that the greatest problem the Nazis faced was "how to overcome...the animal pity by which all normal men are affected in the presence of physical suffering." Most of the German perpetrators were by and large not sadists or moral degenerates or even political fanatics — yet they became conscious collaborators in the process of mass murder. How was it possible to create torturers out of next door neighbors? (How could our clean-cut young boys napalm other humans, or target them via drones?)

In the early sixties, A Yale psychologist named Stanley Milgram began a series of experiments which sought to clarify these problems. The basic question was narrowed to "if an experimenter tells a subject to act with increasing severity against another person, under what conditions will the subject comply, and under what conditions will he disobey?" Subjects were recruited from all walks of life to "help us complete a study of memory and learning." An actor-scientist greeted pairs of volunteers, and lots were drawn to pick who would be the "teacher" and who would be the "learner". The subject would always choose the "teacher" slip (all the slips said "teacher"); the other "volunteer" was a plant who then became the "learner"/victim. The "scientist" explained that there has been some association of punishment with learning, but that there had never been any quantitative studies on how much punishment would give the best results.

After orientation, the "learner" was strapped into a chair in the next room, and an electrode glued to his wrist. The "teacher" could see and communicate with him via a glass panel and microphone. In front of the "teacher" was a bogus control panel consisting of 30 switches enabling him to deliver shocks from 15 to 450 volts in 15 volt increments. The groups of switches were marked Slight Shock, Moderate Shock, Strong Shock, Very Strong Shock, Intense Shock, Extreme Intensity Shock, Danger: Severe Shock. Two switches after this last designation were simply marked XXX.

The basic experimental design was this: the "teacher" would read groups of word pairs to the "learner", and then ask him to correctly identify the pairing word from lists of four. If the "learner" made a mistake, the "teacher" was to administer a shock. For each mistake, the "teacher" was instructed to "move one level higher on the shock generator". The victim (who, of course, was feeling no shock at all) greeted the increasing "voltage levels" with a full range of response, indicating no discomfort until the 75 volt shock was administered. At 120 volts he would shout to the experimenter that the shocks were becoming painful. Painful groans at 135 volts. At 150 volts. he would cry out, "Get me out of here! I refuse to go on!" By 180 volts, "I can't stand the pain", and by 270, agonizing screams. After 300 volts he would no longer provide answers to the test questions. The "teacher" was told that no answer constituted a wrong answer, and was instructed to raise the shock level.

How far would these "teachers" go? In spite of there being no coercion or threat (as there was in Nazi Germany), and without any animosity toward the victim (unlike Nazi Germany), these average Americans far, far exceeded the expectations of all psychologists in their obedient compliance with instructions. Despite the fact that many questioned or even protested what they were doing, a substantial proportion continued to the last level of shock despite the "learner's" screams. Almost 2/3 of the subjects — ordinary people drawn from working, managerial and professional classes — were "obedient subjects", willing to go to almost any length at the command of an authority. Their explanations at post-experiment interview echoed those of Adolf Eichmann — "I was just doing my job. I was doing what I was told. I was only doing my duty."

Milgram was profoundly disturbed by his findings, (as were many members of the scientific community who attacked him personally.)

> *What is the limit of such obedience? At many*
> *points we attempted to establish a boundary. Cries from*
> *the victim were inserted: they were not good enough.*
> *The victim claimed heart trouble; subjects continued to*

shock him on command. The victim pleaded to be let free, and his answers no longer registered on the signal box; subjects continued to shock him. At the outset we had not conceived that such drastic procedures would be needed to generate disobedience, and each step was added only as the ineffectiveness of the earlier techniques became clear. The final effort to establish a limit was the Touch-Proximity condition [where the "learner" sat, screaming, shoulder to shoulder with the subject.] But the very first subject in this condition subdued the victim on command, and proceeded to the highest shock level. A quarter of the subjects in this condition performed similarly.

The results, as seen and felt in the laboratory, are to this author disturbing. They raise the possibility that human nature or — more specifically — the kind of character produced in America democratic society, cannot be counted on to insulate its citizens from brutality and inhumane treatment at the direction of malevolent authority. A substantial proportion of people do what they are told to do, irrespective of the content of the act and without limitations of conscience, so long as they perceive that the command comes from a legitimate authority.

In spite of Milgram's despair, the findings did have their bright side. A number of experiments were done in which the subjects were exposed to several experimenters who disagreed among themselves and argued about continuing the shocks. Another series was performed not at Yale, with its aura of authority, but in a minimal office, under the auspices of the fictitious, unknown, "Bridgeport Research Associates". A third series was performed in which the "teachers" were not instructed to increase the shock level with each wrong answer, but could choose their own levels throughout the experiment. The outcomes of these series was illuminating: given any hint of disagreement among the authorities, subjects immediately discarded their slavish obedience, and were no longer willing to engage in behavior they found morally questionable. When authority became questionable ("Bridgeport" vs. Yale), compliance dropped significantly. And without prompting from authority, "teachers" maintained shocks well under the discomfort level of the victim.

The casting off of "animal pity" was sustainable only under seamless monolithic authority. For all its fragility, it seems that it is not human nature *per se* that is malevolent, but that human malevolence, at least in part, is socially constructed. Under the right system, even here and now in the United States, obedience to authority can prevail against the "better instincts" of the population. The trouble is that such a system is currently alive and well throughout the land.

The System There and Then, and Here And Now

It is commonly assumed that outbreaks of bestial violence — the Holocaust, or what we have seen in Rwanda, Syria, Afghanistan or Israel's attacks on Palestine — are the result of primitive eruptions into a civilization insufficient to contain them. If people could only become "more civilized", there would be no such behavior. But what if civilization itself were the problem — not the solution?

Again and again we have to confront the difficult fact that Nazi Germany was an advanced industrial culture quite like our own. The death machines were put into operation by people quite like us, living in comparable surroundings. Certified architects and engineers in well-lit rooms drew up plans for crematoria. Government bureaucrats, some trained in Kant and Hegel, purchased tickets for each passenger in the cattle cars. Had there been computers, there would have been excellent data bases. Nazi soldiers played Beethoven sonatas to entertain the troops, to lift their spirits and help them return to guard duty at the camps. Out of this modern, rational society, with a history of the highest culture, the Holocaust was born. Can we ever understand this? What can it tell us about our own situation?

One of the most crucial insights here came from a man who died well before Hitler came to power. Contemplating the industrialization of late 19th century Germany, Max Weber, "the father of sociology", came to the conclusion that "Reason" — the ideal of the Enlightenment — was evolving dangerously into *Zweckrationalität* — instrumental reason, reason driven by a goal. In the service of its goals, modern society was becoming efficiently bureaucratic and scientific, but was losing its sense of values. In fact, "value-free" had become a test of objectivity and scientific legitimacy, as technique replaced moral responsibility.

Recent times have certainly proven Weber correct. Marxists and postmodern thinkers have taken Weber many steps further, as they deconstruct the goals we have inherited, and the stories we tell ourselves. Whose goals are they? If society is a garden, who decides on who gets weeded?

The important point is that Weber's analysis of modern society — clearly increasingly applicable as the years push on — in no way excludes the possibility of another Nazi state. *Nothing in the rules of the reigning instrumental rationality would disqualify Holocaust methods of social engineering*, nor would its actions even seem improper. After all, social problems must be solved.

Milgram, too, found Weberian mechanisms at play in his subjects. To avoid confronting the victim's pain, his "teachers" became absorbed in the technical aspects of voltage control and memory testing. "The experiment *requires* that you continue" was often sufficient explanation to overcome any hesitations. "Scientific truth" as defined by "authority" was a goal so persuasive that its perceived legitimacy overwhelmed humane behavior.

Outside the laboratory, for instance in the military, we find parallel mechanisms at work. Boot camp is not so much a training in military technique as it is in absolute acceptance of monolithic authority. Patriotism *requires* such acceptance. Once in the field, attention to technical details blinds the perpetrator to the effects of his violence. The bombing sequence in *Dr. Strangelove* is a brilliant satire on the efficient calm of men about to destroy the world. Similar comparisons can easily be made with the instrumental rationality of the corporate board room, where the lives of millions are part of the calculus of maximizing profit.

How The Nazis Did It

I know one is not allowed to use the word "Nazism" in any discussion of current practices, that the holocaust is unique, etc., etc. — but if you don't see the similarities between the structures put into place in Germany in the mid- and late-1930s and those evolving here, now, well then, you don't see structural similarities.

National Socialist Strategy

What were the moves the Nazis evolved to "overcome animal pity" with regard to Jewish victims?

Step 1. Defining the enemy. Jewishness was clearly and legally defined as part of a problem. Thus the Jews were made "other" to the rest of the population.

Step 2. Eliminating the enemy from the economy. Jews were not allowed to work in state-affiliated institutions. Jewish stores were boycotted and vandalized. "Otherness" was thereby increased, as the Jews were forced from the normal productive economy, and were now an ever-increasing problem — and not just by definition.

Step 3. Ostracism by custom and law. Many other discriminatory laws were put into place. No Jews allowed, here or there, this place or that.

Step 4. Removal from view. Ghettos were created to wall the problem off from the rest of the population. Jews thus became less visible. When they began to disappear, there was often little to notice. As intolerable conditions developed in the ghettos, inhuman measures were justified as humane. Jews were killed in "acts of mercy" — in order to "spare them the agony of famine". In deliberately intolerable conditions, the stage was set for even more radical steps.

Step 5. Transport to slave labor camps, using these "outsiders" to support the economy.

Step 6. Transport to death camps. The "Final Solution".

Potential Holocaust in America : The Here and Now

Laws are being made here, too. And Presidential Enabling Acts, aka "signing statements". And court seats being filled.

The cast of characters is somewhat changed. Instead of Jews, we have the poor and soon-to-be-poor, the homeless, the disabled, the aged, the immigrant "Other" — an open-ended, potentially unruly, group, getting larger with each job loss and foreclosure.

We have very few overt Nazis, only Republicans and Democrats in Congress. Both parties agree that the foremost task is to eliminate the deficit, and both agree that the main hit will be on services to the poor, without tapping the military budget or corporate welfare. Both agree that taxes for the most part need to be cut — it's good for getting re-elected. Asses and Pachyderms (from Gr: "thick-skinned") may argue over numbers or priorities, but the fundamental assumptions — and the potential victims — are precisely the same. And outside the beltway is a population of Good Americans, voting their pocketbooks, not paying much attention to details evolving inside. How could they? All they know is what the government- and corporate-controlled media choose to tell them.

All the propensities of the Authoritarian Personality are still at large in this social consciousness, along with the tendency to behave as Milgram's subjects did with respect to "legitimately constituted" authority. Weber's analysis accurately describes what is going on today: bureaucracy, science, efficiency, and value-free thought running the show in the interest of "Progress" and "Freedom and Democracy" — and maximization of profit.

Social forces and individual thought habits are distressingly similar to those in Nazi Germany. The poor and the "Others" are as despised as were the Jews. Helping them is as verboten. *There are no cultural safeguards in place which would prevent a holocaust-like social cannibalism, a society-wide suspension of morality with regard to the designated "problem".*

There would be no help on a global level, either, since every national state claims the right to dispose of its citizens as it will, starving them, imprisoning them, executing them as it finds necessary. The United States refuses to recognize judgments of the World Court except when such judgments suit its purposes, and refuses to ratify several international treaties concerning human rights. International objectors like Amnesty International are delegitimized as "interfering in the internal affairs of sovereign nations". National sovereignty is built into the United Nations. Besides, who would take on the United States, militarily or economically for any mere human rights issue?

Thus, all the pieces are in place for another holocaust — this time against the poor and "Other". Native racism adds to the potential, since — no surprise — many of the poor are immigrants and people of color, and code words overlap: "End welfare as we know it" = "Get the minorities under control." Hence the ominous double significance of our move toward prison expansion. The vast preponderance of prisoners are poor people of color.

A comparative check on where we are now in the six historical steps above is sobering — and frightening.

Step 1. *Defining the enemy*. The poor are clearly defined as "the problem". Not the profit-driven economy. Not the culture of violence. Not the controlled information system. Studies focus on the pathology of the "underclass". The Poor are the problem. They are "other" to "normal Americans". Consequently they must to be "dealt with". Highest priority: "excess" population, a drain on the nation, unviable.

Step 2. *Eliminating the enemy from the economy*. By national policy, there are fewer and fewer jobs available to the poor, and fewer and fewer salaries that could raise a family out of poverty. Wall Street is bailed out, while money for public sector employment is denied, and corporate profits recover, with CEOs reaping massive benefits at taxpayer expense. Education funding is similarly squelched, so that the problem army of the poor can only swell. "Otherness" is increased as the media focus in on the predictably rising problems of crime, the inner city, and immigrant workers, ignoring problems elsewhere, and their root causes.

Step 3. *Ostracism by custom and law*. It is frightening to make such a list, but almost every step taken by the Third Reich has some parallel here and now — with no built-in limits:

— Laws passed by Congress can be overridden by executive orders, presidential "findings", National Security directives, or simply aborted by not disbursing committed funds.

— Courts are routinely packed with obedient federal appointees. The current composition of the Supreme Court is the biggest scandal of all. Legal rights of poor defendants are being systematically reduced, and money for good lawyers diminished.

— The current push in Congress is for law to serve the state and its rich financiers at the expense of individuals. Corporate personhood triumphs. Surveillance technology and "anti-terrorism" stand guard at the gates. The government moves to limit consumer and environmental protection. These laws are being made deliberately, without even pretending to be a democratic response to the will of the people. There is increasing governmental readiness to evade constitutional law.

— The many Nazi restrictions on employment are all replaced by the fact that — for the poor and uneducated above all — there are simply *no* jobs. Affirmative action is increasingly questioned. The situation has worsened catastrophically with jobs exported and capital flight, and its attendant dog-eat-dog resentments. With no money for private transportation, no money for parking, and increasingly expensive, inadequate public transportation, the poor are deprived of the mobility necessary to find and maintain employment — even if there were employment to be had.

— Municipal services are neglected or abandoned in poor neighborhoods, and the police remain an occupying army, protecting and serving the threatened rich. Consequently, living conditions and ghettos become ever more intolerable.

— Student loans have exorbitant conditions at the same time that tuitions are skyrocketing. Thus education increasingly excludes the poor as effectively as discriminatory laws did the Jews. Without an educated workforce, the vicious spiral continues downward.

— "Economics of scale" are driving out smaller, local businesses in favor of large corporate operations — if they even choose to locate in poorer neighborhoods.

Remember: such policies are not accidents. They are designed and signed by upper-class men and women, and approved by well-prepped voters.

Step 4. *Removal from view.* In addition to long-existing ghettoization, foreclosures on housing toxically mortgaged, and increasing inter-racial suspicion, many municipalities are now enacting draconian laws to "get the poor out from under our noses." Sleeping in public spaces, panhandling, even accepting free food have been criminalized. Here in Burlington, Vermont, an ordinance was floated to make it illegal to sit in a street, or even lean against a building. When there are no more poor on the streets or in the subways, how will we know when there are no more poor at all? As the plight of the poor is made ever more intolerable, ever less visible, radical solutions become ever more thinkable.

Steps 5 and 6 — *slave labor and death camps* have not yet been literally established. Nevertheless there is recognizable social movement in that direction. Prisons are currently the greatest growth industry, and there is increasing practice of substituting prison labor for outside workers — at substantially lower wages. As someone once said to me, "Why should I support those criminals? Let 'em earn their keep." (She would also kill everyone on death row right away, so that her taxes wouldn't be used to support murderers.)

And the attachment to capital punishment continues. Less legal protection for prisoners, less chance for appeal, more designated-capital crimes, destruction of *habeus corpus* and Miranda protections in the name of "fighting terrorism"; micro-fascism at the airport, greater surveillance, Obama giving himself permission to assassinate Americans without trial, Trump doubling down on all the above...

Given the above array of conditions, what can we surmise about the likely American future?

Holocaust Thinking In America

There is a scent of pre-holocaust in the air. It is a mood, a direction faced, a lingo, haze of assumptions. And look! — there is a Jack-in-the-box with a box's six sides: authoritarianism, consumo-conformity, efficiency, moralism, patriotism, and a penchant for punishment.

Turn the crank:

> All around the mulberry bush
> the monkey chased the weasel,
> the monkey thought 'twas all in fun...

Now just hold it there. What will pop out at the very next move?

We don't really know. The mind rebels. Tens of millions of children in poverty experiencing a "greater sense of personal responsibility"? Welfare cut-offs flooding an already non-existent job market getting people "back to work"? Or giving them back their "self-esteem"?

There is discontinuity in the curve of thought here — except for one constant — it is definitively the poor and "Other" that are poised to fall off the line into god-knows-what abyss. And the numbers of those impoverished are growing as the middle class shrinks away into unknown territory.

The number of officially poor is now approaching 40 million. The most vulnerable families are those headed by single mothers, and among them the hardest hit are those headed by single women of color. Two-thirds are employed. But in addition to chronic low wages, many single mothers have seen their work hours cut in the recession.

Where have the jobs gone, the money? The current income gap is the largest it's been since the late 1920s, the result of a long series of policy decisions by legislators bought and paid for by the high-class bandits making out. The race to the bottom is fueled by a race to the top. The dynamics seem irreversible.

The assault on America is a bipartisan operation. Whatever their deceitful rhetoric, neither party is willing to place serious limits on corporate speculation and profitability. Neither will question the need for public austerity and private profit, nor the enormous damage done by the military industrial complex.

Trump's budgets are most importantly calls to continue tax cuts for the rich to grow the income gap and protect its well-heeled beneficiaries. Secondarily, it is a plan to repeal even the pathetic Affordable Health Care Act, itself written by lobbyists from insurance and pharmaceutical companies. Republicans have blocked benefits for homeless vets, health care for 911 first responders, a jobs bill that gives tax breaks to companies hiring new employees, an act to ensure women are paid the same wages as men, have tried to block unemployment benefits extension, and have succeeded in blocking stricter regulations for financial institutions. Their ultimate goal, often stated, is privatization of Social Security, Medicare and Medicaid. The Democrats have put up no fight in the interest of "compromise". Is there a pattern here?

Such an immiseration project must be protected by spreading fear of "terrorism", and the use of illegal surveillance now openly practiced, with sweeping new regulations for the internet. Robert Mueller, ex-director of the FBI has stated that, "There is a continuum between those who would express dissent and those who would do a terrorist act." One spokesperson from an FBI/police "information fusion center" claimed that the protest of a war against "international terrorism" is *itself* "a terrorist act". The USAPATRIOT Act (Uniting and Strengthening America by Providing Appropriate Tools Required to Intercept and Obstruct Terrorism — 1st prize for acronyms) stands behind him. And for good measure, Obama came up with approved "kill lists" of suspected terrorists — including Americans — he claims he can exterminate with impunity, and has handed the capacity over to Trump. The final solution, no doubt.

Holocaust and Totalitarianism

Many of the classic structures of a totalitarian state are already in place in contemporary America, Land of the Free. Many new ones, too — modern and post-modern. Official lawlessness no longer bothers to hide itself, and is tolerated or approved by the population at large. Criminal investigations into state crimes are blocked in the interests of "national security". Checks and balances among the three branches of government have been manipulated into a seamless, self-validifying whole. Make that four, as the media becomes ever more embedded in the corporate beltway.

But while totalitarianism is almost certainly a necessary context for holocaust, genocide, nakba, shoah, it is not a *sufficient* condition: the cooperation of the population is necessary. And that is where the Milgram Experiments come in. When the authorities say "do it!", a population of authoritarian personalities, born and bred, will do it.

American murder, massive and limited, even if openly criminal, seems to have widespread support by a population ready to lash out at designated victims. Americans know about torture of detainees in hidden prisons. They know of American slaughter in Iraq and Afghanistan, even if they are only discovering such activities in Pakistan, Yemen, Somalia and well-supported in Palestine. Hey, freedom isn't free. They know, too, about the slave labor of prisoners, and of undocumented workers, frightened and hiding. Let the torture, war and racist attacks proceed, I guess, if USA is once again to be Number One. *Gott mit uns!*

Should some object, they, like Germans in the thirties, will find no levers of change in their much-vaunted political process, all of whose candidates stand behind the American project of victory, "democracy", and control of resources. As Jay Gould said back in the 1880's, "I don't care who they vote for as long as I get to pick the candidates."

And those candidates are — with notable exceptions — no dummies. They can see as clearly as anyone the general direction in which we are headed. Why else reduce or remove the safety net for Americans while pouring trillions into armaments, corporations, and banks? A group — the poor and Other, Muslim immigrants above all — has been identified as the problem and the need for a "solution" given highest priority — Step 1, above.

Now we are poised at the edge of the precipice. "Terrorism" and its attendant and well-tended-to fear make Step 2 certain: they virtually guarantee that most people will not be able to make the transition into productive work. They further assure galloping immiseration of the Other as they are cut off from food and cash assistance, childcare and nutrition for their children. The consequent desperation will require more policing, desperate, more "final" and effective solutions, solutions which can ensure that the misery of the poor does not inflict itself on the top 10%.

Steps 1 and 2 have been taken. Steps 3 and 4 are underway. The smell of holocaust is in the air. Our civilization provides no safeguards. The *Zweckrationalität* dynamic described by Max Weber — the very one that nourished the Jewish holocaust in a most civilized, advanced-industrial Germany — still rules. Is it realistic to say "It can't happen here"?

We have the Jewish holocaust behind us, and the words "Never Again" engraved in our collective heartminds. But our own history — previous and subsequent to the holocaust is not reassuring. Native Americans were wiped out to make room for middle America. "Pioneers" were rewarded by the government with land deeds for expropriating Native American territory and violating treaties. It is not necessary to go over the "social suspension of morality" with respect to African Americans, or the atrocities committed during the Civil War.

In our own time, we have seen World War II with its mass fire-bombings and atomic attacks, then ten more wars, wiping out gooks and towel-heads with high-tech weapons. They don't value life like we do. I don't have much faith in home-grown American morality resisting commands to solve a problem by slaughter.

Richard Miller notes that

> Most Germans did not believe the final steps would be taken. They saw each measure as a discrete event and failed to understand that each step prepared the way for the next. The SS Journal *Das Schwarze Korps* noted in 1938, "What is radical today is moderate tomorrow." In 1933 the Nazis had no plan to kill all the Jews, and even militants would have shrunk in horror from such a suggestion. Gradually, over the next decade, "reasonable people" found that they had to become a little harsher. By 1943, the context of the war against Jews had escalated to the point where warriors could blandly pass bureaucratic memos back and forth about behavior that would have seemed unconscionable in 1933. (*Nazi Justiz*, p.3)

Our leaders are now passing such notes, and setting in place such laws concerning our current "Others". Proposals are being negotiated which would have horrified officials of earlier administrations. Will we allow a similar denouement? It *can* happen here.

Cycling Around

Beware of Riding a Nazi Bike

I used to ride a BMW, an R-50, in the days when motorcycles looked like motorcycles, and not crotch rockets. It was sleek, and above all, quiet. Double cylinders reaching out toward either side, and a driveshaft, not a chain. Beautiful black, white and blue roundel either side of the gas tank. German engineering. Bayerische Motoren Werke.

I often thought I was some kind of ironic retribution: a Jew gaily riding his Nazi-designed bike down the Pacific Coast Highway, the pre-helmet law wind blowing through my hair. What would they have done had they caught me?

So — little did they know: me, riding atop, as punishment to them. And not just them. Had I owned a Moto Guzzi, or a Honda, a Ducati or a Yamaha, I would have had, between my legs, controlled by my will, the entire Axis, once out to get me.

We ride these things, but though they are under us, they are also above us, and on every side. What else do we ride?

First, and most determinative, capitalism. We have sown its wind, and are reaping its whirlwind. What blows in our victorious yet defeated faces, breaths grit into our eyes? The big C, its wars and poisoned food, all policies, foreign and domestic, devised and enforced by The Wild

Ones, led by self-identified, boasting gangsters ready to *step outside*, beyond any limp-wristed, fairy-world manners of so-called civilization,

women clinging on behind, presenting breasts to spine. You know the drill.

Now we ride Israel, whirlwind Israel, the land that once demanded a king to quell it.

Once, we thought WE were that king. Once, we could pretend to ride Israel. But blowing the dust of her sands into our eyes, the rider has become the ridden.

Who the gods would destroy, they first make mad.

Acromegalic Patriotism

Or Pulling a Joshua 10

Acronyms, I think, bring out the worst in people. For example, the USAPATRIOT act is not an act for American Patriots as it would appear, but rather the U.S.A.P.A.T.R.I.O.T. Act — Uniting and Strengthening America by Providing Appropriate Tools Required to Intercept and Obstruct Terrorists. Act. Imagine the wordsmithing over that one.

Imagine how many taxpayer dollars went into the choice of those acronymic wonders. And the marvelous mendacities therein — "uniting", "strengthening", "appropriate", "required" — all hidden behind the mask.

Truly a work of the devil. There are masks that hide, like that one, and masks that reveal. It's important to distinguish them.

Acromegaly is a disease resulting from a pituitary tumor overproducing growth hormone. In children it produces giants, and in adults, overgrown jaws, thick skulls and thick skin. You can see an acromegalic giant in action in Kurosawa's great film, *Yojimbo*. He wields a mean sledge hammer against his enemies.

Big jaw, thick skull, thick skin. Could this syndrome describe the US approach to the world?

Our president is about to pull a Joshua (10:8-14), to try to stop the sun from setting. During one campaign in an early Operation Cast Lead, while the children of Israel were smiting the Amorites, man, woman, and child, Joshua, in a fit of chutzpah, bade the sun stand still so smiting time might be longer and smiting more complete.

And behold,
the sun stood still,

517

and the moon stayed,
until the people had avenged themselves upon their enemies.
The sun stood still in the midst of heaven,
and hasted not to go down about a whole day.
And there was no day that like that before it or after it,
that the LORD hearkened unto the voice of a man:
for the LORD fought for Israel.

The 342-page USA PATRIOT ACT — clearly already prepared and lying in wait — was passed by Congress (357-66 in the House, and 98-1 in the Senate), and signed by George W. Bush on October 26, 2001. Many legislators admitted to not having read it through before voting. Most of the bill's provisions were due to sunset after December 31, 2005, four years after passage, and safely after the 2004 election. But by March 2006, Congress had voted to reauthorize the bill so as not to tie the president's hands in his Global War on Terror.

Sunset now [19] years late.

Though having campaigned for greater oversight, the White House is now out-republiing the Republicans by asking to further delay its sunset until December, 2013, giving the new Republican majority, and perhaps a new Republican president plenty of time to authorize permanent status.

The Children of Israel no doubt approve.

And it's not as if the abuses of the bill have disappeared as GWOT has aged and mellowed.

Rather, the jawbone and skin continue to thicken, and the skull grows ever more dense as we Patriots resist and punish those on the side of freedom.

ESSAYS POLITICAL

Leadershipwreck

Obama

The Evolution of the Band-Aid

What is "Flesh"-Colored, and Looks Like a Band-Aid?

When was the last time you saw a white band-aid? White — as in the color of adhesive tape. Actually, when was the last time you saw adhesive tape?

It was a good, simple idea Earle Dickson had back in 1920 — to attach a dressing to a cloth that didn't have to be wrapped and tied — usually one-handed, or with the help of teeth. Add sterility to the cotton, and you have a perfect little gizmo — protecting a small wound from dirt and germs, reducing the likelihood of its reopening, and maintaining a moist environment for the migration of new skin cells.

The evolution of the band-aid gives us a metaphorical glimpse into the dynamics of the American cultural/political system.

At the beginning of the ebullient fifties, along with chrome, fins, and anti-Communism, came the first decorative band-aids. Stars and Strips® on plastic. Conspicuous consumption. Be proud you were wounded. Then the corporations — all with their ®s attached — moved in with Super-, Spider-, and Bat-man, then Barbie and Ken, and now Rug-Rats, Smiley Faces, and Sponge Bob. Band-aids were no longer wound care, but fashion accessories for toddlers.

Enter the current deadly combination of irony and infantilization, and the grown-ups followed hard upon with unicorn, Jesus, and bacon strip band-aids at four to five times the generic price.

That was one very American direction — as Max Bialystock says in The Producers, "If you've got it, flaunt it!"

Parallel evolution: for the more decorous among us, or young urban professionals not wanting proletarian-looking hands, the sixties saw the spreading use of disguise: transparent band-aids, to which was added the patina of political correctness, since "flesh colored" might be any color flesh (if you ignore the white, colorblind rectangle under it).

Now we have special shapes for knuckle and fingertip, though only God, and perhaps Johnson&Johnson knows which is to be used where. We have giant band-aids for knee scrapes, and the stirring of high-tech medicalization with the introduction of home-use gel-impregnated burn dressings.

Let's apply these categories to the recent difficult birth and passage of the health reform bill, an Obama accomplishment commonly seen as a band-aid.

So we have this wound in America called disastrous health care — at least for the vast majority. The simple, practical, white-adhesive tape band-aid would have been to adopt any variation on the national health care systems used worldwide by advanced industrial countries not afflicted with exceptionalism. That would still be a band-aid because it would largely address disease post-facto, and not the physical and mental pollution and economic causes behind it. Nevertheless, it would have been straight-forward, still practical.

Conspicuous consumption, corporate profit. What would we do without them? The president and his party are trying hard to pass a health reform bill. The president and his party are battling. The stars and stripes are unfurled on both sides. The president and his party has passed a health reform bill! Yea! Boo! And corporate Scooby-doo. If you've passed it, flaunt it.

At the same time — disguise, and the opacity of CNN transparency. (The opacity is the white rectangle covering the wound.) Let the many colors of wounded flesh show through. Discarded children and cancer victims, the poor, the old, most of the currently uninsured. Under the white rectangle, big pharma and the insurance companies.

In Germany, Band-Aids® are called "plasters" — and they are white. Germans also have universal, national health care.

Big Lie, Endless Lie

A tale told by an idiot, full of sound and fury, signifying nothing

Obama's Escalate-Afghanistan speech turned, as did all of Bush's on the tired and depleted justification of "9/11". "We did not ask for this fight," the president intoned. "On September 11, 2001, nineteen men hijacked four airplanes and used them to murder nearly 3,000 people. They struck at our military and economic nerve centers. They took the lives of innocent men, women and children without regard to their faith or race or station. Were it not for the heroic actions of the passengers on board one of those flights, they could have also struck at one of the great symbols of our democracy in Washington, and killed many more." And so we need 100,000 soldiers plus 110 "contractors" to fight the "less than 100 operatives" (Gen. Jones) left in Afghanistan.

Aside from the absurdity of proportion, the demonstrated ineffectiveness of the approach, and the barbaric "collateral damage" always accompanying it, the entire package is based on a most problematic "fact" — the official story of 9/11, 19 Arab hijackers with boxcutters, etc. Absolutely every one of the major and minor elements of this tale has been shown to be inconsistent with physical events and surrounded with suspicious behavior.

After eight years of study, thousands of serious researchers in many technical and response areas can confidently assert the complete falsity of the official story, along with slightly differing alternatives, diffuse along the edges, but solidly agreeing at the core. (Google "9/11 truth" for many professional websites devoted to exploration and discussion of details. This is not "crackpot" material.)

And yet the same, tired, much-wounded story continues to justify the exercise of our killing machines, military and financial, around the globe — including here at home where our own population is still starved of humane goods and services. The "war on terror" (by whatever Obama chooses to call it) remains the be all and end all of our existence — all based on a set of demonstrated, manipulated falsities. The media has enshrined the official story; any challenge to it — at least in this country — is off the table of the mind.

I've tried to make an end-run around the general censorship by writing *Skulk*, a comic novel about 9/11. The characters are a bit silly, but the things they rant about are not. And the websites they mention in their "calls to the people" are real. I call this approach "Fighting Fiction with Fiction" — an essay I appended to the back of the book. See it above.

Trump

Fattening the Curve

The Once and Future Trump

At first glance it would not seem that the present occupant of the White House would need any fattening, but that depends on where, and how closely one looks. You may recall that last November, the president went for "an unscheduled visit" to Walter Reed National Military Hospital. He explained to the nation (https://www.cnn.com/2019/11/19/politics/donald-trump-hospital-visit-white-house/index.html) that he "had some extra time," and wanted to get a head start on his annual physical exam.

But a trusted White House source reported that the first lady had noticed a slight facial drooping, and encouraged him to have it checked out. A head MRI, done on November 16, 2019 demonstrated significant shrinkage and flattening of both amygdalae.

(The amygdalae (> Gr. *amygdala*, almond) are two almond-shaped clusters of neuronal nuclei deep within the temporal lobes of the brain, and which play a primary role in the processing of memory, decision-making and emotional response, including fear, anxiety, and aggression.)

All almond eaters among us know that they will occasionally find a "double almond", with a smaller, flatter, yet still brown-surfaced almondette, curved and clinging to the side of its fully developed partner. It is easily separable as a dwarf stand-alone. That comparison was a major part of the Walter Reed radiology report.

The White House assumed correctly that the whole amygdala story would be Greek to an uncomprehending public who can barely read English ("I love the poorly educated." DT February 24, 2016 https://www.youtube.com/watch?v=Vpdt7omPoa0) — and the medical results were hidden as a matter of confidentiality and national security. Nevertheless, the president's medical team made the following recommendation:

The president's amygdalae must be fattened up toward the pleasant curve of a mature and well-developed almond. While he does not tolerate much change to his normal diet, one of his Secret Service valets, reported off the record, that his assignment was to add chocolate-covered almonds to the president's golf course trail mix.

In addition, Hope Hicks, counselor to the president, collaborating with Kayleigh McEnany, his new "Superwoman" press secretary, have told Mark Meadows, the president's new Chief of Staff, that they will continue adding almond milk to their boss's Coke. Though it discolors the original, when he drinks it without knowing, via a Trump straw from an opaque McDonalds Supersize cup (32 oz.), the president is, as another one of his Secret Service valets put it, "happy as a pig in s..t."

Let us hope that fattening the (almond) curve may lead to surprisingly bright national and international outcomes.

Happy Birthday, Albert

Blanchot : « *La réponse est le malheur de la question.* " (The answer is the sorrow of the question.)

ALBERT EINSTEIN SAID

Sometimes I ask myself how it came about that I happened to be the one to discover the theory of relativity. The reason is, I think, that the normal adult never stops to think about space and time. Whatever thinking he or she did about these things will already have been done as a small child. I, on the other hand, was so slow to develop that I only began thinking about space and time when I was already grown up. Naturally I then went more deeply into the problem than an ordinary child.

THE ANSWER IS THE SORROW OF THE QUESTION

There exists a remarkable photograph of Einstein and Marie Curie standing together on a naked, blasted heath, both dressed in black — he in a cape, she in a hooded cloak. They look like allegorical figures from an early Bergman film — set eternally there for us to ponder their meaning, their relationship to one another, their relationship to us.

I'd been carrying that mysterious image around for a long time when I came upon a poem by Adrienne Rich that explained it to me:

Today I was reading about Marie Curie

She must have known she suffered from radiation sickness
her body bombarded for years by the element
she had purified.
It seems she denied to the end
the source of the cataracts on her eyes

the cracked and suppurating skin of her
finger ends
till she could no longer hold a test tube or a
pencil

She died a famous woman denying her wounds
denying her wounds came from the same source
as her power.

Einstein, too, suffered from radiation sickness. Einstein, too, denied. Two kinds of radiation sickness, actually. Sickness over his unintended contribution — in theory and in practice — to the deaths of so many and the poisoning of the planet. And sickness about from-radiation-born physics, a disease within the whole swing of science which left him behind, an oddball, a hermit, a naysaying party pooper, a pathetic, has-been, once-important old man.

His wounds came from the same source as his power. The power to imagine an entirely other view of the world, of the universe, the view of someone who rides on a light beam. The power of the light-beam-rider to see the light also enabled him to envision a world without war, a world beyond nations, beyond power, greed and corruption. One can't see these visions without being seriously wounded. One can't be wounded without denying.

"God does not play at dice," he said. Events in the world must have a cause, in spite of what the quantum mechanics were saying. At its deepest level the universe must be orderly, not random. If he could only find this statement which would describe it. "Forget it," said the mechanics.

He wouldn't forget it. His eyes were glued on the universe and the possibility of penetrating to the ultimate core where all secrets would be resolved and understood as the emanation of a single law. This law, the unified field theory, would be for him the name of God. He could never name the Name. His wounds came from the same source as his power. He could never name the Name

ALBERT EINSTEIN SAID

Everyone who is seriously involved in the pursuit of science becomes convinced that a spirit is manifested in the laws of the Universe — a spirit vastly superior to that of humanity, and one in the face of which we, with our modest powers, must feel humble. In this way the pursuit of science leads to a religious feeling of a special sort, which is quite different from the religiosity of someone more naïve.

THE ANSWER IS THE SORROW OF THE QUESTION

Moses and Aron

He could never name the name of God. It is a remarkable coincidence that just at the time Einstein was leaving the physics community, beginning his retreat into the desert of his solitary vision quest, another German seeker was articulating something very similar. Let's switch our eyes over to the power and wounds of Arnold Schoenberg, the great revolutionary who broke open a millennium of Western tradition to lead music into uncharted territory. Between 1923 in 1928 he worked on his largest, most ambitious and shattering work, his opera, *Moses and Aron*. This piece is a radical and comprehensive act of the imagination, an attempted human song in the face of the unspeakable immensity of God.

At the opening of the first act, Moses hears the wordless voice of God, and understands that it is *einziger, ewiger*, everywhere, invisible and inconceivable. Standing in relation to such a God, he cannot sing, he is almost dumb, he can express himself only in a halting, halfway manner, using a vocal technique of Schoenberg's called *Sprechstimme* — half singing, half speaking, limited, frustrated, fallen. The voice from the burning bush instructs him to prophesy the name of the eternal God. But he resists. He is too simple, he cannot speak, he cannot express the infinite.

No prob. Aron, his brother, sizes up the situation, and is ready for the job. He has a beautiful tenor voice, sight-sings well, and although describing the infinite God is a difficult task, he'll give it a shot. Granted, it may be only an approximation, but it's close enough for church work, and besides, the people need an image to hang onto, or they just won't buy the whole business.

The opera concerns the conflict between Moses and Aron over trying to enclose the boundless in a finite image. Like Einstein.

ALBERT EINSTEIN SAID

I do not believe in a personal God. If something is in me which can be called religious, it is the unbounded admiration for the structure of the world so far as science can reveal it. My religiosity consists in a humble admiration of the infinitely superior spirit that reveals itself in the little that we, with our weak and transitory understanding, can comprehend of reality.

THE ANSWER IS THE SORROW OF THE QUESTION

The Retreat from the Word

A nine-year-old asked me the other day "What did Einstein do?" I found it hard to describe. If he had invented the steam engine or discovered penicillin, or the charge on the electron, I could've explained more easily. But just try telling a child what Einstein did — it ain't easy. And that is in large part because what he did is not in English. It's not in German either. As his futile search dragged on, it was conducted more and more in the language of mathematical symbols, unrepresented by the tongue.

This was new, but not, perhaps, inappropriate. New because until relatively recently, our Judeo-Christian culture bore witness to the belief that all truth and realness — with the exception of a small, clear margin at the very top — could be housed inside the walls of spoken language. Until the 17th century, the predominant bias and content of the natural sciences were descriptive. But with the invention of analytic geometry and the theory of algebraic functions, with the development of calculus, mathematics transcended being an instrument to characterize certain aspects of nature, and became its own independent language, one of progressive untranslated ability. Mathematical forms and meanings have receded from spoken language at an ever accelerating pace. For no dictionaries to relate the vocabulary and grammar of contemporary higher mathematics to ordinary speech. One cannot even paraphrase.

This was the world in which Einstein ended. No more railroad cars and flashing lights of special relativity. Gone were the elevators of general relativity. Just pages and pages of reiterative tensor equations. The small, queer margin at the top. No song; beyond speech; never expressible even in its own terms. Einstein. Moses. The Unspeakable, Unreachable Absolute Idea of God.

ALBERT EINSTEIN SAID

The religious feeling engendered by experiencing the logical compre-hensibility of profound interrelations is a somewhat different sort from the feeling that one usually calls religious. It is more a feeling of awe at this scheme that is manifested in the material universe. It does not lead us to fashion a godlike being in our own image — a personage who makes demands of us and to take some interest in us as individuals. There is in this neither will nor goal, but only sheer being.

THE ANSWER IS THE SORROW OF THE QUESTION

THE TRIAL OF ALBERT EINSTEIN

PROSECUTOR

Is it not true that your discoveries of mass and energy equivalence led directly to the production of atomic weapons?

EINSTEIN

(Shakes his head vehemently)

PROSECUTOR

Is it not true that you wrote a series of letters to President Roosevelt recommending that the United States develop an atomic bomb?

EINSTEIN

(Thinks, then shakes his head decisively)

GEORGE GAMOW

When Einstein accepted a consultingship with the Bureau of Ordinance he said he would be unable to travel to Washington regularly, and that someone from the Division of High Explosives would have to come up to meet him at Princeton. I was selected to carry out the job. And so, on every other Friday, I took a morning train to Princeton, carrying a briefcase packed with secret Navy projects. Einstein would meet me in his study at home, and we would go through all the proposals one by one. He approved practically all of them, saying, "Oh, yes, very interesting, very, very ingenious," and the next day the admiral in charge was quite happy with Einstein's comments.

EINSTEIN (screams out)
I have never worked in the field of applied science, let alone for the military! I condemn the military mentality of our time just as you do! I have been a pacifist all my life, and I regard Gandhi as the only truly great political figure of our time!
(Pause, quietly...)
I just served as a mailbox. They brought me a letter and all I had to do was sign...

AUDIENCE APPLAUSE FOR FAMOUS SPEAKER EINSTEIN

EINSTEIN
Our time is distinguished by wonderful achievements in the fields of scientific understanding and technical application. But let us not forget that knowledge and skills alone cannot lead humanity to a happy and dignified life. What humanity owes to Buddha, Moses and Jesus ranks for me higher than all the achievements of the inquiring and constructive mind. What these blessed men have given us we must guard and tried to keep alive with all our strength if humanity is not to lose its dignity, the security of its existence, and the joy in living.

APPLAUSE

EINSTEIN

The unleashed power of the atom has changed everything save our ways of thinking, and thus we drift toward unparalleled catastrophe. A new way of thinking is essential if humanity is to survive and move toward higher levels.

HUGE APPLAUSE

EINSTEIN

The big political doings of our time are so disheartening that one feels quite alone. It is as if people had lost the passion for justice and dignity and no longer treasured what better generations have won by extraordinary sacrifice. The foundation of all human value is morality. To have recognized this clearly in primitive times is the unique greatness of our Moses. In contrast, look at the people today...

POLITE APPLAUSE

EINSTEIN
(Yelling)
It is easier to change the nature of plutonium than people's evil spirit!
(He looks at the clappers, who do not respond)
People grow cold faster than the planet they inhabit.
(He looks for God)
Mine eyes fail with looking upward.
(Pause)
Three great powers rule the world: stupidity, fear and greed.

SILENCE

THE ANSWER IS THE SORROW OF THE QUESTION

ALBERT EINSTEIN SAID
People like you and me, though mortal like everyone else, do not grow old no matter how long we live. What I mean is that we never cease to stand like curious children before the great Mystery into which we are born.

THE JEWISH QUEST FOR THE ABSOLUTE

Aron puts forth a comprehensible image so that Israel may live and not fall into despair. Moses loves an idea, an absolute vision, relentless in its purity. He would make of Israel the hollow, tormented vessel of an inconceivable presence.

Here, in George Steiner's imagination (in *The Portage to San Cristóbal of A.H.*), is Hitler's self-defense after he was captured as an old man in the Brazilian jungle:

"There had to be a solution, a FINAL solution. For what is the Jew if he is not a long cancer of unrest? Gentlemen I beg your attention. Was there ever a crueler invention, a contrivance more calculated to harrow human existence, than that of a non-impotent, all seeing, yet invisible, impalpable, inconceivable God?... the Jew emptied the world by setting his God apart. No image. No concrete embodiment. No imagining even. A blank emptier than the desert. Yet with a terrible nearness. Spying on our every misdeed, searching out the heart of our heart for motive... the Jew mocks those who have pictures of their God. HIS God is purer than any other. And because His inconceivable, unimaginable presence and develops us, we must obey every jot and tittle of the Law. We must bottle up our rages in desires, chastise the flesh and walk bent in the rain. You call me a tyrant, and enslaver. What tyranny, what enslavement has been more oppressive, has branded the skin and soul of man more deeply than the sick fantasies of the Jew? You are not God killers, but GOD makers. And that is infinitely worse. The Jew invented conscience and left humanity guilty serfs.

"But that was only the first piece of blackmail. There was worse to come. The white-faced Nazarene. Gentleman, I find it difficult to contain myself. But the facts speak for themselves. What did that epileptic rabbi ask of us? That we renounce the world, that we leave mother and father behind, that we offer the other cheek when slapped, that we render good for evil, that we love our neighbor as ourselves, no, far better, for self-love is an evil thing to be overcome. Oh grand castration! Note the cunning of it. Demand of human beings more than they can give, demand that they give up their stained, selfish humanity in the name of a higher ideal, and

you will make of them cripples, hypocrites, mendicants for salvation. The Nazarene said that his kingdom, his purities were not of this world. Lies, honeyed lies. It was here on earth that he founded his slave-church. It was men and women, creatures of flesh, he abandoned to the blackmail of hell, of eternal punishment. What were our camps compared to THAT? What can be crueler than the Jew's addiction to the ideal?

First the invisible but all seeing, the unattainable but all demanding God of Sinai. Second the terrible sweetness of Christ. Had the Jew not done enough to sicken man? No, gentlemen, there is a third act to our story.

"'Sacrifice yourself for the good of your fellow man. Relinquish your possessions so that there may be equality for all. So that justice may be achieved on earth. So that history may be fulfilled and society be purged of all imperfection.' Do you recognize that sermon, gentlemen? Rabbi Marx. Was there ever a greater promise? 'The classless society, to each according to his needs, brotherhood for all humanity, the earth made a garden again, a rational Eden.' In the name of which promise tyranny, torture, war, extermination were a necessity, a historical necessity! It is no accident that Marx and his minions were Jews, that the congregations of Bolshevism — Trotsky, Rosa Luxembourg, the whole fanatic, murderous pack — were of Israel. Look at them: prophets, martyrs, smashers of images drunk with the terror of the absolute. It was only a step, gentleman, a small inevitable step, from Sinai to Nazareth, from Nazareth to the covenant of Marxism. The Jew had grown impatient. Let the kingdom of justice come here and now, next Monday morning. Let us have a secular messiah instead. But with a long beard and his bowels full of vengeance.

"You are not humanity's conscience, Jew. You are only its bad conscience. And we shall vomit you so we may live and have peace."

The Nazis set a price of 50,000 marks on Albert Einstein's head.

ALBERT EINSTEIN SAID

You believe in a God who plays dice, and I in complete law and order in a world which objectively exists, and which I, in a wildly speculative way, am trying to capture. I hope that someone will discover a more realistic way, or rather a more tangible basis than it has been my lot to find.

THE ANSWER IS THE SORROW OF THE QUESTION
The physicists walked away from Einstein to follow Schrodinger's cat. The old man was left alone on his deathbed, pad and pencil in hand.

ALBERT EINSTEIN SAID
God does not play at dice.

THE ANSWER IS THE SORROW OF THE QUESTION

Six Possibilities of Other

The Sustainable Energy of the Bread & Puppet Theater

Post-revolutinary existance in a pre-revolutionary world

I read somewhere that the average lifespan of an independent theater group is about seven years. I don't know where such figures originate, but from my experience it seems plausible to me. The average lifespan of a poorly maintained urban tree is seven years.

If seven years is an average lifespan, equivalent to a human life of 75, and if Bread & Puppet has been around since 1963, that would make the Bread & Puppet Theater approximately 470 human years old. So, as you might ask about any 470-year-old person, what is it that sustains the Bread & Puppet theater? Why has it lived so long and so energetically? And more generally what is it that makes <u>any</u> organization — political, social and artistic, educational — long-term sustainable? Perhaps Bread & Puppet can do some radical teaching here.

Unlike most things in the depleting world, this group seems to run on a battery that is ever recharging and ever recharged. And like a battery, its strength is directly proportional to the difference, the tension, between opposite poles. My thought, after working with them for forty years, is that the secret of Bread & Puppet's survival is its continual feeding on six opposites in the universe. A Marxist or a Hegelian might call it eating dialectical tension.

1. Beauty — Ugliness.

Since 1974 the theater has lived in one of the most inspiring landscapes in the gorgeous state of Vermont. Open fields — with a built-in natural amphitheater — are surrounded by rolling meadows and hills, and capped by a mysterious evocative pine forest — out of all of which milieu the plays and puppets emerge. At night, without ambient light, the sky is so clear one can see fourth-order stars with the naked eye. If one stops working, and looks around in any direction, it is breathtaking.

At the same time, the theater thinks about, and portrays gross ugliness — the ugliness of the contemporary world, polluted with ugly intentions and ugly effects. There are lots of "bad guys" among the puppets — butchers or suits we call them, and lately billionaires. They have their airplanes which mow down vast populations of helpless bas-relief figures. The theater was born in the lower East side, and performs in low-income neighborhoods, with low-income people around the world. Bur its current bucolic setting has never made it forget its origins or the people and values for whom it fights. Rather the opposite: I believe that the dialectical tension between the ugliness ever present to the minds of the puppeteers and the beauty which they see when they look around them fuels their energy.

Were Bread & Puppet to be a city theater, living in the slums, scratching for leftover food, they would never know or imagine the possibilities of health for the world or for the wretched of the earth. On the other hand, were they just to live in the beautiful countryside, they might make a theater of Ooooohs and Aaaaahs, but they might easily forget the issues that surround them — the way many of us do. It is the constant tension between the beauty and the ugliness that keeps the theater on track, making, consistently over the years, their unique, signature productions.

2. Hardness — Happiness.

By and large, puppeteers are terribly hard working, but terrifically happy. That pairing is not uncommon, but it is too often enervating and alienating if one is not working at what one loves. Unlike factory workers, the puppeteers work 16 hours a day six days a week, and on the seventh they do their laundry. That is, the life is all consuming — researching, imagining, making shows, building puppets, rehearsing, practicing their instruments, all that plus the exhausting life involved in touring and in producing 16 different shows over eight weeks in the summer time. In short, work is hard, and the simple, rural life is hard. When there is no hammer, one has to use a stone, when there is no wood, one must harvest it from local trees on the land. The water runs out in the summer, and there are no showers. When the toilets no longer flush, it's the outhouse or the woods. A rushed dinner on tour might be nothing but bread and garlic. But that is puppeteer macho.

Even — and often — the weather conspires against them. Bread & Puppet shows have a history of affecting the weather, stopping rain, and bringing "god rays" down out of a black sky, on cue, to illuminate certain scenes. It's a gag among puppeteers. "See? It happened again. Circus energy." But not always.

I remember one Saturday performance when Peter decided to play chicken with God under a threatening sky. Midway through a performance, the rain came torrenting down, and an entire flock of paper-maché sheep were ruined, along with many masks and other figures. All had to be rebuilt and repainted from scratch, overnight. Unhappiness reigned. And puppeteer resignation. But a later circus featured the following act:

The Vermont Sky presents: THE WEATHER.
Starring the Federal Union of United Clouds
and the Absolute Happiness Weather System.
(Sing):
Whatever
the weather,
we'll weather
the weather.
whether
we like it
or not.

That'll learn 'em.

What with puppeteer resignation and puppeteer macho, people are happy most of the time. If they weren't happy, if they weren't fulfilling and feeling fulfilled, they wouldn't be doing, wave after wave of them, generation after generation including us geezers, what they have been doing for the last 45 years. The volunteers would have stopped coming, and Peter Schumann would find himself working alone, unsupported by a hundred co-conspirators.

And yet, with difficulty, puppeteers <u>can</u> be made unhappy. Typical anecdote: Back in the seventies, in an era quite dedicated to hedonism, I was sitting among a group of exhausted puppeteers, the night before our return home from a two-month European tour. Folks were griping about almost everything — the food (largely bread with garlic and onions), the accommodations (from hostels to floors), the schedule (outdoor shows in the morning, rehearsals in the afternoons, with constant changes for performances in the evenings, no time to relax or sight-see). If you've ever been on too-long a tour, you can imagine. All during the gripe session, Peter was sitting quietly at the table, puffing on his pipe, listening. After a long pause in the conversation — some dejected angel passing over — he quietly said the only words he was to say: "Happiness is not important."

"Happiness is not important." It was at that moment that I realized what I was dealing with. Schumann and his theater were not only out of their time with respect to style and message and *modus operandi*, they were displaced — bodily — from the entire *Zeitgeist*. In *Human, All-too Human*, Nietzsche describes a condition of "free, fearless hovering over people, customs, laws, and traditional assessments of things." <u>That</u> was the universe into which The Shu was leading, dragging his bleary-eyed troops. Not only were we to continually speak truth to power, to operate on garlic, spit and duct tape, to try to live "inside the bubble" of insecure poverty with no eyes on "success" — we were even to repudiate happiness as important in the scheme of things. I think I grew up then and there. It didn't take an unhappy love affair, or a Platonic dialogue, or more than five seconds. It was the whole context of the tour and the quietness of Peter's short summation. Changed my life.

3. Richness — Poverty

Perhaps the core of both the ethic and the aesthetic of Bread & Puppet is the idea of "cheap art". According to Peter Schumann, cheap art is "sloppy, unsightly, unframed, unmatted; non-valuable art, because of slap-dash execution with poor materials; ephemeral art with no eternal ambitions." In a flyer called "The Importance of Cheap Art", Peter writes, "Cheap art defies, ridicules, undermines and makes obsolete the sanctity of affluent-society economy." It attacks the art of privilege, which does nothing but decorate "dull spaces", and "is meant to affect nothing — even in the face of the most horrendous violations of the sense, beauty and dignity of the world."

And cheap art inspires the cheap art life. Dressing out of the costume room is a time-honored custom among puppeteers who for many years made a "high two figure" salary. The boxes and racks are labeled "Men's pants, colored", "Women's shirts, white", "Men's hats", "Warm coats," "Fancy shoes"... There are a hundred different boxes, and fifty feet of racks. And it's all FREE. The clothing, donated by friends and fans, is supposed to be for shows, but "borrowing from the costume room" is the only practice that can explain puppeteer high fashion.

Do puppeteers feel poor for this practice? Hell no. The ball gowns hanging on the rack are used for a team of "fancy ladies with sledge-hammers", or for the revealed undergarments of one of Ben Franklin's singing turkeys. That's what elegant clothing is for.

It's back to basics for puppeteers. Confounding the poverty of plenty — the plenty of poverty. In my favorite New Yorker cartoon, two Neanderthals are standing at the mouth of a huge cave in which children are seen playing drums, dancing, painting on walls. "Things are really tight," says one, "so we had to get back to basics — music and art."

Bread & Puppet takes that one step further: not only music and art, but the most basic music and art of puppetry. Not grand opera, not cinemascope, not even the Vermont Youth Orchestra. Just rough paper maché, its clay still clinging, ragged and uninteresting to the powers-that-be or wanna be. Basic, innocent, stupid — and dangerous.

We had a wonderful contrast experience on one tour. The theater showed up in Frankfurt on the fancy main stage of the Stadttheater, a rag-tag bunch of puppeteers with their roughly lettered plywood boxes full of bashed-around masks and tattered costumes. Our leader went out to locate a friendly bread oven while we were left to unpack and set up. The German stage hands in their white, spanking jumpsuits regarded us with unconcealed scorn. They were deployed in qua-si-miltary manner, with *ober*-thises barking orders to *unter*-thats. They could sense martians when they saw them. Unfriendly, supercilious, efficient. Lemme out of here.

Our next stop was Warsaw. We were playing on the main stage in the main theater building in town, one of those grotesque, wedding-cake skyscrapers towering over a city of six-story buildings or smaller. Again the boxes were carried from trucks to stage, the puppets unpacked, and we looked for repairs that needed to be made. Ah, here's some fabric which has become detached from its frame. As usual, there are not enough staple guns in the tool box. We asked an old stage hand if he had one we could borrow. "Oh," he laughed, "we don't have staple guns," and he ambled over, reached into his overalls for some used small nails ("pre-owned" we would say in capitalism), and without being asked, hammered the cloth onto the wood, bending the top over to make an ersatz staple. Warm, helpful, skilled. Several of the crew invited us to their homes for supper.

"We don't have staple guns." In the biggest theater of the biggest city in Poland! We were all moved by that fact, so easy to connect with the invitations home. At dinner that night, I remarked on the simple beauty of my particular host's shirt. "You like it?" he asked. "Here. For you. Take." And in spite of my "No, no, I couldn't", he pulls the shirt off his back and gives it to me. A poor man, having dressed up for his guests, feeding poor fare to his poor family — he feels he must give me the shirt off his back. Never in my life had I so felt the inhumanity of my own grasping, rich society.

Back home, shortly thereafter, we had a contrast experience to that contrast experience: We were playing in New Haven, in some Yale-connected building, a huge, beautiful, well-equipped room. The students were behind in striking the previous setup and were still clearing the stage space when we arrived, pulling apart a large, irregular platformed structure, and tossing the wood into what looked like a pile of miscellaneous junk. "What are you going to do with that wood?" we asked. "Oh, toss it," a student answered.

Now this was almost-virgin 2X4 that any puppeteer would have killed for. In Glover, we bought wood when absolutely necessary, but mostly made do with remnants of lumber-yard scraps, or saplings cut from the woods or fallen limbs gathered in the pine forest. It was used over and over and over, until finally, shortened or splintered beyond building, it gave up its wooden ghost in the ballroom stove to heat Peter's winter painting studio. At Yale, we looked at the growing pile of 2X4s in the corner, and debated asking whether we could have the wood. I don't remember what we did. It likely depended on whether there was room on the bus.

The accumulation of these kind of experiences, sinking into Peter's already-monkish heart, led to the great revolution: Bread & Puppet, already poor, was to stop acting rich. No more buying hinges at the hardware store. We would learn the knotting and folding techniques used by third-world people who don't <u>have</u> hardware stores. We would unbend every nail, or wire things together. We would use rocks if there were not enough hammers. And most of all, we would stop using Celastic, that popular resin-impregnated cloth with which we were making our large puppets, our weather-resistant, permanent puppets, the ones the theater was famous for.

Here is the glory of Celastic: you tear strips of fabric from the bolt. You soak them in acetone, and lay them onto the clay. You go away and come back. Voilá, there is your puppet in fine sculptural detail, ready to be painted, light, strong, as "forever" as a puppet can be. Here is the hell: acetone fumes are toxic, the material costs an arm and a leg, buying it supports Union Carbide, and third-world peasants don't use it.

Out with acetone and Union Carbide. Out with expensive celastic and the The Celastic Corporation of Arlington, NJ. In with cardboard and experiments on how to make weather-resistant, stronger-than-anywhere-else paper maché. We discovered that a-lot-stronger paper maché was a lot heavier than Celastic, especially with the extra framing it required to support large shapes. We discovered that nothing we did could make paper maché really weatherproof. We lost a lot of puppets. The logic then was clear: make puppets you can afford to lose, and which can be easily replaced. Make lots of them. Light bas-reliefs, or figures simply painted on big-box cardboard, perhaps with hanging-off arms and legs. The entire look of the theater changed. A few big, sculpted art objects were replaced by many rough ones equally, if not more powerful. The plenty which comes from poverty.

4. Great — small

Good and evil, life and death, these are the themes of Bread & Puppet. Big themes, almost infinite. Yet to portray them: paper-maché? Cardboard? House paint? Are these the materials of greatness? Ay! there's the rub. So huge the problems, so few the actual resources.

But unlike those stymied by their inability "to raise just a couple of hundred thousand dollars more to...", Bread & Puppet has no illusions about potential achievements. Because their lances are wooden, their targets automatically become mere windmills — institutions whose much-vaunted power becomes — poof! — imaginary.

The simplicity of the puppeteer vision is that of the child in "The Emperor's New Clothes", saying things that no one else can say with self-evidential truth. "Even a worm may speak to God," says Wozzeck, and yes, the Bread & Puppet worm is more likely to be heard — at least in heaven — than, say, Dick Cheney or Henry Kissinger.

Many folktales tell stories of lions and mice, of the power of the small in the world of the great, of smallness's ability to disappear when necessary into the cracks of the world, to be laughed at when to be taken seriously might be fatal. Bread & Puppet's is the power of Feste, or of the fool in Lear, greater than that of his Lord — precisely because of paper maché's deceptive smallness.

The theater is capable of walking — marching — in where angels or NGOs fear to tread. When the saints go marching in, puppeteers rush to be in that number.

Great and small are related as yin and yang, mutually empowering. Great and wannabe great are not. For Bread & Puppet, small is not only beautiful, it is survival itself, the triumph of paper maché over steel.

5. Now — then — soon

Faulkner: "The past is not dead, it is not even past."

I've never been involved with an organization where the continuity between time past and time future is so active. The agent of pastness is Death; that of futurity, Hope. Death is the concierge of the B&P necropolis — the little houses and monuments for dead puppeteers proliferating yearly in the pine forest. It is the casting agent for all the skeletons dancing over surfaces, sculpted into masks and puppets. It is the patron saint of all the recycling — sculptures smashed and watered back to clay, paintings painted over, puppets harvested for their parts. Back, back into memory, into the elements from which they were fashioned.

Along the way, there is even a kind of practical worship of old age. We have the honorific of being "a geezer", a long-ago puppeteer come back to manifest. Things, oddly enough, are rarely repaired. There are rips in fabric that are decades old, tears in cardboard never mended. Laziness is the last thing puppeteers can be accused of, yet there is great reluctance to patch things up. In those rips and tears is active history. Look as you will in storehouse or shed, you will never find anything brand spanking new.

And yet archives are hard to come by. Very little gets written down. "How did we do that before?" is the eternal question. And therefore one is always misremembering and reinventing.

And then that clay takes another shape, the bent nails, straightened, restructure the amputated wood, new shows are invented, and three-year olds on 2" stilts become pre-teens, and narrate their own cantistorias.

Past, present and future are in active, creative tension in puppetland. The kids like it enough to stay or return, to marry other puppeteers, or bring their partners in, and to generate their own little ones for those 2" stilts. The battery keeps charging.

6. Leadership — independence.

Without Peter Schumann there could be no Bread & Puppet. No puppeteer imagines he or she can take over and continue when Peter goes. That he has been so energetic, idiosyncratic, and persistent over the decades accounts for the unique and identifiable continuing style of the theater. There is evolution in the imagery, but not evolution by committee, or wanderings off here and there with the cultural winds.

Working with Peter is, I imagine, quite similar to working with the great Renaissance masters: Schumann is likely the only sixteenth century human stalking planet Earth today. His art is of that time, as is his thinking. For what sane mind these days is swirling with gods and demons and swimming among archetypes? We mostly exist in our little world of images and simulacra, fed to us by the media masters — look, honey, I shrunk the universe, major credit cards accepted. But Peter's world is as large as it was for Luther or Michelangelo, or Giordano Bruno, as full of portents, images, characters, all speaking, listening, to be embraced or exorcised. He runs a workshop, as did Leonardo, laying out the big ideas, and nourishing his apprentices as they grow toward his vision. But he is still, at 75, far beyond any of them — the best stilter, the most graceful dancer, the most music-filled musician, the most visionary painter and sculptor, the most lateral-thinking inventor, the funniest, the most serious, the most innovative with language. And thus he is the consummate "Renaissance man", broadly accomplished, promethean, challenging heaven and earth as did the geniuses of old.

But Bread & Puppet is not just Peter. Without decades of devoted help from others sharing his vision, Peter would be constrained, an extraordinary painter and sculptor, perhaps, exhibiting large pieces and installations in galleries around the world. But could he fill 10 acres with huge dancing puppets, could he fashion flocks of birds and herds of beasts that would roam the fields and forest, could he create year after year, an irreverent circus taking on huge themes in act after act? No.

Not only are many bodies needed to animate the puppets, many minds are needed to mine Peter's suggested themes, many instincts to invent the performance details that make the shows so wonderful.

This past summer, there was a puppet who announced herself as The Anarchist Fairy of Revolutionary Intervention, and whose job was to wave her magic wand and transform the office of Bernie Madoff into the office of Karl Marx. Each week of the summer the role was played by a different puppeteer, each bringing his or her own persona to the part. The last performance was done by a geezer who had never learned to stilt. Would it be lacking in pizzazz? Unlike any of her predecessors, before touching the office door, she spit on her magic wand to shine it up. Who needs stilts with such imagination?

So yes, one serves a master in puppetland, but the master is not always Peter Schumann — it is often the puppet. Rehearsals for a new circus act or show usually begin with a mere theme. "Find some puppets," Peter says, and the museum and sheds are raided, and unexpected congeries of figures carried out into the backyard. "OK, let's see what they do." The puppeteers pick them up and start to move. The power transfers from puppeteer to puppet, and it is the puppet who quickly begins to call the shots. Metaphors emerge like sparks from the unpredicted interactions; Peter chooses, sorts and shapes what he sees and hears. "Try some sounds," he says. And out come the "instruments", some recognizable, others invented and crazed — flapping things, and wind machines, and scrapers and bangers and blocks. All of a sudden the dance fills out into a world generated from a supra-human dimension.

Sometimes the effects are predictable, and can be called upon at will. Political leaders must come undone when impersonated by dancing bears in tutus, or by Kaspars oozing malignant chaos. Put on a Kaspar head, and a puppeteer may come up with God-knows what Kasparized lines. One of my favorites: The Rotten Idea Theater Company of Kaspars was acting out a string of US withdrawals from international agreements. The ABM Treaty, The International Criminal Court, the Kyoto Protocol, and others were hauled out and Kaspars holding their cardboard signs were serially bashed to the ground by Kaspar Dubya. The action proceeded to the Bill of Rights ("I paid that already!"), the Magna Carta, and finally the Ten Commandments. "Ten Commandments — way too many," said the president, swinging his foam rubber club. "Ten Commandments — way too many." No mere human in a Kaspar could come up with such a line. Only the Kaspar could do it.

To summarize: my feeling is that the Bread & Puppet battery stays fiercely charged by being aware of, understanding, and embracing the oppositions of beauty <u>and</u> ugliness, hardness <u>and</u> happiness, richness <u>and</u> poverty, great <u>and</u> small, forward <u>and</u> back, individualism <u>and</u> community. Founding one's output on only half of these dialectical tensions leads to Hallmark cards, loss of charge, and a speedy organizational death.

Bread & Puppet's **Radical Lessons For Aliveness**:

— stay aware of destructive ugliness and the potential of transformational beauty.

— value hardness for the happiness of its call to creativity.

— understand the poverty of richness and the richness of poverty.

— note the real smallness of the "great", and the substantial greatness of the small.

— honor the ancestors and geezers who keep the tradition, yet bash them continually with newness.

— follow the leader when and if there is a truly great one, but without strangling one's own potential to contribute.

On Money and Cheap Art

Fleshing Out the Dialectic

Money is a tool, and like any tool, its effects depend on how it is used. But tools have an inherent relationship to danger. Though both can be instruments of death, a chainsaw is a more dangerous device than, say, an Allen wrench, and a car can be more malign than a filing cabinet can ever think of being.

What then of money? Where does it sit in the potentially dangerous continuum?

A key text to consider is the Pardoner's tale in Chaucer's *Canterbury Tales*. Hie thee directly thither, reader, as my synopsis will lack many telling details.

Three guys are drinking it up at a tavern, gambling, cursing, steeped in what the Pardoner condemns as the "tavern sins" of gluttony. A burial bell is heard, and the rioters realize it is for a friend of theirs, killed by the "privee theef" named Deeth — that bad hombre, that mass murderer, who they've heard has likely killed thousands. Someone should end this plague once and for all, and why not they? So they set out *"sleen this false traytour Deeth.*

He shal be slayn, which that so manye sleeth,

By Goddes dignitee, er it be nyght!"

Outside the tavern, they meet an Olde Man who has been begging Death to take him. They rudely tease him, and ask why he's lived so long. He answers,

> *"For I ne kan nat fynde*
> *A man, though that I walked into Ynde,*
> *Neither in citee nor in no village,*
> *That wolde chaunge his youthe for myn age;*

And therfore mooth I han myn age stille,
As longe tyme as it is Goddes wille.
Ne Deeth, allas, ne wol nat han my lyf.
Thus walke I lyk a restelees kaityf,
And on the ground, which is my moodres gate,
I knokke with my staf bothe erly and late,
And seye, "Leeve mooder, leet me in!
Lo, how I vanysshe, flessh and blood and skyn!
Allas, whan shul my bones been at reste?"

A wonderful Chaucerian touch, as you will see. The Olde Man instructs them that he had last left Deeth up under yonder oak. Our three *burschen* run to the tree so as not to miss their prey, but no Death do they find, but "Wel ny an eighte busshels" of golden florins. My God, what luck!

"No lenger thanne after Deeth they soughte,
But ech of hem so glad was of that sighte,
For that the floryns been so faire and brighte,

That doun they sette hem by this precious hoord."

The stage is set for MONEY to do its thing. They decide to spend the night at the oak so as to guard their find. They draw straws, and one of them is sent to town to bring food and drink for their overnight camping. I'll bet you can smell what's coming.

The two under the tree plot to kill the third upon his return so that the'll each have a larger share of the gold, while the one out buying decides to flavor the wine with rat poison before returning.

"O lorde," quod he, "if so were that I myghte
Have al this tresor to my-self allone,
Ther is no man that lyveth under the trone
Of God, that sholde lyve so murye as I."

Back at the oak, he is greeted by his friends, who promptly kill him according to plan, then celebrate their enlarged riches by drinking up the fatal wine.

"Thus ended been thise homycides two,
And eek the false empoysoner also."

Well. There's a money plot for you.

You might say that if they were more rational fellows like Elon Musk or Bill Gates, they would have gathered up the florins and invested them in a Flanders Building Supply company, or an arms factory. The problem isn't with money, you say, but with human greed. *Radix malorum est cupiditas* (the root of evil is greed) (as it says on our front porch.)

But that Latin is an insufficient translation of the Biblical Greek ""ῥίζα γὰρ πάντων τῶν κακῶν ἐστιν ἡ φιλαργυρία" (1Timothy 6:10). While cupidity can mean all forms of greed, the Greek φιλαργυρία"(*philaguria*) can mean *only* love of money.

There it is, way back then, misdirection — don't let's look at money, let's just call it greed and blame the greedy, not the rich, and not their money.

Money. The ultimate taboo. People are more prone to tell you about their sex lives than about how much money they have at their command.

There is, of course, conspicuous consumption, lighting Havana cigars with hundred dollar bills, or as Zero Mostel's character, Max Bialystock in *The Producers*, newly rich, says, "If ya got it, FLAUNT it!" But what's being flaunted is usually not money, per se, but what it can buy, the life style it can bring. What remains hidden is the ecological destruction, and human wage slavery that supports not the yacht, but the money that went into shaping, buying, and maintaining it. It's at the money level that things get suspicious, and had best remain hidden.

So what is it about money *qua* money that becomes and attracts the problematical? My theory is that it's a problem of surface to volume ratio. The rioters' florins would likely fill a small to medium sack, but that's far less than the volume of trouble it can cause. With that sack you have a relatively tiny surface of burlap enclosing a huge volume of trouble. Surface to volume ratio dangerously low.

If worth were measured, say, in cattle, rather than in gold florins, it would be hard to imagine that the number of cattle gatherable under the oak, even if planted there by Deeth, could cause as much havoc as a bag full of gold. The problem is that gold contains great, in Chaucer's example, too much, concentrated wealth or power. It has been *defined* at that high-power density to save space, grassland, feed, and to make trading more defined and possible.

Great. Who wants to lug three cows and a pig to Hannafords to pay for a Sunday shop? Who even needs gold florins at Hannafords? Swipe your card and the electrons are there. Easy. What $E=mc^2$ tells us is that you can pack a lot of energy into a tiny mass. Too much of that, and things get dangerous.

The problem with money — not greed, but money — is that there is too much energy contained in too little mass. That mass can be moved around too easily, it hides a lot of nasty things that otherwise would never sell, it buys a lot of high-quality things that easily sell, and it attracts crooks. As in crooked, bent.

I think it was Chuang-tzu that said something like, "You cannot cut a straight board from a crooked tree." And worse is Kant's more pointed version:

"Out of the crooked timber of humanity, no straight thing was ever made."

Immanuel Kant, *Idea for a Universal History with a Cosmopolitan Purpose*

So in the 21st century, living within rampant capitalism, can we detach, at least somewhat, from "the cash nexus", that "agglomerate of impersonal monetary factors specifically considered as the basis for human relations" (Webster)?

The best example I know of that practice, sixty years old and still thriving, is the Bread & Puppet Theater. The secret contained in its burlap sack is the WHY CHEAP ART? Manifesto:

> *PEOPLE have been THINKING too long that*
> *ART is a PRIVILEGE of the MUSEUMS & the*
> *RICH. ART IS NOT BUSINESS!*
> *It does not belong to banks & fancy investors*
> *ART IS FOOD. You cant EAT it BUT it FEEDS*
> *you. ART has to be CHEAP & available to*
> *EVERYBODY. It needs to be EVERYWHERE*
> *because it is the INSIDE of the*
> *WORLD.*
> *ART SOOTHES PAIN!*
> *Art wakes up sleepers!*

ART FIGHTS AGAINST WAR AND STUPIDITY!
ART SINGS HALLELUJAH!
ART IS FOR KITCHENS!
ART IS LIKE GOOD BREAD!
Art is like green trees!
Art is like white clouds in blue sky!
ART IS CHEAP!
HURRAH!
Bread & Puppet Glover, Vermont, 1984

Cheap art is "sloppy, unsightly, unframed, unmatted; non-valuable art, because of slap-dash execution with poor materials; ephemeral art with no eternal ambitions." But it's terrific! Fierce, strong, lovely, inventive — a cardboard and bent wire uprising.

In a flyer called "The Importance of Cheap Art", Peter Schumann, the B&P director, writes, "Cheap art defies, ridicules, undermines and makes obsolete the sanctity of affluent-society economy." It attacks the art of privilege, which does nothing but decorate "dull spaces", and "is meant to affect nothing — even in the face of the most horrendous violations of the sense, beauty and dignity of the world." It's the sourdough rye art squadron against the "degenerate tastebuds of the fluffy white-bread-eaters".

And cheap art models and inspires the cheap art life. Rough bread feeds rough puppeteers who play rough, making rough art for rough times.

If puppeteers can do it to make theater, why not the rest of us, the puppeted, to make real life? Why can we not refashion our own lives out of cardboard and wire, the paint and junk in attics and basements and brains, making WORTH instead of MONEY, sharing our outputs as the theater shares its shows and its bread, participating warily and minimally in the capitalism that surrounds, but does not define us, acting as if life is ART, the inside of the world easing its way through the concrete? If you haven't got it, flaunt that instead, and share with those with even less.

On a "Free University"

Fighting Stupidity, Fear, and Greed

I have this crackpot theory that the insane, deadly, calamitous decisions made by "deciders" are what they are not because of Einstein's insightful trinity of "great powers that rule the world" — stupidity, fear, and greed — but because they are made under fluorescent light.

Fluorescent light — cold, buzzing, flickering at electronic speed beyond the senses, but still itchy and far from comforting. Contrast this to the warm light of incandescence, modern cousin to candle, fireplace and hearth, generously available at the flick of a switch, and not after the stingy decisions of some judgmental ballast. One is warm, one is cold. That in itself is enough to start with.

The Germans have a wonderful word, *"gemütlich"* — cozy, comfortable, snug, homelike, unhurried, pleasant and cheerful. It comes, interestingly enough, from *"Mut"* (say *moot*) — a noun meaning courage, audacity, spirit, valor, pluck. In *gemütlich* surroundings, *Mut* develops, humor and creativity thrive. Heidegger talks about calculative vs. meditative thinking. Which do you think reigns in a White House or Pentagon war room?

Connected with the acrid brilliance of fluorescent lights are hallways with rooms coming off them, rooms in which stand tables and comfortless chairs. Here, discourse takes on the stringency of flow charts and right angles, strategies and definitions, metrics and grades. What is taught in such rooms? What is learned? Whatever it is, these hallways, these rooms seem a poor and ailing incubator for education, for *ed-ducare*, the drawing out of what is within.

Name a space that is generally not lit with fluorescence, whose hallways may be darkish, but whose rooms are fitted as best they can be, for comfort, *Gemütlichkeit*. If not in a coffee shop, it's probably where you're sitting right now, reading *05401* — your home. A house is not a home. What is the difference? *Gemütlichkeit*, with or without family. A warm home is an optimal place to be educated, drawn out, inspired. It always was, from cave to kitchen, bedroom to barn — in those homes, humanity has always learned its language, its hopes, its skills. Why, then, did we ever decide that for our children, and now our life-long-learning adults to be drawn out, they have to be marched into institutions of long hallways and fluorescent rooms to sit around tables being tested? Follow the money, I suppose.

So here we are, yearning for "home schooling", but not in the sense of an enriched or protected curriculum, but optimal for any curriculum at all, the home and yard as a where for human learning of any kind, for meditative, not just calculative thinking, for discussing, imagining, provoking.

Hold that thought for a moment. I want to come round the other side and tell you about a lovely and complete failure of good intentions. Two springs ago, our little "free university" group that is writing in this issue of *05401*, decided to just *do* it, to start a "free university" for the community at large. We arranged for ourselves and others to offer nine free activities of "Life Skills" and "Critical Intellectual Inquiry". Instructors or group leaders volunteered to lead study and practice in the following: Legal and Political Analysis of the Legal and Political Systems and Rule of Law; Organic Gardening; Latin America Today; How the Events of 9/11 Changed the World; Greenhouse Vegetable and Flower Production; Indigenous Alternatives to Neoliberal Development in Mexico; The Design and Construction of Solar Collectors for Home Heating; Imaging the City: Architecture and Urban Life; Mushroom Foraging.

Not bad for a first calling around and a little arm-twisting. The instructors or group leaders provided a short course or activity description, made their homes or gardens available, along with an email address for anyone interested to contact. All courses and activities were free of charge. We posted flyers on the bulletin boards around town, and in the area colleges. Guess how many inquiries we got.

None. Zero. Hmm.

Not an institutional fluorescent light or hallway involved. Living rooms more comfortable than classrooms. And no doubt the potlucks would have been fabulous. All free. Not one call.

Four likely suspects might explain our results:

1. Not enough advertising, wrong time, wrong places.

2. Bad choice of course offerings.

3. No academic or other credit offered for work done under incandescence.

4. No time or interest available for any more life activities.

Or of course all of the above.

It was #3 that piqued the most discussion. We, as a group of community individuals, were "unaccredited", regardless of our skills. Why would that make a difference to a potential learner? Things and skills would be learned regardless. But then, the work would not be "counted" on a resumé submitted for a job. Were resumés the choke point where education was shaped and manacled? The need for "accreditation"? Who were the accreditors? What were their "metrics"? Fluorescent or incandescent? Calculative or meditative? Who or what accredited them to accredit in the first place? How the hell did we get here at their feet on our knees?

Jobs, jobs, jobs. A capitalist economy which needs unemployment and debt pressure to keep wages low and profits maximized. Workers pre-stressed and vetted in schools. BAs flipping burgers, MAs selling lingerie, PhDs driving cabs. But real education does not have to be accredited, and probably can't be. So why is it connected to job search and jobs? Why do employers prefer a gentleman's C from Yale to calloused hands from a working farm? Smarts?

It is a cliché that you don't want those calloused hands managing a scalpel in your brain. Not at least, until washed and trained over eight years of medical school and residency. But let us distinguish training from education. We're talking about education. Basta.

Let's leave that as we work our way around a triangular circle that leads back to fluorescent lighting, institutions, and a manufactured playground for stupidity, fear and greed.

The "free" in "free university" or "free school" is certainly not restricted to cost. It is more related to the French Revolutionary ideal of Liberté — being uncontrolled by authoritarian forces from above, and following both one's own path and service to the collective good. I taught at Goddard College during it's "golden years", 1969-1979. Some would say they were the craziest years, the most uncontrolled, drug-ridden, chaotic and destructive — but I wouldn't be one of them.

Talk about community! Everyone in the whole school — students, faculty, administrators, staff — was majoring in the same thing, all together, all at the same time, and the major was called "What is education, and how can a college be involved in it?" Pretty basic, but with results far more profound than following prescriptions from those who "already know" the answer.

That being said, there *were* no majors. There were no departments. Students pursued areas of interests with the help of faculty they deemed relevant to guide their quests. Faculty taught things they wanted to learn more about, their paid expertise being proven skills in how to learn, plus whatever was their "field". I was hired to teach theater, and while I did lead theater groups, I also wound up teaching English, music, math, physics, writing, Finnegans Wake, health care, and a collection of seminars for students who listened to taped lectures while washing dishes in the cafeteria. We called it "the Dishwashing Seminar". I taught a community class on the Beethoven String Quartets in Plainfield homes. I conducted a Goddard Community Chorus, working with student and local musicians. When Bread & Puppet came to be theater in residence, we did shows together based on choral masterpieces. I learned a lot in pursuing these activities, the most important being that if I want to learn something, or do something new, I should *just do it*. I didn't need a degree. I didn't need to be accredited. How else would I start writing novels at age 63, and have a dozen published in a dozen years? I'm not boasting — I'm attributing my rich life path to a formative Goddard education.

There were community meetings up the gazoo. Anyone could post a call for a meeting, and lo and behold, the cafeteria was filled, on "Goddard time" perhaps, but there were always enough students and faculty for substantive discussion of the many, many issues involved in living out an educational community.

Some of the students couldn't handle so much self-direction, and wanted more telling what-to-do. But many students can't handle Harvard, or UVM, or Johnson State, or CCV for similar and different reasons. Education is hard, and like quitting smoking, one may need multiple runs at it.

The level of questioning at Goddard was foundational. My favorite Goddard story (I'm not making this up) is that of the pink memo that came down from the president's office calling for a community meeting to discuss a "unisalary". The president — the new president! — an ex-tax commissioner for the state of Vermont — proposing we take the entire college income, and divide it equally among all employees, administrators, faculty, and staff, including maintenance and cleaning staff. When you did the math, it came out to $8,500/year. At the time I, as full-time faculty, was making $10K, and the president $22.5K. We were both willing, indeed happy, to take the cuts as part of our commitment to "the Goddard experiment". Some of the other faculty went along; some objected. The most widespread objections came from the staff — all of whose salaries would have increased. (Quite the political lesson for the proposers.) The unisalary did not pass a community vote. But it was actually and seriously discussed over months. And it came from the president. Imagine that. In short, there was nothing out-of-bounds at Goddard, and anything was possible. *That* for me came to be the goal and fruit of my experience with a free university right here in Vermont.

Sandy Baird jumps on the inequality of payer and paid — all involved in the same thing. Why is that? Why are some paid, while others pay? she rightly demands. Why does thinking and experimentation stop at the salary door? So yes, let's try to think past it. We can start with a thought-experiment proposed by Charles Simpson:

Let's put jobs and accreditation-toward-jobs aside, and just assume a *guaranteed minimum income* where society shares its great wealth not primarily with the military and the 1% (or the 15%) — but pays out a unisalary to all citizens, say $30K/year to live on, doing whatever one wants, including salaried work as desired. Don't worry about where the money is coming from — it's coming from the imagination. This is a thought experiment to facilitate a certain question:

Under those conditions — where one didn't have to go to school to get a job — would anyone go to school? To do what? How would education be understood in a society without the stricture of need? If you could do and learn whatever you wanted, what would that be?

Such a question gets to the heart of the issue. Mannie, our editor, is not comfortable with that investigative method. Such a society does not exist, he avers, and never will, certainly not under the present power structure. So why consider it, even as a hypothetical?

First, the idea of a guaranteed minimum income *has* been seriously studied along with its many psychological and economic implications. Just google the expression, or start by examining the many writings of Robert Theobald. While his prescriptions for the "post-scarcity model" and the "economics of abundance" may seem archaically quaint in our world of increasing scarcities, the basic qualitative possibilities remain the same — since much of today's scarcity is created and enforced via intentional mal-distribution.

But beyond economic juggling, utopian or not, consider the riches unearthed (sans pollution) by seriously asking the question: If I could do or learn anything I wanted, what would it be, and how would I do that? Spending more than a minute with that question is revelatory. Effecting it, whatever it is, would go far to combatting stupidity, fear and greed as the powers that rule the world. And unless it is specific job training for a job you always wanted, it is not necessarily to be undertaken in fluorescent-lit rooms off fluorescent-lit halls.

For a start, I suggest that we open up our living rooms, backyards and fields to study groups and workshops, and locate community members to offer and attend them. I suggest that, as workers, we demand to be interviewed and hired for our capacities, not just our credentials, and that, as employers, we seek the real potential of colleagues beyond their "accredited" resumés. I suggest that employees and employers see themselves as exploring together, the way student, faculty and staff did at Goddard, the larger institutions we want to flourish. Work and home would become the main worlds of education. And free. Our living rooms, our work spaces are "shovel ready" with a *gemütlich* variety of shovels.

And in this *gemütlich* atmosphere, we can develop our *Mut*, and aim at the goal of true education — freedom. Not just freedom from oppression and exploitation, but freedom to envision a world beyond existing systems of power, freedom to imagine new forms of association and action.

Incandescence. Gemütlichkeit. Unaccreditation. Concerning a "free university", as the walls read in May '68: "BE REALISTIC: DEMAND THE IMPOSSIBLE!"

The U in Education

Something not-at-all rotten in the state of Denmark

As noted earlier in this book, between 1969 and 1979 I was hired to teach theatre at Goddard College, but wound up also teaching music, writing, Finnegans Wake, math, physics, medical self-help and "crazy courses" like Philosophy for Dishwashers. Yet in this setting, tuned for several surprises a day, there came still a flash of something, someone more astounding still: Aage (pron. Oh-ah) Nielsen and his New Experimental College in Snested, Denmark.

I met Aage at some conference I had attended on radical education. We hit it off right away (he fifty-ish, I thirty), and he invited me to come see what he was up to in a little town near the northwestern tip of Denmark. Since Goddard was all about "What is education?", the school gave me its blessing, and the airfare for the trip, so I could bring back some news. It was one of the more remarkable weeks of my life. I wrote a fictional account to try to catch the flavor of it, as Julius Marantz, spends a college year there. The documents quoted are real:

1968 was a good year to start college. Especially in Denmark. Especially at New Experimental College, the brainchild of a nisseman named Aage Rosendal Nielsen. Cross Aage's Santa with his Imp of Perversity and you'd likely generate his admissions questionnaire. Among normal, Harvardish questions it asked:

> 1. What is a question?
> 9. What ambitions do you have for your life?
> 22. What do you want the world to be like after you have left it?

23. Where will you be then?

26. Under what circumstances do people scare you?

27. How beautiful is your anger?

31. What is infatuation?

36. How are you godlike?

38. How are you learning to take in your suffering?

47. How sneaky can you be?

49. Why are you such a good person?

Julius's answers convinced Aage they could use him. It was the Hamletness of Denmark that convinced Julius to go. That, plus a letter sent to Coney Island, addressed to Philip and Florence Marantz, and opened by their orphan:

> Dear Parents [it began],
> You may be reluctant to see your child at an institution such as ours. Such concern is natural and good, and you do not want your children wasting time or money at a school unhelpful to maturing, to becoming responsible, or for acquiring an education which will help them make a living. I share your concerns.
> Most children who have come so far, have come here, rather than to the schools you might prefer, because you have not been good enough parents or because they are better children than you expected them to be. It is likely that your behavior did not match your stated ideals, or that there was a lack of genuine relationship in the family. These are terrible things to subject children to for years on end.
> Children are so wonderful and idealistic that if they don't find authentic behavior or genuine relationships in their homes, they will look for them for the rest of their lives, look harder for them than for success as you understand it. As a result of attending NEC, they may reject you, and your lives. This will be painful, and will require your utmost understanding and support.
> One thing I consistently try to do is encourage

*students to write their parents — and everyone else —
in the most open and frank way possible Sometimes
parents respond indignantly, saying that they were good
parents, always had a good relationship, always tried to
do their best. But you know your best never suffices. If
you are lucky enough to have children who can express
their discontent and their dreams, then listen to them,
be proud of them, and realize how much they are helping you, even if it hurts.*

  Sincerely yours,
  Aage Rosendal Neilsen, Rector,
  New Experimental College.
  Skyum Bjerge, 7752 Snedsted, Thy, Danmark

At the end of his first semester, Julius made the following presentation for the approval of the community:

"Aage, Sara, Tom, Ruth, John, Pippy, Terri, Kelly, Bill, Jim, Hennig,
Mogens,

Elmo, Elaine, Jane, Emil, Alan, Doris...

I feel it's important for me to have both definite goals and indefinite ones. The definite ones will be best met at the University of
Copenhagen physics department, with three full semesters of their
normal undergraduate curriculum — mechanics, electromagnetism,
thermodynamics, relativity, quantum theory, etc. I have already begun
my study in many of these areas, and I trust will be able to manage a
heavy courseload, and pass the normal examinations. And during my
three residencies here at NEC, I will teach three courses in "Physics for
the Inquiring Mind". With this background, I should get into whatever
graduate school I choose.

More important, however, and the reason I came to NEC, is that I
wish to develop — and I'm serious — the cardinal and theological vir-
tues: courage and excellence, temperance and justice, faith, hope and
charity. I expect my stay at NEC to lead me in that direction.

At the moment I am nothing. I am, as Aage says, empty and stupid.
I would like to put others before myself, and I'm miserable because
I find that hard to do. Sometimes I think crazy things like joining a

565

motorcycle gang, or what it might be like to sleep with God. Some of my screws may be missing. I want to find them here. So in addition to my career goals, I also want to study a quite indefinite thing, area, cloud, wisp: Julius Marantz.

I invite you all to instruct me in this subject, in classroom or kitchen or bedroom, in person, or in correspondence during my Copenhagen semesters. I will choose my work-study so as to learn most about myself. I will teach you physics so that we may both discover ourselves in the teaching. Why should learners be left out of the learning? Are we afraid education will become too involving, endless, unfathomable? NEC is the place to extend the variables. Yet I expect nothing from NEC per se. I expect it all from us, especially myself. *Mange tak.*"

His proposal was enthusiastically accepted by the school assembly, the *Ting*. He went off to Copenhagen for fall semester.

(from *The Lamentations of Julius Marantz, 2007*)

Chop Wood, Carry Water

A Review of a Book, and Reflection on the Life

A review of *Chop Wood, Carry Water: A Guide to Finding Spiritual Fulfillment in Everyday Life*, by Rick Fields, with Peggy Taylor, Rex Weyler, and Rick Ingrasci, Tarcher, 1984

Everyday life — alarm clock, toothbrush and toaster; transport and time clock and boss; working, hacking, yelling, juggling a life with harried others — everyday life in America.

A thousand years ago, a Chinese Zen master wrote:

> *Magical power,*
> *marvelous action!*
> *Chopping wood,*
> *carrying water...*

What has this to do with us? Where is magic today, and action to marvel over? In our magical, marvelous machines? No — say these four editors of the *New Age Journal*. The magic is still where it always was, in our own lives and actions, properly considered, and properly done.

And so they have produced a book to help contemporary westerners clear a path in the chaotic jungle of our civilization. The title poem suggests one of the keys — simplicity. We are not all in a position to chop wood and carry water, but each of our daily actions — even if embedded in a complex web — can help us see and serve the grand design. The result: mindfulness, service and meaning.

This is not an extensive philosophical text, but rather a compilation of short reflections and tactics for would-be travelers on the path called Tao. There are chapters on the obvious themes: relationships and sex, family, work, money, and play, tuning the body and healing. Then, looking outward from self and family, technology, the earth, and social action. The authors begin with a beginner (and who is not a beginner?), and speak, encouragingly about beginnings in the process of learning. And they return, finally, to where they began — the individual quest, inner resources, and, finally, the perils of the path

This last chapter is a worthwhile reflection on a new chaos, which the book itself could represent: the ever-growing "spiritual supermarket" — open 24 hours a day for your enlightenment pleasure. We want results, and fast, and there are those who are willing to sell us anything we want. And so "cutting through spiritual materialism" is an apt theme, with which to close a wise and — for all its reach — fundamentally modest book. Beware, say the authors, beware of those who have all the answers.

Beside the main body of the text, chop wood, carry water has two features which make it especially attractive. The word margins are sprinkled with aphorisms like gorgeous and surprising flowers along the side of the road. Any one of the hundreds of these may be worth the whole price of the book — for who can put a price on gems that glow forever in the memory? Bravo for this remarkable side-collection! And then, each chapter closes with a short annotated bibliography of recommended reading, and a list of organizational resources for further involvement.

In sum, *Chop Wood Carry Water* is a short, but rich sifting of the gifts the "New Age" has made available as an antidote to the late 20th century. It speaks to everyone — not just to spiritual devotees — about how everyday lives can become "paths," transforming self and world into

> *Magical power.*
> *marvelous action!*
> *Chopping wood*
> *carrying water…*

Charles Ives' Disconcordia

It seems appropriate to end this collection as it began with the ur-American composer, Charles Ives. His father, George, was the town bandmaster of Danbury, CT, his town band generally considered to be the best in the Northern Army. George was also a spectacular pedagogue, and his son, Charlie, the beneficiary.

One famous anecdote, and likely true, is that George sent Charlie up to the top of the Danbury Soldier's Memorial tower to experience an "acoustical experiment" — his town band, divided evenly in two, each half playing different pieces, in different rhythms, in different keys, the two halves marching toward and past one another, with Charlie's tower at the midpoint. Charles reported as to how the bands were "brought together in cacophonous conflict", an effect that he loved, and that permanently shaped his acoustic world as a composer.

The generally cacophonous conflicts which have become the subjects of this book have yet to find the gorgeous resolution Ives imagined at the end of his Concord Sonata:

Not a bang, and certainly not a whimper. Who in authority can conceive of such a thing?

About the Author

Marc Estrin was hired to teach theater at Goddard College, but in this departmentless utopia, wound up also teaching music, writing, Finnegans Wake, math, physics, medical self-help and "crazy courses" like Philosophy for Dishwashers, an audio-based lecture/discussion series to sweeten the life of cafeteria volunteers. Such are the fruits of liberal education.

Fomite

Writing a review on social media sites for readers will help the progress of independent publishing. To submit a review, go to the book page on any of the sites and follow the links for reviews. Books from independent presses rely on reader-to-reader communications.

For more information or to order any of our books, visit:
fomitepress.com/our-books.html

More essays from Fomite...

William Benton — *Eye Contact: Writing on Art*

J. Malcom Garcia — *A Different Kind of War: Uneasy Encounters in Mexico and Central America*

Stephen Langfur — *Confession from a Jericho Jail*

Douglas W. Milliken — *Any Less You*

George Ovitt & Peter Nash — *Trotsky's Sink: Ninety-Eight Short Essays on Literature*

Robert Sommer — *Losing Francis: Essays on the Wars at Home*

www.ingramcontent.com/pod-product-compliance
Lightning Source LLC
Chambersburg PA
CBHW021601120626
46545CB00001B/13